ID0788232

VOLUME FIFTY-FIVE

THE PSYCHOLOGY OF LEARNING AND MOTIVATION

Cognition in Education

Series Editor

BRIAN H. ROSS

Beckman Institute and Department of Psychology, University of Illinois at Urbana-Champaign, Urbana, Illinois

VOLUME FIFTY-FIVE

THE PSYCHOLOGY OF LEARNING AND MOTIVATION

Cognition in Education

Edited by

JOSE P. MESTRE
*Beckman Institute and Departments of
Physics and Educational Psychology, University of Illinois
at Urbana-Champaign, Urbana, Illinois*

BRIAN H. ROSS
*Beckman Institute and Department of Psychology,
University of Illinois at Urbana-Champaign, Urbana, Illinois*

ELSEVIER

AMSTERDAM • BOSTON • HEIDELBERG • LONDON
NEW YORK • OXFORD • PARIS • SAN DIEGO
SAN FRANCISCO • SINGAPORE • SYDNEY • TOKYO
Academic Press is an imprint of Elsevier

Academic Press is an imprint of Elsevier
525 B Street, Suite 1900, San Diego, CA 92101-4495, USA
225 Wyman Street, Waltham, MA 02451, USA
32 Jamestown Road, London, NW17BY, UK
Radarweg 29, PO Box 211, 1000 AE Amsterdam, The Netherlands

Copyright © 2011 Elsevier Inc. All rights reserved

No part of this publication may be reproduced, stored in a retrieval system or transmitted
in any form or by any means electronic, mechanical, photocopying, recording or
otherwise without the prior written permission of the publisher

Permissions may be sought directly from Elsevier's Science & Technology Rights
Department in Oxford, UK: phone (+44) (0) 1865 843830; fax (+44) (0) 1865 853333;
email: permissions@elsevier.com. Alternatively you can submit your request online by
visiting the Elsevier web site at http://elsevier.com/locate/permissions, and selecting
Obtaining permission to use Elsevier material

Notice
No responsibility is assumed by the publisher for any injury and/or damage to persons
or property as a matter of products liability, negligence or otherwise, or from any use or
operation of any methods, products, instructions or ideas contained in the material
herein. Because of rapid advances in the medical sciences, in particular, independent
verification of diagnoses and drug dosages should be made

ISBN: 978-0-12-387691-1
ISSN: 0079-7421

For information on all Academic Press publications
visit our website at elsevierdirect.com

Printed and bound in USA
11   12   13   10   9   8   7   6   5   4   3   2   1

Working together to grow
libraries in developing countries

www.elsevier.com | www.bookaid.org | www.sabre.org

ELSEVIER   BOOK AID
             International   Sabre Foundation

Contents

Contributors

Sian L. Beilock
Department of Psychology, University of Chicago, Chicago, IL, USA

Daniel M. Belenky
Department of Psychology and Learning Research and Development Center,
University of Pittsburgh, Pittsburgh, PA, USA

Jennifer L. Docktor
Department of Physics, University of Illinois at Urbana-Champaign,
Urbana, IL, USA

Lisa K. Fazio
Department of Psychology, Carnegie Mellon University, Pittsburgh, PA, USA

Andrew F. Heckler
Department of Physics, The Ohio State University, Columbus, OH, USA

Richard E. Mayer
Department of Psychology, University of California, Santa Barbara, CA, USA

Jose P. Mestre
Departments of Physics and Educational Psychology, University of Illinois at
Urbana-Champaign, Urbana, IL, USA

Timothy J. Nokes
Department of Psychology and Learning Research and Development Center,
University of Pittsburgh, Pittsburgh, PA, USA

Adam L. Putnam
Department of Psychology, Washington University in St. Louis, St. Louis,
MO, USA

Aryn Pyke
Department of Psychology, Carnegie Mellon University, Pittsburgh, PA, USA

Gerardo Ramirez
Department of Psychology, University of Chicago, Chicago, IL, USA

Bethany Rittle-Johnson
Department of Psychology and Human Development, Peabody College,
Vanderbilt University, Nashville, TN, USA

Henry L. Roediger, III
Department of Psychology, Washington University in St. Louis, St. Louis, MO, USA

Brian H. Ross
Beckman Institute and Department of Psychology, University of Illinois at Urbana-Champaign, Urbana, IL, USA

Robert S. Siegler
Department of Psychology, Carnegie Mellon University, Pittsburgh, PA, USA

Megan A. Smith
Department of Psychology, Washington University in St. Louis, St. Louis, MO, USA

Jon R. Star
Graduate School of Education, Harvard University, Cambridge, MA, USA

Natalie E. Strand
Department of Physics, University of Illinois at Urbana-Champaign, Urbana, IL, USA

John Sweller
School of Education, University of New South Wales, Sydney, New South Wales, Australia

Preface

Education and cognitive psychology are natural companions, albeit ones with the minor frictions that arise from slightly different goals. A major goal of education is to teach students to learn and think. We want students to learn particular content information, to learn to think within particular domains, to learn to approach situations and problems (and to reflect upon them) in productive ways, and to learn how to learn new information on their own. A major goal of cognitive psychology is to understand how people acquire and process new information, how people learn and think. An understanding of learning and thinking seems an important consideration to teaching learning and thinking. For over a hundred years, some psychologists have focused on examining learning and thinking within educational contexts or applying psychological principles to education, but it has been a relatively small group.

Why has there not been more collaboration between education and cognitive psychology? The answers depend on whom one asks but we can point to a number of partial answers. From the psychologists' perspective, the goal of constructing theories of learning and thinking requires carefully controlled experiments and manipulations, both rather difficult to achieve in real-world educational situations. Testing in schools is messy and cumbersome compared to the usual reliance on college subject pools. To develop theories requires much back and forth between thinking and testing, so having tests that can be done quickly, over an hour or a few hours, not over the course of a semester or school year, is a big advantage. From the educators' perspectives, psychological theories that have been tested in controlled experiments often leave open how to apply them in authentic educational settings as well as concerns about whether the effect in such settings will warrant the effort. From the perspective of both, there is usually little collaborative effort—little experience working with people from "the other side."

Much has changed in the past several years and the goal of this volume is to provide some illustrations of these changes. Again, the reasons for the change depend on whom one asks, but we can again point to some partial answers. From the psychologists' perspectives, the theoretical development over the past few decades has been great and there has been much expansion on topics closely related to education—complex learning, memory, reasoning, and problem solving. The theories have developed sufficiently within the laboratory to enable us to understand many of the conditions under which particular effects might be realized. In addition, there is greater interest in examining theories in more complex, authentic contexts—not only to show their viability but also to provide true tests of where they might succeed or fail. From the educators' perspective, in addition to their usual motivation to improve instruction, an important factor has been the push to adopt evidence-based educational practices. In addition to these separate reasons, there has been a strong funding-related push, principally from the Institute of Education Sciences (IES) and the National Science Foundation (NSF), to develop theories for such practices, to adopt evidence-based practices, and to promote collaborations between researchers and educators. The combination of interests and funding is a potent one, helping foster new collaborations.

In fact, this book would not have come about were it not for one such collaboration between the two editors. We met partly by happenstance 6 years ago-Mestre is a physicist with a long-term interest in physics education and Ross is a cognitive scientist with interests in learning, concepts, and problem solving. The meeting has led to a productive collaboration at the intersection of cognitive science and physics learning, including IES support to study conceptual learning in physics. It has been, more so than the usual collaboration, a major learning experience. Mestre has learned much about experimental cognitive science, a welcome opportunity given his professional trajectory, from physicist, to educational researcher, to pseudocognitive scientist. Ross has (kind of) learned some physics, often painfully and accompanied by smiles and laughs from physics students and postdocs. We have learned much about both cognition and physics learning by examining our ideas from another perspective and trying to apply them in classroom settings.

Over the past several years, we have seen changes in attitudes and research, as more cognitive researchers examine theoretical ideas in educational settings, often with education collaborators. We see this work being developed in at least two ways. First, educators and researchers interested in specific educational domains often notice a large problem in educational settings (e.g., the lack of conceptual understanding in physics students). This observation is then followed by asking: "what do we know from research on cognition that might provide a way to close this gap?" Second, cognitive researchers may have an effect or principle that has been well studied in the laboratory and want to test its efficacy in a more complex setting. To apply this idea to an educational setting may require a careful consideration of what variables might be most important, how much control one might have on them, and how the setting might influence examining this effect. Researchers often learn much about their ideas by being forced to construct an instructional intervention and apply it in a classroom.

This volume contains overviews of research projects from a breadth of researchers: cognitive psychologists, developmental psychologists, educational psychologists, and science educators. The contributors were chosen both for the quality of their work and the variety of their contributions—general principles; influence of affect and motivation; focus on math and science education. In the chapter by Roediger, Putnam, and Smith, testing is given a fresh look from the perspective of benefits to the student. If used by students as a study strategy they argue that self-testing in various forms can provide many benefits, from improving memory retrieval and retention, to identifying gaps in knowledge, to enhancing metacognitive monitoring.

Two chapters offer broad-ranging perspectives on instructional design. Sweller's chapter on cognitive load theory links human cognitive architecture to evolutionary theory and argues for two different types of knowledge that humans acquire, biologically primary and biologically secondary, the latter being the type learned through schooling. By considering how cognitive architecture operates, cognitive load theory can be used to test empirically instructional procedures designed to increase knowledge in long-term memory, while reducing unnecessary load on working memory. Mayer argues that the design of effective multimedia instruction should apply principles from the science of learning, the science of assessment, and the science of instruction, and presents examples of successful multimedia instruction based on applications of those principles.

The impact of affective factors in math and science performance is explored in two chapters. Nokes and Belenky begin by reviewing a theoretical framework for transfer that blends both a classical and modern perspective, and then incorporate into the framework the notion of competence motivation as manifested in achievement goals. The predictions of performance based on achievement goals in a transfer task were empirically supported. Beilock and Ramirez discuss ways of mitigating the impact of negative-emotion-inducing factors such as choking under pressure, math anxiety, and stereotype threat in test performance. Combining ideas from a variety of research areas, they show how such seemingly deep-seated problems may be improved in surprisingly simple ways.

Interventions for improving mathematical performance are explored in two chapters. Siegler, Fazio, and Pyke report on a theoretically based intervention that they devised for helping preschoolers develop a sense for the relationship between counting and magnitude. Their short intervention resulted in an impressive boost in low-income children's mathematical knowledge. Rittle-Johnson and Star begin by discussing how different types of comparison (e.g., which between two correct methods for solving a problem is more efficient?) have been used to promote learning across different domains, and then discuss their efforts in designing instructional activities that exploit comparison to support math learning in classrooms. Their research and analysis of the literature indicate that different types of comparison support different learning outcomes, and that degree of learning from comparison depends on individual differences.

Two chapters explore problem solving and conceptual understanding in physics. Heckler discusses common error patterns in physics reasoning and argues that the canonical attribution of those patterns to faulty reasoning or misconceptions (top-down processes) may be too simplistic. He hypothesizes that error patterns are also influenced by competition between relevant and irrelevant information (bottom-up processes) in the problems/questions/graphs/diagrams that students process in route to answering scientific questions. Mestre, Docktor, Strand, and Ross address how one can get physics students to go beyond problem solving and develop a conceptual understanding. They outline three research projects that encourage the student to perform conceptual analyses of problems and provide evidence for improvement in students' conceptual learning.

We see these chapters as illustrations of what we hope will be a growing field applying cognitive principles in education. Education will be improved both by broadening the consideration of new practices and by adopting evidence-based practices. Cognition will be improved both by another means of generating important issues to study and by testing ideas in more complex real-world settings. Best of all, student learning and thinking will be improved.

CHAPTER ONE

TEN BENEFITS OF TESTING AND THEIR APPLICATIONS TO EDUCATIONAL PRACTICE

Henry L. Roediger III, Adam L. Putnam *and* Megan A. Smith

Contents

Abstract

Testing in school is usually done for purposes of assessment, to assign students grades (from tests in classrooms) or rank them in terms of abilities (in standardized tests). Yet tests can serve other purposes in educational settings that greatly improve performance; this chapter reviews 10 other benefits of testing. Retrieval practice occurring during tests can greatly enhance retention of the retrieved information (relative to no testing or even to restudying). Furthermore, besides its durability, such repeated retrieval produces knowledge that can be retrieved flexibly and transferred to other situations. On open-ended assessments (such as essay tests), retrieval practice required by tests can help students organize information and form a coherent knowledge base. Retrieval of some information on a test can also lead to easier retrieval of related information, at least on

Psychology of Learning and Motivation, Volume 55

ISSN 0079-7421, DOI 10.1016/B978-0-12-387691-1.00001-6

© 2011 Elsevier Inc.

All rights reserved.

delayed tests. Besides these direct effects of testing, there are also indirect effects that are quite positive. If students are quizzed frequently, they tend to study more and with more regularity. Quizzes also permit students to discover gaps in their knowledge and focus study efforts on difficult material; furthermore, when students study after taking a test, they learn more from the study episode than if they had not taken the test. Quizzing also enables better metacognitive monitoring for both students and teachers because it provides feedback as to how well learning is progressing. Greater learning would occur in educational settings if students used self-testing as a study strategy and were quizzed more frequently in class.

1. INTRODUCTION

Benefits of testing? Surely, to most educators, this statement represents an oxymoron. Testing in schools is usually thought to serve only the purpose of evaluating students and assigning them grades. Those are important reasons for tests, but not what we have in mind. Most teachers view tests (and other forms of assessment, such as homework, essays, and papers) as necessary evils. Yes, students study and learn more when given assignments and tests, but they are an ordeal for both the student (who must complete them) and the teacher (who must construct and grade them). Quizzes and tests are given frequently in elementary schools, often at the rate of several or more a week, but testing decreases in frequency the higher a student rises in the educational system. By the time students are in college, they may be given only a midterm exam and a final exam in many introductory level courses. Of course, standardized tests are also given to students to assess their relative performance compared to other students in their country and assign them a percentile ranking. However, for purposes of this chapter, we focus on the testing that occurs in the classroom as part of the course or self-testing that students may use themselves as a study strategy (although surveys show that this practice is not widespread).

Why might testing improve performance? One key benefit is the active retrieval that occurs during tests. William James (1890, p. 646) wrote:

> A curious peculiarity of our memory is that things are impressed better by active than by passive repetition. I mean that in learning (by heart, for example), when we almost know the piece, it pays better to wait and recollect by an effort from within, than to look at the book again. If we recover the words in the former way, we shall probably know them the next time; if in the latter way, we shall very likely need the book once more.

James presented no evidence for this statement, apparently basing it on introspection. However, experimental reports appearing in the next 20 years showed he was right (Abbott, 1909; Gates, 1917). The act of retrieving when taking a test makes the tested material more memorable, either relative to no activity or compared to restudying the material. The size of the testing effect, as it has been named, also increases with the number of tests given.

Throughout the twentieth century, examination of the testing effect occurred in fits and starts. Gates (1917) provided the first thorough examination, but other important studies were done by Jones (1923/1924), Spitzer (1939), Tulving (1967), and Izawa (1970). In 1989, Glover bemoaned the fact that the testing effect had not been applied to education and the subtitle of his paper on the testing phenomenon was "not gone, but nearly forgotten." Since this rather gloomy appraisal, interest in testing and retrieval practice has made a great comeback. Carrier and Pashler (1992) developed a particular paired-associate learning paradigm that has been used extensively since then, and their study may serve as a landmark for a resurgence of interest in testing over the past 20 years.

Roediger and Karpicke (2006b) provided a thorough review of the early testing work as well as research conducted since that time. But even in the half-dozen years since that review was published, research on retrieval practice and testing has grown rapidly. Many papers cited in this chapter answer important questions that came after 2006, as will become obvious over the course of the chapter.

1.1. Direct and indirect effects of testing

One critical distinction is between the direct effects tests have on retention and the indirect effects provided by tests (Roediger & Karpicke, 2006b). We will refer to this distinction throughout the chapter. Briefly, as the name implies, direct effects arise from the test itself. So, for example, if a student is asked "Which kings fought in the Battle of Hastings in 1066?" and she correctly answered the question, her retrieval of this fact would lead to it being better recollected again later than if she had no practice or had simply studied the answer. This is an example of the direct effect of testing (e.g., Carrier & Pashler, 1992). Incidentally, in case you need it, the answer is that the forces of Duke William II of Normandy overwhelmed King Harold II's English forces at Hastings, hence "the Norman conquest."

The indirect effects of testing refer to other possible effects that testing might have. For example, if students are quizzed every week, they would probably study more (and more regularly) during a semester than if they were tested only on a midterm and a final exam. Thus, testing would have an indirect effect on apportionment of study activities. We return to evidence bearing on this issue later (Section 11).

The above two examples are clear, but in some cases tests may have both direct and indirect benefits. We will revisit this issue from time to time throughout the chapter. We now consider the 10 benefits of testing (see Table 1), but we have a section at the end outlining possible detriments to testing, too.

2. BENEFIT 1: THE TESTING EFFECT: RETRIEVAL AIDS LATER RETENTION

In this section, we review several experiments demonstrating the basic testing effect, the fact that information retrieved from memory leads to better performance on a later test. There are perhaps a hundred experiments we could choose from, but we have selected two straightforward ones from our own lab to make the case. The first experiment used easily nameable pictures as materials (the kind of material that experimental psychologists like to use) whereas the second experiment used nonfiction prose materials more relevant to education. However, the basic testing effect has been obtained with many other types of materials, such as foreign language vocabulary, map reading, general knowledge questions, and so on.

Wheeler and Roediger (1992) conducted an experiment in which a strong testing effect occurred, although the experiment was mostly about a different topic. We present selected conditions here from their experiment to make our points about testing. Their subjects saw 60 pictures

Table 1 Ten Benefits of Testing

Benefit	1	The testing effect: retrieval aids later retention
Benefit	2	Testing identifies gaps in knowledge
Benefit	3	Testing causes students to learn more from the next learning episode
Benefit	4	Testing produces better organization of knowledge
Benefit	5	Testing improves transfer of knowledge to new contexts
Benefit	6	Testing can facilitate retrieval of information that was not tested
Benefit	7	Testing improves metacognitive monitoring
Benefit	8	Testing prevents interference from prior material when learning new material
Benefit	9	Testing provides feedback to instructors
Benefit	10	Frequent testing encourages students to study

while they listened to a story, with instructions that they would later be asked to recall the names of the pictures. The pictures were integrated into the story so that when an object was named in the story, the picture appeared on the screen. Subjects were told that paying attention to the story would help them retain the pictures (which was true). After hearing the story and seeing the pictures, subjects were given free recall tests in which they were given a blank sheet of paper and had to recall as many of the names of the 60 pictures as possible.

After hearing the story, one group of subjects was told that they could leave and return a week later for a test. A second group was given a single test that lasted 7 min and then they were excused. The third group was given three successive 7-min tests after the learning phase; that is, they recalled the pictures once, were given a new blank sheet and recalled as many items as possible a second time, and then repeated the process a third time. The group that recalled pictures once recalled about 32 pictures and the group that recalled them three times recalled 32, 35, and 36 pictures (i.e., performance increased across tests, a phenomenon called hypermnesia; Erdelyi & Becker, 1974).

For present purposes, the data of most interest are those on the final retention test 1 week later when the students returned to the lab for more testing. Students in all three groups had heard the story and seen the pictures once, so the only difference among the three groups was how many tests they had taken just after studying the materials (0, 1, or 3). How did this manipulation affect recall? The data to answer this question are shown in Figure 1, where it can be seen that those who had not been tested recalled 17.4 pictures, those who had been tested once recalled 23.3 pictures, and those who had previously been tested three times recalled 31.8 pictures. Thus, taking three tests improved recall by nearly 80% a week later relative to the condition with no tests.

Another way to consider the data is by comparing the scores on the immediate test just after study to those a week later. Recall that on the first test after study, subjects produced about 32 items. We can assume that those subjects who were not tested immediately after study could have recalled 32 had they been tested, yet a week later they could recall only 17, showing 45% forgetting. However, the group that was tested three times immediately were still able to recall 32 items a week after study, thus giving three tests essentially eliminated forgetting after a week. This outcome shows the power of testing.

Yet a critic might complain that the Wheeler and Roediger (1992) results could be due to an artifact. Perhaps, the critic would maintain, the outcome in Figure 1 has nothing to do with testing per se. Rather, all "testing" did was to permit selective restudy of information. The group that did not take a test did not restudy any material, whereas the group that took the single test restudied 32 of the 60 pictures, and the group with

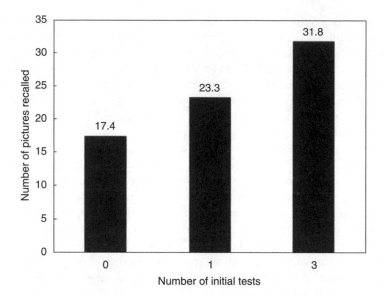

Figure 1 The number of pictures recalled on a final recall test after a 1-week delay, adapted from Table 1 of Wheeler and Roediger (1992). The number of initial tests strongly influenced final test recall. On the first immediate recall test, subjects recalled, on average, 32.25 pictures. The results indicate that taking three immediate recall tests will effectively eliminate forgetting over a 1-week period.

three tests restudied 32, then 35, and finally 36 pictures (mostly studying the same items each time). Perhaps it was merely this process of restudying that led to good performance a week later. After all, it is hardly a surprise to find that the more often a person studies material, the better they remember it. Thompson, Wenger, and Bartling (1978) voiced this interpretation of testing research. In a similar vein, Slamecka and Katsaiti (1988) argued that repeated testing may create overlearning on a certain subset of items and that such overlearning is somehow responsible for the effect.

These criticisms of the testing effect are often voiced, but dozens of studies have laid them to rest by including a "restudy" control group in addition to a testing group. That is, in the comparison condition, students restudy the set of material for the same amount of time that others are engaged in taking a test. When this procedure is followed, the testing group is at a disadvantage in terms of restudy of information compared to the restudy group. The reason is that in the testing condition subjects only have the opportunity to restudy the amount of information they can recall (about 53%—32 ÷ 60 × 100—in the Wheeler and Roediger study), whereas in the restudy condition subjects usually receive the entire set of material again (100%). Thus, if the testing effect were due to restudying, using such a restudy control should make the testing effects disappear or even reverse. However, this does not happen, at least on delayed tests.

Consider an experiment by Roediger and Karpicke (2006a). They used relatively complex prose passages on such topics as "sea otters" that were full of facts. The test given was free recall; subjects were asked to recall as much as they could from the passage when given its name and the protocols were scored in terms of the number of idea units recalled from the passage. In one condition, subjects studied the passage once and were tested on it three times; on each test, they recalled about 70% of the material. Another group studied the passage three times and was tested once (recalling 77%). Finally, a third group studied the passage four times, so subjects had the greatest study exposure to the material (reading the passage four times) in this condition. Thus, subjects in the three conditions were exposed in one form or another to the material four times via various numbers of studies and test events. We can label the conditions STTT, SSST, and SSSS, where S stands for study of the passage and T stands for its testing.

The data of critical interest were those that occurred on a final criterion test, which was given 5 min or 1 week after the learning session. As can be seen in the left-hand side of Figure 2, when the final test was given shortly after the initial four study/test periods, recall was correlated with the number of study episodes: the SSSS condition led to better performance than the SSST condition that in turn was better than STTT condition. As students have known for generations, cramming does work if a test occurs immediately after studying. However, for subjects given the final test a week later, exactly the opposite ordering of performance emerged: the more students had been tested during the learning session, the better was performance. This outcome occurred despite the fact that subjects who had repeatedly studied the material had received much more exposure to it. Once again, receiving tests greatly slowed down forgetting (see also Karpicke, 2009; Karpicke & Roediger, 2008; Wheeler, Ewers, & Buonanno, 2003). Another point to take from Figure 2 is that a testing effect is more likely to emerge at longer delays after study. On a test given soon after studying, repeated studying can lead to performance greater than that with testing.

We could add dozen more experiments to this section on the basic testing effect (e.g., Carpenter & DeLosh, 2005, 2006; Cull, 2000; Pyc & Rawson, 2007), but we will desist. Many experiments will be reviewed later that have the same kind of design and establish conditions in which testing memory produces a mnemonic boost relative to a restudy control condition (as in Roediger & Karpicke, 2006a) or relative to a condition with no further exposure (as in Wheeler & Roediger, 1992). However, even in the latter case, we can rest assured that the testing effect is mostly due to causes other than restudying the material.

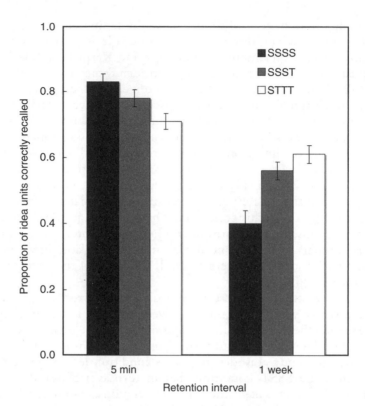

Figure 2   Mean number of idea units recalled on the final test taken 5 min or 1 week after the initial learning session. During learning, subjects studied prose passages and then completed a varying number of study (S) and test (T) periods. Error bars represent standard errors of the mean (estimated from Figure 2 of Roediger and Karpicke (2006a)).
Adapted from Experiment 2 of Roediger and Karpicke (2006a).

3. Benefit 2: Testing Identifies Gaps in Knowledge

The testing effect represents a direct benefit of testing; the second benefit is indirect. Taking a test permits students to assess what they know and what they do not know, so that they can concentrate study efforts on areas in which their knowledge is deficient. Students may take a practice quiz, realize which questions or items they got wrong, and then spend more time studying the items they missed. For example, Amlund, Kardash, and Kulhavy (1986) found that subjects corrected errors on a second test if they had an intervening study session after the first test. Other research shows that when students receive opportunities to restudy material after a test, they spend longer on restudying items that were missed than those that were correctly retrieved (see Son & Kornell, 2008).

Kornell and Bjork (2007) provided evidence from a laboratory experiment that students are typically unaware that learning can occur during testing. In one experiment, students learned a set of Indonesian–English vocabulary words by repeated trials. They had the option of studying the pairs or being tested on them (with feedback) on each occasion and could switch between the two modes at any point. Most students began in the study mode, although nearly everyone changed to the test mode after the first two trials. Kornell and Bjork interpreted this outcome as indicating that students wanted to achieve a basic level of knowledge before testing themselves. In addition, Kornell and Bjork also reported the results of a survey in which students were asked whether they quizzed themselves while studying (using a quiz at the end of a chapter, a practice quiz, flashcards, or something else); 68% of respondents replied that they quizzed themselves "to figure out how well I have learned the information I'm studying" (Kornell & Bjork, 2007, p. 222). Only 18% of respondents recognized that testing actually facilitated further learning.

In another survey on study habits, Karpicke, Butler, and Roediger (2009) asked college students to list their most commonly used study habits (rather than asking directly if they used testing, as in the Kornell and Bjork (2007) survey). When the question was framed in this open-ended manner, only 11% of students listed retrieval practice as a study technique they used, suggesting that students may be generally unaware of the direct or indirect benefits of testing. On a forced response question, students had to choose between studying and testing in a hypothetical situation of preparing for a test. Only 18% of students chose to self-test and more than half of those explained that they chose to self-test to identify what they did or did not know to guide further study. Thus these two points are in broad agreement with the Kornell and Bjork (2007) findings.

In further surveys, McCabe (2011) found that college students' knowledge of effective study strategies is quite poor without specific instruction. She provided students with educational scenarios and asked them to select study strategies that would be effective. She based her strategies on findings from cognitive psychology studies, including such principles as dual coding and retrieval practice. McCabe found that students were generally unaware of the effectiveness of the strategies. If this is the case with college students, one can only assume that high school students and others in lower grades would, at best, show the same outcome.

Testing one's memory allows one to evaluate whether the information is really learned and accessible. Karpicke et al. (2009) suggested that one of the reasons students reread materials rather than testing themselves is that rereading leads to increased feelings of fluency of the material—it seems so familiar as they reread it they assume they must know it. Also, in contrast to self-testing, restudying is easy. In short, students may lack metacognitive awareness of the direct benefits of testing, while at the same time understand that self-testing can be useful as a guide to future studying. Testing helps students learn because it helps them understand what facts they might not know, so they can allocate future study time accordingly.

4. BENEFIT 3: TESTING CAUSES STUDENTS TO LEARN MORE FROM THE NEXT STUDY EPISODE

Another benefit of retrieval practice is it can enhance learning during future study sessions. That is, when students take a test and then restudy material, they learn more from the presentation than they would if they restudied without taking a test. This outcome is called test-potentiated learning (Izawa, 1966). The benefits of test potentiation are distinctly different from the direct benefits of testing per se, although in many practical situations (e.g., receiving feedback after tests) the two are mixed together.

Izawa (1966) was perhaps the first researcher to study the test potentiation effect and has contributed much to our understanding of test potentiation. Her initial forays into the area emerged after asking questions about whether learning could occur during a test. She proposed three specific hypotheses. First, neither learning nor forgetting occurred on tests. Second, learning and forgetting (as well as learning of incorrect information) could occur on test trials. Finally, although learning and forgetting might not occur on a test session, taking a test might influence the amount of learning during a future study session. Izawa studied how different patterns of study, test, and neutral trials affected later performance.

Across many experiments (e.g., Izawa, 1966, 1968, 1970), Izawa concluded that neither forgetting nor learning occurred on test trials, but taking a test could improve the amount of material learned on a subsequent study session. While this conclusion may appear to contradict the basic finding of the testing effect, the contradiction is resolved by examining how learning and forgetting are defined in Izawa's basic paradigm. Izawa's conclusion was that no learning or forgetting occurred during a test trial, but she made no assumptions about how learning or forgetting would be affected *after* the test trial; the testing effect can be interpreted as a slowing of forgetting after the test.

Other researchers have continued to explore test potentiation in different contexts. Pyc and Rawson (2010) showed that subjects formed more effective mediators (mnemonic devices that link a cue to a target) when they were tested before a study session compared to when they were not. Karpicke and Roediger (2007) found that subjects learned more from a single study session after being tested three times relative to completing one test prior to study. Similarly, Karpicke (2009) showed a test potentiation effect by comparing three different patterns of study and test on how students learned foreign language vocabulary. One condition was the standard cycle alternating between study and test trials; during a study trial, subjects saw both a Swahili word and its English translation, and on a test trial, they saw the Swahili word and were asked to recall the English word, without any corrective feedback. The standard cycle consisted of three alternative study–test trials, or STSTST. Another group studied three times before the first test and had one intervening study session before the final test (SSSTST). Finally, a third group had five study sessions before the final test period (SSSSST).

Figure 3 shows the results of the experiment. Clearly, alternating study and test trials caused subjects to recall more word pairs on the final test than for others who spent equivalent time studying. This outcome can be

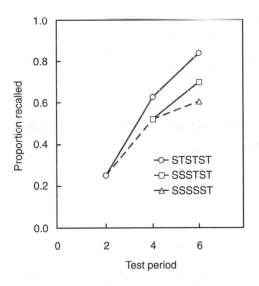

Figure 3 The potentiating effects of testing on learning. Subjects alternated study and test (STSTST), studied with only one intervening test (SSSTST), or studied with no intervening tests (SSSSST). The dashed line connects performance on the first test across conditions to show the effect of repeated studying on recall. The solid lines connect performance within each condition. The results show that inserting test trials leads to greater learning by the final test.
Adapted from Experiment 1 of Karpicke (2009).

interpreted as the test potentiating later learning, because tests enabled learning from the later study episode.

Other researchers, however, have had difficulty obtaining test potentiation effects when they are examined in more complex designs that discount the fundamental testing effect (McDermott & Arnold, 2010). For example, all the experiments described in the previous paragraph could be interpreted as exemplifying direct effects of testing because the two effects are mixed together in those designs (e.g., the design of Karpicke and Roediger (2007) and others described above). Thus, the major difficulty in examining test potentiation is separating its effects (enhanced learning from restudying) from other factors related to testing (such as the direct effect of testing on improving recall). However, McDermott and Arnold (2010) have succeeded in replicating Izawa's work showing test-potentiated learning under certain conditions, so both the direct effect and the indirect effect of test-potentiated learning are secure findings.

In many standard studies on testing, feedback is provided after the test and this condition is compared to a condition in which no test is given (but students study the material). The test plus feedback condition usually greatly outpaces the restudy-only condition, even when timing parameters are equated (i.e., subjects are exposed to material for the same amount of time). The benefit of testing probably arises both from the direct effect of testing and from the indirect effect of testing potentiating future learning (from feedback), but further research is needed to establish this point and determine the relative contributions of the testing effect and the test potentiation effect in these circumstances.

5. BENEFIT 4: TESTING PRODUCES BETTER ORGANIZATION OF KNOWLEDGE

Another indirect benefit of retrieval practice is that it can improve the conceptual organization of practiced materials, especially on tests that are relatively open-ended (such as free recall in the lab or essay tests in the classroom). Gates (1917) postulated that one of the reasons retrieval practice leads to increased performance is that retrieval (or recitation, as he called it) causes students to organize information more than does reading. He suggested that as students actively recall material, they are more likely to notice important details and weave them into a cohesive structure.

Masson and McDaniel (1981) showed that an additional testing session after study resulted in higher performance on delayed recall and recognition tests and, more important, that the additional test yielded higher organization on the final recall test. Their primary measure of organization was the adjusted ratio of clustering (ARC), which is a measure of how often words from the same category are recalled together in free recall with an adjustment for the overall level of recall. Scores range from −1 to 1, with 1 representing perfect organization or clustering and 0 representing chance clustering (Roenker, Thompson, & Brown, 1971). Masson and McDaniel's results suggested that the test resulted in improved organization and higher recall on final tests.

More recently, other research (Zaromb, 2010; Congleton & Rajaram, 2010) has explored the relationship between testing and organization. Experiments reported by Zaromb and Roediger (2010), for example, showed that retrieval practice during testing improves both the organization of materials and their recall. In fact, the increased organization from previous retrievals may provide an underlying mechanism of the testing effect, at least in free recall.

In one experiment (Zaromb & Roediger, 2010, Experiment 2), subjects studied categorized word lists in one of several learning conditions (although we are considering only two groups here). One group studied the list of words twice with different encoding instructions; in the first cycle, subjects made pleasantness ratings and in the second cycle, they were given intentional learning instructions. A second group of subjects learned a list of items by making pleasantness ratings, and then they immediately attempted a final free recall of the list (with no feedback). Both groups returned to the lab after a 24-h delay and took both a free recall test and a cued recall test. Table 2 shows the results. In the free recall test, subjects who had taken an intermediate test showed increased performance as measured by total number of words recalled.

The same outcome occurred when total words were decomposed into the number of categories recalled (Rc; subjects are given credit for recalling a category if one item is recalled from that category) and the number of words recalled per category (Rw/c). Most important, the tested group showed greater ARC score compared to the group that studied twice. A similar pattern of results in recall was obtained for the cued recall test where subjects where provided with the category labels as retrieval cues. Zaromb and Roediger also showed that testing improves subjective organization, or recall of items in a more consistent order (Tulving, 1962).

In sum, testing can increase both category clustering and subjective organization of materials compared to restudying, and this may be one of the underlying mechanisms driving the testing effect, at least in free recall and other open-ended kinds of tests (e.g., essay tests). Further research is needed to generalize this result to educational contexts, but extrapolating from the current work, the prediction would be that testing improves organization of knowledge.

Table 2 Mean Proportion of Words Recalled, Number of Categories Recalled (Rc), Number of Words Per Category Recalled (Rw/c), ARC Scores on Delayed Free, and Cued Recall Tests

Measure		Free Recall		Cued Recall	
		S_pS_i	S_pT	S_pS_i	S_pT
Recall	*Prop.*	.21	.45	.37	.61
	CI	(.06)	(.06)	(.06)	(.05)
Rc	*M*	8.19	12.56	15.69	17.25
	CI	(1.32)	(.74)	(1.09)	(.67)
Rw/c	*M*	2.16	3.17	2.09	3.17
	CI	(.35)	(.28)	(.26)	(.27)
ARC	*M*	.60	.85		
	CI	(.17)	(.04)		

Note: Values in parentheses are 95% confidence intervals (CI). Subjects made pleasantness ratings on the first trial and had intentional learning instructions on the second trial (S_pS_i) or made pleasantness ratings on the first trial followed by a recall test on the second trial (S_pT). Adapted from Experiment 2 of Zaromb and Roediger (2010).

6. BENEFIT 5: TESTING IMPROVES TRANSFER OF KNOWLEDGE TO NEW CONTEXTS

One criticism of retrieval practice or testing research is that students may be learning little factoids in a rote, verbatim way. Critics complain that testing is the old "kill and drill" procedure of education from 100 years ago that produces "inert knowledge" that cannot be transferred to new situations. However, proponents of testing argue that retrieval practice induces readily accessible information that can be flexibly used to solve new problems. This issue leads to the crucial question of whether knowledge acquired via retrieval practice (relative to other techniques) can be applied to new settings.

Recent research shows that the mnemonic benefits of taking a test are not limited to the specific questions or facts that were tested; retrieval practice also improves transfer of knowledge to new contexts. Transfer may be defined as applying knowledge learned in one situation to a new situation. Researchers often categorize transfer as being near or far; near transfer occurs if the new situation is similar to the learning situation, whereas far transfer occurs if the new situation is very different from the learning situation. Barnett and Ceci (2002) proposed a taxonomy for transfer studies, arguing that transfer might be measured on many continuous dimensions (e.g., knowledge domain, physical context, temporal context, etc.).

The topic of transfer is an old one—Ebbinghaus (1885) conducted transfer experiments—but there has been a large growth in research over the past decade. Furthermore, transfer is extremely important in education; the purpose of education is to teach students information that they will be able to apply later in school, as well as in life after their schooling is finished. However, transfer of knowledge can be difficult to obtain (e.g., Gick & Holyoak, 1980). Far transfer is very difficult to obtain, yet is arguably the most important type of education to apply to settings encountered later in life (Barnett & Ceci, 2002). In fact, Detterman (1993) maintained that experiments investigating transfer are insignificant unless they are able to obtain far transfer on a number of dimensions. Given the important role of transfer in education and the difficulty in promoting its occurrence, the finding that testing can improve transfer is an important one.

Some evidence suggests that repeated testing can facilitate transfer better than restudying. For example, Carpenter, Pashler, and Vul (2006) showed that testing with word–word paired associates (denoted by A–B here) improved performance on a later test relative to additional study opportunities. When given A, subjects could recall B more often when they had previously been tested relative to only studying the pairs. More important, Carpenter et al. also tested subjects' recall for the A member of the pair when they were given B, so they were tested on the member of the pair that was not directly retrieved during initial testing. Recall was improved for these A items when learning had occurred via testing relative to repeated studying. Repeatedly testing with one member of the pair transferred to higher performance in recalling the other member of the pair. This could be considered a case of near transfer.

Similar benefits of testing have been shown with more complex materials, even in learning concepts. Jacoby, Wahlheim, and Coane (2010) showed that testing can improve classification of novel exemplars when students learn categories of birds. Students learned to classify birds by repeatedly studying or repeatedly testing examples of various classes of birds. During a study trial, students were presented with a picture of a bird and the name of the bird family to which it belonged (e.g., warbler presented with a picture of this type of bird). During a test trial, students were presented with only a picture of a bird and asked to name the family to which the bird belonged (like warbler), and then they received feedback (the correct name of the category). Students who were repeatedly tested were better able to classify new birds than those who repeatedly studied them, showing that testing helped subjects better apply their knowledge to new exemplars. In two other generally similar examples of transfer, testing improved transfer relative to restudying using multimedia materials (Johnson & Mayer, 2009) and with elementary school children learning about maps (Rohrer, Taylor, & Sholar, 2010).

In a series of experiments, Butler (2010) recently demonstrated that repeated testing not only increases retention of facts and concepts learned from prose passages, but also increases transfer of knowledge to new contexts (relative to repeated studying). In Experiments 1 and 2, repeatedly testing with questions in one knowledge domain (e.g., information about bats) promoted retention in answering the same questions as well as new questions within the same knowledge domain. Better performance on new questions provided evidence of near transfer. More impressively, in Experiment 3 Butler showed that repeated testing improved far transfer— that is, transfer to new questions in different knowledge domains (again, relative to repeated restudying). In this experiment, subjects studied prose passages on various topics (e.g., bats; the respiratory system). Subjects then restudied some of the passages three times and took three tests on other passages. After each question during the repeated tests, subjects were presented with the question and the correct answer for feedback. One week later subjects completed the final transfer test. On the final test, subjects were required to transfer what they learned during the initial learning session to new inferential questions in different knowledge domains (e.g., from echolocation in bats to similar processes used in sonar on submarines).

Figure 4 depicts the results from the final transfer test. This experiment showed that repeated testing led to improved transfer to new questions in a new domain relative to restudying the material. Butler (2010) also showed through conditional analyses that retrieving the information during the initial test was important in producing transfer to a new domain. Subjects were more likely to correctly answer a transfer question when they had answered the corresponding question during initial testing. According to Butler, retrieval of information may be a critical mechanism producing greater transfer of that information later.

Practicing retrieval has been shown time and again to produce enhanced memory later for the tested material. One criticism in educational circles has been that testing appears to produce enhanced memory for the facts tested, but that such "kill and drill" procedures may produce "inert" or "encapsulated" learning that will not transfer to new settings. However, the experiments reviewed here show that testing does produce transfer, even far transfer (Butler, 2010). Along with the other evidence reviewed, it appears that retrieval practice produces knowledge that can be flexibly transferred, which overcomes this criticism.

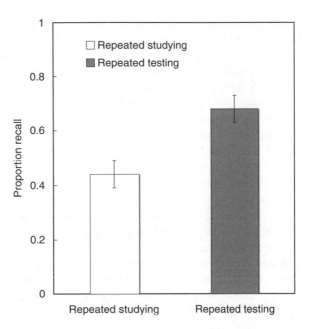

Figure 4 Performance on the final transfer test containing inferential questions from different knowledge domains 1 week after initial learning. Error bars represent the standard error of the mean. During initial learning, subjects repeatedly studied the prose passages or were repeatedly tested on the prose passages.
Adapted from Experiment 3 of Butler (2010).

7. BENEFIT 6: TESTING CAN FACILITATE RETRIEVAL OF MATERIAL THAT WAS NOT TESTED

One potential limiting factor of implementing testing in a classroom setting is choosing which material to test. It is unrealistic for an instructor to test students on everything. Fortunately, research on testing suggests that retrieval practice does not simply enhance retention of the individual items retrieved during the initial test: taking a test can also produce retrieval-induced facilitation—a phenomenon that shows testing also improves retention of nontested but related material.

Chan, McDermott, and Roediger (2006) were the first to coin the term retrieval-induced facilitation, providing evidence for the effect in three experiments. Students studied a prose passage and then completed two initial short answer tests, restudied the passage twice, or did nothing (the control condition). Those in the initial testing group answered questions related to a subset of information from the passage. More important, another subset from the passage was not tested during the initial test, but this material was related to the questions that had been answered on the initial test. In the restudy condition, students read the answers but did not receive a test. After 24 h, all the students returned to complete a final test covering the entire passage. Results of the final test revealed that retention of the nontested information was superior when students had taken a test relative to conditions in which they restudied the material or in which they had no further exposure after study. Chan et al. concluded that testing not only improves retention for information covered within a test, but also improves retention for nontested information, at least when that information is related to the tested information.

In contrast, other researchers have found that retrieving some information may actually lead to forgetting of other information, a finding termed retrieval–induced forgetting (e.g., Anderson, Bjork, & Bjork, 1994). In a typical retrieval–induced forgetting experiment, subjects first study words in categories and then take an initial test. For some categories, half of the items are repeatedly retrieved during the initial test; for other categories, none of the items are retrieved during the initial test. The general finding is that the unpracticed items from the categories cued for retrieval practice are impaired on a later retention test relative to items from the nontested categories.

Retrieval–induced facilitation and retrieval–induced forgetting are obviously contradictory findings. Consequently, Chan (2009) sought to differentiate between conditions causing facilitation and conditions causing forgetting in these paradigms. In two experiments, he demonstrated the importance of integration of the materials and the delay of the test for the retrieval–induced facilitation and retrieval–induced forgetting effects. In his first experiment, subjects studied two prose passages; each passage was presented one sentence at a time on the computer. During study, some subjects were given the sentences in a coherent order and were told to integrate the information (the high integration condition). For another group of subjects, the sentences within each paragraph were scrambled to disrupt integration of information during study (the low integration condition). Similar to the Chan et al. (2006) experiments, an initial test occurred immediately after studying one of the passages, and subjects completed the same test twice in a row. Subjects completed the final test covering material from both the passages 20 min or 24 h after the completion of the initial learning phase.

Figure 5 depicts performance on the final test. Results reveal both a retrieval–induced facilitation effect (see the fourth pair of bars in Figure 5) and a retrieval–induced forgetting effect (see the first pair of bars in Figure 5) within the same experiment. This outcome demonstrates the importance of both integration of materials and delay of the final test for these effects. When subjects were instructed to integrate the information during study (i.e., the high integration condition) and the test was delayed

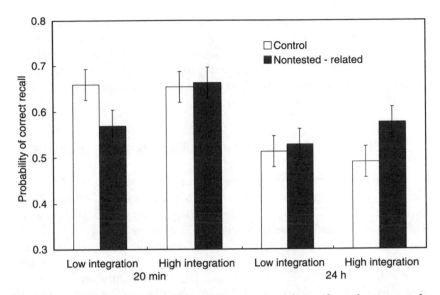

Figure 5 Performance on the final test for questions drawn from the passage that was not tested initially (control items) and questions drawn from the tested passage but were not present on the initial test (nontested related items). During the initial learning session, subjects studied two passages either in a coherent order with integration instructions or in a randomized order (low integration). Subjects completed an initial test for one of the passages. The final test was completed 20 min or 24 h after the initial learning session. Error bars represent standard errors.
Adapted from Experiment 1 of Chan (2009).

24 h, a retrieval-induced facilitation effect was found—subjects' performance was enhanced for the nontested items from the passage that was tested relative to the control items. However, when the ability to integrate during study was disrupted (i.e., the low integration condition) and the final test was only 20 min after the initial learning phase, a retrieval-induced inhibition effect was found—subjects' performance was reduced for the nontested items relative to control items. Despite the fact that contradictory results from retrieval-induced facilitation and retrieval-induced forgetting literatures emerge, it seems that these two effects do occur under different sets of conditions. The other two conditions in the experiment of Chan (2009) produced intermediate results.

Evidence from the retrieval-induced facilitation literature provides additional support for the use of testing to enhance learning and memory in educational settings. Notably, it seems that when conditions are more similar to those in educational settings, retrieval-induced facilitation occurs (see Cranney, Ahn, McKinnon, Morris, and Watts (2009) for further evidence of retrieval-induced facilitation in classroom settings). In addition, these effects seem to be durable—Chan (2010) increased the length of the retention interval, showing that the benefits of retrieval-induced facilitation can last up to 7 days. The experiments reviewed here show that testing can be used in classroom settings to enhance retention of both the tested material and the related but untested material. Retrieval-induced forgetting does not seem to occur on tests delayed a day or more (MacLeod & Macrae, 2001).

8. BENEFIT 7: TESTING IMPROVES METACOGNITIVE MONITORING

Another benefit of testing is improvement of metacognitive accuracy relative to restudying (e.g., Roediger & Karpicke, 2006a; Shaughnessy & Zechmeister, 1992). This point is related to the second one discussed—testing informs students as to what they know and what they do not know. However, in this case, the focus is on students' accurate predictions of their future performance. Testing permits students to have better calibration of their knowledge. If students only study material repeatedly, they may think that their familiarity with the material means that they know it and can retrieve it when needed. However, such familiarity can be misleading. These points have direct implications for educational settings—the better students are at differentiating what they do know and what they do not know well, the better they will be at acquiring new and more difficult material and studying efficiently (Thomas & McDaniel, 2007; Kornell & Son, 2009). Therefore, instead of simply restudying, teachers can administer quizzes and students can self-test to determine what material they know well and what material they do not know well.

Students' ability to accurately predict what they know and do not know is an important skill in education, but unfortunately students often make inaccurate predictions. When students reread material repeatedly, they are often overconfident in how well they know the material. Taking a test, however, can lead to students becoming less confident, a finding known as the underconfidence-with-practice effect (Koriat, Scheffer, & Ma'ayan, 2002; see also Finn & Metcalfe, 2007, 2008). Testing can help compensate for the tendency to be overly confident, which results in a more accurate assessment of learning.

In the first section on the direct effects of testing, we described an experiment by Roediger and Karpicke (2006a), showing that testing produces greater long-term benefits relative to studying. In particular, studying a passage once and taking three tests improved retention a week later relative to studying the passage three times and taking one test or studying the passage four times (see Figure 2, right-hand side). At the end of the first session in the same study, the authors had students judge how well they would do when they were tested in a week (a metacognitive judgment). After learning the passages in their respective conditions (SSSS, SSST, and STTT), subjects completed a questionnaire about the learning phase. They were asked to predict how well they thought they would remember the passage in 1 week, and predictions were made on a scale ranging from 1 (*not very well*) to 7 (*very well*). Even though testing produced greater long-term benefits relative to repeated studying after 1 week, the subjects in the repeated study condition (SSSS) were more confident that they would remember the content of the passage relative to those in the tested groups (SSST and STTT). Thus, repeatedly studying inflated students' predictions about their performance, causing them to be overconfident (see also Karpicke & Roediger, 2008). Put another way, testing reduced students' confidence even while aiding their performance. Interestingly, however, students' predictions do line up with their performance on a test given a few minutes after the learning session (see the left-hand side of Figure 2, where the SSSS condition was best). Thus, when students try to make a long-term prediction (how will I do a week from now?), they may base their judgments on their current retrieval fluency (what Bjork and Bjork (1992) called retrieval strength). They cannot accurately assess the quality that will lead to success a week later (storage strength, in the Bjorks' terms).

Testing is a powerful way to improve retention, but when students are given control over their own learning, they do not often choose to test themselves or do not test themselves very frequently (Karpicke, 2009; Kornell & Bjork, 2007). During paired-associate learning, when students are given the opportunity to drop, restudy, or retest on items they have correctly retrieved, they often choose to drop items despite benefits that would accrue if they continued to test themselves. When given control early in the learning phase, students often choose to study pairs instead of testing themselves on them and receiving feedback. These decisions seem to be guided by their inflated judgments of learning, but they lead to poor learning strategies (Karpicke, 2009; Metcalfe & Finn, 2008).

Students seem to lack a good theory about what study strategies are effective. As noted in a previous section, surveys have shown that university students do not realize the direct benefits of retrieval practice as a study strategy. Future research is needed to determine if students can be educated on this aspect. For example, if students experience the benefits of retrieval practice on learning in one context, will they then adopt this strategy for learning in a different context? While we must await the answer to this question, we can say that testing does cause students to become less overconfident in the judgments of learning (even to the point of underconfidence, as in the underconfidence-with-practice effect). Because tests generally improve metacognition, educators should encourage their students to self-test during learning and while studying.

9. BENEFIT 8: TESTING PREVENTS INTERFERENCE FROM PRIOR MATERIAL WHEN LEARNING NEW MATERIAL

Another indirect benefit of testing is that tests create a release from proactive interference. Proactive interference occurs when sets of materials are learned in succession; the previous material learned influences the retention of new materials in a negative manner. Thus, proactive interference refers to the poorer retention of material learned later, caused by prior learning (Underwood, 1957; see Crowder (1976) for a review). Elongated study sessions may therefore cause a buildup of proactive interference. However, research has shown that when tests are inserted between study episodes, they cause a release from proactive interference and enable new learning to be more successful.

Szpunar, McDermott, and Roediger (2007) reported evidence of a release from proactive interference caused by testing in a paradigm in which subjects learned five lists of words. During learning, each list was separated from the next list by an immediate test or a short break of equivalent length. The group that took tests between each list performed better on a final test relative to the group that took short breaks. In addition, the tested group was able to recall a greater proportion of studied words from the most recent list relative to the no-test control group. Thus, taking tests after learning each list protected the subjects from proactive interference during learning.

In a later experiment, Szpunar, McDermott, and Roediger (2008) directly tested the idea that testing protects against the buildup of proactive interference. In two experiments, subjects studied five lists composed of words that were interrelated across lists or words that were unrelated to one another. (The interrelated words belonged to the same categories across lists, for example, several different types of birds or furniture in each list). Between each list, subjects completed math problems for 2 min or completed math problems for 1 min followed by a 1-min free recall test over the list learned most recently. Both groups were tested on the fifth list after its presentation. In addition, a cumulative final test was given to all subjects. For the final test, subjects were instructed to recall as many words from each of the studied lists as possible.

Figure 6 shows the mean number of words recalled from list 5 on the initial test and the final test. The top panel of the figure shows the results from the experiment with interrelated word lists, while the bottom panel shows the results from the experiment with unrelated word lists. For both interrelated and unrelated materials, taking intervening tests during learning protected against proactive interference. Relative to the nontested group, subjects tested after each list produced more correct words from the list 5 and produced fewer intrusions, thus showing that the tests protected

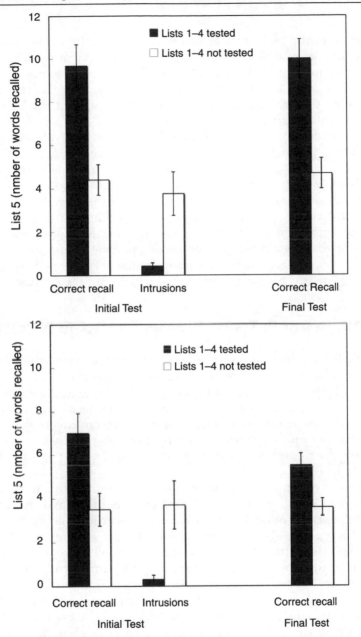

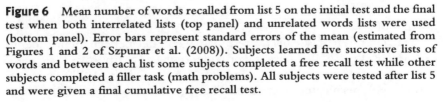

Figure 6 Mean number of words recalled from list 5 on the initial test and the final test when both interrelated lists (top panel) and unrelated words lists were used (bottom panel). Error bars represent standard errors of the mean (estimated from Figures 1 and 2 of Szpunar et al. (2008)). Subjects learned five successive lists of words and between each list some subjects completed a free recall test while other subjects completed a filler task (math problems). All subjects were tested after list 5 and were given a final cumulative free recall test.

subjects from the buildup of proactive interference. In additional experiments, Szpunar et al. (2008) ruled out the hypothesis that the release from proactive interference caused by testing is due to re-exposure to the material because a comparison condition having subjects restudy the lists (rather than receiving tests) did not protect against the buildup of proactive interference.

The results from these and other experiments provide compelling evidence that testing protects subjects from the negative effects of proactive interference, at least when they are required to learn lists of words in succession. While testing causes a release from proactive interference in experimental settings, it is not yet clear whether these results have implications for classroom practice. Bridging experiments using nonfiction prose materials and the like is the next step needed. However, we are optimistic that these results will eventually provide lessons for classroom practice and for self-testing as a study strategy. The next two sections discuss the indirect benefits testing produces within the classroom.

10. BENEFIT 9: TESTING PROVIDES FEEDBACK TO INSTRUCTORS

So far our discussion on the benefits of testing has focused on how testing can have an impact on the learning and memory of students in the classroom. However, classroom testing can do more than help students learn: testing can provide teachers with valuable feedback about what students do and do not know, and teachers in turn can encourage students to change their study behavior. Although these points may seem obvious, they are often overlooked benefits of using frequent testing in the classroom.

Tests and quizzes in the classroom are perhaps one of the most important ways in which teachers can formally assess the knowledge of their students, but of course homework can be used for this purpose, too. Testing is typically seen as an evaluation of what students have learned, and indeed this is true. Conscientious teachers will pay attention to how students perform on tests and use that knowledge to inform their teaching in the future. If many students fail a particular topic on the test, it may be a sign to spend more time covering that material next time or use a different approach to teaching the materials. Teachers can also learn how individual students perform and what the students' respective strengths and weaknesses are. In turn, teachers can use that information to guide further instruction.

Teachers often drastically overestimate what they believe their students to know (Kelly, 1999) and testing provides one way to improve a teacher's estimation of their students' knowledge. The problem of "the curse of knowledge" permeates education. That is, instructors (especially those just beginning) can fail to realize the state of knowledge of their students and pitch their presentations at too high a level. (Most readers can think of their first calculus or statistics course in this regard.) The general idea is that once we know something and understand it well, it is hard to imagine what it was like not to know it. For example, Newton (1990) conducted a study in which students sat across from each other separated by a screen. Each was given a list of 25 common tunes that most Americans know (Happy Birthday to You, the Star Spangled Banner, etc.). One student (the sender) was picked to tap out the tune with his or her knuckles on the table and give an estimate of the likelihood that the other student could name the tune. The other student (the receiver) tried to decipher the tune and name it. This is a classic situation similar to a teacher and student where one person knows the information (tune, in this case) and is trying to communicate it to the other person who does not know it. When the senders judged how well they did in communicating the tune to the other student, they thought they succeeded about 50% of the time. However, the students on the receiving end of the taps could recognize the tune only 3% of the time! When the sender was tapping out Happy Birthday, she was hearing all that music in her mind's ear and tapping in time to it. What the receiver heard, however, was a series of erratic taps. This tale is an allegory of an expert in a subject matter trying to teach it to a novice, especially the first time. Again, it is hard to know what it is like not to know something you know well.

One hopeful new technology may help overcome the instructor's curse of knowledge. The introduction of student response (clicker) systems that permit teachers to quiz students' understanding during lectures may provide assessment on the fly. Teachers can give 2–3-item quizzes in the middle of a lecture to assess understanding of a difficult point; if many students fail to answer correctly, the instructor can go back and try to present the information in a different way. As smart phones increase in use and become more standardized, they may be adapted in classrooms for the same purpose. These new technologies represent a relatively new approach that provides immediate feedback to both students and instructors about students' understanding.

A more formal approach that utilizes testing to understand the current state of individual students is referred to as formative assessment (Black & Wiliam, 1998a, 1998b; for a brief review of formative assessment from a cognitive psychology perspective, see Roediger and Karpicke (2006b)). Formative assessment not only helps teachers better understand what their students know, but also aims to improve the metacognitive judgments of the students' own knowledge. Students will be better able to assess their current knowledge state and their goal knowledge state, as well as understand what steps they need to take to close that gap if they are given proper feedback. Black and Wiliam (1998a) reviewed studies of formative assessment, and one of their major conclusions was that implementing formative assessment programs generally improved performance in the classroom. However, they also concluded that formative assessment programs themselves, as implemented, typically need improvement. One important point is that effective formative assessment programs do not simply add more tests and have teachers pay attention to students' scores, but rather implementing good formative assessment practices typically requires an overhaul of classroom pedagogy geared toward maximizing interactions between the teacher and students. In these interactions, students should have ample opportunity to show understanding, and teachers in turn should provide explicit personalized feedback about how students can improve.

11. BENEFIT 10: FREQUENT TESTING ENCOURAGES STUDENTS TO STUDY

Probably the most influential indirect benefit of testing is the one described in general terms at the beginning of the chapter: Having frequent quizzes, tests, or assignments motivates students to study. Every professor and every student knows that many students procrastinate and often do not study until the night before a test. Often university courses include only a midterm and a final exam, and it is no surprise that the episodes of studying occur primarily just before tests. Mawhinney, Bostow, Laws, Blumenfeld, and Hopkins (1971) documented this point in controlled circumstances, with tests given daily, weekly, or every three weeks. Studying was most copious and evenly spaced with daily testing. With less frequent testing, study behavior occurred only before the tests (see also Michael, 1991). In addition, in their survey of student behaviors described previously, Kornell and Bjork (2007) found that 59% of students, when choosing what to study, chose topics that were due soon or already overdue. More frequent testing across the semester would encourage students to study more and would space their studying over several weeks.

One specific example of how retrieval practice can provide benefits aside from direct mnemonic benefits can be found in Lyle and Crawford (2011; see also Leeming, 2002). The senior author taught two sections of an introductory statistics course and in one session gave students a short two- to six-question quiz at the end of every lecture. The quizzes covered only materials from the current day's lecture and the emphasis was on the quizzes as being for retrieval practice rather than assessment. As such, the quizzes played only a minor role in determining students' final grades.

This conception of daily quizzes alleviates some of students' typical concerns and stresses on testing. In a different section, the students were given the same lectures and main exams, but they did not receive the daily quizzes. In comparing the two groups, the class that had the daily quizzes earned better grades at the end of the semester on the exams than did the group without daily quizzes. More important for present purposes, however, were students' perceptions of how quizzes affected them academically. A year-end survey indicated that students felt that the quizzes (a) gave them a chance to practice questions that would be similar to exam questions, (b) helped identify important topics in the course, (c) caused students to come to lectures more often, (d) caused students to pay more attention, and (e) allowed students to better understand what they had learned during each lecture. Clearly, students had a positive attitude toward the daily quizzes.

As mentioned earlier, self-testing can help students identify what information they do or do not know, which in turn can lead to decisions about how to allocate study time. The relationship between what a student initially learns, their metacognitive judgments of what they think they know, and how they choose to study have a complex relationship with actual test performance. One model of study time allocation is called the discrepancy reduction framework (Dunlosky & Hertzog, 1998). The idea is that students have a goal state of knowledge that they wish to attain and they allocate their study opportunities to reduce the discrepancy between their current knowledge state and that they hope to achieve. Simply put, if students already know some topic reasonably well, they will not study it; if they are quite ignorant of another topic they need to know, they will devote their study efforts to that topic. In short, students will be most likely to study first the most difficult information facing them. Indeed, Nelson, Dunlosky, Graf, and Narens (1994) showed that judgments of learning for studied items were negatively correlated with additional study time; that is, items that subjects thought they knew well were not selected for further study and items that were judged most difficult received the most study time.

However, one criticism of the discrepancy reduction model for study time allocation is the assumption that students will have unlimited time to study. When a time constraint is introduced, the choices students make about what items to study change significantly. Often students tend to study not the most difficult material, but material in the medium range of difficulty, material just out of their current reach. Metcalfe (2002) and Kornell and Metcalfe (2006) developed the region of proximal learning framework to account for these new results. Essentially, their model suggests that students will try and learn the most difficult items that they will be able to learn in the time frame. If time is limited, then students will often not study the most difficult items, since they will not be able to learn them before time is up. Kornell and Metcalfe (2006) provided results supporting the region of proximal learning framework and also showed that student learning was more effective when students chose what to study than when the items were assigned by the experimenter. This outcome suggests that, at least at the level of selecting individual pieces of knowledge to study, students know how to make study choices that will ultimately benefit their own future test performance.

Yet in other ways, students are not good at choosing what, when, how, and how long to study. Nelson and Leonesio (1988) showed that even if subjects are given unlimited time to study, they often continue to study even when the efforts result in no additional gain in performance (an effect they called "labor in vain"). Similarly, Karpicke (2009) showed that if students chose to drop materials from study after an initial recall (which they often did), they would perform worse compared to a repeated retrieval condition.

In conclusion, frequent testing encourages students to study and also permits them to comprehend the gaps in their knowledge (our second benefit). Thus, testing permits students some accuracy in choosing what to study in some circumstances, but in other situations they may make poor choices (Karpicke, 2009; Kornell & Bjork, 2007). Students often choose to stop studying before they have mastered material and will often choose to mass their study immediately before a test rather than spacing it out. Integrating more tests across the course of the semester will encourage students to study more consistently throughout the semester, which will increase performance.

12. POSSIBLE NEGATIVE CONSEQUENCES OF TESTING

We have reviewed 10 benefits that we believe testing confers on learning and memory, directly or indirectly. Yet our message is slow to permeate the educational establishment. Critics have raised a number of objections to any emphasis on testing in the schools (whether achievement testing or giving frequent classroom tests). The arguments against testing range from philosophical to empirical. Some of the latter criticisms are valid, and we have already briefly considered some of the issues in the chapter. Here, we cover this ground rather rapidly because we have touched on these issues in earlier parts of this chapter or in previous writings (see Roediger & Karpicke, 2006b).

First, quizzing in class may take time away from other critical classroom activities, such as lectures, discussion, and demonstrations. Is that a problem? This point is true to an extent, but how does one know (in absence of proper studies) whether these activities are better than retrieval via quizzing? For example, Karpicke and Blunt (2011) showed that retrieval practice produced better retention later than did concept mapping, a widely used study technique. We expect that when other such studies are conducted, they may show that some quizzing is as beneficial as, or more beneficial than, an equal amount of time spent on lecturing (just as testing is better than restudying). In addition, as discussed above, having classroom quizzes may keep motivation up and provide the indirect benefit of having students study more. At any rate, we do not think this criticism holds water, but future research may change our opinion.

Second, critics sometimes argue that retrieval practice through testing produces "rote" learning of a superficial sort, as if the student can parrot back the information but not really understand it or know it in a deep fashion. Learning is said to become "inert" or "encapsulated" in little factoid bubbles. Perhaps this criticism is justified in some cases, but we think that good programs of quizzing with feedback usually prevent this problem. We reviewed evidence previously showing that retrieval (via testing) can lead to deep knowledge that can be used flexibly and transferred to other contexts (e.g., Butler, 2010). Again, the burden is on the critics to show that testing leads to problems rather than simply asserting that these problems might exist. The next two criticisms are based on data and must be taken more seriously.

Third, many studies have documented a phenomenon variously called output interference (Tulving & Arbuckle, 1966), the inhibitory effects of recall (Roediger, 1974, 1978), or retrieval-induced forgetting (Anderson et al., 1994). The basic phenomenon is that while the act of retrieval may boost recall of the retrieved information (the testing effect), it can actually harm recall of nontested information. We discussed this point in Section 7. Thus, in educational settings, the fear is that if students repeatedly retrieve some information, they may actually cause themselves to forget other information.

There is now a vast literature on these topics (see Bäuml (2008) for a review). Although the various phenomena encapsulated under the rubric of retrieval-induced forgetting are highly reliable, as we discussed in Section 7, the implications for educational practice may not be great. For one thing, the phenomenon is often short lived, so if a delay is interposed between retrieval practice and testing, the inhibition dissipates or even evaporates altogether (MacLeod & Macrae, 2001). In addition, most experiments on retrieval-induced forgetting have used word lists. As noted in Section 7, when well-integrated materials such as prose passages are used, the inhibition effect can disappear (Anderson & McCulloch, 1999) or even reverse altogether, leading to retrieval-induced facilitation (Chan et al., 2006). As discussed previously, Chan and his collaborators (see also Chan, 2009, 2010) showed that testing can sometimes enhance recall of material related to the tested material. Thus, although much research remains to be done, the various phenomena showing that testing of some material can have negative effects on retrieval of other material may not have strong implications for the kinds of material learned in educational settings.

   A fourth issue of concern about testing is that the construction of some tests themselves can lead to acquisition of erroneous knowledge. Although educators would never consider knowingly providing erroneous information during lectures or in assigned readings, they do it all the time when they give certain types of tests. In true/false tests, students are given a set of statements and asked to judge which are true and which are false. Of course, false items are often tricky, incorporating some true and some false elements. Thus, students are forced to consider erroneous information and perhaps they will even judge some false statements as true. Similarly, in the more commonly used multiple-choice test, students are given a stem and then four choices to complete the stem. Three of the choices supply incorrect information, so students have to ponder these erroneous statements. Unfortunately, a well-known principle in cognitive psychology is the "mere truth effect," the fact that repeatedly exposed statements gain credibility and are judged more likely to be true regardless of their truth value (Hasher, Goldstein, & Toppino, 1977; see also Bacon, 1979; Begg, Armour, & Kerr, 1985). Thus, because (as we have repeatedly seen in the course of this chapter) students learn from tests, the danger exists that students who are exposed to wrong information on tests will learn that information. Remmers and Remmers (1926) raised the specter of such difficulties long ago and termed possible negative effects of testing the negative suggestibility effect. Ironically, their own research did not show much to worry about, but more recent studies have shown that negative suggestibility is real, at least on true/false and multiple-choice tests.

   Toppino and Brochin (1989) had students take true/false tests. On a later occasion, they then asked the students to judge the truth of objectively false statements they had seen before mixed in with new (equivalent) statements they had not seen before. Sure enough, students judged the previously read statements as truer than the new statements. Toppino and Luipersbeck (1993) extended this finding to multiple-choice tests. The wrong choices on the multiple-choice tests were later judged to be truer than other distracter items (see also Brown, Schilling, & Hockensmith, 1999).

   Roediger and Marsh (2005) had students take multiple-choice tests using a design in which both positive and negative effects of testing could be measured on later cued recall test. Are negative suggestibility effects so great that they will overcome the positive effects of testing? Without going into the details of the experiment, Roediger and Marsh found both positive and negative effects of taking a multiple-choice test on a later cued recall test. When students got an answer right on the multiple-choice test, their performance was boosted on a later cued recall test for the information. However, when they answered erroneously, the negative suggestibility effect occurred: students tended to supply the wrong answer on the cued recall test later at levels much greater than that in the control condition (see also Fazio, Agarwal, Marsh, & Roediger, 2010; Marsh, Roediger, Bjork, & Bjork, 2007). However, the positive effects of testing outweighed the negative suggestibility effect in these studies. Interestingly, the same pattern of results occurs on the widely used Scholastic Assessment Test (the SAT; Marsh, Agarwal, & Roediger, 2009), and in one study in that series in which students did very badly on the initial multiple-choice form of the SAT, the negative effects outweighed the positive effects on the final test given later.

Although these negative suggestibility that effects on multiple-choice tests are quite real, they can be overcome simply by providing feedback on the tests (Butler & Roediger, 2008). Feedback increases the testing effect for items answered correctly and overcomes the negative suggestibility effect for items given erroneous answers (see also Butler, Karpicke, & Roediger, 2007, 2008; Pashler, Cepeda, Wixted, & Rohrer, 2005).

In sum, we have considered four possible negative consequences of testing. The most serious of these is the negative suggestibility effect on true/false and multiple-choice tests, but if feedback is provided after the tests, even this difficulty disappears. As long as students receive feedback on their exams, we see no major drawbacks in using tests as a learning mechanism (either from quizzes in class or self-testing as a study tool).

13. Conclusion

We have reviewed 10 reasons why increased testing in educational settings is beneficial to learning and memory, as a self-study strategy for students or as a classroom tactic. The benefits can be indirect—students study more and attend more fully if they expect a test — but we have emphasized the direct effects of testing. Retrieval practice from testing provides a potent boost to future retention. Retrieval practice provides a relatively straightforward method of enhancing learning and retention in educational settings. We end with our 10 benefits of testing in summary form:

Benefit 1: The testing effect: Retrieval aids later retention.
Benefit 2: Testing identifies gaps in knowledge.
Benefit 3: Testing causes students to learn more from the next learning episode.
Benefit 4: Testing produces better organization of knowledge.
Benefit 5: Testing improves transfer of knowledge to new contexts.
Benefit 6: Testing can facilitate retrieval of information that was not tested.

Benefit 7: Testing improves metacognitive monitoring.
Benefit 8: Testing prevents interference from prior material when learning new material.
Benefit 9: Testing provides feedback to instructors.
Benefit 10: Frequent testing encourages students to study.

Finally, testing can of course be relied on to fulfill its traditional functions: Permitting instructors to assign grades to students.

REFERENCES

Abbott, E. E. (1909). On the analysis of the factors of recall in the learning process. *Psychological Monographs, 11*, 159–177.
Amlund, J. T., Kardash, C. A., & Kulhavy, R. W. (1986). Repetitive reading and recall of expository test. *Reading Research Quarterly, 21*, 49–58.
Anderson, M. C., Bjork, R. A., & Bjork, E. L. (1994). Remembering can cause forgetting: Retrieval dynamics in long-term memory. *Journal of Experimental Psychology: Learning, Memory, and Cognition, 20*, 1063–1087.
Anderson, M. C., & McCulloch, K. C. (1999). Integration as a general boundary condition on retrieval-induced forgetting. *Journal of Experimental Psychology: Learning, Memory, and Cognition, 25*, 608–629.
Bacon, F. T. (1979). Credibility of repeated statements: Memory for trivia. *Journal of Experimental Psychology: Human Learning and Memory, 5*, 241–252.
Barnett, S. M., & Ceci, S. J. (2002). When and where do we apply what we learn? A taxonomy for far transfer. *Psychological Bulletin, 128*, 612–637.
Bäuml, K. H. (2008). Inhibitory processes. In H. L. Roediger (Ed.), *Cognitive psychology of memory* (pp. 195–217). Vol. 2 of *Learning and Memory: A comprehensive reference*, 4 vols (J. Byrne, Ed.). Oxford: Elsevier.
Begg, I., Armour, V., & Kerr, T. (1985). On believing what we remember. *Canadian Journal of Behavioral Science, 17*, 199–214.
Bjork, R. A., & Bjork, E. L. (1992). A new theory of disuse and an old theory of stimulus fluctuation. In A. Healy, S Kosslyn, & R. Shiffrin, (Eds.), *From learning processes to cognitive processes: Essays in honor of William K. Estes* (Vol. 2, pp. 35–67). Hillsdale, NJ: Erlbaum.
Black, P., & Wiliam, D. (1998a). Assessment and classroom learning. *Assessment in Education: Principles, Policy & Practice, 5*, 7–74.
Black, P., & Wiliam, D. (1998b). Inside the black box: Raising standards through classroom assessment. *Phi Delta Kappan, 80*, 139–147.
Brown, A. S., Schilling, H. E. H., & Hockensmith, M. L. (1999). The negative suggestion effect: Pondering incorrect alternatives may be hazardous to your knowledge. *Journal of Educational Psychology, 91*, 756–764.
Butler, A. C. (2010). Repeated testing produces superior transfer of learning relative to repeated studying. *Journal of Experimental Psychology: Learning, Memory, and Cognition, 36*, 1118–1133.
Butler, A. C., Karpicke, J. D., & Roediger, H. L. (2007). The effect and timing of feedback on learning from multiple-choice tests. *Journal of Experimental Psychology: Applied, 13*, 273–281.
Butler, A. C., Karpicke, J. D., & Roediger, H. L. (2008). Correcting a metacognitive error: Feedback increases retention of low-confidence correct responses. *Journal of Experimental Psychology: Learning, Memory, and Cognition, 34*, 918–928.

Butler, A. C., & Roediger, H. L. (2008). Feedback enhances the positive effects and reduces the negative effects of multiple-choice testing. *Memory & Cognition, 36,* 604–616.

Carpenter, S. K., & DeLosh, E. L. (2005). Application of the testing and spacing effects to name learning. *Applied Cognitive Psychology, 19,* 619–636.

Carpenter, S. K., & DeLosh, E. L. (2006). Impoverished cue support enhances subsequent retention: Support for the elaborative retrieval explanation of the testing effect. *Memory & Cognition, 34,* 268–276.

Carpenter, S. K., Pashler, H., & Vul, E. (2006). What types of learning are enhanced by a cued recall test? *Psychonomic Bulletin & Review, 13,* 826–830.

Carrier, M., & Pashler, H. (1992). The influence of retrieval on retention. *Memory & Cognition, 20,* 633–642.

Chan, J. C. K. (2009). When does retrieval induce forgetting and when does it induce facilitation? Implications for retrieval inhibition, testing effect, and text processing. *Journal of Memory and Language, 61,* 153–170.

Chan, J. C. K. (2010). Long-term effects of testing on the recall of nontested materials. *Memory, 18,* 49–57.

Chan, J. C. K., McDermott, K. B., & Roediger, H. L. (2006). Retrieval-induced facilitation: Initially nontested material can benefit from prior testing of related material. *Journal of Experimental Psychology: General, 135,* 553–571.

Congleton, A., & Rajaram, S. (2010, November). *Examining the immediate and delayed aspects of the testing effect.* Paper presented at the meeting of Psychonomic Society, St. Louis, MO.

Cranney, J., Ahn, M., McKinnon, R., Morris, S., & Watts, K. (2009). The testing effect, collaborative learning, and retrieval-induced facilitation in a classroom setting. *European Journal of Cognitive Psychology, 21,* 919–940.

Crowder, R. G. (1976). *Principles of learning and memory.* Hillsdale, NJ: Erlbaum.

Cull, W. L. (2000). Untangling the benefits of multiple study opportunities and repeated testing for cued recall. *Applied Cognitive Psychology, 14,* 215–235.

Detterman, D. K. (1993). The case for the prosecution: Transfer as an epiphenomenon. In D. K. Detterman, and R. J. Sternberg (Eds.), *Transfer on trial: Intelligence, cognition, and instruction* (pp. 1–24). Westport, CT: Ablex Publishing.

Dunlosky, J., & Hertzog, C. (1998). Training programs to improve learning in later adulthood: Helping older adults educate themselves. In D. J. Hacker, J. Dunlosky, and A. C. Graesser, (Eds.), *Metacognition in educational theory and practice* (pp. 249–275). Mahwah, NJ: Erlbaum.

Ebbinghaus, H. (1885). Über das Gedächtnis. Leipzig: Duncker & Humblot.

Erdelyi, M. H., & Becker, J. (1974). Hypermnesia for pictures: Incremental memory for pictures but not words in multiple recall trials. *Cognitive Psychology, 6,* 159–171.

Fazio, L. K., Agarwal, P. K., Marsh, E. J., & Roediger, H. L. (2010). Memorial consequences of multiple-choice testing on immediate and delayed tests. *Memory & Cognition, 38,* 407–418.

Finn, B., & Metcalfe, J. (2007). The role of memory for past test in the under-confidence with practice effect. *Journal of Experimental Psychology: Learning, Memory, and Cognition, 33,* 238–244.

Finn, B., & Metcalfe, J. (2008). Judgments of learning are influenced by memory for past test. *Journal of Memory and Language, 58,* 19–34.

Gates, A. I. (1917). Recitation as a factor in memorizing. *Archives of Psychology, 6*(40).

Gick, M. L., & Holyoak, K. J. (1980). Analogical problem solving. *Cognitive Psychology, 12,* 306–355.

Glover, J. A. (1989). The "testing" phenomenon: Not gone but nearly forgotten. *Journal of Educational Psychology, 81,* 392–399.

Hasher, L., Goldstein, D., & Toppino, T. (1977). Frequency and the conference of referential validity. *Journal of Verbal Learning and Verbal Behavior, 16*, 107–112.

Izawa, C. (1966). Reinforcement-test sequences in paired-associate learning. *Psychological Reports, 18*, 879–919.

Izawa, C. (1968). Function of test trials in paired-associate learning. *Journal of Experimental Psychology, 75*, 194–209.

Izawa, C. (1970). Optimal potentiating effects and forgetting-prevention effects of tests in paired-associate learning. *Journal of Experimental Psychology, 83*, 340–344.

Jacoby, L. L., Wahlheim, C. N., & Coane, J. H. (2010). Test-enhanced learning of natural concepts: Effects on recognition memory, classification, and metacognition. *Journal of Experimental Psychology: Learning, Memory, and Cognition, 36*, 1441–1451.

James, W. (1980). *The principles of psychology.* New York: Holt.

Johnson, C. I., & Mayer, R. E. (2009). A testing effect with multimedia learning. *Journal of Educational Psychology, 101*, 621–629.

Jones, H. E. (1923). The effects of examination on the performance of learning. *Archives of Psychology, 10*, 1–70.

Karpicke, J. D. (2009). Metacognitive control and strategy selection: Deciding to practice retrieval during learning. *Journal of Experimental Psychology: General, 138*, 469–486.

Karpicke, J. D., & Blunt, J. R. (2011). Retrieval practice produces more learning than elaborative studying with concept mapping. *Science, 331*(6018), 772–775.

Karpicke, J. D., Butler, A. C., & Roediger, H. L. (2009). Metacognitive strategies in student learning: Do students practise retrieval when they study on their own? *Memory, 17*, 471–479.

Karpicke, J. D., & Roediger, H. L. (2007). Repeated retrieval during learning is the key to long-term retention. *Journal of Memory and Language, 57*, 151–162.

Karpicke, J. D., & Roediger, H. L. (2008). The critical importance of retrieval for learning. *Science, 319*, 966–968.

Kelly, C. M. (1999). Subjective experience as a basis for "objective" judgments: Effects of past experience on judgments of difficulty. In D. Gopher & A. Koriat (Eds.), *Attention and Performance XVII*, 515–536.

Koriat, A., Scheffer, L., & Ma'ayan, H. (2002). Comparing objective and subjective learning curves: Judgments of learning exhibit increased underconfidence with practice. *Journal of Experimental Psychology: General, 131*, 147–162.

Kornell, N., & Bjork, R. A. (2007). The promise and perils of self-regulated study. *Psychonomic Bulletin & Review, 14*, 219–224.

Kornell, N., & Metcalfe, J. (2006). Study efficacy and the region of proximal learning framework. *Journal of Experimental Psychology: Learning, Memory, and Cognition, 32*, 222–609.

Kornell, N., & Son, L. K. (2009). Learners' choices and beliefs about self-testing. *Memory, 17*, 493–501.

Leeming, F. C. (2002). The exam-a-day procedure improves performance in psychology classes. *Teaching of Psychology, 29*, 210–212.

Lyle, K. B., & Crawford, N. A. (2011). Retrieving essential material at the end of lectures improves performance on statistics exams. *Teaching of Psychology, 38*, 94–97.

MacLeod, M. D., & Macrae, C. (2001). Gone but not forgotten: The transient nature of retrieval-induced forgetting. *Psychological Science, 12*, 148–152.

Marsh, E. J., Agarwal, P. K., & Roediger, H. L. (2009). Memorial consequences of answering SAT II questions. *Journal of Experimental Psychology: Applied, 15*, 1–11.

Marsh, E. J., Roediger, H. L., Bjork, R. A., & Bjork, E. L. (2007). The memorial consequences of multiple-choice testing. *Psychonomic Bulletin & Review, 14*, 194–199.

Masson, M. E., & McDaniel, M. A. (1981). The role of organizational processes in long-term retention. *Journal of Experimental Psychology: Human Learning and Memory*, *2*, 100–110.

Mawhinney, V. T., Bostow, D. E., Laws, D. R., Blumenfeld, G. J., & Hopkins, B. L. (1971). A comparison of students studying-behavior produced by daily, weekly, and three-week testing schedules. *Journal of Applied Behavior Analysis*, *4*, 257–264.

McCabe, J. (2011). Metacognitive awareness of learning strategies in undergraduates. *Memory & Cognition*, *39*, 462–476.

McDermott, K. B., & Arnold, K. M. (2010, November). *Test taking facilitates future learning*. Paper presented at the meeting of the Psychonomic Society, St. Louis, MO.

Metcalfe, J. (2002). Is study time allocated selectively to a region of proximal learning? *Journal of Experimental Psychology: General*, *131*, 349–363.

Metcalfe, J., & Finn, B. (2008). Evidence that judgments of learning are causally related to study choice. *Psychonomic Bulletin & Review*, *15*, 174–179.

Michael, J. (1991). A behavioral perspective on college teaching. *Behavioral Analysis*, *14*, 229–239.

Nelson, T. O., Dunlosky, J., Graf, A., & Narens, L. (1994). Utilization of metacognitive judgments in the allocation of study during multitrial learning. *Psychological Science*, *5*, 207–213.

Nelson, T. O., & Leonesio, R. J. (1988). Allocation of self-paced study time and the "labor-in-vain effect.". *Journal of Experimental Psychology: Learning, Memory and Cognition*, *14*, 676–686.

Newton, L. (1990). *Overconfidence in the communication of intent: Heard and unheard melodies*. Unpublished doctoral dissertation. Stanford, CA: Stanford University.

Pashler, H., Cepeda, N. J., Wixted, J. T., & Rohrer, D. (2005). When does feedback facilitate learning of words? *Journal of Experimental Psychology: Learning, Memory, and Cognition*, *31*, 3–8.

Pyc, M. A., & Rawson, K. A. (2007). Examining the efficiency of schedules of distributed retrieval practice. *Memory & Cognition*, *35*, 1917–1927.

Pyc, M. A., & Rawson, K. A. (2010). Why testing improves memory: Mediator effectiveness hypothesis. *Science*, *330*, 335.

Remmers, H. H., & Remmers, E. M. (1926). The negative suggestion effect on true–false examination questions. *Journal of Educational Psychology*, *17*, 52–56.

Roediger, H. L. (1974). Inhibiting effects of recall. *Memory & Cognition*, *2*, 261–269.

Roediger, H. L. (1978). Recall as a self-limiting process. *Memory & Cognition*, *6*, 54–63.

Roediger, H. L., & Karpicke, J. D. (2006a). Test enhanced learning: Taking memory tests improves long-term retention. *Psychological Science*, *17*, 249–255.

Roediger, H. L., & Karpicke, J. D. (2006b). The power of testing memory: Basic research and implications for educational practice. *Perspectives on Psychological Science*, *1*, 181–210.

Roediger, H. L., & Marsh, E. J. (2005). The positive and negative consequences of multiple-choice testing. *Journal of Experimental Psychology: Learning, Memory and Cognitive*, *31*, 1155–1159.

Roenker, D. L., Thompson, C. P., & Brown, S. C. (1971). Comparison of measures for the estimation of clustering in free recall. *Psychological Bulletin*, *76*, 45–48.

Rohrer, K., Taylor, K., & Sholar, B. (2010). Tests enhance the transfer of learning. *Journal of Experimental Psychology: Learning, Memory, and Cognition*, *36*, 233–239.

Shaughnessy, J. J., & Zechmeister, E. B. (1992). Memory-monitoring accuracy as influenced by the distribution of retrieval practice. *Bulletin of the Psychonomic Society*, *30*, 125–128.

Slamecka, N. J., & Katsaiti, L. T. (1988). Normal forgetting of verbal lists as a function of prior testing. *Journal of Verbal Learning and Verbal Behavior*, *10*, 400–408.

Son, L. K., & Kornell, N. (2008). Research on the allocation of study time: Key studies from 1890 to the present (and beyond). In J. Dunlosky, & R. A. Bjork, (Eds.), *A handbook of memory and metamemory* (pp. 333–351). Hillsdale, NJ: Psychology Press.

Spitzer, H. F. (1939). Studies in retention. *Journal of Educational Psychology, 30,* 641–656.

Szpunar, K. K., McDermott, K. B., & Roediger, H. L. (2007). Expectation of a final cumulative test enhances long-term retention. *Memory & Cognition, 35,* 1007–1013.

Szpunar, K. K., McDermott, K. B., & Roediger, H. L. (2008). Testing during study insulates against the buildup of proactive interference. *Journal of Experimental Psychology: Learning, Memory, and Cognition, 34,* 1392–1399.

Thomas, A. K., & McDaniel, M. A. (2007). Metacomprehension for educationally relevant materials: Dramatic effects of encoding-retrieval interactions. *Psychonomic Bulletin & Review, 14,* 212–218.

Thompson, C. P., Wenger, S. K., & Bartling, C. A. (1978). How recall facilitates subsequent recall: A reappraisal. *Journal of Experimental Psychology: Human Learning and Memory, 4,* 210–221.

Toppino, T. C., & Brochin, H. A. (1989). Learning from tests: The case of true–false examinations. *Journal of Educational Research, 83,* 119–124.

Toppino, T. C., & Luipersbeck, S. M. (1993). Generality of the negative suggestion effect in objective tests. *Journal of Educational Psychology, 86,* 357–362.

Tulving, E. (1962). Subjective organization in free recall of "unrelated" words. *Psychological Review, 69,* 344–354.

Tulving, E. (1967). The effects of presentation and recall of material in free-recall learning. *Journal of Verbal Learning and Verbal Behavior, 6,* 175–184.

Tulving, E., & Arbuckle, T. (1966). Input and output interference in short-term associative memory. *Journal of Experimental Psychology, 72,* 145–150.

Underwood, B. J. (1957). Interference and forgetting. *Psychological Review, 64,* 49–60.

Wheeler, M. A., Ewers, M., & Buonanno, J. F. (2003). Different rates of forgetting following study versus test trials. *Memory, 11,* 571–580.

Wheeler, M. A., & Roediger, H. L. (1992). Disparate effects of repeated testing: Reconciling Ballard's (1913) and Bartlett's (1932) results. *Psychological Science, 3,* 240–245.

Zaromb, F. M. (2010). Organizational processes contribute to the testing effect in free recall. (Unpublished doctoral dissertation). Washington University of St. Louis, Saint Louis, MO.

Zaromb, F. M., & Roediger, H. L. (2010). The testing effect in free recall is associated with enhanced organizational processes. *Memory & Cognition, 38,* 995–1008.

COGNITIVE LOAD THEORY

John Sweller

Contents

Abstract

Cognitive load theory uses evolutionary theory to consider human cognitive architecture and uses that architecture to devise novel, instructional procedures. The theory assumes that knowledge can be divided into biologically primary knowledge that we have evolved to acquire and biologically secondary knowledge that is important for cultural reasons. Secondary knowledge, unlike primary knowledge, is the subject of instruction. It is processed in a manner that is analogous to the manner in which biological evolution processes information. When dealing with secondary knowledge, human cognition requires a very large information store, the contents of which are acquired largely by obtaining information from other information stores. Novel information is generated by a random generate and test procedure with only very limited amounts of novel information able to be processed at any given time. In contrast, very large amounts of organized information stored in the information store can be processed in order to generate complex action. This architecture has been used to generate instructional procedures, summarized in this chapter.

Psychology of Learning and Motivation, Volume 55

ISSN 0079-7421, DOI 10.1016/B978-0-12-387691-1.X0001-4

© 2011 Elsevier Inc.

All rights reserved.

1. INTRODUCTION

Cognitive load theory is an instructional theory based on our knowledge of human cognition (Sweller, Ayres & Kalyuga, 2011). Since its inception in the 1980 s (e.g., Sweller, 1988), the theory has used aspects of human cognitive architecture to generate experimental, instructional effects. These effects are demonstrated when novel instructional procedures are compared with more traditional procedures as part of a randomized, controlled experiment. If the novel procedure facilitates learning, based on test performance, a new effect may have been demonstrated, an effect generated by our knowledge of human cognition. The new instructional procedures that follow from the effect become candidates for relevant professionals such as instructional designers and teachers.

While cognitive load theory is not unique in using human cognition to generate instructional procedures, it is regrettably rare for instructional design to be based on human cognitive architecture. Frequently, instructional design principles are promulgated as though human cognition either does not exist or if it does exist, it has no implications for instruction. An alternative to a theory-free process is to determine instructional design by using well-known cognitive structures such as working memory and long-term memory. These structures and their properties have strong implications for instruction. They can generate hypotheses that can be tested experimentally and if supported, can lead to new effects and novel instructional procedures.

Cognitive load theory, by using our knowledge of the relations between working memory and long-term memory, has been able to generate instructional procedures that to some can appear counterintuitive. Furthermore, a large range of those instructional procedures that otherwise would appear random and unconnected to each other can be seen to be closely related by their common, theoretical base provided by human cognitive architecture. That architecture, discussed in Section 2, not only indicates the relations between the instructional effects discussed in Section 3 but also provides an explanation why an effect is obtained and the conditions under which it can or cannot be obtained.

None of the experimental effects and the instructional procedures that flow from these effects is universal in the sense that it can be obtained under all conditions. All effects depend on variations in cognitive load. For this reason, the effects should not be considered in isolation from human cognitive architecture. An effect that occurs under one set of conditions may disappear under conditions that on the surface appear very similar but in fact differ substantially when considered from the perspective of the cognitive load imposed. Analyzing the instructional conditions discussed in Section 3 using the cognitive architecture of

Section 2 can explain why apparently similar conditions impose a differential cognitive load. As will be seen in Section 3, this analysis has frequently given rise to new experimental effects and so new instructional procedures. The next section will discuss those aspects of human cognitive architecture that have been incorporated into the theory.

2. HUMAN COGNITIVE ARCHITECTURE

In the last few years, cognitive load theory has taken an evolutionary view of human cognitive architecture (Sweller, 2003; Sweller & Sweller, 2006). There are two aspects of this treatment. First, the theory has incorporated Geary's (2007, 2008) categorization of knowledge into biologically primary and secondary knowledge. This categorization assumes that we have specifically evolved to acquire some particular types of information, known as biologically primary knowledge, while we have only needed other types of information, known as biologically secondary knowledge, in more recent times and so have not evolved a specific disposition to acquire that information. Only biologically secondary knowledge is the subject of instruction. Second, the theory has suggested that biologically secondary knowledge is acquired, organized, and in general processed in the same way as evolution by natural selection "processes" information (Sweller, 2003; Sweller & Sweller, 2006). Evolution by natural selection is normally and appropriately considered as a biological theory. In this chapter, it will be suggested that it should also be considered as a natural information processing system. Geary's categorization of knowledge according to its evolutionary status will be discussed next.

2.1. The evolutionary status of knowledge

Knowledge and skill can be classified into an enormous variety of categories. The vast majority of potential classification schemes have failed to yield instructional consequences in that instructional procedures that facilitate learning in one category may equally facilitate learning in another. In contrast, Geary's (2007, 2008) classification of knowledge into biologically primary and secondary knowledge is directly relevant to instructional procedures.

2.1.1. Biologically Primary Knowledge
Consider a young child learning to speak and listen to his or her native language. The child may be given considerable assistance by parents and others. They may repeat key words, speak clearly and distinctly, and use a very restricted range of vocabulary and grammar that heavily emphasizes

"baby-talk." Nevertheless, children are not explicitly taught how to listen and speak. Indeed, with the exception of speech therapists, most people are likely to have little idea how to teach children to speak their native language. For example, children acquire the immensely complex motor actions associated with speech with no tuition whatsoever. An appropriate coordination of tongue, lips, breath, and voice occur without any explicit instruction. For most of us, simple membership of a functioning society is sufficient to learn to speak our native language. Despite the complexity of the task, we do not require explicit tuition.

Learning to listen and speak are biologically primary skills (Geary, 2007, 2008). They are skills that we have evolved to acquire over countless generations. We do not need to be motivated by others to acquire these language skills. We are self-motivated and acquire the skills easily, effortlessly, and unconsciously without instruction. We will automatically take on the accent of our society rather than the accent of, for example, immigrant parents because we have evolved to learn to speak with the accent of our peers.

There are many biologically primary skills. We learn basic social relations and we learn to recognize faces just as easily and automatically as we learn our native language. In each case, external motivational factors are irrelevant because we have evolved to acquire these skills and explicit instruction is unnecessary.

Biologically primary skills are modular. Learning our native language and learning to recognize faces require quite different, unrelated processes. We may have deficits in one biologically primary area with no apparent deficiencies in another. We may have evolved to acquire different biologically primary skills at very different times in our evolutionary history.

2.1.2. Biologically Secondary Knowledge

The nature and acquisition processes of biologically secondary skills are quite different from the processes associated with primary skills. We have evolved to acquire secondary skills but only in a general sense, not as specific modular abilities. Biologically secondary knowledge is knowledge that has become culturally important and needs to be acquired in order to function appropriately in a society. While listening and speaking provided examples of biologically primary knowledge, reading and writing provide equivalent examples of biologically secondary knowledge and can be used to demonstrate some of the characteristics of secondary knowledge.

As indicated above, most of us will learn to listen and speak simply as a consequence of living in a normal, listening/speaking society. In contrast, simply living in a reading/writing society is insufficient to allow most people to learn to read and write. Reading and writing became near universal skills only in some societies with the rise of modern education. The fact that a few people in some cultures could read and write was not sufficient to allow most people to read and write, a state of affairs that persisted for several thousand years. People will learn to listen and speak without explicit tuition. They will rarely learn to read and write without specific tuition.

The difference between listening/speaking and reading/writing is evolutionary. We have evolved to learn to listen and speak. We are able to learn to read and write, but we have not specifically evolved to read and write. The evolved perceptual motor and cognitive skills we use to read and write did not evolve in relation to reading and writing. The skills evolved for other reasons, but we are able to use these skills to learn to read and write. The vastly different evolutionary history of speaking/listening and reading/writing has both cognitive and educational consequences.

2.1.3. Consequences of the Distinction Between Biologically Primary and Secondary Knowledge

With respect to cognitive consequences, while we are internally motivated to learn to listen and speak, and learn to do so relatively effortlessly unconsciously and without external encouragement or explicit tuition, the same ease of acquisition is not apparent in the case of learning to read and write. We may not be motivated to learn to read and write and so learning reading and writing is likely to require considerable conscious effort over long periods of time. A considerable minority of people in a reading/writing culture may never learn to read and write.

The educational consequences of learning to read and write compared to learning to speak and listen are stark. If a society wants most of its people to read and write, it must specifically organize itself through its education systems to ensure that most of its members learn to read and write. We do not need educational systems and procedures to teach people to listen and speak. In contrast, without schools, most people will not learn to read and write. Schools and other educational and training institutions have been established to deal with biologically secondary knowledge such as reading and writing. Every subject taught in educational and training institutions can be virtually classified as incorporating biologically secondary knowledge.

There are other instructional consequences of the distinction between biologically primary and secondary knowledge. In recent years, there has been a heavy emphasis in the research literature on teaching general cognitive and metacognitive strategies. The distinction between primary and secondary knowledge casts some doubt on the relevance of that emphasis. First, it is difficult to find any cognitive or metacognitive strategies around which there is a consensus, rendering it difficult to assess the validity and usefulness of a particular strategy. Second, the whole point of cognitive or metacognitive strategies is that they are very general, applying to a vast array of tasks. It is much easier to classify them as biologically primary than secondary simply because we are likely to have evolved to acquire a skill that has very wide applicability. A metacognitive skill such as learning to organize information is likely to be essential for the survival of the human species. If a university student, for example, cannot organize information, it is more likely that he or she suffers from the complexity of the particular information with which he or she is dealing with rather than an ignorance of how to organize information. A biologically primary skill such as organizing information may not be teachable or learnable because it will have been already acquired by normally functioning people.

Of course, the above argument would be rendered irrelevant if we had a body of evidence based on randomized controlled experiments demonstrating the advantages of being taught general skills. This body of evidence is missing despite there being many studies demonstrating relatively improved performance following instruction in general skills. Unfortunately, almost without exception, these studies are flawed either because they alter multiple variables simultaneously and so eliminate any possibility of determining causality or because they fail to use far transfer tests. Transfer is essential if we are to exclude the possibility that the acquisition of domain-specific knowledge provides the factor determining improved performance. If, for example, we claim that learners who are taught how to organize knowledge subsequently will learn better than students who have not been taught to organize knowledge, we need to demonstrate that improved learning in areas quite unrelated to the area used to teach the strategy. The use of the same or a similar area in teaching and testing cannot exclude the possibility that learners have merely acquired domain-specific knowledge, rather than knowledge of how to organize information. To my knowledge, there is no scientifically acceptable body of evidence for any general strategy indicating that it is teachable and beneficial in a variety of unrelated areas. A likely reason for that failure may be found in the suggestion that general cognitive strategies consist of biologically primary knowledge.

2.2. The acquisition and organization of secondary knowledge

The manner in which the human cognitive system is organized to acquire, retain, and disseminate biologically secondary information is directly relevant to instructional design. As an example that has generated some controversy in recent years, if human cognitive architecture is better suited to discovering secondary information than receiving the same information, then instruction needs to be organized in a manner that encourages discovery. Alternatively, if the human cognitive system is better at acquiring information from other humans than discovering the same information, then instructional systems need to reflect that fact by emphasizing the presentation rather than the discovery of information (Kirschner, Sweller, & Clark, 2006; Klahr & Nigam, 2004). Furthermore, if we acquire biologically primary information in a manner that is very different from the manner in which we acquire biologically secondary information, then the distinction between the two categories of information becomes an important consideration. Accordingly, how we deal with information, especially biologically secondary information, is critical to instructional design.

There are many ways of approaching the issue of how the human cognitive system deals with information, with the most common being to study the components of human cognitive architecture such as working memory or long-term memory. Much of our knowledge about human cognition comes from such critically important work. Nevertheless, there is an alternative, complementary approach. Humans are, of course, part of nature and nature processes information. For example, while well-known theories such as evolution by natural selection are characteristically considered as biological theories, they can just as easily be considered as natural information processing theories (Sweller & Sweller, 2006).

Evolution by natural selection creates novel information, stores that information for later use, and disseminates it across space and time. It can be considered as an example of a natural information processing system. Biological evolution gave rise to humans including the human cognitive system. Unsurprisingly, given its evolutionary origins, the human cognitive system is also a natural information processing system with characteristics similar to that of the evolutionary system. When dealing with biologically secondary information, the human cognitive system also creates novel information, stores it for later use, and disseminates it across space and time.

The characteristics of natural information processing systems such as biological evolution and human cognition can be specified in a variety of ways. In this chapter, five basic principles will be used to describe the systems (Table 1). The *information store principle* indicates the role of stored information in the functioning of natural information processing systems, with the *borrowing and reorganizing principle* providing the major process by which information is acquired. The *randomness as genesis principle* indicates the centrality of random generate and test procedure to the creation of novel information. The importance of processing very small amounts of information when engaging in random generation is covered by the *narrow limits of change principle*, while the ability to handle very large amounts of previously organized information is dealt with by the *environmental organizing and linking principle*. Together, these principles indicate how information can be created, stored, disseminated, and used by natural information processing systems. Each of the principles will be discussed next.

Table 1 Natural Information Processing Principles

Principle	Function
Information store principle	Store information
Borrowing and reorganizing principle	Obtain information from others
Randomness as genesis principle	Generate novel information
Narrow limits of change principle	Restrict the random generation of novel information to protect the information store
Environmental organizing and linking principle	Use stored information to determine appropriate action within an environment

2.2.1. Information Store Principle

In order to function in the normally very complex natural environment, natural information processing systems require very large stores of information that can be used to direct appropriate activity. A genome provides that information store in the case of evolution by natural selection. While there is no agreed upon technique for measuring the size of a genome (Portin, 2002; Stotz & Griffiths, 2004), all genomes, even relatively simple ones, require thousands of units of information. More complex genomes may require billions of units of information. It is appropriate to consider a genome to be a very large information store designed to appropriately organize complex activity using complex processes.

The human cognitive system must also navigate a complex environment, and similar to evolution by natural selection, human cognitive architecture requires a large information store in order to function. Human long-term memory provides that store.

The central importance of long-term memory to cognitive functioning is often overlooked, especially in education. Long-term memory tends to be tacitly dismissed as consisting of little more than isolated, random elements of information. It is, of course, far more important than that depiction. Long-term memory is central to all cognitive functioning. The importance of long-term memory to general cognition became apparent only following seminal work in the field of problem solving. The work not only changed our view of long-term memory but also our view of problem solving and, indeed, the nature of human cognition.

The initial work was published by de Groot (1965) in the 1940 s, but it attracted a wider audience only when it was translated from the original Dutch to English and republished over 20 years later. De Groot was interested in the cognitive factors that distinguished chess grandmasters from weekend players. We know chess grandmasters virtually always defeat weekend players, but it was not clear what skills they had developed to allow this superiority. Better problem-solving skill provided the most likely hypothesis, but we did not really know what that meant. De Groot investigated some obvious hypotheses. Chess experts may plan ahead a larger number of moves than weekend players. That is, they may engage in a greater search in depth. Alternatively, they may consider a greater number of possible moves at each choice point, indicating a greater search in breadth. In the case of either those who increase their search in depth or in breadth, we might expect them to increase their chances of finding good moves and hence to increase their probability of winning. De Groot tested the hypotheses that expert chess players engage in a greater search in depth or breadth compared to weekend players, but essentially found no differences on these measures between different grades of players. Whatever cognitive processes the chess grandmasters engage in to win, looking further ahead or considering a greater range of possible moves than the weekend players was not included in their repertoire of skills.

There was one difference between chess grandmasters and weekend players that De Groot found. He presented grandmasters with a board on which the pieces had been placed in an arrangement taken from a real game. In other words, the board configuration was one that could be found during a game. De Groot showed the grandmasters the board configuration for 5 s before taking it away and asked them to replicate the configuration that they had just seen. They were surprisingly good at this task, accurately replacing about 70% of the pieces. In contrast, weekend players were much poorer, accurately replacing only about 30% of the pieces. Chase and Simon (1973) replicated these findings and found that if the pieces were placed on the board in a random configuration, the differences between grandmasters and weekend players disappeared. Both were able to accurately replace only about 30% of random board configurations. The superiority of chess grandmasters was restricted to board configurations taken from real games.

What do these results tell us about skill in chess in the first instance and, more generally, about long-term memory, problem solving, and cognition? It takes at least a decade to become a chess grandmaster (Ericsson & Charness, 1994). During this period, grandmasters not only play many games but also spend many hours each day studying previous games. While studying and playing games, grandmasters learn to recognize a large number of board configurations and the best moves associated with each configuration. Chess is a game of problem solving, but chess grandmasters' skill does not derive from some mysterious and undefinable problem-solving skill. Rather it derives from a familiarity with a great number of board configurations and the moves associated with those configurations. A chess grandmaster does not have to plan a sequence of moves because he or she knows which moves work well and which do not. It is a weekend player who must plan moves because he or she does not have the large repertoire of moves acquired by grandmasters. The repertoire of moves is held in long-term memory and explains the skill of chess grandmasters. No other skill, particularly no general problem-solving strategies, has been found to differentiate chess grandmasters and weekend players. Neither are other skills required to explain the performance of chess grandmasters.

Grandmasters have been estimated to hold tens of thousands of board configurations in long-term memory (Simon & Gilmartin, 1973). Although impressive, we need to note that many educated people have similar skills due to similar stores of information held in long-term memory but in areas other than chess. The skill exhibited by chess grandmasters is unusual because few people become professional chess players. In contrast, many more people become competent mathematicians and even more learn to read competently. If de Groot or Chase and Simon had demonstrated that competent readers can readily reproduce the letters "chess is a game of problem solving skill" while poor readers or non-readers are far poorer, the influence of the finding would likely have been much reduced. Similarly, demonstrating that the letters "lliks gnivlos melborp fo emag a si ssehc" are equally poorly remembered by good and poor readers is less likely to attract attention than the same finding from the game of chess. The genius of de Groot's and Chase and Simon's findings was their demonstration of the critical importance of long-term memory in an area in which the influence of long-term memory was assumed to be negligible.

The results from chess have been extended to a variety of educationally relevant areas such as understanding and remembering text, designing software, and solving mathematical problems (Chiesi, Spilich, & Voss, 1979; Egan & Schwartz, 1979; Jeffries, Turner, Polson, & Atwood, 1981; J. Sweller & Cooper, 1985). Experts in a given area are able to better remember information associated with that area and are able to better use that information to solve problems. They recognize problem states and the best moves associated with each state.

There are consequences associated with these findings both for our understanding of human cognition and for educational research and practice. With respect to human cognitive architecture, the role of long-term memory is transformed. We do not use long-term memory just to remember items. We use it to determine the bulk of our activity. If we are good at something, it is because we have stored innumerable elements of information concerning that area in our long-term memory. All expertise, on this view, is determined by what is stored in the long-term memory. Activities such as problem solving that traditionally were assumed to be largely unrelated to the characteristics of long-term memory can now be seen to closely depend on it. Long-term memory is a central to, perhaps *the* central structure in, human cognitive architecture.

The nature of learning is also changed by this perspective. A competent person is not someone who has acquired complex, sophisticated, cognitive strategies that can be used in a variety of unrelated areas. Such teachable/learnable general strategies have not been described, probably because they are biologically primary. Rather, competence is domain specific. Some domains may be applicable in a large variety of areas, but it is still the particular domain that is important. Acquiring chess skill may not be usable in any areas other than playing chess. Acquiring reading skill may allow a person to read an unlimited number of unrelated texts. Nevertheless, reading skill applies only to reading. It will not improve a person's chess skill. Neither, in isolation, will it improve a person's knowledge of history. It will, of course, enable one to read historical texts and being able to read historical texts will improve a person's knowledge of history. The point is that in each case, the skill can be clearly specified and so clearly taught. From an educational perspective, the role of education is to increase knowledge held in long-term memory of particular discipline areas. How that knowledge is best acquired is a concern of cognitive load theory. Teaching general cognitive skills, on the other hand, may need to await the specification of such skills.

2.2.2. Borrowing and Reorganizing Principle

If, as indicated by the information store principle, natural information processing systems require a very large store of information in order to function in complex natural environments, the processes by which large stores of information are acquired become a critical issue. In the case of evolution by natural selection, the processes of reproduction, both asexual and sexual, are well known. They constitute the primary procedures by which a store of information is acquired. During asexual reproduction, each genome is copied exactly from the genome of the previous generation, with the exception of occasional mutations. In this sense, the information store that constitutes a particular genome has been borrowed largely in its entirety from the information store of the preceding generation. Borrowing can be seen to be a major procedure for acquiring a large information store.

Borrowing is equally important in the case of sexual reproduction. The major difference between asexual and sexual reproduction is that in the case of asexual reproduction, an information store is borrowed with no or minimal change, while in the case of sexual reproduction, the information is reorganized. Not only is the information reorganized, in addition, that reorganization provides the major reason for the existence of sexual reproduction. The reorganization of information during sexual reproduction results in a logical structure ensuring that each generation is necessarily different from the previous generation. Sexual reproduction occurs in order to ensure that, unlike the case of asexual reproduction, generational variation is a logical necessity of the procedure. During sexual reproduction, information is obtained and combined from both male and female parents resulting in offspring that necessarily differ from either parent. Information is not only borrowed, it is also reorganized.

The acquisition and storage of information in long-term memory more closely resembles sexual than asexual reproduction. We rarely remember information with minimal or no change in the same way as asexual reproduction or as an electronic recording device "remember" information. We do acquire or borrow the vast bulk of the information held in long-term memory from other people, but we alter that information depending on what we have already stored in long-term memory.

The processes by which we borrow information from others are well known. We imitate other people (Bandura, 1986), listen to what others tell us, read what they write, and look at diagrams and pictures that they produce. Listening, reading, and looking at diagrams and pictures are particularly important in the acquisition of the biologically secondary information that is the subject of education and training. The vast bulk of the biologically secondary information that is stored in long-term memory is acquired by one of the processes or a combination of these processes.

Although information is borrowed from others, it is reorganized in a manner analogous to sexual reproduction. We combine new information with information already stored in long-term memory and it is the new, reorganized information that is stored rather than an exact copy of the information that was presented. In other words, we store information as schemas rather than as precise copies (Chi, Glaser, & Rees, 1982). Each schema stored is likely to be different from the schema held in the long-term memory of the person from whom it was borrowed because it is a combination of the borrowed information combined with information already held in long-term memory.

Cognitive load theory has been used to generate many instructional effects and these effects rely heavily on the borrowing and reorganizing principle. The effects are largely concerned with techniques for presenting information to learners that are most likely to result in the facilitation of schema acquisition. In addition to the acquisition of schemas, cognitive load theory is also concerned with their automation so that they can be used without conscious processing in working memory (Kotovsky, Hayes, & Simon, 1985; Schneider & Shiffrin, 1977; Shiffrin & Schneider, 1977). In the case of schema acquisition, the theory assumes that learners acquire domain-specific information that is best obtained from other people. All the cognitive load instructional effects depend on these assumptions.

The theory has been concerned with the generation of novel information, the topic of the next section, to a far lesser extent. There are good reasons for that emphasis on obtaining information from others rather than generating it oneself. Contrary to many educational assumptions, humans rarely generate novel information (Kirschner et al., 2006). We almost always prefer to obtain information from others if it is available. If information is required but not available from others, only then do we need to generate it ourselves by, for example, conducting research.

In contrast, constructivist teaching procedures place a far heavier emphasis on learners generating information. The emphasis on generating information during constructivist learning and teaching in the past two decades ignores much of what we have learned about human cognition. There are two issues: whether we need to be taught how to construct knowledge and whether knowledge we have constructed during constructivist teaching sessions is superior to knowledge we have acquired from others.

With respect to teaching learners how to construct knowledge, while we must construct schematic knowledge in long-term memory in order to learn, it is a fallacy to assume that we need to be taught how to construct knowledge. We have evolved to construct knowledge. It is a biologically primary skill. There is no body of evidence based on properly conducted, randomized, controlled studies that teaching learners how to construct knowledge results in better learners. Neither is there a body of experimental evidence that teaching procedures such as discovery learning that require learners to discover or generate information for themselves constitute a better form of learning in comparison to the explicit presentation of information. Evidence that information that is discovered for ourselves is superior to studying the same information presented to us is missing (Klahr & Nigam, 2004). We have neither theoretical reasons nor empirical evidence that withholding information from learners results in better learning. On the contrary, based on the worked example effect, discussed below, we have strong evidence from a large variety of learning areas using very young to adult students that learning is facilitated by direct, explicit instruction.

2.2.3. Randomness as Genesis Principle
As indicated by the borrowing and reorganizing principle, natural information processing systems have powerful techniques for disseminating information, but that information must be created in the first instance in order to have something to disseminate. The randomness as genesis principle provides the necessary machinery for creating novel information.

In biological evolution, random mutation is the ultimate source of all genetic variation. While there are a variety of mechanisms, such as sexual reproduction, for handling and distributing the variations that occur due to mutation, without mutation none of these mechanisms could function. For example, sexual reproduction relies on combining different alleles from male and female parents. Random mutation accounts for the fact that alleles differ. If they did not differ, combining them would have no function. Ultimately, evolution by natural selection assumes that all the variation, not only within species but also between species, can be sourced to random mutation.

There are important consequences that flow from the fact that all genetic variation ultimately derives from random mutation. Evolution by natural selection is a creative system. It has created the entire biological world. The source of that creativity is the randomness as genesis principle. The randomness as genesis principle has a basic problem-solving process, random generate and test, as its creative engine. Random generation creates novelty and it is this novelty that has given rise to the immense diversity of the biological world. Nevertheless, the "test" part of random generate and test is just as important to creativity as the "random generation" part. While random mutation is essential, in isolation it would not and could not generate the diversity and complexity that we see in biological structures and functions. Mutations are randomly generated, but whether a mutation has any substantive biological consequences depends on whether it is adaptive. If a mutation increases the adaptivity of an organism to its environment, it is likely to be retained for future generations. In other words, it is added to the information store, in this case a genome. If it is maladaptive, it is not added to the information store and is likely to be lost. In this manner, mutations are tested for effectiveness with effective mutations added to the genome and retained while ineffective mutations are jettisoned. Thus, when applied to evolution by natural selection, the randomness as genesis principle is closely tied to a problem-solving process, random generate and test.

The randomness as genesis principle functions in an analogous way in human cognition and is equally important (Sweller, 2009). While most of the knowledge held in long-term memory is acquired via the borrowing and organizing principle, the knowledge is created in the first instance during problem solving. When dealing with familiar problems, problem solving largely consists of retrieving schematic information from long-term memory. Our schemas allow us to recognize a problem as belonging to a particular class of problems that require a particular solution (Chi et al., 1982). Dealing with familiar problems in this manner is critical to problem-solving skill but is unlikely to result in the generation of new knowledge. In contrast, dealing with novel, unfamiliar problems has the potential to create new knowledge. New knowledge can be generated when we discover a new procedure or concept during problem solving. Random generate and test is central to solving unfamiliar problems. All problem-solving procedures intended to deal with novel problems, at some point, incorporate a random generate and test process that is indistinguishable from the random generate and test process used by evolution by natural selection.

The logical status of random generate and test needs to be considered. It is argued that when faced with a potential problem-solving step that we have not previously carried out, or faced with an entire problem for which we do not have a solution stored in long-term memory, then we have no choice but to engage in a random generate and test procedure. Assume that knowledge is unavailable to generate a known move or assume that there is sufficient knowledge to generate two or more potential moves but insufficient knowledge to rank them in terms of their likelihood of success. Faced with the lack of information held in long-term memory, we must randomly choose a move and attempt to test that move for effectiveness. There appear to be no logical techniques available to generate a move under conditions where knowledge is unavailable other than random generation.

We can rationally deduce moves, but all techniques for doing so require knowledge. As an example, we may have a new algebra problem that we have not seen previously but which conforms to the structure $a/b = c$, solve for a. Our knowledge, stored in long-term memory, tells us that the new problem conforms with the structure of $a/b = c$, solve for a, and we also know how to solve problems of this type. We can use this knowledge to generate a problem solution.

Without this knowledge, generating a solution would be more difficult and random generate and test provides the only available generative technique. We can use the rules of algebra to try several moves until we find one that either solves the problem or takes us closer to solving the problem. We might attempt to subtract b from both sides or add b to both sides, but discover these moves are ineffective. We might then discover that multiplying both sides by b is effective and solves the problem.

It should be noted, that even with knowledge, it might be argued that aspects of random generate and test are being used. Assume that we are solving the problem analogically. If we have not seen the relevant problem previously, we cannot be certain that it really does conform to the structure of $a/b = c$, solve for a. In other words, there can be no certainty that the analogy works. We can only be certain that the two problems are analogous once we have chosen the move of multiplying out the denominator and checked to see if it works. Certainty is impossible prior to making the relevant move or moves. Often we may only find that the problem looks as though it is a problem of a certain type but when we try to solve it accordingly, we may discover that the solution does not work, an example of Einstellung (Luchins, 1942; Sweller & Gee, 1978). Einstellung occurs when problem solvers, categorizing a problem incorrectly, fail to see a very simple solution and attempt to solve the problem using a complex or, in extreme cases, an impossible solution. Even when using knowledge to generate a successful solution, we can have no certainty that the knowledge is relevant and that it is properly used until we have attempted to use it.

In the absence of appropriate knowledge, the knowledge may need to be generated and random generate and test is the only available procedure. If alternatives to random generate and test when faced with novel problems are suggested, the procedures must be specified. To this point, random generate and test is the only generative process that has been specified when faced with novel problems for which a complete series of moves is not available in long-term memory.

The randomness as genesis principle provides the source by which new knowledge is created (Sweller, 2009). Once created and shown to be effective, that knowledge can be stored in the information store. While likely to be quantitatively, comparatively small, it has the same status as knowledge stored via the borrowing and reorganizing principle. From evolution by natural selection, we know it is the ultimate source of creativity in the biological world and we also know by observing the biological world that it is a highly effective source of creativity.

There is every sign that the randomness as genesis principle plays the same role in human cognition as in evolution by natural selection. If so, there are educational implications. Calls to encourage generative processes in education or to encourage creativity need to be made in light of the nature of generative processes and creativity. We need to understand that teaching learners to be flexible and creative requires us to teach them to engage in random generate and test. At this point, it is unclear whether encouraging learners to engage in random generate and test is likely to be productive. The question needs to be answered using appropriate experiments. Simply asserting that encouraging learners to engage in generative, constructivist, creative activities will be beneficial is inappropriate in the absence of data.

2.2.4. Narrow Limits of Change Principle

The randomness as genesis principle has structural implications. Random generation and test is concerned, in all cases, with the manner in which elements of information should be combined. Some combinations of elements prove to be effective when tested, others do not. The number of combinations that need to be tested can be critical. For example, there are six permutations of three elements ($3! = 6$). In contrast, there are 3,628,800 permutations of 10 elements ($10! = 3,628,800$). A random generate and test process that must find an appropriate permutation of 10 elements is vastly more difficult than a random generate and test process that must find the permutations of 3 elements. The implication of this arithmetic is that random generation and test should only deal with very small numbers of elements at a time.

This logic is directly relevant to the randomness as genesis principle and so structures are required that take that logic into account. The narrow limits of change principle provides these structures. The randomness as genesis principle is concerned with how natural information processing systems deal with novel information not previously stored in the information store. The novel information is obtained from the external environment and so the structure provided by the narrow limits of change principle is needed to deal with information from the external environment. In the case of evolution by natural selection, the relevant structure is the epigenetic system (Jablonka & Lamb, 2005; West-Eberhard, 2003). This system intercedes between the genetic system and the external environment. It manages the interaction between the genetic system based on DNA and the environment external to the DNA. The epigenetic system may be as equally important as the genetic system, although much less is known of it than the genetic system. Both systems are distinct (Jablonka & Lamb, 1995, 2005; West-Eberhard, 2003) and although they act independently, they closely interact.

The epigenetic system is able to transmit information from the external environment to the DNA-based genetic system in order to affect genetic alterations. Information from the environment can alter DNA by affecting when and where mutations occur. Environmental signals can facilitate or inhibit mutations in particular parts of a genome. For example, stressful environments may require changes in a genome in order to deal with the stress. These changes can occur via mutations and some organisms are able to increase the number of mutations when they find themselves in stressful environments. With increased mutations, there is a greater likelihood of a change to a genome that increases the chances of survival. As another example, mutations may be thousands of times higher than the average in some sections of a genome. Venomous animals such as snakes need to frequently change the composition of their venom to ensure their prey do not become immune to it. The epigenetic system can both facilitate these mutations and ensure they are not repaired.

It needs to be noted that while the epigenetic system can determine when and where mutations occur, it cannot determine the nature of a particular mutation. Beyond the epigenetic system's determining influence, each mutation is random and must be tested for effectiveness before being added to the DNA-based information store. Critically, even where the rate of mutations is increased, mutations are relatively rare. For the reasons outlined above, random generation and test must result in small changes to the genome. Large changes are likely to have catastrophic effects on the current store of information found in DNA because, based on the above arithmetic, there are a huge number of large changes that are possible and only a very few of these changes are likely to be adaptive. Accordingly, all effective changes are small and incremental.

The human cognitive system similarly must reduce the number of novel elements with which it deals for the same arithmetic reasons that apply to evolution by natural selection. In the case of human cognition, the relevant structure is human working memory. We probably know more about human working memory than about the epigenetic system because working memory has been studied more intensively for a longer period (Miller, 1956) than the epigenetic system. In particular, we have known for a long time that working memory, when dealing with novel information, is very limited in both capacity (Miller, 1956) and duration (Peterson & Peterson, 1959). These are exactly the limitations to be expected given the logic of dealing with novel information.

One of the major functions of working memory is to act as a conduit between the external environment and long-term memory in the same way as the epigenetic system acts as a conduit between the external environment and the DNA-based genetic system. The characteristics that we normally associate with working memory, its capacity and temporal limitations, occur when working memory must deal with novel information from the external environment. We know that working memory is unable to store more than about seven items of novel information (Miller, 1956) for more than about 20 s (Peterson & Peterson, 1959).

The processing capacity of working memory is considerably less than its storage capacity with no more than about three–four items of information being able to be processed at a time (Cowan, 2001). Processing refers to combining, contrasting, or dealing in some manner with multiple elements. The processing capacity limits of working memory are the limits we must expect of any natural processing system that must deal with novel information using a random generate and test procedure.

The narrow limits of change principle is critical to instruction and central to cognitive load theory. Instructional procedures need to take into consideration the capacity and duration limits of working memory. Recommended procedures that unnecessarily increase working memory load run the risk of severely constraining the ability of students to learn, where learning is defined as a positive change in long-term memory. Information that cannot be fully processed in working memory cannot be fully transferred to long-term memory inhibiting learning. Too many instructional recommendations proceed as though we do not have a working memory or if we do have a working memory, it is irrelevant to instructional considerations. At least in part, cognitive load theory was developed as an alternative to such instructional recommendations.

2.2.5. The Environmental Organizing and Linking Principle
The epigenetic system and working memory not only deal with novel information from the external environment but also use information from the external environment to organize information in the information

store and determine how that information is to be used and translated into action. The characteristics of the epigenetic and working memory systems are vastly different when organizing novel information from the environment compared to when using environmental information to organize the information store. The environmental organizing and linking principle covers the relation between the external environment and the information store. It permits a natural information processing system to use environmental signals to determine appropriate action. This principle is the final, natural information processing principle and provides the ultimate justification for the preceding principles.

The importance of the epigenetic system in organizing the genetic system can be demonstrated readily. A major function of the epigenetic system is to turn genes on and off. Consider the genetic material that can be found in the nuclei of human cells. For a given person, the nucleus of each cell has exactly the same genetic material as the nucleus of every other cell for those cells that contain nuclei. For example, the nucleus of a skin cell has exactly the same DNA as the nucleus of a liver cell, barring mutations. Of course, the structure and function of a skin cell bears little resemblance to the structure and function of a liver cell. If the genetic structure of these two cells is identical, what causes the immense differences in their characteristics? The answer is the epigenetic system. This system, via the environment external to the nucleus that holds the genetic material, controls which genes are to be turned on and which genes are to be turned off. By selectively turning genes on and off depending on environmental signals, vastly different cell structures with vastly different functions are built despite all cells having an identical genetic structure. In this sense, the epigenetic system is at least as important in biological systems as the genetic system.

The epigenetic system, when influencing the rate or location of mutations, must deal with relatively small amounts of information at a time, for reasons indicated above when discussing the narrow limits of change principle. In contrast, when the epigenetic system deals with the previously stored and previously organized information of the genetic system, the strictures imposed by a random generate and test process are absent. Accordingly, there are no limits to the amount of genetic material that can be dealt with by the epigenetic system. Very large amounts of DNA that constitute some genes can be turned on or off by the epigenetic system.

It can be seen that the epigenetic system links environmental signals to the genetic system. In this sense, it links the environment to the information store. The environmental organizing and linking principle is the general principle used by natural information processing systems to allow signals from the environment to influence the operation of the information store. Working memory has the same role in human cognition as the epigenetic system has in biological systems. Working memory uses signals from the environment to determine which aspects of long-term memory are relevant to current processing. For example, assume that we are familiar with problems of the form $(a + b)/c = d$, solve for a. When we see a problem of this form, it acts as a signal or cue triggering those aspects of long-term memory relevant to this particular problem with the rest of long-term memory left unaffected. In this manner, working memory determines which aspects of long-term memory are triggered and which are ignored. Its function is identical to the epigenetic system in biological systems.

As is the case for the epigenetic system, the characteristics of working memory are very different when it is dealing with stored, previously organized information compared to when it is dealing with novel information from the environment. The capacity and duration limits of working memory found when it deals with novel information disappear when working memory deals with information from long-term memory. Just as there are no known limits to the amount of stored DNA that can be handled by the epigenetic system, there are similarly no known limits to working memory when it processes familiar information organized in a familiar manner, that is, information stored in long-term memory. In other words, there are no known limits to the amount of organized information held in long-term memory that can be cued by appropriate environmental signals.

The different characteristics of working memory when dealing with familiar as opposed to novel information has resulted in some theorists suggesting a different structure when working memory handles familiar as opposed to novel material. Ericsson and Kintsch (1995) suggested "long-term working memory" as the structure that accounts for the manner in which working memory handles previously learned information held in long-term memory. Long-term working memory describes the characteristics of working memory when it deals with information stored in long-term memory. Because these characteristics bear little resemblance to the characteristics of working memory when it deals with novel information from the environment, we must either postulate different structures to deal with familiar and unfamiliar information or postulate different processes engaged in by the same structure. With respect to current concerns, either characterization results in an identical outcome. Information held in long-term memory allows us to carry out actions that we otherwise could not possibly consider.

The environmental organizing and linking principle provides the ultimate justification for natural information processing systems. Via this principle, the information created by the randomness as genesis and narrow limits of change principles, transmitted by the borrowing and reorganizing principle and stored by the information store principle, can be used to determine action that is appropriate to a particular environment. This action provides the purpose for a natural information processing system.

Based on the conception of a natural information processing system, the purpose of instruction is to increase biologically secondary knowledge held in long-term memory. That knowledge changes us. It changes the characteristics of working memory by eliminating its capacity and duration limits and allows us to engage fluently and efficiently in actions that we otherwise could not dream of carrying out. Cognitive load theory uses this cognitive architecture to devise instructional procedures.

3. Element Interactivity and Categories of Cognitive Load

Biologically secondary information varies in the extent to which it imposes a working memory load. There are two basic sources of instructional cognitive load. Some information imposes a heavy cognitive load because of its intrinsic nature. That load is referred to as intrinsic cognitive load. It can only be changed by changing what is learned or by changing the knowledge levels of learners. Other information imposes a heavy cognitive load not because of its intrinsic nature but rather because of the way it is presented. That load is referred to as extraneous cognitive load. It can be reduced by changing the instructional procedures. Both categories of cognitive load are determined by the same underlying factor: element interactivity (Sweller, 2010). High element interactivity occurs when learners process a large number of elements of information simultaneously in working memory with low element interactivity requiring few elements. The number of elements of information being processed due to the intrinsic nature of the information determines intrinsic cognitive load, while the number of elements of information due to instructional design factors determines extraneous cognitive load. Details concerning intrinsic cognitive load will be discussed next.

3.1. Intrinsic cognitive load

Intrinsic cognitive load refers to the complexity of the knowledge that is being acquired without reference to how that knowledge is acquired. How knowledge is acquired refers to extraneous cognitive load and will be discussed below. One of the critical features of intrinsic cognitive load is that it is fixed and unalterable for given information to be processed by learners with given levels of expertise. Because intrinsic cognitive load refers to the intrinsic complexity of the information being processed, it cannot be altered other than by altering what is learned or the levels of expertise of the learners. Once knowledge that is to be learned and what the learner already knows are determined, intrinsic cognitive load is fixed.

We can determine levels of intrinsic cognitive load by determining element interactivity. Some information is very high in element interactivity and so imposes a very high working memory load, while other information is low. For example, consider students who must learn chemical symbols. There are many symbols and the task is difficult. Nevertheless, the difficulty is not caused by a heavy intrinsic cognitive load and so working memory is not overloaded by this task. Each symbol can be learned independent of every other symbol because there is minimal element interactivity between the learning elements. For example, students can learn that Cu is the symbol for copper without any reference to the fact that the symbol for iron is Fe. Working memory resources can be devoted entirely to learning the symbol for copper without any reference to other symbols. Element interactivity is low and so working memory load due to intrinsic cognitive load is also low.

In contrast, other information can be very high in element interactivity, imposing a high working memory load due to a high intrinsic cognitive load. As an example, learning to balance a chemical equation requires consideration of a large number of elements of information in working memory simultaneously. When dealing with any unfamiliar equation in any discipline area, element interactivity is likely to be high. No change can be made to any element of information in an equation without considering the consequences of that change for every other element in the equation. Since the elements interact, all elements must be considered simultaneously prior to any manipulation of an equation.

Consider students who must learn to solve the algebra problem, $(a + b)/c = d$, solve for a. In order to understand and solve this problem, each of the elements that constitute the problem must be processed in working memory. Because they interact, they cannot be processed serially. They must be processed simultaneously. Each algebraic symbol must be considered in relation to every other algebraic symbol and the problem goal. For novice algebra students, these interacting elements may overload working memory resulting in a failure to solve the problem. This heavy working memory load is not caused by the need to process many elements, but rather by the need to process many elements simultaneously. Some tasks, such as learning the chemical symbols, require many more elements to be processed and so are difficult. This difficulty has a cause different from that of the difficulty imposed by the need to process many elements simultaneously. Simultaneous processing imposes a heavy working memory load, while successive processing does not. Whether information can be processed simultaneously or successively depends on element interactivity.

Levels of expertise also determine element interactivity via the information store and environmental organizing and linking principles. For readers of this chapter for whom the above algebra problem may be familiar because they hold a schema for the equation in long-term memory, the problem and its solution may be processed with little working memory load. The load may be so low that the problem may be solved without recourse to written materials because the interacting elements are incorporated in a schema that can be treated as a single element in working memory. A schema, due to the environmental organizing and linking principle, allows us to readily remember the equation, the problem goal, and to correctly manipulate the equation in working memory because the schema held in long-term memory includes the original problem state and all subsequent states.

Cognitively, learning to balance a chemical equation or manipulate an algebraic equation is analogous to learning to make a good move in chess. In each case, there are many elements of information that must be processed simultaneously in working memory. If these elements are not incorporated into a schema that can be treated as a single element using the environmental organizing and linking principle, the element interactivity and intrinsic cognitive load will be high. Learning requires the acquisition of large numbers of schemas incorporating interacting elements and stored in long-term memory via the information store principle. Once stored, they can be transferred to working memory via the environmental organizing and linking principle, thus permitting cognitive activities that otherwise would be impossible to even contemplate.

3.1.1. Understanding

This analysis of element interactivity and intrinsic cognitive load can be used to explain understanding and the distinction between learning with understanding and learning by rote. Counterintuitively for some, long-term memory is central to understanding and this fact has bedevilled an analysis of the concept. *Understanding* does not apply to low element interactivity information. It applies exclusively to high element interactivity information. For example, with respect to low element interactivity, if a learner is unable to indicate the symbol for copper, we might say they have forgotten the symbol or never learned the symbol, but we would not refer to the failure as a failure of understanding. The role of memory is clear-cut and obvious in the case of low element interactivity material. In contrast, if a person is unable to balance a chemical equation or solve an algebra problem, the term *understanding* is readily applied. It is quite appropriate for us to refer to a person understanding or not understanding an equation. It is inappropriate to refer to understanding a chemical symbol. Nevertheless, the difference between knowing a correct symbol and knowing how to deal with an equation can be expressed entirely in element interactivity terms. The cognitive processes in both cases are identical with both relying on memory.

Consider a student learning to multiply two numbers such as $3 \times 4 = 12$. Some students may treat learning this process as nothing more than memorizing the answer to 3×4. If so, the task is treated as a low element interactivity or "rote-learned" task. Other students may learn that 3×4 means 3 lots of 4 or $4 + 4 + 4$. These learners are beginning to *understand* the procedure. But note the process of understanding. It relies on long-term memory in exactly the same way as the rote learning with the only difference being in what is memorized. Rote learning simply means learning that $3 \times 4 = 12$, while learning with some degree of understanding means that in addition to learning that $3 \times 4 = 12$, students have also learned that $3 \times 4 = 4 + 4 + 4 = 12$. Both learning by rote and learning with understanding require changes to long-term memory with the only difference being that learning with understanding requires that more be memorized. If more is memorized, for example, that $3 \times 4 = 4 + 4 + 4 = 3 + 3 + 3 + 3 = 12$, then even more is understood. Further understanding occurs when $3 \times 4 = 12$ can be related to subtraction, division, and more general mathematical systems. In each case, further understanding consists of more information stored in long-term memory.

Before this high element interactivity information can be stored in long-term memory in order for the environmental organizing and linking principle to apply, it must of course be processed first in working memory. Processing high element interactivity information in working memory imposes a high intrinsic cognitive load. Acquiring the information requires a greater use of either the randomness as genesis principle if the information is discovered by learners or the borrowing and reorganizing principle if the information is presented. In either case, the working memory load (narrow limits of change principle) is increased compared to not having to process the additional information, especially if the randomness as genesis principle must be used. Learners can avoid processing the additional information by just learning that $3 \times 4 = 12$, resulting in a high element interactivity task being turned into a low element interactivity task. Of course, what has been learned has been changed. Changing what is learned from high to low element interactivity has the obvious advantage of reducing intrinsic cognitive load. There are obvious disadvantages to reducing intrinsic cognitive load when learning by rote instead of learning with understanding. Nevertheless, some students under some circumstances may have little choice in the matter. They may be unable to process the large number of interacting elements that need to be processed in order to learn with understanding. The intrinsic cognitive load imposed by learning with understanding may be overwhelming.

3.2. Intrinsic cognitive load effects

Cognitive load theory has been used to generate a large number of instructional procedures designed to alter cognitive load and, indeed, the generation of novel instructional procedures provides the ultimate purpose of the theory. A cognitive load effect is demonstrated when the theory is used to suggest ways of altering the number of interacting elements resulting in a new instructional procedure with better test outcomes than a traditional procedure. Most cognitive load effects are due to reductions in extraneous cognitive load (see below). There are few intrinsic cognitive load effects because intrinsic cognitive load cannot be altered except by altering the nature and goals of what is learned or by altering the levels of expertise. The variability effect and the isolated elements effect provide examples of effects due to changing levels of intrinsic cognitive load. Table 2 lists the cognitive load effects discussed in this chapter.

3.2.1. The Variability Effect
The variability effect, unlike all other cognitive load effects specified to date, occurs due to an increase rather than a decrease in cognitive load, in this case intrinsic cognitive load. Assume that learners are presented with a set of problems that are very similar. For example, they may vary only in the numerical values that need to be plugged into equations. In contrast, assume another set of problems in which, in addition to numerical values changing, equations have to be manipulated. The second set has greater variability resulting in increased element interactivity since more elements must be processed. Intrinsic cognitive load is increased because learners must not only learn how to solve a particular class of problems but must also learn to distinguish between problem types and learn which types require essentially the same solution and which types require a different solution. Providing that learners have sufficient working memory capacity to process the additional elements, there should be advantages to learning with more rather than less variable problems.

Paas and van Merriënboer (1994) obtained the variability effect with learners provided more variable problems learning more and performing better on transfer problems than the learners provided less variable problems. The effect is due to intrinsic cognitive load because what students were required to learn changed resulting in a change in element interactivity due to changed goals. Rather than just learning how to use an equation, a task that is relatively low in element interactivity, learners also had to learn which equations were appropriate at which time, a task that requires the processing of many more interacting elements. In terms of the cognitive architecture discussed in Section 2, increasing variability increased the amount of information stored so increasing the effectiveness of the environmental organizing and linking principle. The cost is an increased working memory load and so the procedure can be effective only if sufficient working memory resources are available.

Table 2 Cognitive Load Theory Effects

Effect	Description
Variability	Under low intrinsic cognitive load, increased variability increases intrinsic load resulting in increased learning if working memory resources are available
Isolated elements	Under high intrinsic cognitive load, presenting interacting elements as though they are isolated can decrease intrinsic load
Goal-free	Eliminating a problem goal eliminates the use of means–ends analysis reducing extraneous cognitive load
Worked example	Demonstrating a problem solution reduces the extraneous cognitive load associated with problem solving
Split-attention	If mental integration is required, extraneous cognitive load may be reduced by physically integrating disparate sources of information
Modality	Mental integration can be facilitated by presenting material using audiovisual rather than a visual only format
Redundancy	Processing unnecessary information imposes an extraneous cognitive load
Element interactivity	If intrinsic cognitive load is low, a high extraneous cognitive load may not exceed working memory capacity, reducing extraneous cognitive load effects
Expertise reversal	Information that is essential for novices may be redundant for experts reversing the relative effectiveness of instructional designs
Problem completion	Similar to the worked example effect based on partial worked examples and can be used during guidance fading
Guidance fading	Due to expertise reversal, as expertise increases, the guidance provided by worked examples should be decreased and eventually eliminated
Imagination	With sufficient expertise, imagining procedures or concepts can be more effective than studying
Transient information	The use of technology can transform permanent into transient information increasing extraneous cognitive load

3.2.2. The Isolated Elements Effect

While the variability effect is due to instructional procedures increasing intrinsic cognitive load, the isolated elements effect is due to instructional procedures decreasing intrinsic cognitive load. Assume that what students are required to learn is very high in element interactivity due to intrinsic cognitive load. It may be so high that the number of elements that must be processed exceeds working memory capacity. In this case, understanding and learning cannot proceed until levels of expertise are attained that permit interacting elements to be incorporated into schemas and treated as single elements using the environmental organizing and linking principle. It may be preferable to initially present the interacting elements in isolated form so that they can be processed even though they cannot be fully understood. Each element can be presented without reference to the other interacting elements. Once learned, the material can be presented again, but on this occasion in fully interacting rather than isolated form so that students can learn the interactions. Pollock, Chandler, and Sweller (2002) presented students with very complex information in isolated elements form thus reducing the intrinsic cognitive load followed by a presentation of the same information with the links between elements indicated. Another group was presented with the fully interacting material twice. The students who were presented with the elements in isolated form first performed better on subsequent test problems, providing an example of the isolated elements effect.

3.3. Extraneous cognitive load

Just as element interactivity determines intrinsic cognitive load, it also determines extraneous cognitive load. While the interacting elements that generate an intrinsic cognitive load are unavoidable other than by changing the task or levels of expertise, extraneous load is under the control of instructors and so the interacting elements due to extraneous cognitive load can be reduced or eliminated by changing instructional procedures. Some instructional procedures require learners to unnecessarily process many elements of information simultaneously resulting in a heavy, extraneous cognitive load that interferes with learning. These interacting elements should be eliminated because unlike intrinsic cognitive load, extraneous cognitive load should always be reduced with no conditions under which it should be increased. There are many cognitive load effects based on instructional techniques designed to reduce extraneous cognitive load.

3.3.1. The Goal-Free Effect

This cognitive load effect was the first to be demonstrated and the first to indicate the negative consequences of a means–ends problem–solving strategy (Sweller, 1988; Sweller, Mawer, & Ward, 1983). The effect occurs when students who are provided problems without a conventional goal outperform students presented with conventional problems on subsequent tests. A goal-free problem will require students to, for example, "calculate the value of as many variables as you can" or "calculate the value of as many angles as you can" rather than, for example, "How fast was the car traveling?" or "What is the value of angle ABC?"

In order to solve a conventional problem, learners must use a means-ends problem-solving strategy in which they consider both the current problem state and the goal state, find differences between the current problem state and the goal state, and find problem-solving operators to reduce these differences. The many interacting elements associated with this process impose an extraneous cognitive load that can overwhelm working memory and interfere with learning. In contrast, goal-free problem solving only requires learners to consider their current problem state and any operator that can alter that state. The reduction in extraneous working memory load due to the reduction in the number of interacting elements by the use of goal-free problems increases the information transferred to the long-term memory store.

While the goal-free effect is an interesting effect, goal-free problems can only be used under conditions where calculating as many variables as possible results in the calculation of a limited number of instructionally relevant variables. Some problems meet this requirement but many do not. For this reason, the worked example effect, discussed next, was devised as a universal procedure.

3.3.2. The Worked Example Effect

The worked example effect (Renkl, 2005) is probably the best known among the cognitive load theory effects. It is demonstrated when students learn more by studying a problem and its solution rather than solving the problem themselves. For example, learners may be presented with the problem, $(a + b)/c = d$, solve for a, for which they are required to find a solution. This problem-solving condition can be compared with a worked example condition in which learners are presented with the same problem along with its worked solution:

$$(a + b)/c = d$$
$$a + b = dc$$
$$a = dc - b$$

The worked example effect is demonstrated when the worked example condition performs better on subsequent problem-solving tests.

Since its demonstration by Sweller and Cooper (1985), the worked example effect has been replicated on a large number of occasions. It occurs because, as is the case with the goal-free effect, problem-solving search is associated with a large number of interacting elements that generate a heavy extraneous cognitive load. In contrast, studying a worked example reduces the number of interacting elements that need to be processed in working memory. Consider a person who does not have a solution schema and so cannot use the environmental organizing and linking principle when attempting to solve the above problem, $(a + b)/c = d$, solve for a. To solve the problem, a sequence of moves that will isolate a must be found. The addend b and the denominator c must be removed from the left side of the equation. What procedure could be used to remove b? Using the randomness as genesis principle, either subtracting b or dividing by b might work. In fact, neither of these procedures seems possible. Perhaps attending to c might work. As can be seen, there are a large number of elements that must be considered when searching for a problem solution. When knowledge is unavailable, the randomness as genesis principle must be used. In contrast, the elements required to study the worked example are all essential for someone who is learning to solve this category of problems and do not extend beyond the elements incorporated in the example. The randomness as genesis principle is not required to generate moves, the use of worked examples reduces the number of interacting elements associated with solving a problem and so reduces extraneous cognitive load, facilitating learning as indicated on subsequent test problems.

Most of the early studies on the worked example effect used curriculum materials from mathematics, science, and other technical areas. The problems were well defined as is common with problems in these areas. There are no cognitive reasons why the worked example effect should not be equally effective in areas that usually deal with ill-defined problems. There are now an increasing number of demonstrations of the worked example effect in ill-defined areas associated with language-based curricula or design issues. For example, Rourke and Sweller (2009) demonstrated the worked example effect when teaching learners to recognize furniture designers' styles.

The worked example effect follows closely from the principles used above to describe human cognitive architecture. Studying worked examples allows us to accumulate the large number of schemas associated with skill in an area in accordance with the information store principle. These schemas are best acquired by borrowing information provided by others in accordance with the borrowing and reorganizing principle. We learn more slowly if we attempt to acquire the same information by problem solving via the randomness as genesis principle. The narrow limits of change principle ensures that reducing working memory load by presenting learners with worked examples rather than having them solve problems facilitates learning. Once problem-solving schemas have been stored in long-term memory, we can solve problems that we otherwise would have great difficulty in solving as indicated by the environmental organizing and linking principle.

3.3.3. The Split-Attention Effect

A large number of other cognitive load theory effects are related to the worked example effect. The split-attention effect was the first of those satellite effects. Worked examples can be effective provided they reduce the need to process interacting elements that are extraneous to learning. Algebra worked examples of the type exemplified above do reduce extraneous cognitive load. Nevertheless, if a worked example is structured in a manner that does not reduce extraneous cognitive load, it will not be effective. Consider a typical geometry worked example. It usually consists of a diagram and a set of statements next to or under the diagram that indicate geometric relations such as "Angle ABC = Angle XBZ (vertically opposite angles are equal)." In order to understand this statement, learners must search for the two relevant angles using the randomness as genesis principle since the angles could be anywhere on the diagram. Search, as indicated above, can be expected to involve a large number of elements of information and processing these elements imposes an unnecessary working memory load—an extraneous cognitive load. That extraneous cognitive load is imposed because learners must split their attention between the diagram and the statements. Alternatively, if the statements are placed at appropriate locations on the diagram or if arrows link the statements with appropriate diagram locations, a search for referent locations no longer is necessary, reducing extraneous cognitive load due to the elimination of the need to use the randomness as genesis principle to process the statements. We might expect such physically integrated worked examples to be superior to conventional, split-attention versions.

Comparing worked examples presented in a split-attention format with a physically integrated format indicates that the integrated format facilitates learning (Sweller, Chandler, Tierney, & Cooper, 1990; Tarmizi & Sweller, 1988; Ward & Sweller, 1990). The effect is relevant to all forms of instruction, not just worked examples. Any instructional procedure including initial instruction prior to the presentation of worked examples and including forms of instruction other than diagrams and text such as multiple sources of text, multiple diagrams, or even physical equipment such as computers (Sweller & Chandler, 1994) should be analyzed from the perspective of the split-attention effect with the aim of physically integrating split-attention materials so that learners do not have to mentally integrate them. Ayres and Sweller (2005) provide a review of the split-attention effect.

It needs to be noted that the split-attention effect applies only to sources of information that are unintelligible in isolation. In order to understand a diagram and a text, for example, both should only become intelligible once they have been physically or mentally integrated. If they do not have to be integrated in order to be understood because, for example, the text merely redescribes the diagram, there are no grounds for assuming that the split-attention effect applies. Under these circumstances, the diagram or text may be redundant, leading to the redundancy effect described below.

3.3.4. The Modality Effect

This effect is closely related to the split-attention effect. When faced with two sources of information that cannot be understood in isolation, rather than physically integrating the two sources, they can be presented in different modalities. One source can be presented visually, while the other source can be presented aurally. Dual modality presentation should increase effective working memory and so decrease cognitive load.

There are theoretical grounds for suggesting that dual modality presentation should increase effective working memory capacity. According to Baddeley's model (Baddeley, 1999), working memory includes an auditory loop for processing speech and a visual–spatial sketchpad for processing visual material. These two processors are partially independent and both are limited in capacity. By using both, working memory capacity should increase (Penney, 1989).

Consider again, geometry instruction presented entirely visually with text presented in written rather than spoken form. The visual channel must be used to process diagrams and must also be used to initially process the written text. The written text then will need to be converted into auditory form for further processing. The visual channel has a limited processing capacity and so it can readily be overloaded. The need to initially process the written text using the visual channel and then to convert the written text into auditory text can be expected to impose an extraneous cognitive load that can interfere with the transfer of information to long-term memory. As an alternative, assume that the written text is presented in spoken rather than written form. The visual channel is no longer needed to process the text nor is there a need to convert the information into auditory form for further processing. The auditory channel only needs to be used to process spoken text. The consequence should be a reduction in the cognitive load imposed on the visual channel that can be expected to enhance learning.

This hypothesis was first tested by Mousavi, Low, and Sweller (1995) using geometry problems. They obtained the modality effect with students performing better on subsequent tests after learning using an audio-visual format rather than a visual only format. These results have been replicated on many occasions (see Ginns, 2005, for a meta-analysis). While the effect is very robust, there are many conditions under which it is known not to occur, with many of these conditions leading to new cognitive load effects. The modality effect will occur only under the same conditions required for the split-attention effect. The two sources of information must be unintelligible in isolation. If text, for example, merely restates the information in a diagram, it will lead to redundancy, not to the modality effect. In addition, the effect will not be obtained if intrinsic cognitive load is low due to the element interactivity effect. Neither will the effect be obtained if levels of expertise are high, due to the expertise reversal effect. Finally, in a very recent work, it was indicated that if text is lengthy and complex, a reverse modality effect is obtained due to the transient information effect. Each of these effects is separately discussed below.

3.3.5. The Redundancy Effect

The redundancy effect occurs when the addition of redundant information interferes with learning. The effect can be obtained using sources of information that on the surface appear similar to those that lead to the split-attention effect. The distinction between the two effects derives from the relation between the multiple sources of information. In the case of the split-attention effect, the multiple sources of information are unintelligible in isolation and must be integrated, mentally or physically, before they can be understood. In the case of redundancy, the sources of information are intelligible in isolation and do not need to be integrated in order to be understood. For example, a text may merely redescribe a diagram that is intelligible in its own right. Such text is redundant. The redundancy effect occurs when any additional information is presented that is not required. Often, but not always, the redundant information redescribes other information. Redundant information is defined as any unnecessary information.

The redundancy effect is caused by the introduction of unnecessary interacting elements resulting in an extraneous cognitive load. For example, if learners are presented with a self-explanatory diagram along with text that redescribes the diagram, they will attempt to process both the elements that constitute the diagram and the elements that constitute the text. They are likely to attempt to relate the diagram and the text. Such attempt to relate diagrams and text is likely to unnecessarily require the use of random generate and test via the randomness as genesis principle. The additional elements that need to be processed in working memory introduce an extraneous cognitive load.

The redundancy effect was first demonstrated using diagrams and redundant text (Chandler & Sweller, 1991). A diagram alone demonstrating the flow of blood in the heart, lungs, and body resulted in more learning than the same diagram with text redescribing the diagram. The effect has been replicated many times using a variety of materials other than diagrams and text. For example, learning to use machinery such as computers can be facilitated by the use of diagrams without the presence of the computer (Sweller & Chandler, 1994). As another example, verbal material should not be presented simultaneously in spoken and written form (Kalyuga, Chandler, & Sweller, 2004). There are many other examples. A review of the redundancy effect may be found in Sweller (2005).

3.3.6. The Element Interactivity Effect

All cognitive load effects rely on the information that is being processed imposing a heavy, intrinsic cognitive load. The information must be complex. If element interactivity due to intrinsic cognitive load is low, any element interactivity due to extraneous cognitive load may have few instructional consequences. It may be possible to process the interacting elements due to extraneous cognitive load without exceeding working memory capacity. If so, cognitive load effects will not be obtained when element interactivity due to intrinsic cognitive load is low. Information can be processed in working memory and transferred to the long-term store even under the presence of elements imposing an extraneous cognitive load. Neither the split-attention nor the redundancy effects are likely to be obtained using intrinsically low element interactivity information (Sweller & Chandler, 1994). Similarly, the modality effect is unlikely to be obtained with such material (Tindall-Ford, Chandler, & Sweller, 1997) along with several other cognitive load effects (Leahy & Sweller, 2005, 2008).

3.3.7. The Expertise Reversal, Problem Completion, and Guidance Fading Effects

The element interactivity effect is concerned with changes in the complexity of information presented to learners. The expertise reversal effect, in turn, is concerned with changes in learners' levels of expertise. The two effects are complementary because the complexity of information and the levels of expertise can compensate for each other with opposing effects on element interactivity. According to the environmental organizing and linking principle, increases in knowledge result in decreases in element interactivity and complexity as interacting elements are incorporated into schemas that are treated as a single element. Thus, intrinsic element interactivity can be decreased either by changing to a task with lower element interactivity or by increasing levels of learner expertise.

The expertise reversal effect (Kalyuga, Ayres, Chandler, & Sweller, 2003) occurs under the following conditions. Assume that instructional procedure A is superior to instructional procedure B using novice learners. With increasing expertise, the difference between the two procedures narrows and then disappears, before reappearing as a reverse effect with instructional procedure B proving superior to instructional procedure A. The expertise reversal effect has been demonstrated with many cognitive load effects including the worked example (Kalyuga, Chandler, Tuovinen, & Sweller, 2001), split-attention (Kalyuga, Chandler, & Sweller, 1998), and modality effects (Kalyuga, Chandler, & Sweller, 2000).

The expertise reversal effect relies on the redundancy effect. The inclusion of material that may be essential for novices to understand information may be redundant for more knowledgeable learners and so interfere with rather than facilitate learning. Consider the worked example effect. For novices, studying worked examples may facilitate learning compared to solving the equivalent problems. Searching for problem solutions increases extraneous element interactivity that interferes with learning. As expertise increases, learners may still need additional practice but may have sufficient knowledge to no longer need to search for solutions. It may be easier for them to generate a problem solution rather than study a solution provided by someone else. For example, most readers of this chapter are likely to find it easier to solve the problem $(a + b)/c = d$, solve for a, rather than study a worked example. Studying a worked example is likely to be redundant and so increase rather than decrease working memory load. As a consequence, for novices who have just begun to learn algebra, it may be easier to study a worked example than solve the equivalent problem; while for more knowledgeable learners, it may be easier to solve the problem than study the equivalent worked example, resulting in an expertise reversal effect. This effect was demonstrated by Kalyuga et al. (2001) using worked examples.

It follows from the worked example effect that novices should initially be presented with worked examples to study. With increasing expertise, these worked examples should be replaced by problems. Initially, worked examples can be replaced by completion problems that include part of the solution with the rest to be completed by learners (Paas, 1992; van Merrienboer, 1990). The *completion effect* is similar to the worked example effect and occurs when students presented with completion problems learn more than students presented with full problems. With further increases in expertise, completion problem may be replaced by full problems. This process of fading worked examples is superior to either just solving problems or just studying worked examples and is known as the *problem fading effect* (Salden, Aleven, Schwonke, & Renkl, 2010).

3.3.8. The Imagination Effect
This effect is also subject to expertise reversal. It occurs when learners are asked to imagine a concept or procedure rather than study it (Cooper, Tindall-Ford, Chandler, & Sweller, 2001). For example, learners may be presented with a worked example of an algebra problem. Rather than being asked to study the worked example, learners under *imagination* conditions are asked to look at the example and then turn away from it and try to imagine the solution to the problem. The imagination effect occurs when imagining a concept or procedure is superior to studying the relevant material. In order to imagine a concept or procedure, it is necessary to process the information in working memory. Novices may

have difficulty in processing all the required interacting elements in working memory and so imagining concepts or procedures may be difficult or even impossible. More knowledgeable learners may be able to imagine information more readily because many of the interacting elements are already incorporated into schemas via the environmental organizing and linking principle. As a consequence, the effect can be demonstrated only if levels of expertise are sufficiently high. For novices, studying the information tends to be superior to imagining it because imagining all the necessary interacting elements may overload working memory.

3.3.9. The Transient Information Effect

This effect is a new cognitive load effect. The use of educational technology sometimes has unintended cognitive load consequences. For example, a frequent side effect of using technology is that previously permanent information that can be repeatedly and easily accessed becomes transient and can only be reaccessed with difficulty or cannot be accessed at all. Information is transient if it disappears with the passage of time. Shifting from permanent written text to transitory auditory text or from permanent sets of diagrams to animation provides examples. Auditory information or most animated information disappears as new information is presented and so is transitory. If the information being conveyed is high in element interactivity, presenting it in transient form can have negative consequences. Having to remember previous, high element interactivity information that is no longer available and integrate it with currently appearing information can severely overload working memory.

Evidence for this hypothesis was obtained by Leahy and Sweller (in press) when testing for the modality effect. They ran two experiments comparing dual modality with visual only presentations. Primary school students were taught how to interpret time/temperature graphs showing the variations in temperature during the day. The first experiment included relatively lengthy, complex spoken statements such as "Find 35C on the temperature axis and follow across to a dot" while referring to a graph. The second experiment provided exactly the same information except that the statements were divided into smaller segments. The above statement, for example, was divided into "Find 35C on the temperature axis" and "Follow across to a dot." The first experiment with the longer statements demonstrated a reverse modality effect with the visual only material that included written statements proving superior to the audiovisual presentation. The second experiment with the shorter statements indicated a conventional modality effect.

The Leahy and Sweller work was not the first to obtain a reverse modality effect. Tabbers, Martens, and van Merriënboer (2004) also obtained a reverse modality effect using relatively lengthy, complex verbal information. These results can be explained readily from a cognitive load theory perspective. Assume that learners are faced with a relatively complex statement such as "Find 35C on the temperature axis and follow across to a dot." Holding this statement in working memory while referring to a graph may overload working memory. If presented in spoken form, the entire statement will need to be held and processed in working memory. In contrast, if it is presented in written form, learners can easily divide and return to the statement in part or in whole whenever they need to. For example, they can quickly scan the entire statement once and then return to the first clause, "Find 35C on the temperature axis...," process that statement with respect to the graph by finding the 35C point, and then return to the statement to process the rest of the statement "...and follow across to a dot." If presented in auditory form, learners would need to have memorized the entire statement using the information store and environmental organizing and linking principles in order to engage in a similar activity. Accordingly, a visual text along with a visual diagram is superior to an audiovisual presentation.

If the statements are presented in shorter form, they are likely to be automatically held in working memory irrespective of whether they are presented in spoken or in written form. For shorter statements, the expansion of working memory due to the use of both auditory and visual channels should result in the conventional modality effect obtained in a large number of studies over many years (Ginns, 2005).

The transient information effect should apply equally to any transient information such as complex, high element interactivity animations. Preliminary results confirm that the length of animations can determine their relative effectiveness compared to static graphics.

3.4. Summary of element interactivity and the cognitive load effects

Element interactivity is central to cognitive load theory and the cognitive load effects. When we must process multiple, interacting elements in working memory simultaneously, an excessive or inappropriate cognitive load may be generated. If cognitive load is intrinsic to the information being assimilated as it occurs for the variability and isolated elements effects, it needs to be altered. Altering intrinsic cognitive load will alter what is learned and understood. Intrinsic cognitive load cannot be altered if what needs to be learned is unaltered and if levels of expertise remain the same.

The vast majority of cognitive load effects are due to a reduction of extraneous cognitive load. If instructional procedures require learners to unnecessarily process interacting elements because of the manner in which information is presented, especially if the presentation of information requires learners to use the randomness as genesis rather than the borrowing and reorganizing principle, extraneous cognitive load will be high and should be reduced. A reduction in extraneous cognitive load will permit working memory resources to be mobilized to deal with intrinsic load that is germane to learning. Extraneous cognitive load can be reduced by altering instructional procedures as indicated in this section (see Table 2).

4. Conclusions

The cognitive load effects provide the ultimate justification for cognitive load theory. Nevertheless, they should not be considered in isolation. Human cognitive architecture and the categories of cognitive load are essential. There has been a tendency for some in the field to assume that the cognitive load effects can be considered in isolation from the cognitive architecture that gave rise to the effects. This view is misguided. We cannot automatically assume that, for example, studying worked examples is superior to solving problems or presenting information in a split-source format is worse than presenting information in an integrated format. None of the effects should be considered in isolation from the theoretical constructs that gave rise to them. Studying worked examples is frequently superior to solving problems but only if extraneous cognitive load is reduced. If it is not reduced because, for example, worked examples are presented in split-source format or student knowledge is sufficiently high to not require worked examples, then the use of worked examples will be ineffective. Similarly, while we know that dual mode presentations of information can be very effective, we also know that if verbal information is redundant, using a dual mode presentation will not be effective because the redundant information increases extraneous cognitive load. We now also know that lengthy, complex, high element interactivity verbal material needs to be presented in written, not spoken form. The modality effect does not provide an excuse to use audiovisual presentations irrespective of other cognitive load factors. If dual modality presentation leads to a heavy, extraneous cognitive load as will happen if lengthy, complex statements are presented in auditory form, we should not expect to obtain a modality effect. A reverse modality effect is more likely.

The cognitive architecture of Section 2 can be used to assess the likely effects of any instructional intervention. According to this architecture, the purpose of instruction is to increase usable knowledge held in long-term memory via the information store principle. This knowledge allows our working memory to function at a high level according to the environmental organizing and linking principle, permitting us to engage in activities that otherwise would be difficult or impossible. Obtaining information from others is the best way of acquiring knowledge according to the borrowing and organizing principle. If knowledge is not held in long-term memory, we must process information in working memory that is limited in capacity and duration when dealing with novel information according to the narrow limits of change principle. We can acquire novel information while problem solving in accord with the randomness as genesis principle, but that process requires working memory resources that consequently are unavailable for learning. Instructional procedures that do not meet the objective of increasing knowledge in long-term memory while decreasing any unnecessary load on working memory are likely to be ineffective.

We should never ignore human cognitive architecture when designing instruction. It is not an optional extra.

REFERENCES

Ayres, P., & Sweller, J. (2005). The split-attention principle. In R. E. Mayer (Ed.), *Cambridge handbook of multimedia learning* (pp. 135–146). New York: Cambridge University Press.

Baddeley, A. (1999). *Human memory.* Boston, MA: Allyn & Bacon.

Bandura, A. (1986). *Social foundations of thought and action: A social cognitive theory.* Englewoods Cliffs, NJ: Prentice Hall.

Chandler, P., & Sweller, J. (1991). Cognitive load theory and the format of instruction. *Cognition and Instruction, 8,* 293–332.

Chase, W. G., & Simon, H. A. (1973). Perception in chess. *Cognitive Psychology, 4,* 55–81.

Chi, M., Glaser, R., & Rees, E. (1982). Expertise in problem solving. In R. Sternberg (Ed.), *Advances in the psychology of human intelligence* (pp. 7–75). Hillsdale, NJ: Erlbaum.

Chiesi, H., Spilich, G., & Voss, J. (1979). Acquisition of domain-related information in relation to high and low domain knowledge. *Journal of Verbal Learning and Verbal Behaviour, 18,* 257–273.

Cooper, G., Tindall-Ford, S., Chandler, P., & Sweller, J. (2001). Learning by imagining. *Journal of Experimental Psychology: Applied, 7,* 68–82.

Cowan, N. (2001). The magical number 4 in short-term memory: A reconsideration of mental storage capacity. *Behavioral and Brain Sciences, 24,* 87–114.

De Groot, A. (1965). *Thought and choice in chess.* The Hague, Netherlands: Mouton (original work published in 1946).

Egan, D. E., & Schwartz, B. J. (1979). Chunking in recall of symbolic drawings. *Memory & Cognition, 7,* 149–158.

Ericsson, K. A., & Charness, N. (1994). Expert performance: Its structure and acquisition. *American Psychologist, 49,* 725–747.

Ericsson, K. A., & Kintsch, W. (1995). Long-term working memory. *Psychological Review, 102,* 211–245.

Geary, D. (2007). Educating the evolved mind: Conceptual foundations for an evolutionary educational psychology. In J. S. Carlson, & J. R. Levin (Eds.), *Psychological perspectives on contemporary educational issues* (pp. 1–99). Greenwich, CT: Information Age Publishing.

Geary, D. (2008). An evolutionarily informed education science. *Educational Psychologist, 43,* 179–195.

Ginns, P. (2005). Meta-analysis of the modality effect. *Learning and Instruction, 15*, 313–331.

Jablonka, E., & Lamb, M. J. (1995). *Epigenetic inheritance and evolution.* New York: Oxford University Press.

Jablonka, E., & Lamb, M. J. (2005). *Evolution in four dimensions: genetic, epigenetic, behavioral, and symbolic variation in the history of life.* Cambridge, MA: MIT Press.

Jeffries, R., Turner, A., Polson, P., & Atwood, M. (1981). Processes involved in designing software. In J. R. Anderson (Ed.), *Cognitive skills and their acquisition* (pp. 255–283). Hillsdale, NJ: Erlbaum.

Kalyuga, S., Ayres, P., Chandler, P., & Sweller, J. (2003). The expertise reversal effect. *Educational Psychologist, 38*, 23–31.

Kalyuga, S., Chandler, P., & Sweller, J. (1998). Levels of expertise and instructional design. *Human Factors, 40*, 1–17.

Kalyuga, S., Chandler, P., & Sweller, J. (2000). Incorporating learner experience into the design of multimedia instruction. *Journal of Educational Psychology, 92*, 126–136.

Kalyuga, S., Chandler, P., & Sweller, J. (2004). When redundant on-screen text in multimedia technical instruction can interfere with learning. *Human Factors, 46*, 567–581.

Kalyuga, S., Chandler, P., Tuovinen, J., & Sweller, J. (2001). When problem solving is superior to studying worked examples. *Journal of Educational Psychology, 93*, 579–588.

Kirschner, P., Sweller, J., & Clark, R. (2006). Why minimal guidance during instruction does not work: An analysis of the failure of constructivist, discovery, problem-based, experiential and inquiry-based teaching. *Educational Psychologist, 41*, 75–86.

Klahr, D., & Nigam, M. (2004). The equivalence of learning paths in early science instruction: Effects of direct instruction and discovery learning. *Psychological Science, 15*, 661–667.

Kotovsky, K., Hayes, J., & Simon, H. (1985). Why are some problems hard? Evidence from Tower of Hanoi. *Cognitive Psychology, 17*, 248–294.

Leahy, W., & Sweller, J. (2005). Interactions among the imagination, expertise reversal, and element interactivity effects. *Journal of Experimental Psychology: Applied, 11*, 266–276.

Leahy, W., & Sweller, J. (2008). The imagination effect increases with an increased intrinsic cognitive load. *Applied Cognitive Psychology, 22*, 273–283.

Leahy, W., & Sweller, J. (in press). Cognitive load theory, modality of presentation and the transient information effect. Applied Cognitive Psychology.

Luchins, A. (1942). Mechanisation in problem solving: The effect of Einstellung. *Psychological Monographs, 54*, (Whole No. 248).

Luchins, A. (1942). Mechanisation in problem solving: The effect of Einstellung. *Psychological Monographs, 54*, (Whole No. 248).

Miller, G. A. (1956). The magical number seven, plus or minus two: Some limits on our capacity for processing information. *Psychological Review, 63*, 81–97.

Mousavi, S. Y., Low, R., & Sweller, J. (1995). Reducing cognitive load by mixing auditory and visual presentation modes. *Journal of Educational Psychology, 87*, 319–334.

Paas, F. (1992). Training strategies for attaining transfer of problem-solving skill in statistics: A cognitive-load approach. *Journal of Educational Psychology, 84*, 429–434.

Paas, F., & van Merrienboer, J. (1994). Variability of worked examples and transfer of geometrical problem-solving skills: A cognitive-load approach. *Journal of Educational Psychology, 86*, 122–133.

Penney, C. G. (1989). Modality effects and the structure of short-term verbal memory. *Memory & Cognition, 17*, 398–422.

Peterson, L., & Peterson, M. J. (1959). Short-term retention of individual verbal items. *Journal of Experimental Psychology, 58*, 193–198.

Pollock, E., Chandler, P., & Sweller, J. (2002). Assimilating complex information. *Learning and Instruction, 12*, 61–86.

Portin, P. (2002). Historical development of the concept of the gene. *Journal of Medicine and Philosophy, 27*, 257–286.

Renkl, A. (2005). The worked out example principle in multimedia learning. In R. E. Mayer (Ed.), *The Cambridge handbook of multimedia learning* (pp. 229–245). New York: Cambridge University Press.

Rourke, A., & Sweller, J. (2009). The worked-example effect using ill-defined problems: Learning to recognise designers' styles. *Learning and Instruction, 19*, 185–199.

Salden, R., Aleven, V., Schwonke, R., & Renkl, A. (2010). The expertise reversal effect and worked examples in tutored problem solving. *Instructional Science, 38*, 289–307.

Schneider, W., & Shiffrin, R. M. (1977). Controlled and automatic human information processing: I. Detection, search, and attention. *Psychological Review, 84*, 1–66.

Shiffrin, R. M., & Schneider, W. (1977). Controlled and automatic human information processing: II. Perceptual learning, automatic attending and a general theory. *Psychological Review, 84*, 127–190.

Simon, H., & Gilmartin, K. (1973). A simulation of memory for chess positions. *Cognitive Psychology, 5*, 29–46.

Stotz, K., & Griffiths, P. (2004). Genes: Philosophical analyses put to the test. *History and Philosophy of the Life Sciences, 26*, 5–28.

Sweller, J. (1988). Cognitive load during problem solving: Effects on learning. *Cognitive Science, 12*, 257–285.

Sweller, J. (2003). Evolution of human cognitive architecture. In B. Ross (Ed.), *The psychology of learning and motivation* Vol. 43, (pp. 215–266). San Diego, CA: Academic Press.

Sweller, J. (2005). The redundancy principle. In R. E. Mayer (Ed.), *Cambridge handbook of multimedia learning* (pp. 159–167). New York: Cambridge University Press.

Sweller, J. (2009). Cognitive bases of human creativity. *Educational Psychology Review, 21*, 11–19.

Sweller, J. (2010). Element interactivity and intrinsic, extraneous and germane cognitive load. *Educational Psychology Review, 22*, 123–138.

Sweller, J., Ayres, P., & Kalyuga, S. (2011). *Cognitive load theory.* New York: Springer.

Sweller, J., & Chandler, P. (1994). Why some material is difficult to learn. *Cognition and Instruction, 12*, 185–233.

Sweller, J., Chandler, P., Tierney, P., & Cooper, M. (1990). Cognitive load as a factor in the structuring of technical material. *Journal of Experimental Psychology: General, 119*, 176–192.

Sweller, J., & Cooper, G. (1985). The use of worked examples as a substitute for problem solving in learning algebra. *Cognition and Instruction, 2*, 59–89.

Sweller, J., & Gee, W. (1978). Einstellung, the sequence effect, and hypothesis theory. *Journal of Experimental Psychology: Human Learning & Memory, 4*, 513–526.

Sweller, J., Mawer, R. F., & Ward, M. R. (1983). Development of expertise in mathematical problem solving. *Journal of Experimental Psychology: General, 112*, 639–661.

Sweller, J., & Sweller, S. (2006). Natural information processing systems. *Evolutionary Psychology, 4*, 434–458.

Tabbers, H. K., Martens, R. L., & van Merriënboer, J. J. G. (2004). Multimedia instructions and cognitive load theory: Effects of modality and cueing. *British Journal of Educational Psychology, 74*, 71–81.

Tarmizi, R. A., & Sweller, J. (1988). Guidance during mathematical problem solving. *Journal of Educational Psychology, 80*, 424–436.

Tindall-Ford, S., Chandler, P., & Sweller, J. (1997). When two sensory modes are better than one. *Journal of Experimental Psychology: Applied, 3*, 257–287.

van Merrienboer, J. (1990). Strategies for programming instruction in high school: Program completion vs. program generation. *Journal of Educational Computing Research, 6*, 265–285.

Ward, M., & Sweller, J. (1990). Structuring effective worked examples. *Cognition and Instruction, 7*, 1–39.

West-Eberhard, M. (2003). *Developmental plasticity and evolution.* New York: Oxford University Press.

CHAPTER THREE

APPLYING THE SCIENCE OF LEARNING TO MULTIMEDIA INSTRUCTION

Richard E. Mayer

Contents

Abstract

Multimedia instruction refers to learning environments that contain both words and pictures with the intention to promote learning, such as illustrated textbooks, narrated slideshow presentations, online narrated animations, and educational computer games. The design of effective multimedia instruction should be guided by the science of learning (i.e., the scientific study of how people learn), the science of assessment (i.e., the scientific study of how to know what people learn), and the science of instruction (i.e., the scientific study of how to help people learn). Concerning the science of learning, the

Psychology of Learning and Motivation, Volume 55
ISSN 0079-7421, DOI 10.1016/B978-0-12-387691-1.00003-X

© 2011 Elsevier Inc.
All rights reserved.

cognitive theory of multimedia learning is based on three principles from cognitive science (i.e., dual channels, limited capacity, and active processing); five cognitive processes during learning (i.e., selecting words and pictures, organizing words and pictures, and integrating); and five kinds of representations during learning (i.e., external representations, sensory copies in sensory memory, images and sounds in working memory, pictorial and verbal models in working memory, and knowledge in long-term memory). Concerning the science of assessment, the focus is on transfer in the context of three kinds of learning outcomes (i.e., no learning, rote learning, and meaningful learning); experimental comparisons of instructional effectiveness, including the role of effect size; and individual differences in learning, including the role of prior knowledge. Concerning the science of instruction, the triarchic theory of multimedia instruction distinguishes among three goals in instruction and corresponding research-based techniques—reducing extraneous processing, managing essential processing, and fostering generative processing. Applying the science of learning to multimedia instruction is a success story for educational psychology, pointing to the reciprocal relation between cognitive psychology and educational practice.

1. Introduction to Multimedia Instruction

This section defines multimedia instruction, provides a rationale for multimedia instruction, and gives a brief historical overview of multimedia instruction.

1.1. What is multimedia instruction?

Suppose you become interested in solar energy, particularly solar cells, as a way of improving the environment. You go to your local library and find a magazine article that explains how solar cells work using words and diagrams. You go online and find a site that has a narrated animation describing how solar cells work, along with a simulation game that allows you to see how varying the number of cells, orientation of the cells, and amount of sunlight affects the production of electricity. You even attend a meeting by solar cell companies at your civic center in which a speaker presents a PowerPoint presentation on solar cells.

Each of these learning venues—printed text and illustrations, narrated animation, computer simulation game, or slideshow—is an example of multimedia instruction because each presents words and pictures intended to promote learning. The words may be printed (as in a magazine article) or spoken (as in a narration); and the pictures may be static (such as diagrams, illustrations, or photos in PowerPoint slides) or dynamic (such as an animation or video in an online lesson or simulation game).

1.2. The promise and challenge of multimedia instruction

The promise of multimedia instruction is that people can learn better from words and pictures than from words alone—which can be called the *multimedia principle* (Fletcher & Tobias, 2005; Mayer, 2009). In a recent meta-analysis based on 11 experimental comparisons of transfer test performance, people learned better from lessons containing words and pictures than from lessons containing only the identical words. The median effect size was $d = 1.39$, which is considered a large effect (Mayer, 2009).

Although adding pictures to words can improve learning, not all graphics are equally effective and some are even detrimental (Harp & Mayer, 1997, 1998; Mayer, Heiser, & Lonn, 2001). The challenge of multimedia instruction is to figure out how to design effective lessons using words and pictures. The goal of this chapter is to meet this challenge by drawing on advances in the science of learning, science of assessment, and science of instruction. In short, the goal is to develop principles of multimedia instructional design that are grounded in cognitive theory and supported by credible experimental research evidence.

1.3. Historical overview of multimedia instruction

For hundreds of years, instruction has been mainly a verbal endeavor—involving, for example, an instructor talking to a group (i.e., lecturing), an instructor talking with an individual student about a problem or issue (i.e., tutoring), or an author writing to share his or her knowledge (i.e., textbooks). Is there any value added by incorporating pictorial modes of instruction to complement these verbal modes of instruction that have such a long history in education?

The first major practical attempt to accomplish this goal occurred in 1658 with the publication of *Pictus Orbis* ("The World in Pictures") by John Comenius. Each section of the book contained a line drawing of some aspect of the world—for example, a carriage, a butcher shop, or the planets—with each part of the drawing numbered along with a corresponding description of the numbered part in the reader's native language and Latin. The editor's preface to an English language version of the book calls it "an educational classic of prime importance" and notes "it was the first picture book ever made for children and was for a century the most popular textbook in Europe" (Comenius, 1887, p. iii).

Pictus Orbis can be seen as a forerunner of today's textbooks, which devote up to 50% of their space to dazzling color graphics, many of which—unlike *Pictus Orbis*—serve questionable pedagogic purposes (Levin & Mayer, 1993; Mayer, Sims, & Tajika, 1995). Technological advances in the 20th century enabled the educational use of motion pictures beginning in the 1920s, educational television in the 1950s, and computer-based instruction involving words and pictures in the 1960s (Cuban, 1986). However, the history of using graphics-based technologies in education has been somewhat disappointing as reflected in cycles of high hopes followed by lack of instructional effectiveness (Cuban, 1986). Instructors who adopted these technologies for infusing pictorial modes of instruction tended to take a technology-centered approach by focusing on cutting edge technology rather than a learner-centered approach by focusing on how to use technology as an aid to human cognition (Mayer, 2009).

Recent advances in computer-based visualization and communication technologies again afford many exciting possibilities for *e-learning*—computer presented words and pictures intended to promote learning (Clark & Mayer, 2008). Some examples of e-learning venues for multimedia instruction include computer-based training, online multimedia lessons, hypermedia, interactive simulation, intelligent tutoring systems, animated pedagogical agents, virtual environments, and serious games (Graesser, Chipman, & King, 2008). Yet, in spite of Comenius's promising start to the field of multimedia instruction, there is still a need for an approach to multimedia instructional design that is guided by science rather than opinion, fads, and ideology. The remainder of this chapter explores the scientific basis for designing multimedia instruction, including a theory of how people learn (i.e., science of learning), a valid methodology for how to assess what people learn (i.e., science of assessment), and a theoretically grounded evidence base for how to help people learn (i.e., science of instruction).

2. Science of Multimedia Learning: Cognitive Theory of Multimedia Learning

This section describes a cognitive theory of how people learn from words and pictures that is based on three principles from cognitive science, involves five cognitive processes during learning, and involves a progression of five kinds of representations.

2.1. Three principles from cognitive science

Figure 1 summarizes a research-based framework of the cognitive architecture for how people learn from words and pictures, called the cognitive theory of multimedia learning (Mayer, 2005, 2009). It is based on three fundamental principles from research in cognitive science: dual channel principle, limited capacity principle, and active processing principle.

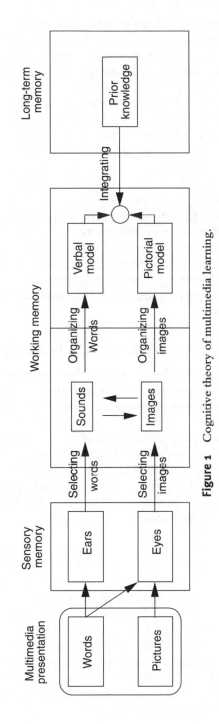

Figure 1 Cognitive theory of multimedia learning.

The *dual channel principle* is that people have separate channels for processing words and pictures (Paivio, 1986, 2006; Sadoski & Paivio, 2001). In Figure 1, the top row corresponds to auditory/verbal processing and the bottom row corresponds to visual/pictorial processing. The *limited capacity principle* is that people can engage in only a limited amount of active cognitive processing in each channel at any one time (Baddeley, 1999; Sweller, 1999). In Figure 1, the column labeled "working memory" represents the bottleneck in human information processing system in which people have limited capacity to engage in cognitive processes such as selecting, organizing, and integrating within each channel. The *active processing principle* is that meaningful learning outcomes depend on the learner engaging in active cognitive processing during learning including attending to relevant incoming information, mentally organizing it into coherent cognitive representations, and integrating the representations with each other and with appropriate prior knowledge from long-term memory (Mayer, 2008a; Mayer & Wittrock, 2006; Wittrock, 1989). In Figure 1, these cognitive processes are represented by the arrows labeled "selecting," "organizing," and "integrating," respectively.

2.2. Five cognitive processes during learning

The arrows in Figure 1 denote five active cognitive processes that the learner can choose to engage in during learning: selecting words, selecting images, organizing words, organizing images, and integrating. *Selecting words and images* occurs when the learner attends to aspects of relevant incoming words and pictures held briefly in sensory memory and transfers them to working memory for further processing. *Organizing words and images* occurs when the learner builds a coherent mental representation in working memory from the words (into a verbal model) or from the images (into a pictorial model). *Integrating* occurs when the learner mentally combines the verbal and pictorial models with each other and with appropriate knowledge from long-term memory, thereby creating knowledge that can be stored in long-term memory. According to the cognitive theory of multimedia learning, the meaningful learning outcomes are created when learners engage in these five cognitive processes during learning in a coordinated way.

Motivation and metacognition play an important role in multimedia learning (Hacker, Dunlosky, & Graesser, 2009; Mayer, 2010; Moreno & Mayer, 2005; Wentzel & Wigfield, 2009). Motivation is needed to energize and maintain the learner's effort to engage in active cognitive processing (Wentzel & Wigfield, 2009). Metacogniton is needed to guide and coordinate the learner's process active cognitive processing during learning (Hacker, Dunlosky, & Graesser, 2009).

2.3. Five kinds of representations

Information goes through a series of transformations in Figure 1. First, on the left side of Figure 1, an *external representation* is presented to the learner in the form of a multimedia instructional message—such as an on-screen narrated animation, a slideshow presentation, or a textbook chapter. In the second column of Figure 1, as the spoken words impinge on the ears, they are held as an *auditory sensory copy* in auditory sensory memory, and as the pictures and printed words impinge on the eyes, they are held as a *visual sensory copy* in visual sensory memory. In the third column of Figure 1, if the learner attends to parts of the fleeting sensory copies they are transferred to working memory as *sounds* or *images* for further processing. In the fourth column of Figure 1, the learner can organize the sounds into a *verbal model* and can organize the images into a *pictorial model* in working memory. In the fifth column of Figure 1, the learner can integrate the verbal and pictorial models with each other and with appropriate knowledge from long-term memory to create *knowledge* for storage in long-term memory at the right of the figure. Overall, in the cognitive theory of multimedia learning, information is changed from an external representation to sensory copies in sensory memory to sounds and images in working memory to verbal and pictorial models in working memory to knowledge in long-term memory.

3. SCIENCE OF MULTIMEDIA ASSESSMENT: FOCUSING ON TRANSFER

This section is concerned with the scientific study of determining what people know (Pellegrino, Chudowsky, & Glaser, 2001), and in particular with assessing the learner's deep understanding of content (Mayer, 2010).

3.1. Three kinds of learning outcomes

Two common kinds of learning outcome assessment instruments are retention tests and transfer tests. Retention tests focus on what the learner remembers from the lesson either in the form a recall test (e.g., "Please write down all you can remember about this chapter said about the cognitive theory of multimedia learning.") or a recognition test (e.g., "According to the cognitive theory of multimedia learning, which of the following is not an active cognitive process during learning? a. selecting, b. organizing, c. integrating, d. navigating"). Transfer tests focus on how well the learner can use the material in the lesson to solve a new problem (e.g., "What kind of learning outcome would result if the learner selects relevant words and images but does not engage in much organizing and integrating?"). Transfer tests can vary from near transfer (e.g., solving problems that are similar to those in the lesson) to far transfer (e.g., solving problems that are different from those in the lesson).

Table 1 lists the names and descriptions of three kinds of learning outcomes—no learning, rote learning, and meaningful learning. *No learning* occurs when the learner fails to engage in selecting, organizing, and integrating during learning, resulting in nothing new being added to long-term memory. The signature test performance for no learning is poor performance on both retention and transfer tests.

Rote learning occurs when the learner selects some relevant aspects of the presented material and mentally organizes it as presented without engaging in reorganizing or integrating the material. The resulting learning outcome is rote in the sense that it is essentially a representation of what was presented without any attempt by the learner to make sense out of it, such as memorizing the definition of a technical term. The signature test performance for rote learning is good retention test performance and poor transfer test performance. Rote learning can be an appropriate instructional objective under some circumstances, such as when someone is expected to do the same procedure the same way repeatedly or simply must know an arbitrary list such as the days of the week.

Meaningful learning occurs when the learner engages in selecting, organizing, and integrating in a coordinated way in order to make sense of the presented material. Sense making involves the two parallel processes of organizing (i.e., putting the pieces of the presented material together into a coherent structure that has logical internal structural integrity) and integrating (combining the cognitive representations with appropriate prior knowledge in a way that has logical externally structural integrity). The signature test performance for meaningful learning is good performance on transfer tests and retention tests. Thus, transfer tests are particularly important assessment instruments when the goal of instruction is to promote meaningful learning. Most instructional objectives in education seek meaningful learning because educators want their students to be able to adapt to new challenges they will face once they leave school, that is, to succeed on transfer tasks. For this reason, this chapter focuses on transfer

Table 1 Three Kinds of Learning Outcomes

Learning outcome	Cognitive processes during learning	Retention	Transfer
No learning	None	Poor	Poor
Rote learning	Selecting and initial organizng	Good	Poor
Meaningful learning	Selecting, organizing, integrating	Good	Good

test performance as the key dependent measure in analyses of instructional effectiveness.

3.2. Experimental comparisons of instructional effectiveness

The research reported in this chapter takes a *value-added approach*, which aims to determine whether adding an instructional feature to a multimedia lesson improves student learning. When the goal is to determine which of two (or more) instructional methods is most effective (as measured by a relevant measure of learning outcome), then the most appropriate research methodology is an *experimental comparison* (Shavelson & Towne, 2002). Although debates about research methodology among educational researchers can become heated, there is consensus that experiments are the most appropriate method for making conclusions about whether a particular instructional method causes learning (Phye, Robinson, & Levin, 2005; Shavelson & Towne, 2002). Overall, wide scale application of experimental methodology to human research represents one of the major scientific accomplishments of the 20th century, and stands as one of psychology's greatest gifts to education.

Three fundamental requirements of an experimental comparison are experimental control, random assignment, and appropriate measures. *Experimental control* means that the experimental and control treatments are identical except for one factor (i.e., the independent variable). For example, in comparing the test performance of a group that listens to an explanation of how a pump works (words only group) to a group that listens to the same explanation along with a concurrent animation depicting the same events as in the verbal explanation (words and pictures group), what is being varied is the addition of pictures. *Random assignment* means that each learner in the study is selected by chance from a pool to be in one of the treatment groups. For example, if there are 100 students in a study, 50 are randomly selected for the control group and 50 are randomly selected for the experimental group. *Appropriate measures* means that the results include the mean (M), standard deviation (SD), and sample size (n) of the experimental and control groups on a relevant measure of learning. In many cases, a relevant measure of learning is performance on a transfer test. For example, on a 10-item comprehension test, the 50 students in the experimental group score higher ($M = 8.0$, $SD = 2.0$) than the 50 students in the control group ($M = 6.4$, $SD = 2.0$).

Based on the means and standard deviations of the experimental and control groups, it is possible to compute *effect size*—the number of standard deviations by which the experimental group scores higher (or lower) than the control group. Effect size (represented as d) is computed by subtracting the mean score of the control group from the mean score of the experimental group and dividing by the pooled standard deviation (Cohen, 1988;

Rosenthal, Rosnow, & Rubin, 2000). For example, using the data from the previous paragraph, $d = (8.0 - 6.4)/2.0 = 0.8$. According to Cohen, effect sizes of 0.8 or greater are considered large effects and those below 0.2 are negligible. Hattie (2009) suggests that any effect size above $d = 0.4$ is practically important for education, and notes that effect size gauges the practical significance of instructional effects rather than simply the statistical significance. Effect size is useful for educational research on instructional effectiveness because it provides a common metric for all experimental comparisons involving the same independent variable, and is particularly useful for meta-analyses in which the effect sizes are averaged across all available experimental comparisons (Hattie, 2009).

It is important to note that there may be boundary conditions for various multimedia instructional methods such that they work best for certain kinds of learners (e.g., low- versus high-knowledge learners), certain kinds of instructional objectives (e.g., science concepts versus arithmetic procedures), certain kinds of dependent measures (e.g., transfer versus retention), and certain kinds of learning environments (e.g., computer-paced versus learner-paced; Mayer, 2009). Thus, research on instructional effectiveness should be broadened to examine what works for which kinds of learners, learning which kinds of material, based on which kinds of measures, and in which kinds of learning environments.

3.3. Individual differences in learning

Consider the role of learner characteristics in evaluating the effectiveness of multimedia instructional methods, such as the learner's prior knowledge or the learner's cognitive style. With respect to prior knowledge, Kalyuga (2005) has reported the *expertise reversal effect* for multimedia instructional methods in which multimedia instructional methods that are effective for low-knowledge learners are not effective for high-knowledge learners, and in some cases are even detrimental to high-knowledge learners. For example, Mayer and Gallini (1990) found that adding graphics to text greatly improved the transfer test performance in lessons on how various mechanical devices work for low prior knowledge learners but not for high prior knowledge learners. Apparently, the high-knowledge learners were able to mentally build their own images based on the text whereas the low-knowledge learners needed the instructor's help.

In contrast, Pashler, McDaniel, Rowher, and Bjork (2009) report that research on *cognitive style*—learners' preferred mode for processing information—has not produced reliable *attribute x treatment interactions* (ATIs) in which one instructional method is better for students with one kind of cognitive style and a different instructional method is better for students with a different cognitive style. For example, Massa and Mayer (2006) asked visualizers and verbalizers to learn from a multimedia lesson on electronics that used a verbal instructional mode or a pictorial instructional mode. In a series of experimental comparisons, the pictorial mode (which used words and pictures) was more effective than the verbal mode (which used mainly words) for all learners, and there was no indication that verbalizers learned better with the verbally based lessons and visualizers learned better with the pictorially based lessons.

Overall, the research on individual differences in multimedia learning implicates prior knowledge as an important consideration but does not show that cognitive style plays an important role.

4. Science of Multimedia Instruction: Triarchic Theory of Multimedia Instruction

This section explores evidence-based techniques for reducing extraneous processing, managing essential processing, and fostering generative processing during learning.

4.1. Three goals in multimedia instructional design

As noted in the cognitive theory of multimedia learning, the learner's cognitive capacity during learning is limited so the learner is able to engage in only a limited amount of cognitive processing in each channel at any one time. According the triarchic theory of multimedia instruction, drawn from cognitive load theory (Plass, Moreno, & Brunken, 2010; Sweller, 1999, 2005a), learners may experience three kinds of demands on their limited processing capacity—extraneous processing, essential processing, and generative processing (Mayer, 2009, 2010; Mayer & Moreno, 2003).

Extraneous processing is cognitive processing that does not serve the instructional objective and is caused by poor instructional design. For example, including interesting but irrelevant stories and graphics may draw learners' precious processing resources. As another example, placing text on one page and corresponding graphics on another page can cause the learners to have to scan back and forth, finding their place each time, and wasting precious cognitive resources.

Essential processing is cognitive processing required to mentally represent the essential material in the lesson as presented and is caused by the complexity of the to-be-learned material. As an example, an explanation of how a complex system works (e.g., a system with eight interacting parts) requires more essential processing than an explanation of how a simple system works (e.g., a system with three interacting parts).

Generative processing is cognitive processing required to make sense of the essential material and depends on the learner's motivation to exert effort during learning. For example, thinking of related knowledge or mentally reorganizing the material as learners explain the material to themselves are examples of generative processing. These three kinds of processing demands are summarized in Table 2.

Figure 2 presents three kinds of instructional scenarios that can occur: extraneous overload, essential overload, and generative underutilization. First, in *extraneous overload* situations, the amount of extraneous processing and essential processing exceeds the learner's cognitive capacity, so there is no capacity available for engaging in generative processing or even all needed essential processing. As a result, the learner is not able to engage in the sense making necessary for a meaningful learning outcome. In this situation, an important goal of instructional design is to *reduce extraneous processing*.

Second, in *essential overload* situations, the amount of essential processing required to mentally represent the essential material as presented exceeds the learner's cognitive capacity, even if all extraneous processing is eliminated. There is not enough capacity to support generative processing or even all needed essential processing, because of the complexity of the essential material. As a result, the learner is not able to engage in the sense making during learning that is necessary for a meaningful learning outcome. In this situation, essential processing cannot be reduced because learning the essential material is the instructional objective; thus, an important goal of instructional design is to *manage essential processing*.

Finally, *generative underutilization* occurs when learners have cognitive capacity available to engage in generative processing but choose not to do so. For example, a learner might not be motivated to engage in deep cognitive processing necessary to make sense of the essential material or

Table 2 Three Kinds of Processing Demands

Kind	Description	Cognitive processes
Extraneous	Does not support instructional objective; caused by poor instructional design	None
Essential	Mentally represent the essential material; depends on the complexity of the material	Selecting (and some organizing)
Generative	Make sense of the representation; depends on the learner's motivation to exert effort	Organizing and integrating

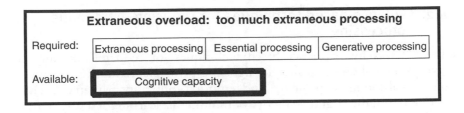

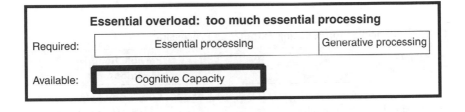

Figure 2   Three instructional scenarios.

might not believe that deep understanding is possible. As a result, the learner does not build a meaningful learning outcome. In this situation, an important goal of multimedia instructional design is to *foster generative processing*.

For the past 20 years, my colleagues and I at the University of California, Santa Barbara have been conducting dozens of experimental comparisons aimed at identifying multimedia design principles that reduce extraneous processing, manage essential processing, and foster generative processing. I share the fruits of this research program with you in the next three sections of this chapter.

In general, we focus mainly on teaching how various physical, mechanical, or biological systems work in short lessons followed by immediate post-tests, using paper-based lessons, computer-based presentations, and computer games. We compare the transfer test performance of students who received the control version of the lesson versus those who received a treatment version that was modified in line with a design principle. I report the median effect size (d) for each of 12 principles, based on multiple experimental comparisons carried out in our lab.

4.2. Evidence-based techniques for reducing extraneous processing

Table 3 lists five evidence-based techniques for reducing extraneous processing: coherence principle, signaling principle, redundancy principle, spatial contiguity principle, and temporal contiguity principle. Each is derived from the cognitive theory of multimedia learning as a way to free up limited cognitive capacity so the learner can use it for essential and generative processing rather than extraneous processing.

Table 3   Principles for Reducing Extraneous Processing

Principle	ES	Tests	Possible boundary conditions
1. *Coherence Principle*: People learn better when extraneous words, pictures, and sounds are excluded rather than included	0.97	13 of 14	Low-knowledge learners; low working memory learners
2. *Signaling Principle*: People learn better when cues are added that highlight the organization of the essential material	0.52	5 of 6	Moderate amounts of highlighting*; low-knowledge learners; complex material
3. *Redundancy Principle*: People learn better from animation and narration than from animation, narration, and on-screen text	0.72	5 of 5	Printed text placed far from graphic*; printed text is long*; spoken text given before printed text
4. *Spatial Contiguity Principle*: People learn better when corresponding words and pictures are presented near rather than far from each other on the page or screen	1.12	5 of 5	Low-knowledge learners*; complex material; system-paced
5. *Temporal Contiguity Principle*: People learn better when corresponding words and pictures are presented simultaneously rather than successively	1.31	8 of 8	Segments are long*; system-paced

Note. Asterisk (*) indicates boundary condition identified in research by Mayer and colleagues.

4.2.1. Coherence Principle

Consider a narrated animation on how lightning storms develop that runs for about 2.5 min and describes 16 steps in the process. Perhaps, you might wish to spice up the lesson by adding some interesting facts (e.g., "Each year 150 people are killed by lightning in the United States."), some interesting video of lightning storms, or even some background instrumental music. However, according to the triarchic theory of instruction and the cognitive theory of multimedia learning, in doing so you might create extraneous processing because the learner wastes limited processing capacity on processing the extraneous material you added and therefore does not have enough remaining capacity for essential and generative processing. In short, your well-intentioned changes to the multimedia lesson can create an extraneous overload situation, as summarized in the top of Figure 2.

The coherence principle is that people learn better from multimedia lessons when extraneous words, pictures, and sounds are excluded rather than included. In 13 out of 14 experimental comparisons conducted in our lab, students who learned from a concise lesson performed better on a transfer test than students who learned from an embellished lesson, yielding a median effect size of $d = 0.97$. For example, students learned better from a computer-based narrated animation on how lightning forms when interesting but irrelevant video clips and spoken facts about lightning were excluded rather than included (Mayer, Heiser, et al., 2001, Experiment 3) or when interesting but irrelevant photos and printed facts about lightning were excluded rather than included from a paper-based multimedia lesson on how lightning forms (Harp & Mayer, 1997, Experiment 1; Harp & Mayer, 1998, Experiments 1–4). Similarly, students learned better from computer-based narrated animations on how lightning forms or how car braking systems work when background instrumental music or instrumental sounds were excluded rather than included (Moreno & Mayer, 2000a, Experiments 1 and 2). Finally, students learned better from a paper-based lesson on lightning consisting of text and illustrations when the text was cut down to a summary (Mayer, Bove, Bryman, Mars, & Tapangco, 1996, Experiments 1, 2, and 3) and students learned better form paper-based and computer-based multimedia lessons on how ocean waves work when technical details about the underlying mathematical formulas were eliminated (Mayer & Jackson, 2005, Experiments 1a, 1b, and 2). There is some preliminary evidence that the coherence principle may be most effective for learners who lack prior knowledge in the domain (Ploetzner, Fehse, Kneser, & Spada, 1999) and have low working memory capacity (Sanchez & Wiley, 2006).

4.2.2. Signaling Principle

Suppose you have a multimedia lesson that contains some extraneous material that you cannot eliminate. As in the previous section, this situation could lead to extraneous overload in which the learner spends so much cognitive capacity on processing the extraneous material that not enough capacity is left for essential and generative processing. A possible solution to this problem is to direct the learner's attention to the essential material by inserting appropriate highlighting, which can be called signaling. When essential material is highlighted, learners can use their limited cognitive capacity for essential and generative processing.

The signaling principle is that people learn better from multimedia lessons when cues are added that highlight the organization of the essential material. Signaling cues include outlines, headings keyed to the outlines, and pointer words such as "first, second, third," as well as typographical highlighting of printed text such as using bolding, italics, or underlining. In five out of six experimental comparisons, students who learned with a signaled lesson performed better on a transfer test than did students who learned with a nonsignaled lesson, yielding a median effect size of $d = 0.52$. For example, in a computer-based narrated animation on how airplanes achieve lift, students learned better when the narrator included an outline, headings, and vocal emphasis on key words (Mautone & Mayer, 2001, Experiments 3a and 3b) and in a paper-based lesson on lightning formation, students learned better when the text included an outline and headings (Harp & Mayer, 1998, Experiment 3a). Similarly, students learned better from a paper-based biology lesson that included graphic organizers that highlighted the organization of the material (Stull & Mayer, 2007, Experiments 1–3). There is some preliminary evidence that the signaling principle is most applicable to situations in which highlighting is used sparingly (Stull & Mayer, 2007), the learners lack reading skill (Meyer, Brandt, & Bluth, 1980), and when the material is complex (Jeung, Chandler, & Sweller, 1997).

4.2.3. Redundancy Principle
Let's again consider a narrated animation that explains how lightning storms develop. You might be tempted to add concurrent on-screen captions that contain the same sentences as in the narration, perhaps to better accommodate people's preferences for printed or spoken text. This well-meaning modification, however, can create an extraneous overload situation because the learner has to scan back and forth between the printed words and graphics and because the learner may try to reconcile the printed and spoken text. By adding on-screen text, you may have caused learners to engage in so much extraneous processing that they do not have enough remaining cognitive capacity for essential and generative processing, as shown in the top portion of Figure 2.

The redundancy principle is that people learn better from animation and narration than from animation, narration, and on-screen text. In five out of five experimental comparisons conducted in our lab, learners performed better on transfer tests when they learned from a narrated animation explaining how some system works than from the same narrated animation along with concurrent on-screen text that was identical to the words in the narration. The median effect size was $d = 0.72$ favoring the nonredundant lessons (i.e., narration and animation without on-screen text). For example, students learned better with a narrated animation on lightning formation than from the same narrated animation with concurrent on-screen text (Mayer, Heiser, et al., 2001, Experiments 1 and 2; Moreno & Mayer, 2002a, Experiment 2). Similarly, students learned better from an on-screen agent in a botany computer game when the agent narrated an animation rather than when the agent narrated an animation with concurrent on-screen captions (Moreno & Mayer, 2002b, Experiments 2a and 2b). There is some preliminary evidence that the redundancy principle is strongest when the on-screen text is long and placed far from the graphic (Mayer & Johnson, 2008) or when the spoken text is presented before the printed text (Kalyuga, Chandler, & Sweller, 2004). Sweller (2005b) has a broader definition of the redundancy principle in multimedia learning, but reports similar findings.

4.2.4. Spatial Contiguity Principle

Consider a lesson consisting of graphics and printed text, presented either as an annotated narration on a computer screen or a series of annotated frames in a book. Common practice is to place the words at the bottom of the screen or figure as a caption or to present the words in a paragraph with directions to "see the figure." According to the cognitive theory of multimedia learning, this can create an extraneous overload situation in which the learner must visually scan back and forth between the printed words and the corresponding part of the graphic. The required scanning is a form of extraneous processing that leaves less cognitive capacity for essential and generative processing. A solution to this kind of extraneous overload situation is to move segments of the printed text next to the part of the corresponding part of the graphic, so the need for visual scanning is reduced.

The spatial contiguity principle is that people learn better from a multimedia lesson when corresponding words and pictures are placed near rather than far from one another on the screen or page. In five out of five experimental comparisons, students learned better from integrated lessons (with words placed near the part of the graphic they described) than from separated lessons (with words placed as captions or in paragraphs far from the graphic). The median effect size was $d = 1.12$ favoring the integrated lessons. For example, students learned better from an annotated animation on lightning when the on-screen text was placed within the graphic next to the element it described rather than at the bottom of the screen as a caption

(Moreno & Mayer, 1999a, Experiment 1). Similarly, in paper-based lessons on brakes (Mayer, 1989, Experiment 2) and lightning (Mayer, Steinhoff, Bower, & Mars, 1995, Experiments 1, 2, and 3) students performed better on a transfer test when printed descriptions were placed next to the corresponding part of the graphic than when the words were printed as a caption or paragraph away from the graphic. In another meta-analysis of 37 experimental comparisons testing the spatial contiguity principle, Ginns (2006) reported a mean effect size of $d = 0.72$. Preliminary research suggests that the spatial contiguity principle applies most strongly for low-knowledge learners (Kalyuga, 2005; Mayer et al., 1995), when the material is difficult for the learner (Ayres & Sweller, 2005), and when the learner cannot control the pace of the lesson (Bodemer, Ploetzner, Feuerlein, & Spada, 2004).

4.2.5. Temporal Contiguity Principle

Let's again consider a multimedia lesson that consists of a narrated animation on how lightning storms develop. You might want to provide longer exposure to the material by allowing the learner to hear the narration before (or after) viewing the animation—effectively presenting the same explanation twice in different modalities. However, according to the cognitive theory of multimedia learning, this modification would require the learner to hold the entire narration in working memory until the animation was presented (or vice versa) in order to mentally integrate corresponding words and pictures. Given the limitations on cognitive capacity in working memory, the learner's cognitive capacity would become overloaded because of the extraneous processing task of trying to maintain the narration in working memory. The result of successive presentation should be less opportunity for mentally integrating corresponding words and pictures in working memory, and therefore poorer transfer performance.

The temporal contiguity principle is that people learn better from a multimedia lesson when corresponding words and pictures are presented simultaneously rather than successively. In eight out of eight experimental comparisons, students performed better on transfer tests when they received simultaneous presentations (e.g., narrated animation) rather than successive presentations (e.g., narration before or after animation), yielding a median effect size of $d = 1.31$. This pattern was found in a computer-based multimedia lesson on how tire pumps work (Mayer & Anderson, 1991, Experiments 1 and 2a; Mayer & Anderson, 1992, Experiment 1; Mayer & Sims, 1994, Experiment 1), how brakes work (Mayer, Moreno, Boire, & Vagge, 1999, Experiment 2; Mayer & Anderson, 1992, Experiment 2), how the human respiratory system works (Mayer & Sims, 1994, Experiment 2), and how lightning storms develop (Mayer, Moreno, Boire, & Vagge, 1999, Experiment 1). In another meta-analysis involving 13 experimental comparisons of the temporal contiguity principle, Ginns (2006) reported a mean effect size of $d = 0.87$. The temporal contiguity principle applies to situations in which the segments of animation and narration are long rather than short (Mayer, Moreno, Boire, & Vagge, 1999; Moreno & Mayer, 1999a) and in which the learners cannot control the pace of a fast-paced presentation (Michas & Berry, 2000).

4.3. Evidence-based techniques for managing essential processing

Sometimes the to-be-learned material is complex for the learner, but unlike extraneous material this complex essential material cannot be excluded from the lesson. Instead, what is needed are instructional design techniques for managing essential processing—that is, techniques that help people learn the essential material in a way that does not overload their cognitive systems. Table 4 lists three evidence-based techniques for managing essential processing: segmenting principle, pretraining principle, and modality principle. Each is derived from the cognitive theory of multimedia learning.

Table 4   Principles for Managing Essential Processing

Principle	ES	Tests	Possible boundary conditions
6. *Segmenting Principle*: People learn better when a multimedia lesson is presented in user-paced segments rather than as a continuous unit	0.98	3 of 3	Low-knowledge learners; complex material; fast-paced
7. *Pretraining Principle*: People learn better from a multimedia lesson when they know the names and characteristics of the main concepts	0.85	5 of 5	Low-knowledge learners; material; fast-paced
8. *Modality Principle*: People learn better from animation and narration than from animation and on-screen text	1.02	17 of 17	Familiar words*; complex material; fast-paced; corresponding part of graphic is highlighted

Note. Asterisk (*) indicates boundary condition identified in research by Mayer and colleagues.

4.3.1. Segmenting Principle

Consider again how you might improve the instructional effectiveness of a 2.5-min narrated animation on lightning formation. The presentation is fast-paced and complex, consisting of a chain of 16 events. Learners may not be able to build a causal model of the system if the lesson moves on to the next event before the learner has completely digested the event that was just presented. In short, the learner is likely to experience an essential overload situation as shown in middle portion of Figure 2, in which the amount of required essential processing exceeds the learner's cognitive capacity. In order to help learners manage the flow of essential information, you could break the narrated animation into 16 segments, each about 8–10 s long and describing one step in the process. After each segment, the computer could display a "CONTINUE" button on the screen, which must be clicked to go on to the next segment. In this way, the learner can manage essential processing in a way that relieves an essential overload situation.

The segmenting principle is that people learn better when a multimedia lesson is presented in user-paced segments rather than as a continuous unit. In three out of three experimental comparisons conducted at our lab, students performed better on transfer tests after receiving a segmented lesson (e.g., segments of a narrated animation paced by the learner) rather than a continuous lesson (e.g., a narrated animation), yielding a median effect size of $d = 0.98$. For example, students performed better on a transfer test after viewing a narrated animation about lightning formation in which they had to click a "CONTINUE" button after each of 16 segments as compared to students who viewed the narrated animation as a continuous 2.5-min presentation (Mayer & Chandler, 2001, Experiment 1). Similarly, students performed better on a transfer test when they were able to click to see each segment of narrated animation on how an electric motor works rather than view a continuous narrated animation (Mayer, Dow, & Mayer, 2003, Experiments 2a and 2b). The segmenting principle may be strongest for low experience learners (Ayres, 2006) or when complex material is presented at a fast pace (Mayer, 2009).

4.3.2. Pretraining Principle

Are there other ways to help learners when they are presented with a fast-paced narrated animation that is so complex it threatens to create an essential overload situation for the learner? When learners view a narrated animation on how a system works—such as how a car's braking system works—they must build *component models*—that is, representations of each part, such as a piston or brake shoe, and how it works—as well as *causal models*—that is, a cause-and-effect model of how a change in one component, such as the piston moving forward, affects a change in another component, such as an increase in fluid pressure, and so on. All that essential processing may overload the learner's cognitive capacity. To help manage essential processing, you could provide pretraining to the learner concerning the name and characteristics of each component in the system (e.g., a piston can move forward and back, a brake shoe can press against the drum or not, etc.), before presenting the narrated animation. When the narrated animation is presented, some of the essential processing—i.e., building component models—has already been carried out so learners can focus all their essential processing on building a causal model of the system.

The pretraining principle is that people learn better from a multimedia lesson when they have received pretraining in the names and characteristics of the main components. In five out of five experimental comparisons conducted at our lab, students who received pretraining learned better from a multimedia lesson explaining how a complex system works than did students who did not receive pretraining, yielding a median effect size of $d = 0.85$. For example, with a fast-paced narrated animation on how car brakes work or how a tire pump works, students performed better on a transfer test if they were given pretraining in the names and characteristics of each major part of the system before they received the narrated animation (Mayer, Mathias, & Wetzell, 2002, Experiments 1–3). Similarly, in a geology simulation game, students learned geology principles better if they received pretraining before the game in which they learned the name and description of each kind of geological formation in the game (Mayer, Mautone, & Prothero, 2002, Experiments 2 and 3). There is some preliminary evidence that the pretraining principle is most effective for low-knowledge learners (Clarke, Ayres, & Sweller, 2005; Pollock, Chandler, & Sweller, 2002), and the principle is likely to be most effective for fast-paced presentations containing complex material (Mayer, 2009).

4.3.3. Modality Principle

Let's consider a slightly different version of an essential overload situation in which the learner views a fast-paced animation on lightning formation along with corresponding on-screen captions describing the events depicted in the animation. This situation can cause a form of essential overload in the learner's visual channel. Ayres and Sweller (2005) refer to this situation as *split attention* because the learner's cognitive processing in the visual channel must be split between looking at the animation and looking at the caption. When learners look at the caption they may miss something in the animation and when they look at the animation they may not be able to finish reading the caption. In short, the amount of essential processing required in the visual channel may exceed the learner's processing capacity. In this case, a useful way to manage essential processing is to offload some of the processing to the verbal channel by presenting the words in spoken form rather than printed form. When a narrated animation is presented, the learner can use the visual channel for processing the animation and the verbal channel for processing words, thereby managing essential processing in the visual channel.

The modality principle is that students learn better from animation and narration than from animation and on-screen text. In 17 out of 17 experimental comparisons conducted by our lab, students performed better on a transfer test when they learned with animation and narration rather than animation and on-screen text, yielding a median effect size of $d = 1.02$. The modality principle is the most studied multimedia design principle in our lab and around the world (Low & Sweller, 2005). It has been confirmed in our lab using fast-paced lessons with unfamiliar material involving how lightning forms (Mayer & Moreno, 1998, Experiment 1; Moreno & Mayer, 1999a, Experiments 1 and 2), how brakes work (Mayer & Moreno, 1998, Experiment 2), and how electric motors work (Mayer, Dow, et al., 2003, Experiment 1); multimedia biology lessons in schools (Harskamp, Mayer, Suhre, & Jansma, 2007, Experiments 1 and 2a); desktop computer games on botany (Moreno & Mayer, 2002b, Experiments 1a and 2a; Moreno, Mayer, Spires, & Lester, 2001, Experiments 4a, 4b, 5a, and 5b); and virtual reality games on botany (Moreno & Mayer, 2002b, Experiments 1b, 1c, and 2b) and aircraft fueling (Neil, Mayer, Herl, Thurman, & Olin, 2000, Experiment 1). In another meta-analysis of 39 experimental comparisons involving the modality principle, Ginns (2005) reported a mean effect size of $d = 0.72$ based on a variety of test measures. There is preliminary evidence that the modality principle is most effective when the words are familiar (Harskamp et al., 2007), when the material is complex (Tindall-Ford, Chandler, & Sweller, 1997), when relevant portions of the animation are highlighted (Jeung et al., 1997), and when the lesson is fast-paced and not under learner control (Tabbers, Martens, & van Merrienboer, 2004).

4.4. Evidence-based techniques for fostering generative processing

Suppose that a multimedia lesson is well designed (i.e., it is designed to reduce extraneous processing and manage essential processing) so that the learner has cognitive processing capacity available for essential and generative processing. However, even though the learner has capacity available, he or she does not use it to make sense of the material. This is an example of generative underutilization as shown in the bottom of Figure 2. Table 5 lists four evidence-based techniques for fostering generative processing: multimedia principle, generation principle, personalization principle, and voice principle. Each is derived from the cognitive theory of multimedia learning.

Table 5 Principles for Fostering Generative Processing

Principle	ES	Tests	Possible boundary conditions
9. *Multimedia Principle*: People learn better from words and pictures than from words alone	1.39	11 of 11	Low-knowledge learners*
10. *Generation Principle*: People learn better from multimedia lessons when they generate words or drawings or self-explain during learning	0.91	5 of 5	
11. *Personalization Principle*: People learn better from multimedia lessons when words are in conversational style rather than formal style	1.11	11 of 11	Low computer experience learners*; moderate amount of personalization*
12. *Voice Principle*: People learn better when the narration in multimedia lessons is spoken in a friendly human voice rather than a machine voice	0.78	3 of 3	Preferred accent*

Note. Asterisk (*) indicates boundary condition identified in research by Mayer and colleagues.

4.4.1. Multimedia Principle

Presenting words and pictures on the page or screen may encourage learners to mentally integrate verbal and pictorial representations in working memory and may even encourage them to think of related knowledge from long-term memory (i.e., engage in the process of integrating and, to some extent, organizing). Thus, adding pictures to words is a way of fostering generative processing—helping learners build connections among representations. When only words are presented, learners must create their own images—a process that may be too difficult for novices thus resulting in rote learning. According to the cognitive theory of multimedia learning, students will learn more deeply—and thereby perform better on transfer tests—when they are encouraged to engage in generative processing during learning (i.e., integrating and organizing). Multimedia presentations are intended to foster generative processing.

The multimedia principle is that people learn better from words and pictures than from words alone. In 11 out of 11 experimental comparisons carried out in our lab, students performed better on transfer tests if they received lessons about how mechanical, physical, or biological systems work containing words and pictures (e.g., computer-based narration and animation or paper-based printed text and illustrations) rather than words alone (e.g., computer-based narration or paper-based printed words). The median effect size was $d = 1.39$. The modality principle is the most fundamental multimedia design principle because it provides the rationale for multimedia instruction (Fletcher & Tobias, 2005). For example, in our lab, students performed better on transfer tests if they received narration and animation rather than narration alone in lessons explaining how pumps work (Mayer & Anderson, 1992, Experiment 1), how brakes work (Mayer & Anderson, 1992, Experiment 2), how lightning works (Moreno & Mayer, 2002b, Experiment 1), or within an arithmetic simulation game (Moreno & Mayer, 1999b, Experiment 1). Similarly, students performed better on transfer tests after they read a booklet containing printed text with illustrations rather than printed text alone in lessons explaining how brakes work (Mayer, 1989, Experiments 1 and 2; Mayer & Gallini, 1990, Experiment 1), how pumps work (Mayer & Gallini, 1990, Experiment 2), how generators work (Mayer & Gallini, 1990, Experiment 3), and how lightning works (Mayer et al., 1996, Experiment 2). An important boundary condition for the multimedia principle is that it appears to be most effective for low-knowledge learners (Kalyuga, Chandler, & Sweller, 1998, 2000; Mayer & Gallini, 1990).

4.4.2. Generation Principle
Another way to foster generative processing of a multimedia lesson is to ask learners to engage in learning activities that require deep processing of the presented material (Mayer, 2009; Mayer & Wittrock, 2006; Wittrock, 1989). For example, self-explanation refers to asking learners to explain the presented material to themselves during learning (Roy & Chi, 2005), self-testing refers to asking learners to take practice tests (without feedback) during learning (Roediger & Karpicke, 2006), and drawing refers to asking learners to create drawings of the material in the lesson (Schwamborn, Mayer, Thillmann, Leopold, & Leutner, 2010). In each case, these learning activities are intended to encourage the learner to make sense of the presented multimedia lesson. Generation activities such as these have been recommended as effective instructional techniques in recent guidebooks on applying cognitive science to education (Halpern, Graesser, & Hakel, 2007; Pashler et al., 2007), and are the basis of Wittrock's (1989) generative theory of learning.

The generation principle is that people learn better from multimedia lessons when they are prompted to generate words or drawings during learning. In five out of five experimental comparisons, we found that people performed better on transfer tests when they were prompted to engage in a generative activity during learning, yielding a median effect size of $d = 0.91$. For example, students learned better from a multimedia game on electric circuits if they were prompted to engage in self-explanation throughout the game (Johnson & Mayer, 2010, Experiments 1 and 2; Mayer & Johnson, 2010, Experiment 1). Similarly, students performed better on a delayed transfer test if they had been prompted to write answers to practice questions after receiving a narrated animation on lightning formation (Johnson & Mayer, 2009, Experiment 1). Finally, students performed better on a transfer test, if they had been asked to create drawings while viewing a narrated animation on how detergents clean clothes (Schwamborn et al., 2010; Experiment 1). In short, the generation principle in multimedia learning was manifested in a self-explanation effect, a testing effect, and a drawing effect.

4.4.3. Personalization Principle

Social cues in a multimedia message can cause the learner to view the computer as a conversational partner. When in a conversation, people tend to adhere to a social contract in which they make an effort to understand what they are being told, which in turn should lead to a meaningful learning outcome that supports transfer performance. This is the proposed mechanism by which social cues such as personalization can be used to foster generative processing (Mayer, 2009; Reeves & Nass, 1996).

The personalization principle is that people learn better from multimedia lessons when words are in conversational style rather than formal style. In 11 out 11 experimental comparisons carried out in our lab, students performed better on transfer tests from multimedia lessons with words in conversational style (such as using first or second person constructions) rather than formal style (such as using third person constructions), with a median effect size of $d = 1.11$. For example, in learning from a narrated animation on how the human respiratory system works, students performed better on a transfer test if the narrator's voice used phrases such as "your bronchial tube" and "your bloodstream" rather than "the bronchial tube" and "the bloodstream" (Mayer, Fennell, Farmer, & Campbell, 2004, Experiments 1–3). In learning from an animation on lightning, students performed better on a transfer test if the accompanying narration or captions used conversational style such as "your cloud" rather than formal style such as "the cloud" (Moreno & Mayer, 2000b, Experiments 1 and 2). Similarly, in learning from an educational computer game in botany, students learned better from narrated or annotated animations in which an on-screen agent used conversational style rather than formal style (Moreno & Mayer, 2000b, Experiments 3–5; Moreno & Mayer, 2004, Experiments 1a and 1b). Finally, in learning from an educational computer game in industrial engineering, students learned better from multimedia lessons in which an on-screen agent phrased directions and feedback with polite wording, such as "Shall we press the ENTER key?", rather than direct wording, such as "Press the ENTER key" (Wang et al., 2008). There is some preliminary evidence that the personalization principle is most effective when conversational style is used sparingly (Mayer et al., 2004) and when the learners are not accustomed to interacting with computers (Mayer, Johnson, Shaw, & Sandhu, 2006; Wang et al., 2008).

4.4.4. Voice Principle

Another social cue that can prime a learner's feeling of social partnership with a computer is a friendly human voice (Nass & Brave, 2005). When the learners feel they are in a conversation with the computer, they try harder to make sense of the message—that is, they engage in generative processing (Mayer, 2009). This is the proposed mechanism by which social cues such as voice can be used to foster generative processing (Mayer, 2009).

The voice principle is that people learn better from narrated graphics when the words are spoken in a likable human voice rather than a machine voice. In three out of three experimental comparisons, we found that students learned better from a narrated animation when the speaker had a standard-accented human voice than a machine voice, yielding a mean effect size of $d = 0.78$. For example, in a narrated animation on lightning formation (Mayer, Sobko, & Mautone, 2003, Experiment 3) and a narrated animation on solving mathematics problems (Atkinson, Mayer, & Merrill, 2005, Experiments 1 and 2), students performed better on transfer tests when the speaker used a standard-accented human voice rather than a machine voice. There is also preliminary evidence that the voice principle may not apply when the human voice has a strong accent that students do not prefer (Mayer, Sobko, et al., 2003; Nass & Brave, 2005).

It is also worthwhile to note that not all social cues are equally effective. In particular, the image principle is that people do not necessarily learn more when a speaker's image is added to the screen. In five experimental comparisons carried out in our lab, the median effect size caused by adding the agent's image on screen was $d = 0.22$, which is too small to be of educational significance (Mayer, Dow, et al., 2003, Experiment 4; Moreno et al., 2001, Experiments 4a, 4b, 5a, and 5b). Perhaps, having a nongesturing agent on the screen reminds the learner that the agent is not acting like a human and thereby does not help create a social bond.

5. THE FUTURE OF MULTIMEDIA INSTRUCTION

This chapter is intended as an example of the benefits of applying the science of learning to education (Mayer, 2008b, 2010). The benefits to education are reflected in advances in the science of multimedia instruction—namely, a collection of 12 evidence-based principles for how to design effective multimedia instruction. The benefits to psychology are reflected in the science of multimedia learning—namely, a cognitive theory of how people learn from educationally relevant situations involving words and pictures. In short, this chapter demonstrates that applying the science of learning to education is a reciprocal activity that mutually challenges and benefits both psychology and education.

This chapter is also an example of how the same research project can have both a basic research goal and an applied research goal. In his book, *Pasteur's Quadrant*, Stokes (1997) argues that instead of viewing applied and basic research as two poles on a continuum, it makes more sense to view them as two potentially overlapping research goals. Research that has only a basic goal is pure basic research and research that has only an applied goal is pure applied research, but research that has both goals—as exemplified by Pasteur's research—can be particularly powerful. Stokes refers to this kind of research as "use-inspired basic research" (p. 73). The research presented in this chapter falls within Pasteur's quadrant—having an applied goal of discovering principles for how to design effective multimedia instruction and having a basic goal of contributing to a cognitive theory of multimedia learning.

If this chapter serves to stimulate further work on applying the science of learning to education (Mayer, 2011), I will consider it to have been a success. The future of multimedia research is bright to the extent that it continues to serve the twin goals of contributing to both the science of instruction and the science of learning.

ACKNOWLEDGMENTS

Preparation of this chapter was supported by Grant N000140810018 from the Office of Naval Research.

REFERENCES

Atkinson, R. K., Mayer, R. E., & Merrill, M. M. (2005). Fostering social agency in multimedia learning: Examining the impact of an animated agent's voice. *Contemporary Educational Psychology, 30,* 117–139.

Ayres, P. (2006). Impact of reducing intrinsic cognitive load on learning in a mathematical domain. *Applied Cognitive Psychology, 20,* 287–298.

Ayres, P., & Sweller, J. (2005). The split-attention principle in multimedia learning. In R. E. Mayer (Ed.), *The Cambridge handbook of multimedia learning* (pp. 135–146). New York: Cambridge University Press.

Baddeley, A. D. (1999). *Human memory.* Boston: Allyn & Bacon.

Bodemer, D., Ploetzner, R., Feuerlein, I., & Spada, H. (2004). The active integration of information during learning with dynamic and interactive visualisations. *Learning and Instruction, 14,* 325–341.

Clark, R. C., & Mayer, R. E. (2008). *e-Learning and the science of instruction*. San Francisco: Pfeiffer.

Clarke, T., Ayres, P., & Sweller, J. (2005). The impact of sequencing and prior knowledge on learning mathematics through spreadsheet applications. *Educational Technology Research and Development, 53*, 15–24.

Cohen, J. (1988). *Statisical power analysis for the behavioral sciences*, 2nd ed. Hillsdale, NJ: Erlbaum.

Comenius, J. A. (1887). *Orbis pictus*. Syracuse, NY: C. W. Bardeen.

Cuban, L. (1986). *Teachers and machines: The classroom use of technology since 1920*. New York: Teachers College Press.

Fletcher, J. D., & Tobias, S. (2005). The multimedia principle. In R. E. Mayer (Ed.), *The Cambridge handbook of multimedia learning* (pp. 117–134). New York: Cambridge University Press.

Ginns, P. (2005). Meta-analysis of the modality effect. *Learning and Instruction, 15*, 313–332.

Ginns, P. (2006). Integrating information: A meta-analysis of spatial contiguity and temporal contiguity effects. *Learning and Instruction, 16*, 511–525.

Graesser, A. C., Chipman, P., & King, B. G. (2008). Computer-mediated technologies. In J. M. Spector., M. D. Merrill., J. van Merrienboer, and M. P. Driscoll (Eds.), *Handbook of research on educational communications and technology*, 3rd ed. (pp. 211–224). New York: Erlbaum.

Hacker, D. J., Dunlosky, J, and Graesser, A. C. 2009 (Eds.), *Handbook of metacognition in education*. New York: Routledge.

Halpern, D. F., Graesser, A., & Hakel, M. (2007). *25 learning principles to guide pedagogy and the design of learning environments*. Washington, DC: American Psychological Society Taskforce on Life-Long Learning at Work and Home.

Harp, S. F., & Mayer, R. E. (1997). The role of interest in learning from scientific text and illustrations: On the distinction between emotional interest and cognitive interest. *Journal of Educational Psychology, 89*, 92–102.

Harp, S. F., & Mayer, R. E. (1998). How seductive details do their damage: A theory of cognitive interest in science learning. *Journal of Educational Psychology, 90*, 414–434.

Harskamp, E., Mayer, R. E., Suhre, C., & Jansma, J. (2007). Does the modality principle for multimedia learning apply to science classrooms? *Learning and Instruction, 18*, 465–477.

Hattie, J. (2009). *Visible learning*. New York: Routledge.

Jeung, H., Chandler, P., & Sweller, J. (1997). The role of visual indicators in dual sensory mode instruction. *Educational Psychology, 17*, 329–433.

Johnson, C. I., & Mayer, R. E. (2009). A testing effect with multimedia learning. *Journal of Educational Psychology, 101*, 621–629.

Johnson, C. I., & Mayer, R. E. (2010). Applying the self-explanation principle to mulimedia learning in a computer-based game-like environment. *Computers in Human Behavior, 26*, 1246–1252.

Kalyuga, S. (2005). Prior knowledge principle in multimedia learning. In R. E. Mayer (Ed.), *The Cambridge handbook of multimedia learning* (pp. 325–337). New York: Cambridge University Press.

Kalyuga, S., Chandler, P., & Sweller, J. (1998). Levels of expertise and instructional design. *Human Factors, 40*, 1–17.

Kalyuga, S., Chandler, P., & Sweller, J. (2000). Incorporating learner experience into the design of multimedia instruction. *Journal of Educational Psychology, 92*, 126–136.

Kalyuga, S., Chandler, P., & Sweller, J. (2004). When redundant on-screen text in multimedia technical instruction can interfere with learning. *Human Factors, 46*, 567–581.

Levin, J. R., & Mayer, R. E. (1993). Understanding illustrations in text. In B. K. Britton., A. Woodward, and M. Binkley (Eds.), *Learning from textbooks* (pp. 95–113). Hillsdale, NJ: Erlbaum.

Low, R., & Sweller, J. (2005). The modality principle in multimedia learning. In R. E. Mayer (Ed.), *The Cambridge handbook of multimedia learning* (pp. 147–158). New York: Cambridge University Press.

Massa, L. J., & Mayer, R. E. (2006). Testing the ATI hypothesis: Should multimedia instruction accommodate verbalizer–visualizer cognitive style? *Learning and Individual Differences, 16*, 321–336.

Mautone, P. D., & Mayer, R. E. (2001). Signaling as a cognitive guide in multimedia learning. *Journal of Educational Psychology, 93*, 377–389.

Mayer, R. E. (1989). Systematic thinking fostered by illustrations in scientific text. *Journal of Educational Psychology, 81*, 240–246.

Mayer, R. E. 2005 (Ed.), *The Cambridge handbook of multimedia learning.* New York: Cambridge University Press.

Mayer, R. E. (2008a). *Learning and instruction*, 2nd ed. Upper Saddle River, NJ: Pearson Merrill Prentice Hall.

Mayer, R. E. (2008b). Applying the science of learning: Evidence-based principles for the design of multimedia instruction. *American Psychologist, 63*(8), 760–769.

Mayer, R. E. (2009). *Multimedia learning*, 2nd ed. New York: Cambridge University Press.

Mayer, R. E. (2011). *Applying the science of learning.* Upper Saddle River, NJ: Pearson Merrill Prentice Hall.

Mayer, R. E., & Anderson, R. B. (1991). Animations need narrations: An experimental test of a dual-coding hypothesis. *Journal of Educational Psychology, 83*, 484–490.

Mayer, R. E., & Anderson, R. B. (1992). The instructive animation: Helping students build connections between words and pictures in multimedia learning. *Journal of Educational Psychology, 84*, 444–452.

Mayer, R. E., Bove, W., Bryman, A., Mars, R., & Tapangco, L. (1996). When less is more: Meaningful learning from visual and verbal summaries of science textbook lessons. *Journal of Educational Psychology, 88*, 64–73.

Meyer, B. J. F., Brandt, D. M., & Bluth, G. J. (1980). Use of top-level structure in text: Key for reading comprehension of ninth-grade students. *Reading Research Quarterly, 16*, 72–103.

Mayer, R. E., & Chandler, P. (2001). When learning is just a click away: Does simple user interaction foster deeper understanding of multimedia messages. *Journal of Educational Psychology, 93*, 390–397.

Mayer, R. E., Dow, G. T., & Mayer, S. (2003). Multimedia learning in an interactive self-explaining environment: What works in the design of agent-based microworlds? *Journal of Educational Psychology, 95*, 806–813.

Mayer, R. E., Fennell, S., Farmer, L., & Campbell, J. (2004). A personalization effect in multimedia learning: Students learn better when words are in conversational style rather than formal style. *Journal of Educational Psychology, 96*, 389–395.

Mayer, R. E., & Gallini, J. (1990). When is an illustration worth ten thousand words? *Journal of Educational Psychology, 82*, 715–726.

Mayer, R. E., Heiser, H., & Lonn, S. (2001). Cognitive constraints on multimedia learning: When presenting more material results in less understanding. *Journal of Educational Psychology, 93*, 187–198.

Mayer, R. E., & Jackson, J. (2005). The case for coherence in scientific explanations: Quantitative details hurt qualitative understanding. *Journal of Experimental Psychology: Applied, 11*, 13–18.

Mayer, R. E., & Johnson, C. I. (2008). Revising the redundancy principle in multimedia learning. *Journal of Educational Psychology, 100,* 223–234.

Mayer, R. E., & Johnson, C. I. (2010). Adding instructional features that promote learning in a game-like environment. *Journal of Educational Computing Research, 42,* 241–265.

Mayer, R. E., Johnson, W. L., Shaw, E., & Sandhu, S. (2006). Constructing computer-based tutors that are socially sensitive: Politeness in educational software. *International Journal of Human-Computer Studies, 54,* 36–42.

Mayer, R. E., Mathias, A., & Wetzell, K. (2002). Fostering understanding of multimedia messages through pretraining: Evidence for a two-stage theory of mental model construction. *Journal of Experimental Psychology: Applied, 8,* 147–154.

Mayer, R. E., Mautone, P. D., & Prothero, W. (2002a). Pictorial aids for learning by doing in a multimedia geology simulation game. *Journal of Educational Psychology, 94,* 171–185.

Mayer, R. E., & Moreno, R. (1998). A split-attention effect in multimedia learning: Evidence for dual processing systems in working memory. *Journal of Educational Psychology, 90,* 312–320.

Mayer, R. E., & Moreno, R. (2003). Nine ways to reduce cognitive load in multimedia learning. *Educational Psychologist, 38,* 43–52.

Mayer, R. E., Moreno, R., Boire, M., & Vagge, S. (1999). Maximizing constructivist learning from multimedia communications by minimizing cognitive load. *Journal of Educational Psychology, 91,* 638–643.

Mayer, R. E., & Sims, V. K. (1994). For whom is a picture worth a thousand words? Extensions of dual-coding theory of multimedia learning. *Journal of Educational Psychology, 84,* 389–401.

Mayer, R. E., Sims, V., & Tajika, H. (1995a). A comparison of how textbooks teach mathematical problem solving in Japan and the United States. *American Educational Research Journal, 32,* 443–460.

Mayer, R. E., Sobko, K., & Mautone, P. D. (2003a). Social cues in multimedia learning: Role of speaker's voice. *Journal of Educational Psychology, 95,* 419–425.

Mayer, R. E., Steinhoff, K., Bower, G., & Mars, R. (1995). A generative theory of textbook design: Using annotated illustrations to foster meaningful learning of science text. *Educational Technology Research and Development, 43,* 31–43.

Mayer, R. E., & Wittrock, M. (2006). Problem solving. In P. A. Alexander, and P. H. Winne (Eds.), *Handbook of educational psychology* (pp. 287–304). Mahwah, NJ: Erlbaum.

Michas, I. C., & Berry, D. (2000). Learning a procedural task: Effectiveness of multimedia presentations. *Applied Cognitive Psychology, 14,* 555–575.

Moreno, R., & Mayer, R. E. (1999a). Cognitive principles of multimedia learning: The role of modality and contiguity. *Journal of Educational Psychology, 91,* 358–368.

Moreno, R., & Mayer, R. E. (1999b). Multimedia-supported metaphors for meaning making in mathematics. *Cognition and Instruction, 17,* 215–248.

Moreno, R., & Mayer, R. E. (2000a). A coherence effect in multimedia learning: The case for minimizing irrelevant sounds in the design of multimedia messages. *Journal of Educational Psychology, 92,* 117–125.

Moreno, R., & Mayer, R. E. (2000b). Engaging students in active learning: The case for personalized multimedia messages. *Journal of Educational Psychology, 92,* 724–733.

Moreno, R., & Mayer, R. E. (2002a). Verbal redundancy in multimedia learning: When reading helps listening. *Journal of Educational Psychology, 94,* 156–163.

Moreno, R., & Mayer, R. E. (2002b). Learning science in virtual reality multimedia environments: Role of methods and media. *Journal of Educational Psychology, 94,* 598–610.

Moreno, R., & Mayer, R. E. (2004). Personalized messages that promote science learning in virtual environments. *Journal of Educational Psychology, 96,* 165–173.

Moreno, R., & Mayer, R. E. (2005). Role of guidance, reflection, and interactivity in an agent-based multimedia game. *Journal of Educational Psychology, 97*, 117–128.

Moreno, R., Mayer, R. E., Spires, H. A., & Lester, J. C. (2001). The case for social agency in computer-based teaching: Do students learn more deeply when they interact with animated pedagogical agents? *Cognition and Instruction, 19*, 177–213.

Nass, C., & Brave, S. (2005). *Wired for speech: How voice activates and advances the human-computer relationship.* Cambridge, MA: MIT Press.

O'Neil, H. F., Mayer, R. E., Herl, H., Thurman, R., & Olin, K. (2000). Instructional strategies for virtual environments. In H. F. O'Neil, and D. H. Andrews (Eds.), *Aircraft training: Methods, technologies, and assessment* (pp. 105–130). Mahwah, NJ: Erlbaum.

Paivio, A. (1986). *Mental representations: A dual-coding approach.* Oxford, England: Oxford University Press.

Paivio, A. (2006). *Mind and its evolution: A dual coding approach.* Mahwah, NJ: Erlbaum.

Pashler, H., Bain, P., Bottage, B., Graesser, A., Koedinger, K., & McDaniel, M., et al., (2007). *Organizing instruction and study to improve student learning.* Washington, DC: National Center for Educational Research, U.S. Department of Education.

Pashler, H., McDaniel, M., Rowher, D., & Bjork, R. (2009). Learning styles: Concepts and evidence. *Psychological Science in the Public Interest, 9*, 105–119.

Pellegrino, J. W., Chudowsky, N, and Glaser, R. 2001 (Eds.), *Knowing what students know.* Washington, DC: National Academy Press.

Phye, G. D., Robinson, D. H, and Levin, J. 2005 (Eds.), *Empirical methods for evaluating educational interventions.* San Diego: Elsevier Academic Press.

Plass, J. L., Moreno, R, and Brunken, R. 2010 (Eds.), *Cognitive load theory.* New York. Cambridge University Press.

Ploetzner, R., Fehse, E., Kneser, C., & Spada, H. (1999). Learning to relate qualitative and quantitative problem representations in a model based setting for collaborative prob lem solving. *Journal of the Learning Sciences, 8*, 177–214.

Pollock, E., Chandler, P., & Sweller, J. (2002). Assimilating complex information. *Learning and Instruction, 12*, 61–86.

Reeves, B., & Nass, C. (1996). *The media equation.* New York: Cambridge University Press.

Roediger, H. L., & Karpicke, J. D. (2006). The power of testing memory: Basic research and implications for educational practice. *Perspectives on Psychological Science, 1*, 181–210.

Rosenthal, R., Rosnow, R. L., & Rubin, D. B. (2000). *Contrasts and effect sizes in behavioral research.* New York: Cambridge University Press.

Roy, M., & Chi, M. T. H. (2005). The self-explanation principle in multimedia learning. In R. E. Mayer (Ed.), *The Cambridge handbook of multimedia learning* (pp. 271–286). New York: Cambridge University Press.

Sadoski, M., & Paivio, A. (2001). *Imagery and text: A dual coding theory of reading and writing.* Mahwah, NJ: Erlbaum.

Sanchez, C. A., & Wiley, J. (2006). An examination of the seductive details effect in terms of working memory capacity. *Memory & Cognition, 34*, 344–355.

Schwamborn, A., Mayer, R. E., Thillmann, H., Leopold, C., & Leutner, D. (2010). Drawing as a generative activity and drawing as a prognostic activity. *Journal of Educational Psychology, 102*, 872–879.

Shavelson, R. J, and Towne, L. 2002 (Eds.), *Scientific research in education.* Washington, DC: National Academy Press.

Stokes, D. E. (1997). *Pasteur's quadrant: Basic science and technological innovation.* Washington, DC: Brookings Institution Press.

Stull, A., & Mayer, R. E. (2007). Learning by doing versus learning by viewing: Three experimental comparisons of learner-generated versus author-provided graphic orga-nizers. *Journal of Educational Psychology, 99*, 808–820.

Sweller, J. (1999). *Instructional design in technical areas.* Camberwell, Australia: ACER Press.

Sweller, J. (2005a). Implications of cognitive load theory for multimedia learning. In R. E. Mayer (Ed.), *The Cambridge handbook of multimedia learning* (pp. 19–30). New York: Cambridge University Press.

Sweller, J. (2005b). The redundancy principle in multimedia learning. In R. E. Mayer (Ed.), *The Cambridge handbook of multimedia learning* (pp. 159–168). New York: Cambridge University Press.

Tabbers, T. K., Martens, R. L., & van Merrienboer, J. J. G. (2004). Multimedia instructions and cognitive load theory: Effects of modality and cueing. *British Journal of Educational Psychology, 74,* 71–81.

Tindall-Ford, S., Chandler, P., & Sweller, J. (1997). When two sensory modes are better than one. *Journal of Experimental Psychology: Applied, 3,* 257–287.

Wang, N., Johnson, W. L., Mayer, R. E., Rizzo, P., Shaw, E., & Collins, H. (2008). The politeness effect: Pedagogical agents and learning outcomes. *International Journal of Human Computer Studies, 66,* 96–112.

Wentzel, K. R, and Wigfield, A. 2009 (Eds.), *Handbook of motivation at school.* New York: Routledge.

Wittrock, M. C. (1989). Generative processes of comprehension. *Educational Psychologist, 24,* 345–376.

CHAPTER FOUR

Incorporating Motivation into a Theoretical Framework for Knowledge Transfer

Timothy J. Nokes *and* Daniel M. Belenky

Contents

Abstract

Knowledge transfer is critical to successfully solving novel problems and performing new tasks. Several theories have been proposed to account for how, when, and why transfer occurs. These include both classical cognitive theories such as identical rules, analogy, and schemas, as well as more recent views such as situated transfer and preparation for future learning. Although much progress has been made in understanding specific aspects of transfer phenomena, important challenges remain in developing a framework that can account for both transfer successes and failures. Surprisingly, few of these approaches have integrated motivational constructs into their theories to address these challenges. In this chapter, we propose a theoretical framework that builds on the classical cognitive approaches and incorporates aspects of competence motivation. In the first part of the chapter we review the classical and alternative views of transfer and discuss their successes and limitations. We then describe our transfer framework that begins to address some of the issues and questions that are raised by

Psychology of Learning and Motivation, Volume 55

ISSN 0079-7421, DOI 10.1016/B978-0-12-387691-1.00004-1

© 2011 Elsevier Inc.

All rights reserved.

the alternative views. In the second part, we describe how our proposed framework can incorporate aspects of competence motivation—specifically, students' achievement goals. We then describe an initial test of the framework and the implications for both psychological theory and educational practice.

1. INTRODUCTION

Solving a problem on a math final. Driving a rental car in a foreign city. Filling out tax forms after a recent move. Planning a backpacking trip. What do all of these activities have in common? *Knowledge transfer*. In each case prior knowledge and experience is used to attempt to solve a new problem or perform a new task. Success depends on a myriad of factors including the amount and type of prior relevant experience, our goals and expectations for success, our level of engagement and persistence, how important it is to succeed, and the perceived difficulty of the task or problem. In some cases success may be achieved with little effort while in others it may require much effort and persistence. In some situations we want to succeed because we want to demonstrate our abilities, or because we are trying to overcome a challenge. In each situation, transfer is determined by the interaction between our past knowledge and experience, the structure and demands of the task, and our motivations for success.

Having a deep understanding of how people transfer their knowledge from one situation to another is critical for both psychological theory and educational practice. A psychological theory of transfer must weave together research on learning, knowledge representation, memory, and problem solving in a principled and coherent way to make predictions for how and when we use our prior knowledge to perform new tasks and solve new problems. Such a theory has obvious implications for education and, for many educational theorists and practitioners, facilitating successful knowledge transfer *is* the critical goal of education (see Packer, 2001 for a historical analysis).

Although much progress has been made in the past 100 years of research on this topic, important challenges remain ahead. There are questions as to how to best account for the wide array of transfer phenomena observed in the literature, including the transfer of procedural skills versus declarative concepts and the transfer of simple versus complex knowledge representations. How do we account for near transfer to similar contexts versus far transfer across contexts and domains, and should these two types of transfer be accounted for by a single theory? How do we account for both transfer successes and failures? Can we construct a general theoretical framework that provides answers to all of these questions?

Much previous work has addressed these challenges from a cognitive perspective as being related to the application conditions of prior knowledge and the specific cognitive processes used to transfer that knowledge (see Barnett & Ceci, 2002; Gick & Holyoak, 1987 for reviews). This work has focused on the underlying knowledge representations and cognitive mechanisms including rules (Singley & Anderson, 1989), analogies (Gentner, 1983; Gick & Holyoak, 1983), schemas (Thorndyke, 1984), and declarative to procedural transfer processes (Anderson, 1987; Ohlsson, 1996). Other research has met these challenges by rejecting the classical cognitive view and proposing alternative perspectives such as situated transfer (Greeno, 1998; Lave, 1988), and preparation for future learning (PFL) (Schwartz & Bransford, 1998). Interestingly, the majority of this work has not included motivational constructs as central factors in their theories to address these challenges (but see Lave & Wenger, 1991).

This absence of motivational factors is not for a lack of research on motivation; as any review of the motivational literature is quick to turn up, there are many potentially relevant theoretical constructs such as intrinsic motivation (Malone, 1981), achievement goals (Elliot & Dweck, 2005), interest (Hidi & Renninger, 2006), task value (Eccles & Wigfield, 2002), affect (Blanchette & Richards, 2010), arousal (Eysenck, 1976), self-efficacy (Bandura, 1997), attributions (Weiner, 1985), the need for cognitive closure (Kruglanski & Webster, 1996), to name a few. Perhaps it is precisely for this reason that these constructs have not been explored and integrated into classical transfer theories; there are simply too many possibilities, making the task of integrating too daunting and unwieldy. Or perhaps this lack of integration reflects more traditional research divisions between cognitive, social, and educational psychology. Whatever the reason, we aim to address this issue in this chapter.

Our goals for this chapter are twofold, and so we divide the chapter into two corresponding parts. In the first part, we give an overview of three classical cognitive theories of transfer and two more recent approaches and discuss their successes and limitations. We then describe our theoretical framework that builds and extends the classical work and begins to address some of the issues and questions raised by the alternative perspectives. In the second part, we describe how theoretical constructs from competence motivation research—specifically, achievement goals—can be incorporated into this framework.

We see this work as an attempt to bridge prior transfer research in the learning and cognitive sciences to research on competence theory as examined in social and educational psychology. This bridging should benefit cognitive theory by incorporating the analysis of individual differences that have largely been ignored in past work and may play a key role in understanding transfer successes and failures. It should also benefit motivational theory by relating motivational constructs to fine-grained cognitive processes of learning and transfer. In the second part, we will describe some initial work testing aspects of this framework and offer some future directions. We end the chapter with the implications for psychological theory and educational practice.

2. KNOWLEDGE TRANSFER

A robust theory of transfer must be able to explain when, why, and how people use prior knowledge to solve new problems and perform new tasks. In this section, we briefly describe three classic cognitive transfer theories and two more recent approaches that have ventured answers to these questions. The purpose is not to provide an in-depth review of each theory, but instead to provide a background and context for our theoretical framework. We then describe how our framework incorporates the classical mechanisms and addresses some of the issues and questions raised by the alternative approaches.

2.1. Classical cognitivist approaches

One of the earliest theories of transfer is the theory of identical elements originally proposed by E. L. Thorndike (Thorndike & Woodworth, 1901). According to this theory, the amount of transfer between any two tasks is determined by the number of shared stimulus elements between those tasks—the more elements in common, the more transfer expected. J. R. Anderson and M. Singley have since given the theory a modern cognitive reconceptualization by recasting the identical task elements as *mental representations* in the form of IF-THEN production rules (Singley & Anderson, 1989). Like the original Thorndikean hypothesis, the amount of transfer is determined by the proportion of rules learned from one situation or task that applies to another. For example, if you have learned the addition rule: IF I am trying to find the sum of 2 + 2, and I know the relevant addition fact, THEN retrieve that fact and output the sum. You could of course use this rule to solve new instances of that same problem, 2 + 2 = ?. You could also use the rule to help solve the subcomponents of more complex problems such as 2 + 2 + 6, where you would first use the 2 + 2 rule before using or creating another rule to add the 6. This type of transfer is often described as vertical transfer in that the simple rule is being applied to solve a subcomponent of a more complex problem (Royer, 1979).

Identical rules are hypothesized to apply automatically, with little cognitive processing, when the application conditions of the rule are satisfied (Anderson & Lebiere, 1998; Anderson et al., 2004). They are also hypothesized to be goal-specific, and only applicable to scenarios in which the same goals are in play (Singley & Anderson, 1989). Given these representation and processing features the theory does well in predicting and explaining procedural transfer to very similar or identical contexts (e.g., Anderson, Conrad, & Corbett, 1989; Kieras & Bovair, 1986; Singley & Anderson, 1989). However, it does not explain how people can transfer knowledge to very different contexts or take advantage of that knowledge to accomplish different goals (Pennington, Nicolich, & Rahm, 1995).

A second classic cognitive approach to transfer is analogy. An analogy is the use of prior exemplar knowledge to solve a new problem or perform a new task (Gentner, 1983, 1989; Gick & Holyoak, 1980, 1983). Gentner (1999) defines analogy as having the following five components: (1) *retrieval*—recalling a prior (source) example or situation based on some similarity to the current context, (2) *mapping*—aligning the objects and relations of the source example and target problem, (3) *inference*—generating an inference based on that mapping for the current context, (4) *re-representation*—searching for new alignment and mapping if the initial mapping failed to result in an adequate solution, and (5) *learning and abstraction*—creating a new representation by abstracting over relations.

Analogy provides a good account for near transfer of prior examples to very similar contexts for novices (see Reeves & Weisberg, 1994 for a review of the empirical findings). Unlike the identical rules theory, the retrieval and application of an example using analogy is not goal dependent and thus frees the example to be used in different ways depending on the application context. Analogy can also account for more rare, across-domain transfer when the specific features do not match but the structural or higher-order relations do (Gentner, 1983, 1989). However, such transfer either requires enough experience in the domain to create an abstract representation that includes structural features of the problem (e.g., Novick, 1988), or the use of abstraction or re-representation processes (e.g., Hummel & Holyoak, 2003), both of which require additional cognitive processing either at the acquisition or application phases (see Forbus, Gentner, & Law, 1995; Holyoak, Novick, & Melz, 1994; Hummel & Holyoak, 2003, for computational models).

A third classic cognitive approach is schema theory (Marshall, 1995; Schank & Abelson, 1977; Thorndyke, 1984). This approach highlights the content and structure of the knowledge representation as the critical factor underlying knowledge transfer. Schemas are knowledge structures that consist of a description of the prototypical features and application conditions of the concept, principle, or skill. Compared to the rules approach, schema representations tend to include abstract features that are true of many examples of the concept, whereas rules include specific features of particular examples or situations. This mechanism can therefore facilitate far transfer to new contexts and across domains because the structural features of the knowledge representation are not tied to any particular instance or context. Although this knowledge structure supports far transfer, it also requires much cognitive processing to interpret how the abstract declarative knowledge should be applied to the new context (Nokes, 2009; Nokes & Ohlsson, 2005). This process of interpreting the declarative knowledge of the schema into a set of procedural actions is called declarative to procedural transfer. Two computational models that illustrate this process are knowledge compilation (Anderson, 1987; Neves & Anderson, 1981) and constraint violation (Ohlsson, 1996; Ohlsson & Rees, 1991), and both require much computational processing to translate abstract declarative knowledge into procedural actions.

Each of these approaches has received independent empirical evidence and can account for some key aspects of transfer phenomena. Common to each view is a focus on the scope of transfer afforded, how knowledge is represented, the cognitive processes for applying the knowledge, and the degree of cognitive processing required. Table 1 provides a summary of the representational and processing characteristics of each approach.

When transfer does not occur as expected it is typically explained as a failure in satisfying the application conditions for the mechanism or a disruption of the cognitive processes involved. Research that has shown transfer failures where transfer was intuitively expected, such as across isomorphic problem structures (i.e., Bassok, 1990), has led to the further development and refinement of these theories. Critically, none of these approaches has incorporated motivational constructs as major components of the theory. We believe that motivations may play a particularly important role in explaining both the transfer failures and successes. We build upon this classic work and articulate a theoretical framework in which the classical mechanisms naturally emerge from sense-making and satisficing processes enacted during transfer. The framework provides a solid foundation to incorporate motivational constructs, specifically competence motivation, into the theory. However, before describing the framework in detail we briefly describe alternative views to the classical cognitive approaches.

2.2. Alternative views

The alternative views were motivated in part by the paradox that although transfer appears to be a ubiquitous aspect of everyday life it proved elusive and difficult to observe in the psychological laboratory (see Bransford & Schwartz, 1999; Lobato, 2006 for reviews). These failures to observe

Table 1 Cognitivist Classical Approaches to Transfer

Approach	Scope of transfer	Knowledge	Transfer process	Efficiency
Identical rules	Very near; applies in situations that match similar application conditions and goals	Production rules	Applied automatically if application conditions of the rule match the current context	High efficiency, applied automatically
Analogy	Near for both novice and expert; far for experts	Exemplars	(1) Retrieve an example, (2) align and map to the current context, (3) generate inference, (4) re-represent, and (5) learn	Moderate efficiency; more similar task representations will result in faster alignment and mapping
Schema	Near to far	Facts, principles, and constraints	Declarative to procedural: knowledge compilation; constraint violation	Low efficiency, requires much cognitive resources and is error prone

transfer in the laboratory raised important questions about the definition, assumptions, and processes of the classical approaches (Lave, 1988; Lobato, 2006). In this section, we briefly describe two of the alternative views including situative transfer and PFL.

The situative perspective postulates that knowledge transfer is deeply interwoven into the individual's activity in the world (Greeno, 1997, 1998; Lave, 1988; Rogoff, 2003; see Gruber, Law, Mandl, & Renkl, 1995 for a review). Transfer is dependent on a set of interrelations between the individual and the environment and it is this set of interrelations that determines the likelihood of transfer (Greeno, 2006). Transfer is described as "patterns of participation" and it is the replication of this pattern that determines transfer to future contexts. Research programs that employ this view examine how the environment affords particular ways of participating in authentic activities (Brown, Collins, & Duguid,

1989). This view shifts the focus from the cognition of the individual to how the individual acts in the world.

In contrast to the classical theories, this view begins to incorporate aspects of motivation into transfer theory by focusing on how individuals participate in legitimate, authentic practices in a community (Lave & Wenger, 1991). With this focus on self-identity and participation in community practices there is great potential to link to work in the social and educational sciences on self-concept, attributions, as well as work on group processes. Similar to this view, we see motivational processes as critical to the transfer story and important to include in a general theory of transfer. Our proposal differs from this in that we focus on a different aspect of motivation, namely, competence motivation and achievement goals, and instead of rejecting the classical mechanisms of transfer, we build upon these mechanisms by incorporating them into our framework.

The second alternative view of transfer is PFL. Here transfer is not viewed as the static transportation of knowledge components from one task or situation to another but instead as the use of prior knowledge and experiences to *learn* from new resources and information that then can affect subsequent performance (Bransford & Schwartz, 1999; Schwartz & Bransford, 1998; Schwartz, Bransford, & Sears, 2005). This view has criticized the classical approach as focusing too narrowly on transfer as a form of sequestered problem solving, with no consideration of additional resources that the initial learning may have prepared people to use more effectively. The authors argue that this limits the types of transfer that one can observe and creates a setting that is not very naturalistic or representative of transfer in daily life.

This view differentiates between transferring knowledge "into" situations versus transferring knowledge "out of" situations. Transferring "into" focuses on how prior knowledge affects the interpretation, encoding, and learning of new information, whereas transferring "out of" focuses on how prior knowledge can be used to solve new problems and perform new tasks (i.e., the classical view). This definition broadens the theoretical conceptualization of transfer and has contributed to the discovery of previously hidden transfer phenomena (Schwartz & Bransford, 1998; Schwartz & Martin, 2004). However, like the classical mechanisms, this approach does not incorporate motivational constructs into the theory.

Although situative and PFL approaches are often discussed as competitors to the classical cognitivist approaches, we believe they are complementary, providing an important focus on components critical to a general theory of transfer but lacking in the specific cognitive processes. We believe that progress in understanding transfer depends on bridging the classical cognitive approaches with these alternative approaches. To move toward this goal, we describe a sense-making framework of knowledge transfer, which consists of cognitive processes that determine when the transfer cycle begins and ends. This framework incorporates interrelations between the learner and the environment, and draws on the classical cognitive mechanisms, which naturally emerge. We believe that this framework can also incorporate motivational constructs that may help to further bridge the classical approach with these alternative views.

2.3. Multiple mechanisms and sense-making transfer framework

Our theoretical framework builds on our prior work on transfer as sense-making and dynamic shifting between multiple mechanisms (Nokes, 2004, 2005, 2009; Nokes, Mestre, & Brookes, submitted) and Mestre and his collaborators' work on coordination processes in transfer (Dufresne, Mestre, Thaden-Koch, Gerace, & Leonard, 2005; Thaden-Koch, Dufresne, & Mestre, 2006). The framework consists of two stages: constructing a representation of context and generating a solution. Each stage is explicitly targeted to account for novice transfer behavior. The construction of context stage consists of generating the frame and activating prior knowledge, and the solution generation stage consists of knowledge application and solution evaluation. These different stages are driven by sense-making and satisficing processes in which one evaluates whether the current representation or problem solving approach "makes sense" and is moving the solver closer to the solution. Figure 1 shows an illustration of the transfer cycle in this framework.

2.3.1. Sense-Making and Satisficing
Sense-making is the act of coordinating an individual's goals and expectations with his or her current understanding of the problem or task and then resolving possible discrepancies. It is an evaluation process that takes place during each stage of the transfer cycle. We hypothesize that sense-making takes place in accordance with H. A. Simon's (1956, 1996) notion of *satisficing*, which is the idea that people will use a solution that suffices to accomplish the goal, even though that solution may not be the most optimal or efficient for the task. Simon (1956) famously described this type of reasoning as "bounded rationality." We take this notion and apply it to transfer. We hypothesize that people satisfice when both constructing a representation and generating a solution, and that these processes determine when the transfer cycle begins and ends.

Applying these ideas to transfer shifts attention from a sole focus on the application conditions of the prior knowledge to determining the cognitive

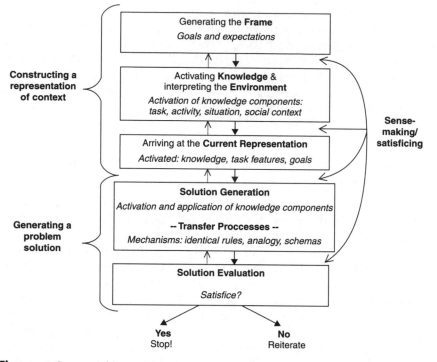

Figure 1   Sense-making transfer cycle adapted from Nokes, Mestre, & Brookes, submitted.

and motivational constraints on the transfer scenario. It also highlights the importance of determining what factors influence a person's *satisficing criteria*. For example, if a person's goal is to understand the solution, then we might expect different kinds of transfer processes than those for a person who simply wants to obtain a correct answer. Specifically, in the former case we might expect a mastery-oriented individual who is concerned with understanding a task to show more engagement and a higher likelihood of generating a deep, relational analogy than a performance-oriented individual who is satisfied with a less optimal surface feature solution. Next we describe the framework in more detail, beginning with constructing a representation of context before discussing solution generation.

2.3.2. Representation of Context

2.3.2.1. Frames   The first component necessary for the construction of context is the generation of the frame. Consistent with other work in the learning sciences, we define a *frame* as an individual's representation of what is being asked or expected of her (Hammer, Elby, Scherr, & Redish,

2005; Redish, 2004; Scherr & Hammer, 2009). For example, a student may frame a physics laboratory group activity as an opportunity to learn more about the underlying physics concepts whereas another student may frame that very same activity as a opportunity to show what she knows and demonstrate her ability to solve physics problems to her classmates and teacher. The first student frames it as an opportunity to develop understanding and the second frames it as an opportunity to perform for others. The frame is often implicit and can be described as answering the question: "What sort of activity is going on here?" We hypothesize that frames are formed as the result of an interaction between a person's goals, expectations, and perception of the target task. We hypothesize that the frame will have a large impact on the satisficing criteria adopted for a particular transfer situation. In the above example, the first student's frame may lead to a deep engagement in the activity and a quest to understand the physics, resulting in collaboration with her classmates; whereas in the latter case, the student's frame may lead to a focus on individual performance and ability, resulting in little collaboration.

2.3.2.2. *Knowledge and Environment*   The second component for the construction of context is the activation of prior knowledge. Consistent with other work in the cognitive and learning sciences, we postulate that knowledge is represented as *knowledge components*. We adopt the classical view that knowledge components include different types of knowledge representations including rules, examples, declarative facts, strategies, principles, and constraints (e.g., Koedinger, Perfetti, Corbett, & the PSLC, 2010). These components get activated in response to perceived cues from the environment and the generated frame. Consistent with classical cognitive theories we view knowledge activation as dependent on memory mechanisms, such as spreading activation, that is, the idea that concepts are related to one another in a semantic network, and activation of one concept activates related concepts as a function of the strength of the relation (Collins & Quillian, 1969). The types of knowledge components activated during this stage depend on perceptions of the cues in the environment. This includes both the physical environment, such as the structure and type of task (e.g., a word problem or an algebraic expression), as well as the social environment including the other individuals present and the social context (e.g., an in-school activity vs. a family function). The environment will provide constraints (e.g., time limitations) and affordances (e.g., books, the internet) that will impact the activation of prior knowledge components.

In sum, the construction of context is highly dynamic, activated by individuals' motivations, prior experiences and knowledge, and the features of the physical and social environment. The context contributes to the sense-making and satisficing processes used throughout the transfer process.

2.3.3. Generating a Solution

2.3.3.1. Transfer Processes In the solution generation stage a person's prior knowledge is brought to bear to generate a solution or to perform some action. Here the various classical cognitive mechanisms naturally emerge from the activated prior knowledge (see Figure 1). If multiple mechanisms are activated the mechanism with the least cognitive cost will be triggered, according to the principle of cognitive economy (Nokes, 2009).

2.3.3.2. Evaluation After a solution attempt has been made, the individual evaluates his or her solution to see whether the solution satisfies the intended goal, which constitutes the last stage in the transfer process. If the solution attempt satisfices, the transfer cycle for that problem is over. If not, some aspects of the transfer cycle will be reiterated. This may result in a change to the frame and the satisficing criteria ("I'm not sure this is right, but I am bored and want to stop") or a new attempt to satisfy the current goal ("Since this formula didn't work, I need to look for a different one that applies here.").

2.4. Answers to initial questions

This transfer framework provides some answers to the questions posed in the introduction. By incorporating multiple transfer mechanisms, the framework can account for both procedural and declarative transfer, as well as near and far transfer (Table 1). The framework makes testable predictions about which mechanisms will be triggered for particular types of transfer scenarios, as well as what behavioral outcomes to expect (e.g., if rules are triggered then one should expect the student to show procedural transfer with minimal cognitive processing).

This framework can also help describe mechanisms that assist in accounting for both transfer successes and failures. According to the framework, transfer failures occur because of either (1) the limited scope of the transfer mechanism or (2) an outcome of satisficing. The first type of failure is consistent with classical work but extends this view to incorporate the notion of multiple mechanisms and that particular mechanisms will have different levels of success dependent on the specifics of the transfer scenario (frames, prior knowledge, and task characteristics). An example of this type of failure is lack of transfer for a production rule to a new context in which it does not apply. The second type of failure is a misalignment of the expectations of the experimenter, teacher, or expert with the novice's satisficing criteria. An example of this type of failure occurs when a student is asked to "explain her/his answer" but instead simply restates or redescribes the answer or gives a surface response such as those common in math and physics classes when a student explains that an answer is the result of applying a particular equation without providing a justification for why they are using that equation or what it means conceptually. This suggests that future work should focus on understanding what factors affect satisficing criteria for particular situations. We believe that motivational factors will play a particularly important role in determining the satisficing criteria for specific types of transfer scenarios.

Next we describe how research in *competence motivation*, specifically students' achievement goals, can be incorporated into the framework. Although other motivational constructs may also be incorporated, we believe achievement goals in particular offer a compelling example of how research on motivational variables can serve to inform our understanding of knowledge transfer.

3. Competence Motivation and Achievement Goals

Much work in social and educational psychology has focused on human motivation, learning, and performance. A large portion of this work falls under the category of what has been called achievement motivation (e.g., Covington, 2000; Dweck, 1986; Nicholls, 1984). This work concerns the factors that affect success in obtaining achievement and encompasses research on intrinsic and extrinsic motivation, attributions, evaluation anxiety, goals, and other constructs. Elliot and Dweck (2005) have recently argued that this literature is better conceptualized as research on competence rather than achievement because competence provides a clearer, coherent, theoretical construct, and target of study.

By focusing on competence as the core of achievement motivation research, Elliot and Dweck (2005) highlight the dual aspects of human ability and success, as well as inability and failure. They argue that competence is a ubiquitous aspect of our daily lives and critical to many human pursuits in work, academic, sports, and social contexts. Furthermore, this construct naturally incorporates both approach motivations, or striving toward competence and avoidance motivations, or moving away from incompetence. We adopt this view and suggest that competence plays a particularly important role in knowledge transfer in academic settings. We examine the role of competence motivation as it is manifest in students' achievement goals.

3.1. Achievement goals and transfer

A prolific amount of research has been conducted on the topic of achievement goals in the past 20 years. Achievement goals are a person's aim in an achievement setting. The dominant framework for considering achievement goals posits two dimensions for goals: definition and valence (Elliot & McGregor, 2001; Elliot & Murayama, 2008). Definition refers to the criterion by which competence is evaluated. When it is based on an absolute standard or some internally set goal, this is considered a mastery goal. When it is based on a normative standard, this is considered a performance goal. Valence refers to the seeking out of positive outcomes (approach) or the avoidance of negative outcomes (avoidance). Combining these dimensions results in four different separable goals: mastery-approach, mastery-avoidance, performance-approach, and performance-avoidance. This framework has been empirically validated, though discussions are still on-going about the reality and utility of the mastery-avoidance construct.

A student in an academic setting can have varying levels of each of these goals, and, as each of these goals are theoretically separate, the independent effect of each can be examined. Over many studies, certain general patterns of student behavior, affect, and achievement outcomes have emerged for each achievement goal. Performance-avoidance goals have been consistently linked with maladaptive outcomes, such as test anxiety, low self-efficacy, poor study habits, avoidance of help-seeking, procrastination, and ultimately, poorer achievement (in the form of test scores, term grades, etc.) (Elliot, McGregor, & Gable, 1999; Urdan, Ryan, Anderman, & Gheen, 2002). The findings for performance-approach goals are more mixed, and have spurred debate about their relative impact on students and achievement (see Harackiewicz, Barron, Pintrich, Elliot, & Thrash, 2002; Midgley, Kaplan, & Middleton, 2001). Performance-approach goals have been linked to negative behaviors and affective variables, such as procrastination, test anxiety, and shallow processing strategies (Elliot & McGregor, 1999) as well as positive behaviors, such as persistence and effort (Elliot et al., 1999). In terms of achievement outcomes, performance-approach goals have been found to predict achievement measures, such as grades, particularly in college settings (Elliot & Church, 1997; Harackiewicz, et al., 2002). Mastery-approach goals have been related to greater use of cognitive and metacognitive strategies, such as elaboration, planning, monitoring, and help-seeking, a preference for challenge, higher levels of effort, less procrastination, greater interest, and long-term retention (e.g., Elliot & McGregor, 1999; Ford, Smith, Weissbein, Gully, & Salas, 1998; Harackiewicz, Durik, Barron, Linnenbrink-Garcia, & Tauer, 2008; Pintrich, 1999; Somuncuoglu & Yildirim, 1999). However, there is only mixed evidence for mastery-approach goals being linked to achievement measures, such as grades.

4. Transfer Framework and Achievement Goals

Given the previous work establishing relationships between achievement goals and student behaviors, cognition, and affect, we hypothesize that students with greater adoption of mastery-approach achievement goals should show a higher probability of knowledge transfer. By incorporating these achievement goals into our transfer framework, we hope to capture variation in transfer performance that is not currently captured by the classical cognitive theories or the alternative views of situated transfer or PFL. We hope that by including these goals they will help further improve the predictions of the framework as well as provide a first step to integrating aspects of motivational and cognitive theories. Second, we hope this integration will further specify the underlying cognitive mechanisms by which achievement goals have their effects.

We view achievement goals as different kinds of cognitive *frames* the student generates for a given transfer scenario. Figure 2 illustrates how various achievement goals could be incorporated into the transfer framework and their potential effect on knowledge activation and satisficing criteria. For example, we predict that a mastery-oriented student might persist until he or she has understood the solution, whereas a performance-oriented student may satisfice after simply generating a plausible answer, whether or not s/he has a deep understanding of the solution.

As the previous section highlights, these different orientations should impact the initial learning and the knowledge acquired, which should also have implications for transfer through creating different prior knowledge that can be activated in the construction of the context. If, for example, a mastery-approach goal facilitates deep cognitive processes, persistence, and engagement, then we might expect this to lead to the acquisition of more abstract knowledge and promote far transfer through the later application of abstract declarative to procedural transfer processes. If one did not initially develop that abstract declarative knowledge, it would be impossible to use a declarative to procedural transfer mechanism. Similarly, a mastery-approach goal may make one actively seek prior knowledge to use, increasing the likelihood of making an analogy.

In the transfer phase itself, these orientations may also play a role by affecting the satisficing criteria of the transfer task. That is, when solving a transfer problem with a mastery-approach goal, one might not be happy with simply arriving at just any solution, but may evaluate the quality ("Do I think the answer makes sense?"). In contrast, if one has a

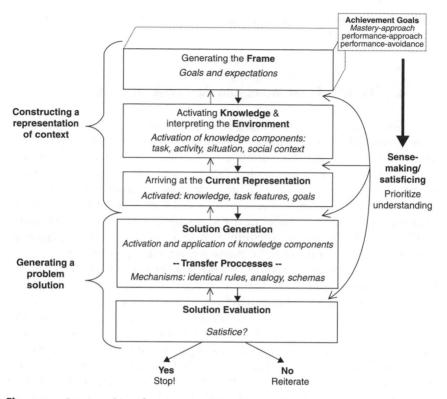

Figure 2 Sense-making framework with achievement goals incorporated. In this illustration a student generates a frame that consists of a mastery-approach achievement goal, which affects her satisficing criteria by focusing on understanding the content of the transfer task.

performance–approach goal and treats each task as a separate demonstration of ability, then one might not be expected to transfer across performances ("Do I think this is what the teacher is looking for here?").

We believe that one reason for incorporating achievement goals into classical theories of transfer is that it adds a new target at which to aim instructional interventions. That is, much of the research on the classical mechanisms has focused on the knowledge representation as the instructional target (see Barnett & Ceci, 2002; Gick & Holyoak, 1987 for reviews). We know from prior work that this has been only partially successful, and is likely not to be the whole transfer story. Even when students acquire the "correct" knowledge components (as defined by the representational scope of application) there have been cases of transfer failure (Nokes, 2009). We hypothesize that sense-making and satisficing processes are one way to account for these failures. If achievement goals affect *satisficing criteria* then one can target instruction at manipulating students' achievement goals as another route to facilitate knowledge transfer.

4.1. Testing the hypothesis

Based on this understanding of how motivation may influence transfer, some predictions are available for empirical testing. One main prediction is that having a mastery goal orientation during learning—which is geared toward the development of understanding—will ultimately lead to better transfer of that knowledge. Although there are theoretical reasons to believe this to be so (Harackiewicz, et al., 2002; Pugh & Bergin, 2006), very few empirical studies have examined this in academic domains (see Bereby-Meyer & Kaplan, 2005; Bereby-Meyer, Moran, & Unger-Aviram, 2004; Ford et al., 1998, for examples in nonacademic domains).

Another set of predictions has to do with how different academic tasks can spur different motivational goals, and what influence this can have on transfer. Specifically, research on the effect of different classroom practices and expectations has found that granting students authority, using different forms of evaluation, and offering challenges increases mastery goal adoption and interest (e.g., Ames, 1992; Ames & Archer, 1988; Malone & Lepper, 1987). As such, one would expect that more open-ended forms of instruction may increase mastery goal adoption for the task at hand. This mastery goal adoption may lead to improvements in transfer, relative to instruction that does not promote this change in goals, particularly for those students who would otherwise not adopt mastery goals on their own.

Together, this leads to the following predictions, which can be empirically tested:

- Students who are more mastery-oriented are more likely to successfully transfer knowledge from instruction to both near and far transfer contexts.
- Students who are not highly mastery-oriented to begin with will transfer better from a more exploratory, open-ended instructional technique relative to a standard direct instruction model. This benefit will be due, at least in part, to an increase in mastery goal adoption during the learning activity.

One study that has examined these possibilities has recently been conducted (Belenky & Nokes, 2009, submitted). This work was based on an earlier study by Schwartz and Martin (2004), which investigated the role of different instructional activities on subsequent ability to transfer knowledge into new learning opportunities and future problems. Belenky and Nokes (2009, submitted) added motivational measures to this paradigm, using the Achievement Goal Questionnaire (Elliot & McGregor, 2001) to assess existing mastery-approach orientation toward mathematics, as well as asking students about their goals and affect during the activities. In this study, students were given one of two types of instructional activities, tell-and-practice or invention. These activities had to do with the concept of standardization, asking students to decide which of two exceptional scores from different given data sets was more impressive. To solve this correctly requires using some conceptualization of the idea of standardizing the values.

In the tell-and-practice condition, students were shown a graphical method for divvying up the distribution to aid in deciding which of the scores was more impressive and told to use it to help them solve the problem. This could be equated with a "direct instruction" form of pedagogy, where the focus is on telling students how to solve problems, and giving them practice doing so. In the invention condition, students were given the same problem to solve, but were not given any explicit aid to solve the problem. Instead, they were instructed to try to come up with a way to solve the problem on their own. Although students struggle and fail to arrive at the correct solution, this sort of problem gives students authority and agency over solving a challenging problem. As such, this type of instruction may have benefits for mastery goal adoption, placing relatively more importance on the development of understanding than on demonstrating ability. This possibility was investigated using a short questionnaire that was administered during the learning activity.

Transfer was assessed by a question that gave students high values from two distributions. For each of these distributions, the descriptive statistics were given (i.e., mean and standard deviation). The students had to decide which of the values was more impressive. While similar to the learning activity, this problem was different in that it did not give the students the data, but rather just the descriptive statistics. As such, the exact method from the tell-and-practice condition could not be used without some adaptation. Also, the problems were constructed in such a way that more intuitive forms of reasoning would arrive at faulty conclusions (i.e., the largest value is not the most impressive, given the distributions).

Additionally, half of each condition received a worked example embedded in the test, which introduced and demonstrated how to use a formula to calculate a standardized score (i.e., [Given value−Mean]/Standard Deviation). No explicit mention was made of how this could be used in relation to the earlier problems or to potential future uses. This worked example was always presented at least two problems prior to the transfer item. If students noticed that this formula could be used in the transfer problem, this would be evidence for initial learning that had

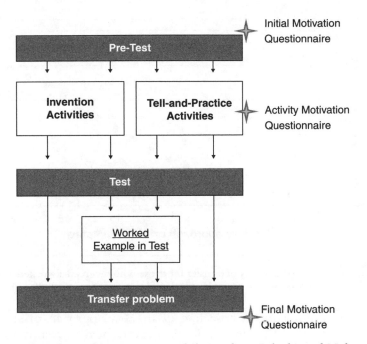

Figure 3   Overview of the experimental design from Belenky and Nokes, 2009, submitted.

prepared the students for future learning of the similar concepts. Students who did not receive this worked example had difficulty solving the transfer problem (11%), but interesting results emerged among those who did receive the worked example. See Figure 3 for an overview of the experimental design.

Among those who received the worked example, the students who were more mastery-oriented at the beginning of the study were more likely to transfer, collapsing across the type of instruction they received. Figure 4 shows the regression model predictions for the likelihood of transfer as a function of students' preexisting mastery orientation scores. For each unit change of the mastery-approach orientation score the odds of successfully solving the transfer problem increase by 29%. This is evidence for the first prediction, that mastery goal orientations can lead students to engage in a way that promotes transfer, as predicted by the sense-making transfer framework.

Evidence for the second prediction required seeing a benefit for invention activities over tell-and-practice for those students who entered lower in mastery orientation. This prediction was also supported. For the tell-and-practice group, the effect mirrored the one seen in Figure 4; the higher one's mastery-approach scores, the higher the likelihood of

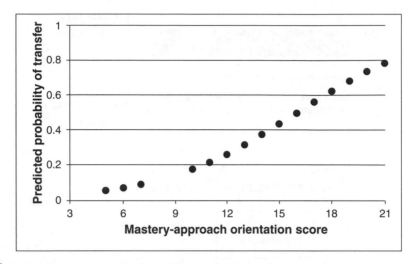

Figure 4 Predicted probability of transfer for those who received a worked example collapsed across condition. Based on data from Belenky and Nokes, 2009, submitted.

successfully transferring. Those low in mastery-approach orientations were unlikely to successfully transfer. However, for the invention group, the relationship between existing mastery-approach orientations and likelihood of transfer was attenuated. Figure 5 shows the regression model predictions of the likelihood of transfer as a function of mastery-orientation score and instructional condition. Students who invented were likely

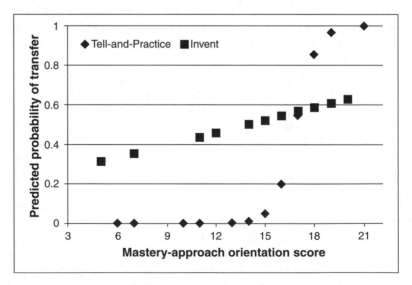

Figure 5 Predicted probability of transfer among those who received a worked example, split by instructional condition. Adapted from Belenky and Nokes, 2009, submitted.

to transfer regardless of whether they were high or low in their initial mastery goal orientations. This effect could be due exclusively to different types of cognitive engagement required by invention activities, rather than having anything to do with a change in mastery goal adoption during the task. However, responses on the questionnaire collected during the learning activities provide evidence against such an argument. The invention activity led to more mastery-related affect and goal responses than did the tell-and-practice, with invention students reporting higher levels of concern for understanding, correctness, and quality of their procedure, as well as feelings of challenge.

This pattern of evidence suggests that the invention form of instruction, which is more open-ended and places greater emphasis on student agency and exploration, influences the adoption of mastery-related goals for a given task. This effect seems particularly beneficial for those lower in mastery orientation to begin with, who, in a more traditional, tell-and-practice form of learning activity, are less likely to transfer. Although only indirect evidence, we believe this leads to more "sense-making" during the learning phase, resulting in more useful prior knowledge to bring to bear on the worked example and subsequent transfer problem. We also believe that the mastery goals may have changed the satisficing criteria on the transfer problem from "Come up with an answer" to something closer to "Come up with a mathematically valid answer," something that was clearly labeled in the instructions but may have been interpreted differently by each student, depending on the frame they generated. This shift could account for the higher likelihood of transfer for those with mastery-approach goals.

To summarize, there is evidence that higher levels of existing mastery-approach goal orientations increase the likelihood of successful transfer. For students lower in these goal orientations, invention activities improve the likelihood of successful transfer. This effect may be due, at least in part, to this type of activity facilitating the adoption of mastery-related goals and affect within the learning environment.

5. CONCLUSION

Transfer is a ubiquitous phenomenon in the real-world and occurs in many situations across many different kinds of tasks. Sometimes we use a prior example to help us solve a new problem; other times, we solve a new problem by applying a general principle. The proposed transfer framework accounts for this variety of transfer phenomena by including multiple transfer mechanisms, each with a different scope of application and efficiency. One aspect that has been missing from prior cognitive theories of transfer is the inclusion of motivational constructs. When a person is solving a new problem, they have particular goals, and these goals will influence the ways in which that person attempts to transfer, and what types of performances they consider adequate.

This framework has two main stages that a novice engages in when attempting to transfer: constructing a representation of the context and generating a solution. Both of these stages are governed by sense-making and satisficing processes, which are used in evaluating each stage. The construction of context involves generation of the frame and relevant prior knowledge, and the frame affects the satisficing criteria for a given transfer scenario. Specifically, we have hypothesized how achievement goals, a form of competence motivation, may play a role in the frame generation and the satisficing process. For example, having a mastery-approach orientation may result in setting a satisficing criterion that requires deep understanding of the solution, which leads to more successful transfer on a novel problem.

This possibility—that mastery-approach goals are more likely to lead to successful transfer—is a research question that has received relatively little empirical study (Pugh & Bergin, 2006). The results of a study in which existing mastery-approach goals led to an increased likelihood of transfer was presented (Belenky & Nokes, 2009, submitted). In addition, the results supported the claim that certain types of instruction (more open-ended, "discovery"-type) led to adoption of mastery-approach goals in that instructional activity. For those students who entered the study lower in such goal orientations, the adoption of mastery-approach goals spurred by the instruction led to an increased likelihood of transfer, relative to those lower in mastery-approach orientations who completed a more standard "direct-instruction" style learning activity.

Although promising, this is only preliminary evidence. Future research should continue to explore this interplay between achievement goals and transfer. In particular, a focus on satisficing criteria may be a fruitful enterprise. Perhaps performance-approach goals, with a focus on demonstrations of competence over development, will create situations in which a fluent use of an existing production rule counts as the satisficing criterion, regardless of whether that production rule actually solves the given problem (i.e., plug and chug). Future work is also necessary to disentangle the effect of these goals on learning from the effect of these goals being present at the time of transfer, something Belenky and Nokes (2009, submitted) did not address (but see Bereby-Meyer & Kaplan, 2005).

Transfer is important to understand for both theories of cognition and for educational practice. Students who are unable to transfer their knowledge to assessments are at a disadvantage for success both inside and outside the classroom. To craft instruction that facilitates transfer, we need to fully understand how it works and the factors that affect it. We believe that the integration of existing theories of transfer with individual difference variables, such as motivation, will be a powerful basis for future studies that will aid our theoretical understanding and our ability to create practical educational interventions.

ACKNOWLEDGMENTS

This work was supported by Grant SBE0354420 from the National Science Foundation, Pittsburgh Science of Learning Center (http://www.learnlab.org) and Grant R305B070085 from the Department of Education, Institute of Education Sciences. No endorsement should be inferred. We would like to thank Brian Ross and Jose Mestre for their many helpful comments and suggestions on the paper.

REFERENCES

Ames, C. (1992). Classrooms: Goals, structures, and student motivations. *Journal of Educational Psychology, 84*(3), 261–271.

Ames, C., & Archer, J. (1988). Achievement goals in the classroom: Students' learning strategies and motivation processes. *Journal of Educational Psychology, 80*(3), 260–267.

Anderson, J. R. (1987). Skill acquisition: Compilation of weak-method problem solutions. *Psychological Review, 94*, 192–210.

Anderson, J. R., Bothell, D., Byrne, M. D., Douglass, S., Lebiere, C., & Qin, Y. (2004). An integrated theory of mind. *Psychological Review, 111*(4), 1036–1060.

Anderson, J. R., Conrad, F. G., & Corbett, A. T. (1989). Skill acquisition and the LISP Tutor. *Cognitive Science, 13*, 467–506.

Anderson, J. R., & Lebiere, C. (1998). *The atomic components of thought.* Mahwah, NJ: Lawrence Erlbaum.

Bandura, A. (1997). *Self-efficacy: The exercise of self-control.* New York: Freeman.

Barnett, S. M., & Ceci, S. J. (2002). When and where do we apply what we learn? A taxonomy for far transfer. *Psychological Bulletin, 128*(4), 612–637.

Bassok, M. (1990). Transfer of domain-specific problem-solving procedures. *Journal of Experimental Psychology: Learning, Memory, and Cognition, 16*, 522–533.

Belenky, D. M., & Nokes, T. J. (2009). Motivation and transfer: The role of achievement goals in preparation for future learning. *Proceedings of the Thirty-First Annual Conference of the Cognitive Science Society* (pp. 1163–1168). Netherlands: Amsterdam, Cognitive Science Society.

Belenky, D. M., & Nokes, T. J. (submitted). Motivation and transfer: The role of mastery-approach goals in preparation for future learning. *Journal of the Learning Sciences.*

Bereby-Meyer, Y., & Kaplan, A. (2005). Motivational influences on transfer of problem-solving strategies. *Contemporary Educational Psychology, 30*, 1–22.

Bereby-Meyer, Y., Moran, S., & Unger-Aviram, E. (2004). When performance goals deter performance: Transfer of skills in integrative negotiation. *Journal of Organizational Behavior and Human Decision Processes, 93*, 142–154.

Blanchette, I., & Richards, A. (2010). The influence of affect on higher level cognition: A review of research on interpretation, judgement, decision making, and reasoning. *Cognition and Emotion, 24*, 561–595.

Bransford, J. D., & Schwartz, D. L. (1999). Rethinking transfer: A simple proposal with multiple implications. *Review of Research in Education, 24,* 61–100.

Brown, J. S., Collins, A., & Duguid, P. (1989). Situated cognition and the culture of learning. *Educational Researcher, 18,* 32–42.

Collins, A. M., & Quillian, M. R. (1969). Retrieval time from semantic memory. *Journal of Verbal Learning and Verbal Behavior, 8*(2), 240–247.

Covington, M. V. (2000). Goal theory, motivation, and school achievement: An integrative review. *Annual Review of Psychology, 51,* 171–200.

Dufresne, R., Mestre, J., Thaden-Koch, T., Gerace, W., & Leonard, W. (2005). Knowledge representation and coordination in the transfer process. In J. Mestre (Ed.), *Transfer of learning from a modern multidisciplinary perspective* (pp. 155–215). Greenwich, CT: Information Age Publishing.

Dweck, C. S. (1986). Motivational processes affecting learning. *American Psychologist, 41,* 1040–1048.

Eccles, J. S., & Wigfield, A. (2002). *Development of achievement motivation.* San Diego, CA: Academic Press.

Elliot, A. J., & Church, M. A. (1997). A hierarchical model of approach and avoidance achievement motivation. *Journal of Personality and Social Psychology, 72,* 218–232.

Elliot, A. J. & Dweck, C. S. (Eds.) (2005). Competence and motivation: Competence as the core of achievement motivation. In *Handbook of competence and motivation* (pp. 3-14). New York, NY: The Guilford Press.

Elliot, A. J., & McGregor, H. A. (1999). Test anxiety and the hierarchical model of approach and avoidance achievement motivation. *Journal of Personality and Social Psychology, 76,* 628–644.

Elliot, A. J., & McGregor, H. A. (2001). A 2 × 2 achievement goal framework. *Journal of Personality and Social Psychology, 80*(3), 501–519.

Elliot, A. J., McGregor, H. A., & Gable, S. L. (1999). Achievement goals, study strategies, and exam performance: A mediational analysis. *Journal of Educational Psychology, 91,* 549–563.

Elliot, A. J., & Murayama, K. (2008). On the measurement of achievement goals: Critique, illustration, and application. *Journal of Educational Psychology, 100,* 613–628.

Eysenck, M. W. (1976). Arousal, learning, and memory. *Psychological Bulletin, 83,* 389–404.

Forbus, K. D., Gentner, D., & Law, K. (1995). MAC/FAC: A model of similarity-based retrieval. *Cognitive Science, 19,* 141–205.

Ford, K. J., Smith, E. M., Weissbein, D. A., Gully, S. M., & Salas, S. (1998). Relationships of goal orientation, metacognitive activity, and practice strategies with learning outcomes and transfer. *Journal of Applied Psychology, 83*(2), 218–233.

Gentner, D. (1983). Structure-mapping: A theoretical framework for analogy. *Cognitive Science, 7,* 155–170.

Gentner, D. (1989). The mechanisms of analogical learning. In S. Vosniadou, and A. Ortony, (Eds.), *Similarity and analogical reasoning* (pp. 199–241). London: Cambridge University Press.

Gentner, D. (1999). Analogy. In R. A. Wilson, and F. C. Keil, (Eds.), *The MIT encyclopedia of the cognitive sciences* (pp. 17–20). Cambridge, MA: MIT Press.

Gick, M. L., & Holyoak, K. J. (1980). Analogical problem solving. *Cognitive Psychology, 12,* 306–355.

Gick, M. L., & Holyoak, K. J. (1983). Schema induction and analogical transfer. *Cognitive Psychology, 15,* 1–38.

Gick, M. L., & Holyoak, K. J. (1987). The cognitive basis of knowledge transfer. In S. M. Cormier, and J. D. Hagman, (Eds.), *Transfer of learning: Contemporary research and applications* (pp. 9–46). Orlando, FL: Academic Press.

Greeno, J. G. (1997). On claims that answer the wrong questions. *Educational Researcher, 26* (1), 5–17.

Greeno, J. G. (1998). The situativity of knowing, learning, and research. *American Psychologist, 53*, 5–26.

Greeno, J. G. (2006). Authoritative, accountable, positioning and connected general knowing: Progressive themes in understanding transfer. *The Journal of the Learning Sciences, 15*, 537–547.

Gruber, H., Law, L., Mandl, H., & Renkl, A. (1995). Situated learning and transfer. In P. Reimann, and H. Spada, (Eds.), *Learning in humans and machines: Towards an interdisciplinary learning science* (pp. 168–188). Oxford, UK: Pergamon Press.

Hammer, D., Elby, A., Scherr, R. E., & Redish, E. F. (2005). Resources, framing, and transfer. In J. Mestre (Ed.), *Transfer of learning from a modern multidisciplinary perspective* (pp. 89–119). Greenwich, CT: Information Age Publishers.

Harackiewicz, J. M., Barron, K. E., Pintrich, P. R., Elliot, A. J., & Thrash, T. M. (2002). Revision of achievement goal theory: Necessary and illuminating. *Journal of Educational Psychology, 94*, 638–645.

Harackiewicz, J. M., Durik, A. M., Barron, K. E., Linnenbrink-Garcia, L., & Tauer, J. M. (2008). The role of achievement goals in the development of interest: Reciprocal relations between achievement goals, interest, and performance. *Journal of Educational Psychology, 100*(1), 105–122.

Hidi, S., & Renninger, K. A. (2006). The four-phase model of interest development. *Educational Psychologist, 41*, 111–127.

Holyoak, K. J., Novick, L. R., & Melz, E. R. (1994). Component processes in analogical transfer: Mapping, pattern completion, and adaptation. In K. J. Holyoak, and J. A. Barden, (Eds.), *Advances in connectionist and neural computation theory volume 2: Analogical connections* (pp. 113–180). Norwood, NJ: Ablex Publishing Company.

Hummel, J. E., & Holyoak, K. J. (2003). A symbolic-connectionist theory of relational inference and generalization. *Psychological Review, 110*, 220–264.

Kieras, D. E., & Bovair, S. (1986). The acquisition of procedures from text: A production system analysis of transfer of training. *Journal of Memory and Language, 25*, 507–524.

Koedinger, K. R., Corbett, A. T., Perfetti, C. & the PSLC. (2010). The Knowledge-Learning-Instruction (KLI) Framework: Toward Bridging the Science-Practice Chasm to Enhance Robust Student Learning. Technical Report: CMU-HCII-10-102. Carnegie Mellon University.

Kruglanski, A. W., & Webster, D. M. (1996). Motivated closing of the mind: "Seizing" and "freezing.". *Psychological Review, 103*(2), 263–283.

Lave, J. (1988). *Cognition in practice.* Cambridge, MA: Cambridge University Press.

Lave, J., & Wenger, E. (1991). *Situated learning: Legitimate peripheral participation.* Cambridge, UK: Cambridge University Press.

Lobato, J. (2006). Alternative perspectives on the transfer of learning: History, issues, and challenges for future research. *The Journal of the Learning Sciences, 15*, 431–449.

Malone, T. W. (1981). Toward a theory of intrinsically motivating instruction. *Cognitive Science, 4*, 333–369.

Malone, T. W., & Lepper, M. R. (1987). Making learning fun: A taxonomy of intrinsic motivation for learning. R. E. Snow, and M. J. Farr, (Eds.), *Aptitude, Learning and Instruction III: Conative and Affective Process Analyses.* Hillsdale, NJ: Erlbaum.

Marshall, S. P. (1995). *Schemas in problem solving.* Cambridge, UK: Cambridge University Press.

Midgley, C., Kaplan, A., & Middleton, M. (2001). Performance-approach goals: Good for what, for whom, under what circumstances, and at what cost? *Journal of Educational Psychology, 93*, 77–86.

Neves, D. M., & Anderson, J. R. (1981). Knowledge compilation: Mechanisms for the automatization of cognitive skills. In J. R. Anderson (Ed.), *Cognitive skills and their acquisition* Hillsdale, NJ: Lawrence Erlbaum.

Nicholls, J. G. (1984). Achievement motivation: Conceptions of ability, subjective experience, task choice, and performance. *Psychological Review, 91*, 328–346.

Nokes, T. J. (2004). Testing three theories of knowledge transfer. In D. Gentner., K. Forbus, and T. Regier, (Eds.), *Proceedings of the Twenty-Sixth Annual Conference of the Cognitive Science Society* (pp. 1029–1034). Mahaw, NJ: Erlbaum.

Nokes, T. J. (2005). An investigation into adaptive shifting in knowledge transfer. In B. Bara., L. Barsalou, and M. Bucciarelli, (Eds.), *Proceedings of the Twenty-Seventh Annual Conference of the Cognitive Science Society* (pp. 1660–1665). Erlbaum: Mahaw, NJ.

Nokes, T. J. (2009). Mechanisms of knowledge transfer. *Thinking & Reasoning, 15*, 1–36.

Nokes, T. J., Mestre, J., & Brookes, D. (submitted). Sense-making as transfer. *Educational Psychologist.*

Nokes, T. J., & Ohlsson, S. (2005). Comparing multiple paths to mastery: What is learned? *Cognitive Science, 29*, 769–796.

Novick, L. R. (1988). Analogical transfer, problem similarity, and expertise. *Journal of Experimental Psychology: Learning, Memory, and Cognition, 14*(3), 510–520.

Ohlsson, S. (1996). Learning from performance errors. *Psychological Review, 103*(2), 241–262.

Ohlsson, S., & Rees, E. (1991). The function of conceptual understanding in the learning of arithmetic procedures. *Cognition and Instruction, 8*, 103–179.

Packer, M. (2001). The problem of transfer, and the sociocultural critique of schooling. *The Journal of the Learning Sciences, 10*(4), 493–514.

Pennington, N., Nicolich, R., & Rahm, J. (1995). Transfer of training between cognitive subskills: Is knowledge use specific? *Cognitive Psychology, 28*, 175–224.

Pintrich, P. R. (1999). The role of motivation in promoting and sustaining self-regulated learning. *International Journal of Educational Research, 31*(6), 459–470.

Pugh, K. J., & Bergin, D. A. (2006). Motivational influences on transfer. *Educational Psychologist, 41*(3), 147–160.

Redish, E. F. (2004). A theoretical framework for physics education research: Modeling student thinking. In E. Redish, and M. Vicentini, (Eds.), *Proceedings of the Enrico Fermi Summer School, Course CLVI* Italian Physical Society.

Reeves, L. M., & Weisberg, W. R. (1994). The role of content and abstract information in analogical transfer. *Psychological Bulletin, 115*, 381–400.

Rogoff, B. (2003). *The cultural nature of human development.* New York: Oxford University Press.

Royer, J. M. (1979). Theories of the transfer of learning. *Educational Psychologist, 14*, 53–69.

Schank, R. C., & Abelson, R. P. (1977). *Scripts, plans, goals, and understanding: An inquiry into human knowledge structures.* Hillsdale, NJ: Lawrence Erlbaum.

Scherr, R. E., & Hammer, D. (2009). Student behavior and epistemological framing: Examples from collaborative active-learning activities in physics. *Cognition and Instruction, 27*(2), 147–174.

Schwartz, D. L., & Bransford, J. D. (1998). A time for telling. *Cognition and Instruction, 16*, 475–522.

Schwartz, D. L., Bransford, J. D., & Sears, D. (2005). Efficiency and innovation in transfer. In J. Mestre (Ed.), *Transfer of learning from a modern multidisciplinary perspective* (pp. 1–51). Greenwich, CT: Information Age Publishers.

Schwartz, D. L., & Martin, T. (2004). Inventing to prepare for future learning: The hidden efficiency of encouraging original student production in statistics instruction. *Cognition and Instruction, 22*, 129–184.

Simon, H. A. (1956). Rational choice and the structure of the environment. *Psychological Review, 63*, 129–138.

Simon, H. A. (1996). *The sciences of the artificial.* Cambridge, MA: The MIT Press.

Singley, M. K., & Anderson, J. R. (1989). *The transfer of cognitive skill.* Cambridge, MA: Harvard University Press.

Somuncuoglu, Y., & Yildirim, A. (1999). Relationship between achievement goal orientations and use of learning strategies. *Journal of Educational Research, 92*(5), 267–277.

Thaden-Koch, T., Dufresne, R., & Mestre, J. (2006). Coordination of knowledge in judging animated motion. *Physical Review E – Special Topics – Physics Education Research, 2*, 020107 11 pages.

Thorndike, E. L., & Woodworth, R. S. (1901). The influence of improvement in one mental function upon the efficiency of other functions. *Psychological Review, 8*, 247–261.

Thorndyke, P. (1984). Applications of schema theory in cognitive research. In J. Anderson, and S. Kosslyn, (Eds.), *Tutorials in learning and memory: Essays in honor of Gordon Bower* (pp. 167–192). San Francisco, CA: W.H. Freeman & Company.

Urdan, T., Ryan, A. M., Anderman, E. M., & Gheen, M. H. (2002). Goals, goal structures, and avoidance behaviors. In C. Midgley (Ed.), *Goals, goal structures, and patterns of adaptive learning* (pp. 55–83). Mahwah, NJ: Erlbaum.

Weiner, B. (1985). An attributional theory of achievement motivation and emotion. *Psychological Review, 92*, 548–573.

CHAPTER FIVE

On the Interplay of Emotion and Cognitive Control: Implications for Enhancing Academic Achievement

Sian L. Beilock *and* Gerardo Ramirez

Contents

Abstract

Whether or not students are able to perform up to their potential in the classroom can be influenced by their perceptions of situational pressures to perform at a high level, their anxiety about succeeding in subjects such as math, and even the awareness of negative academic stereotypes regarding the ability of the gender or racial group to which students belong. In this chapter, we provide an overview of research that has been conducted to date on a diverse set of negative emotion-inducing situations known to influence performance in the classroom. Despite differences in the stressful academic situations that students encounter, we propose that a common set of mechanisms operate to affect performance. We conclude by outlining

Psychology of Learning and Motivation, Volume 55

ISSN 0079-7421, DOI 10.1016/B978-0-12-387691-1.X0001-4

© 2011 Elsevier Inc.

All rights reserved.

work exploring classroom interventions designed to ensure that all students perform at their best in important learning and testing situations.

1. INTRODUCTION

Many students view school as an opportunity to learn and expand their knowledge base. Take a middle school Algebra I class as an example. This class is designed to provide students with basic algebra knowledge and to also give students a foundation for more advanced math they will encounter in the years to come. Of course, sitting in math class not only garners thoughts of learning and achievement in students. For many, school situations also lead to feelings of tension, apprehension, or fear about performing up to the expectations set by the students themselves or the expectations set by others (e.g., parents, teachers, and peers). In other words, learning and performance in school cannot simply be boiled down to acquiring and demonstrating knowledge. Rather, academic performance involves a mix of memory, attention, and cognitive control processes along with motivational and emotional factors.

As an example, think about how a student might go about determining the answer, in his or her head, to a math problem such as "$(32-18) \div 7 = ?$" It involves several steps. First, one must compute the answer to "$32-18 = ?$" Second, one must hold this answer in memory and divide the answer 14 by 7. Although there has been a significant amount of research devoted to investigating the attention, memory, and computational processes that support these types of calculations, less work has addressed how such calculations are impacted by the types of real-world academic situations in which math performance often takes place. How might being in an important testing situation impact performance of the above problem? Or, would working through the problem at the chalkboard as an entire class looks on affect one's success? Finally, what if a female student performed this calculation after being told "everyone knows girls can't do math"?

Although students may be motivated to perform well in such stress-laden situations, these environments often cause students to perform at their worst. The term *choking under pressure* has been used to describe the phenomenon whereby people perform more poorly than expected given their skill level in situations where incentives for optimal performance are maximal and the negative consequences associated with poor performance are high (Beilock & Carr, 2001). The term *stereotype threat* (ST) describes situations in which awareness of a negative stereotype about how one's social group should perform (e.g., "girls can't do math") produces less than optimal execution in group members (Steele, 1997). Finally, the term *math anxiety* describes feelings of tension, apprehension, and fear that some people have when faced with the prospect of performing math (Ashcraft & Kirk, 2001).

Although choking, ST, and math anxiety have all been shown to impact academic performance, these phenomena are often studied in different labs and are largely constrained to separate fields within psychology and education. Nevertheless, many similar conclusions concerning how suboptimal performance arises in academic domains such as math have emerged from their investigation. Our lab is interested in understanding the commonalities among these different phenomena, specifically why they cause performance decrements and for whom poor performance is most likely. Our goal is to leverage this knowledge to devise training regimens, performance strategies, and testing environments to alleviate failure in academic areas such as math.

In this chapter, we bring work together from cognitive psychology, social psychology, developmental psychology, and education in an attempt to understand the interplay of emotion and cognition in education, asking questions about how stressful and emotion-filled academic situations alter the cognitive processes that support performance—processes that, under less-emotion inducing situations, would be readily available for execution. Moreover, we consider implications of the integration of emotion and cognitive control in terms of understanding (a) individual differences in susceptibility to failure and (b) performance sustainability in high-pressure and important situations.

2. Choking Under Pressure

We have all heard the term "choking under pressure" before. In the sports arena, we talk about the "bricks" in basketball when the game-winning free throw is missed. In academics, we refer to "cracking" in important test taking situations. But what exactly do these terms mean and why does less than optimal performance occur—especially when incentives for optimal performance are maximal?

The desire to perform as well as possible in situations with a high degree of personally felt importance is thought to create performance pressure. However, despite the fact that performance pressure often results from aspirations to function at one's best, pressure-packed situations are where suboptimal skill execution may be most visible. The term *choking under pressure* has been used to describe this phenomenon. As mentioned above, choking is defined as performing more poorly than expected given one's skill level, and is thought to occur in many different tasks.

Some of the first attempts to account for unwanted skill decrements can be traced back to investigations of the arousal–performance relationship. According to the models of this relationship (often termed drive theories or the Yerkes–Dodson curve), an individual's performance level is determined by one's current level of arousal or "drive." With too little arousal, the basketball player will not have the tools necessary to make the shot. Similarly, with too much arousal, the shot will be missed. Although drive theories have been useful in accounting for some types of performance failures, they fall short in a number of ways. First, drive theories are mainly descriptive in that they link arousal and performance, but do not explain how arousal exerts its impact. Second, within drive theory models, there are often debates concerning how the notion of "arousal" should be conceptualized (e.g., as a physiological construct, emotional construct, or both). Third, there are situations in which certain types of drive theories have trouble accounting for observed behavior. For example, one derivation of drive theory (i.e., social facilitation) predicts that one's dominant response will be exhibited in high arousal or high drive situations. However, this does not always seem to hold when the pressure is on.

2.1. Two mechanisms of performance failure

Building on drive theory accounts of performance failure, more recent work has attempted to understand how pressure changes how one thinks about and attends to the processes involved in skill performance. These accounts are often termed attentional theories. Two main attentional theories have been proposed to explain choking under pressure.

2.1.1. Distraction Theories

First, distraction theories propose that pressure creates a distracting environment that compromises working memory (WM)—a short-term memory system that maintains, in an active state, a limited amount of information relevant to the task at hand (Miyake & Shah, 1999). If the ability of WM to maintain task focus is disrupted, performance may suffer. In essence, distraction-based accounts of skill failure suggest that performance pressure shifts attention from the primary task one is trying to perform (e.g., math problem solving) to irrelevant cues (e.g., worries about the situation and its consequences). Under pressure then, there is not enough of WM's limited resources for both to successfully support primary task performance and to entertain worries about the pressure situation and its consequences. As a result, skill failure ensues.

Although there is evidence that pressure can compromise WM resources, causing failure in tasks that rely heavily on this short-term memory system, not all tasks do rely heavily on WM. For example, well-learned sensorimotor skills, which have been the subject of the majority of choking research in sport (e.g., simple golf putting, baseball batting, and soccer dribbling), are thought to become proceduralized with practice such that they do not require constant attention and control—that is, such skills are not thought to depend heavily on WM at high levels of learning. How then do such skills fail, if not via the consumption of WM resources? A second class of theories, generally known as explicit monitoring theories, have been used to explain such failures.

2.1.2. Explicit Monitoring Theories

Explicit monitoring theories suggest that pressure situations raise self-consciousness and anxiety about performing correctly. This focus on the self is thought to prompt individuals to turn their attention inward on the specific processes of performance in an attempt to exert more explicit monitoring and control than would be applied in a nonpressure situation. For example, a basketball player who makes 85% of his/her free throws in practice may miss the game-winning foul shot because, in order to ensure an optimal outcome, he/she tried to monitor the angle of his/her wrist as he/she shot the ball. This component of performance is not something that our basketball player would normally attend to. And, paradoxically, such attention is thought to disrupt well-learned or proceduralized performance processes that normally run largely outside of conscious awareness.

From the above description of distraction and explicit monitoring theories, one might conclude that performance pressure exerts one kind of impact on cognitive skill performance and another kind of impact on sensorimotor skill performance. It seems more likely, however, that pressure always exerts at least two different effects—it populates WM with worries and it entices the performer to try to pay more attention to step-by-step control, resulting in a double whammy. These two effects may be differentially relevant to performance depending on the attentional demands of the task being performed. If a task depends heavily on WM but does not involve much in the way of proceduralized routines (e.g., difficult and novel math problem solving), then it will suffer from pressure-induced *disruption* of WM, but it will not be harmed by the attempt to focus what attention remains on step-by-step control that is also induced by pressure. Conversely, if a task relies heavily on proceduralized routines but puts little stress on WM (e.g., a well-learned golf putt), then such tasks will suffer from performance pressure because of the *shift* of attention to step-by-step control and not because WM has been disrupted.

In the context of academic performance (and especially mathematical performance), a majority of work supports distraction theories of choking. One reason for this is that many of the skills performed in the classroom require heavy demands on WM.

To explore how situation–induced pressures undermine math performance, we have created a high–stakes testing environment in our laboratory, using Gauss's (1801, as cited by Bogomolny, 1996) *modular arithmetic* (MA) as a test bed. MA involves judging the truth value of equations [e.g., $34 \equiv 18(\text{mod}4)$]. One way to solve these problems is to subtract the middle from the first number ("34–18"). This difference is then divided by the last number ("16 ÷ 4"). If the dividend is a whole number (here, 4), the statement is *true*. Problems with remainders are *false*. Problem validity can also be determined by dividing the first two numbers by the mod number. If the same remainder is obtained (here, 34 ÷ 4 and 18 ÷ 4 both have remainders of 2), the equation is *true*.

It is important to understand how pressure compromises tasks like MA because careless mistakes on the types of computations inherent in MA contribute to less than optimal performance in testing situations. Moreover, even problems that go beyond the conceptual demands of MA often require mental calculations similar to those needed to compute MA answers. Thus, understanding how stressful situations compromise even relatively simple calculations will shed light on unwanted performance decrements.

In an initial study (Beilock, Kulp, Holt, & Carr, 2004), we asked students to solve MA problems that varied as a function of whether the first problem step involved large numbers (>10) and borrow operations ("45–27"). Larger numbers and borrow operations involve longer sequences of steps and require maintenance of more intermediate products, placing greater demands on WM (Imbo & Vandierendonck, 2007). If pressure impacts WM, then performance should be more likely to decline on high WM–demanding [e.g., $51 \equiv 29(\text{mod}4)$] in comparison to low WM–demanding [e.g., $6 \equiv 3(\text{mod}3)$] problems.

To test this, some individuals (assigned to a low–pressure group) were simply told to try their best. Others were given a scenario based on common pressures (e.g., monetary incentives, peer pressure, and social evaluation). Participants were informed that if they performed at a high level on the math task, they would receive some money. Participants were also told that this award was dependent on both themselves and a partner they were paired with performing well—a "team effort." Participants were then informed that their partner had completed the experiment and improved. Thus, the current participant was entirely responsible for winning (or losing) the money. Participants were also told that their performance would be videotaped and that teachers/students would watch the tapes.

Not surprisingly, this scenario increased participants' reported feelings of pressure and reduced math accuracy relative to individuals in the low–pressure group. However, performance decrements were limited to problems highest in WM demands. This suggests that performance pressure exerts its impact by taxing WM resources necessary for demanding computations.

Although this work implicates WM in math failure, it does not tell us what exactly pressure-filled environments do to WM to produce suboptimal performance. As previously mentioned, the *distraction account* suggests that situation-related worries reduce the WM available for performance. If so, then math problems heavily reliant on the resources that worries also co-opt should be most susceptible to failure. Thus far, we have conceptualized WM as a general capacity system—meaning that it supports cognitive operations regardless of the type of information involved. However, there is also work suggesting that certain components of WM may be devoted more so to either verbal processes (e.g., inner speech and thinking) or to visuospatial processes (e.g., holding a visual image in memory; Baddeley & Hitch, 1974). If worries tax verbal components of WM, and math problems can be differentiated by the demands they make on verbal versus visuospatial resources, then performance on problems heavily reliant on verbal resources should be especially compromised under stress. Of course, this does not mean that tasks with spatial demands (e.g., mental rotation) will show no signs of failure (especially if, for example, one concocts visual images of feared alternatives or uses a verbal procedure for solving a spatial task). Rather, if verbal ruminations and worries are a key component of stress-induced failure, then performance decrements should be most pronounced in tasks that depend heavily on WM and especially verbal aspects of this system.

DeCaro, Rotar, Kendra, & Beilock (2010) examined this hypothesis by varying the type of math problems people performed. We were particularly interested in whether performance of math problems that relied more heavily on verbal versus visuospatial resources would be differentially harmed. Although all arithmetic problems involve general WM resources, Trbovich and LeFevre (2003) demonstrated that math problems presented in a horizontal format depend heavily on phonological or verbal resources because individuals verbally maintain problem steps in memory (e.g., repeating them in their head). Math problems presented in a vertical format rely more on visuospatial resources because individuals tend to solve vertical problems in a spatial mental workspace similar to how such problems are solved on paper (see Figure 1a).

If horizontally oriented MA problems recruit verbal resources that vertical problems do not (Figure 1b) and the performance pressure induces an inner monologue of worries that relies heavily on verbal WM, then horizontal problem performance should be more negatively impacted by pressure than vertical problem performance. This is exactly what was found. People under pressure performed more poorly than people in a nonpressure condition. However, this poor performance was limited to horizontal problems heavily reliant on phonological aspects

(a)

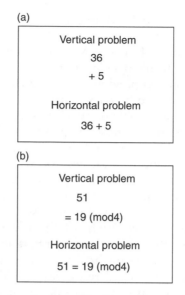

Figure 1   (a) Example of vertically and horizontally oriented arithmetic problems. (b) Example of vertically and horizontally oriented MA problems. Reprinted with permission from DeCaro et al. (2010).

of WM. Performance on vertical problems did not differ as a function of group.

2.2. Individual differences and choking under pressure in math

Establishing a link between WM and math failure not only provides insight into why poor performance occurs but it also hints at important individual differences in susceptibility to failure. Although WM is often portrayed as a general cognitive construct, it is also an individual difference variable—meaning some people have more of this general cognitive capacity than others. The more WM capacity individuals have, the better their performance on academic tasks like problem solving and reasoning (Engle, 2002). Thus, it is important to understand how those who come to the table with more or less of this resource are impacted by the types of high-stakes situations in which math performance often occurs.

To explore this issue, Beilock and Carr (2005) asked individuals lower (Lows) and higher (Highs) in WM to perform MA problems in a low-pressure and a high-pressure test (using the same pressure scenario as above). WM was assessed via measures that capture differences in one's general ability to maintain task-relevant information in the face of less relevant or interfering information (Turner & Engle, 1989). Not surprisingly, higher WM individuals (Highs) outperformed lower WM individuals (Lows) under low-pressure conditions. However, Highs' performance fell to the level of Lows' under pressure. Lows' performance did not suffer under pressure—even though it was not at floor levels to begin with (about 75% correct). Thus, Lows had room to drop.

Why does pressure change the high-level performance of Highs while sparing Lows? To answer this, my colleague and I (Beilock & DeCaro, 2007) examined individuals' perceptions of pressure and their problem solving strategies in low-pressure and high-pressure situations—again, using MA as a test bed. Recall that MA involves judging math equations' truth value. Although one can do this by executing WM-demanding procedures, there are shortcuts that can be employed as well. For example, if one concludes that problems with even numbers are true because dividing two even numbers is associated less often with remainders than dividing two numbers of different parity, this will produce the correct answer on some trials [$34 \equiv 18(\mathrm{mod}4)$] but not always [$52 \equiv 16(\mathrm{mod}8)$]. This shortcut circumvents the demands on WM, but it is not always correct.

If Highs are more likely to rely on demanding procedures (vs. shortcuts) precisely because they have the resources to successfully compute answers in this way—"if you've got it, flaunt it"—then this may be exactly what makes Highs susceptible to failure (i.e., pressure may impact the WM supporting such demanding procedures). In contrast, if Lows rely on shortcuts because they do not have the resources to successfully execute demanding computations, the pressure-induced consumption of WM should not disrupt performance.

Participants performed MA under low-pressure or high-pressure conditions and reported their problem solving strategies and perceptions of pressure during math performance. Under low-pressure conditions, Highs were more likely to use demanding subtraction and division steps to solve MA (vs. simpler shortcuts) and performed more accurately. Under high-pressure conditions, Highs used simpler (and less efficacious) shortcut strategies and their performance suffered. Lows always relied on shortcuts and were not impacted by pressure. Moreover, all individuals, regardless of WM, reported similar feeling under high levels of pressure during the high-pressure test (although see Gimmig, Huguet, Caverni, & Cury (2006), who suggest that Lows and Highs may interpret high-stress situations differently). Thus, Highs appear to be most susceptible to pressure-induced performance decrements precisely because of their reliance on the WM resources that pressure co-opts.

In sum, when individuals find themselves in a high-stakes situation in which there are monetary and social consequences associated with poor performance, these stress-laden environments can negatively impact performance. In the next section, we turn to another type of stressful performance phenomenon, stereotype threat (ST). We review some of the recent research on this phenomenon and show that many similar mechanisms underlie performance failure in choking and ST work.

3. STEREOTYPE THREAT

The fear of confirming an existing negative stereotype about one's social, gender, or ethnic group has been referred to as stereotype threat (*ST*) (Steele & Aronson, 1995). However, ST is not simply a transient concern about how others will see one's performance; it can also shape the quality of task performance of individuals in the stereotyped domain. The term ST was first used by Steele and Aronson, who published a series of studies that attempted to explain the racial achievement gap between African-Americans (AA) and European-Americans (EA). Steele and Aronson reasoned that individuals are motivated to perform well; however, when AA students are called to perform an intellectual task, they must do so against the backdrop of widely held negative expectations and fears of confirming such expectations. Consequently, the researchers suggested that highlighting an existing negative stereotype (whether by direct instruction or subtle cues) can create an added burden of stress that can undermine academic performance and ironically cause students to perform in line with the negative stereotype that they are trying to avoid.

Steele and Aronson (1995) asked a group of AA and EA students to complete a difficult verbal test that was described as problem solving task that was not diagnostic of ability (non-ST condition). However, a separate group of AA and EA students were asked to complete the same difficult verbal test, but it was described as diagnostic of intellectual ability (ST condition). Contrary to societal stereotypes, AA performed equal to EA students when the verbal task was framed as nondiagnostic. But when the test was described as diagnostic of verbal ability, AA students performed significantly worse than their EA peers.

This original study enjoyed wide recognition as it demonstrated how group differences in academic performance between AA and EA could be explained, at least in part, by the performance situation itself rather than inherent differences in ability. Of course, AA are not the only minority group that is stigmatized, which is why researchers wondered whether ST could account for performance difference in other stigmatized groups as well. And indeed, ST has been shown to lead to performance deficits among Latino/a students (Gonzales, Blanton, & Williams, 2002; Schmader & Johns, 2003), women in math (Beilock, Rydell, & McConnell, 2007; Good, Aronson, & Harder, 2008; Inzlicht & Ben-Zeev, 2000; Spencer, Steele, & Quinn, 1999), French Arab students (Chateignier, Dutrevis,

Nugier, & Chekroun, 2009), and students from a lower socioeconomic background (Croizet & Claire, 1998; Desert, Preaux, Jund, 2009).

Importantly, ST should not be thought of as a phenomenon that only individuals from a minority or lower status group experience, since even individuals from a dominant group (e.g., EA males) can suffer from ST in particular contexts. For example, white males perform poorly on a math test when told that their performance will be compared with a group of Asian males (Aronson et al., 1999). Also, men perform more poorly than women at interpreting others' expressive behavior when the task is described as measuring social sensitivity, but not when the task is described as assessing complex information processing (Koenig & Eagly, 2005). This work suggests that ST can be experienced by anybody, provided that they are made aware of an existing negative stereotype about how they are expected to perform in that particular situation.

3.1. Who is most likely to fail under stereotype threat?

It is important to highlight that there are individual differences in the degree to which people are affected by ST—meaning that not all individuals within a group are destined to perform poorly. There are certain factors that have been identified as predictors of ST susceptibility. For example, individuals who strongly value success in a particular domain (e.g., domain identity) typically perform worse under ST than those who do not value the domain (Cadinu, Maass, Frigerio, Impagliazzo, & Latinotti, 2003; Keller, 2007; Levy, 1996; Leyens, Desert, Croizet, & Darcis, 2000; Spencer et al., 1999). Also, the degree to which one identifies with a particular group (e.g., gender identity, and ethnic identity) increases the likelihood that one will perform poorly when faced with a negative group stereotype about performance (Marx, Stapel, & Muller, 2005; Ployhart, Ziegert, & McFarland, 2003; Schmader, 2002). This makes sense as students with low group identity, who place very little value on a stigmatized domain, are likely to feel indifferent about stereotypes that assume how other members within their group should perform. Another major factor that predicts susceptibility to performing poorly under ST is a student's own prior awareness of negative societal expectation of success (what is referred to as stigma consciousness; Pinel, 1999). In other words, it is not merely awareness of a negative expectation of success that produces ST effects but also an activation of what one has previously known themselves (Brown & Lee, 2005; Brown & Pinel, 2003; Pinel, 1999).

3.2. Toward a mechanistic explanation

Work in our lab has primarily contributed to the ST literature by attempting to address the mechanism by which ST impairs performance. Similar to our work on high-pressure situations, we view WM as an essential component of the relationship between stereotypes and performance.

We and others (Cadinu et al., 2003; Schmader, Johns, & Forbes, 2008) posit that ST creates a state of imbalance between one's concept of self and expectation of success that interferes with the WM resources necessary for problem solving success. However, as we have previously discussed, the precise manner by which WM is involved in performance failure depends on the type of activity being performed. We contend that ST can reduce WM availability while at the same time increase attention to performance processes and procedures best left outside WM. Similar to the performance pressure work discussed previously, disruption of WM has been most central to the investigation of poor performance in academic contexts, while enhanced attention helps explain why individuals may perform poorly in proceduralized skills that require very little WM to begin with.

Some of the earliest evidence for the role of WM in ST comes from work that directly implicates WM as an essential element in explaining performance deficits of students under stereotype in the classroom. Schmader and Johns (2003) conducted a study in which female participants were either told that they would complete a task that measures math aptitude between men and women (ST condition) or that they would complete a task for the purpose of obtaining normative data on college students (control condition). In addition, female students in the ST condition completed the study in a room with a male experimenter and two confederates, whereas students in the control condition completed the study in a room with a female experimenter and two female confederates. After receiving the study instructions, all the participants completed a vowel-counting WM test before moving on to the main math task.

As in previous experiments, performance of the women in the ST condition was significantly lower on the math test than that of the women in the control condition. Moreover, performance on the WM test mediated (or accounted for) the effects of the ST manipulation on math accuracy. These results have since been replicated in studies that employ alternative WM tasks (Inzlicht, McKay, & Aronson, 2006; Regner, et al., 2010) and those that use physiological indicators of WM (e.g., heart variability; Croizet et al., 2004).

Additional confirmation of the role of WM in ST comes from work in our own lab showing that ST harms performance for those problems that place a heavy demand on WM (Beilock et al., 2004). In another study, we reasoned that if ST creates worries that impose a demand on the phonological component of WM, then performance for problems that require verbal WM resources should be most susceptible to failure under ST. This is exactly what we have found (Beilock et al., 2007). Thus, similar to choking under pressure, ST appears to exert its impact on a variety of academic tasks via a compromising of WM resources necessary for task performance.

3.3. The developmental approach

Given that we have focused much of our discussion thus far on the impact of negative group stereotypes on the performance of adults, one might wonder when awareness of these stereotypes comes about and the developmental trajectory of their impact. To answer this question, Ambady, Shih, Kim, and Pittinsky (2001) asked young Asian-American girls (in kindergarten through eighth grade) to complete an age-appropriate math task. However, children preceded this task by either coloring a picture of a young child eating with chopsticks (which was meant to prime their ethnic identity) or coloring a picture of a young child playing with a doll (which was meant to prime their gender identity), or coloring a picture of a landscape scene (the control condition). Since Asian-Americans generally share a positive stereotype about their performance in math, the study found that math performance was enhanced when children were given an ethnic identity prime. However, the students' performance was harmed when they were given the gender identity prime. These results are sobering as they indicate that children at a young age have already internalized negative gender stereotypes and their math performance can be impacted by being reminded of such stereotypes. These results also lead one to question where children are getting these stereotypes from.

One source that seems strongly involved in shaping children's ability beliefs and awareness of stereotypes is their parents. For example, parents tend to believe that boys have higher math ability and have greater expectations of success than they do with girls (Eccles, Jacobs, & Harold, 1990). This is also reflected in parents' perceptions that boys have to try less hard in math than girls (Yee & Eccles, 1988). This is despite the fact that gender differences in math performance tend to be nonexistent at the ages of the children for which parents were sampled in these studies.

Recently, we published a study that examined how teachers may also influence young children's gender ability beliefs and math achievement (Beilock, Gunderson, Ramirez, & Levine, 2010). This work was motivated by past research suggesting that teachers also show stereotyped beliefs. For instance, teachers believe that boys like math more than girls (Fennema, Peterson, Carpenter, & Lubinski, 1990) and that boys have greater competency in math than girls (Tiedemann, 2000a, 2000b, 2002). Since the majority of early elementary school teachers are female (>90%; National Education Association, 2003), we wondered if female teachers may be communicating their beliefs about their own insecurities in math to their students (especially to their female students).

Specifically, we speculated that female teachers' insecurities about math (as measured by math anxiety—see later in the chapter) would influence their students' math achievement by way of changing their students' gender abilities beliefs. We also hypothesized that girls should be most influenced by their teachers' insecurities since children emulate same gender behaviors and attitudes (Bussey & Bandura, 1984; Perry & Bussey, 1979). This was exactly what we found. By the end of the school year, teachers' insecurities about math were negatively associated with their girls' math achievement; however, girls gender ability beliefs accounted for (or mediated) this relationship. These effects were not found among boys. This study demonstrates two important points. First, ST and stereotypes in general have a self-perpetuating nature and hence are difficult to put to rest. Second, one way to change a child's negative stereotype may be to provide children with role models that can extinguish widely held negative expectations of success. We will return to this idea in the intervention section later in the chapter.

In the next section, we turn to another factor that impacts academic performance in math, namely, math anxiety. As you will see, there are many commonalities in the mechanisms and sources of math anxiety, ST, and choking under pressure. Such commonalities give us leverage to develop universal interventions that can be used to alleviate poor performance in whatever situation a student might encounter in school.

4. MATH ANXIETY

Thus far, we have discussed two factors that can create a contextually salient form of stress: high-stakes testing situations and reminding students of a personally relevant negative stereotype that challenges their self-concept. However, within the domain of math, some students perform poorly because of prior anxieties they bring with them to the performing table. Specifically, some students are made nervous not by the context of a testing situation as much as the *content* that makes up the test. Math anxiety describes the persistent feelings of tension, apprehension, and fear about performing math (Ashcraft & Ridley, 2005). Math anxiety is important to study, as previous research has shown that students with high math anxiety typically have lower mathematical knowledge, math grades, and perform more poorly on standardized test scores than those with low math anxiety (Ashcraft & Kirk, 2001; Ashcraft & Krause, 2007).

Math anxiety can be particularly problematic to deal with since math anxious individuals need not be put in an evaluative context (that characterizes high-pressure situations) or be reminded of negative societal expectations of failure (which defines ST) to experience stress. In fact, for math anxious individuals, simply the prospect of doing math is enough to elicit a negative emotional response (Ashcraft & Kirk, 2001; Chipman, Krantz, & Silver, 1992; Lyons & Beilock, 2010; Suinn, 1972) that includes increased heartbeat and cortisol (Faust, 1992; Mattarella-Micke, Mateo, Kozak, Foster, & Beilock, 2011), worrisome thoughts (Richardson & Woolfolk, 1980), and an avoidance of situations that involve numerical processing (Krinzinger, Kaufmann, & Willmes, 2009). There are two general interpretations for why higher math anxiety is associated with poor math achievement. The first suggests that highly math anxious students are simply less competent in math to begin with, which leads them to experience a higher degree of stress in this domain (Fennema, 1989). From this account, math anxiety is the *result* of poor proficiency in math and not the *cause* of performance failure. This interpretation is rooted in some truth, since math anxious individuals are typically less motivated in math-related situations than non-math-anxious individuals (Ashcraft & Kirk, 2001) and math anxiety is associated with lower math competence as well as with an avoidance of math classes in general (Hembree, 1990).

However, researchers like Ashcraft and Kirk (2001) contend that math anxiety itself can cause deficits in math problem solving, which can eventually lead to poor math outcomes (Hopko, Ashcraft, Gute, Ruggiero, & Lewis, 1998). Support for this view comes from previous work (Hembree, 1990; see also Kamann & Wong, 1993) showing that counseling interventions designed to treat math anxiety itself (but do not provide math instruction or practice in mathematics) actually increase the posttreatment math achievement scores of math anxious individuals. If math anxiety were simply the by-product of poor math competence, then we would not expect math anxious students receiving anxiety-specific counseling to perform at the level of their low math anxious peers.

Also, other work by Faust, Ashcraft, and Fleck (1996) has shown that while math anxiety can impact how students perform on a timed test with difficult math problems (high-load testing condition), the negative consequences of math anxiety disappear when students are tested in an untimed paper and pencil test (a low-load testing condition). Since paper and pencil tests allow students to reduce the cognitive load associated with math problem solving, this work would suggest that math anxiety may have an online cognitive consequence, which supplements a reduced math competency interpretation of math anxiety.

4.1. A working memory interpretation

By online, we mean that math anxiety has an impact on the *execution* of math problem solving. Specifically, math problem solving situations are thought to encourage an anxiety response among math anxious individuals that disrupts the cognitive processes responsible for math problem solving— namely, WM. Some of the earliest work supporting an online account found that students with high math anxiety took much longer to respond to arithmetic problems with a carry versus no–carry operations than those with low math anxiety (Ashcraft & Faust, 1994; Faust et al., 1996). This is significant because performing a carry operation highly depends on WM (Geary & Widaman, 1992), which led researchers to speculate that math anxiety may be disrupting processes responsible for maintaining superior performance during cognitively demanding math problems.

In a more direct test of this claim, Ashcraft and Kirk (2001) asked a group of college students to solve a series of fairly easy arithmetic problems that varied based on whether they required a carry operation (e.g., 25 + 17) or not (e.g., 23 + 11). Ashcraft and Kirk reasoned that if math anxiety impacts WM processing, then this should be particularly true of problems that require additional mental workload (e.g., arithmetic with a carry operation). However, to really implicate WM as the source of math anxiety failure, they asked students to concurrently solve a secondary task that taxes WM. This secondary task required students to memorize either two (low load) or six (high load) letters as they solved math problems. Their results showed that among students assigned to the two–letter load condition, those with high versus low math anxiety did not differ in amount of errors committed when trying to solve the math problems. This was true in both problems that required carry operation and those that did not. However, among students in the six–letter load condition, those with high math anxiety committed significantly more errors than those with low math anxiety, but these effects were limited to problems with a carry operation.

These results provided strong evidence that while math anxiety may be related to math avoidance in general, it also seems to influence the online execution of math problem solving. Furthermore, math anxiety does not seem to prevent efficient problem solving in all forms of math but is instead particularly detrimental to problems that rely heavily on WM resources (Ashcraft & Kirk, 2001; Faust et al., 1996).

4.2. Math anxiety development

While most studies have concentrated on examining math anxiety in late high school and college populations, there is some work demonstrating that math anxiety is present among both middle (Meece, Wigfield, & Eccles, 1990; Wigfield & Meece, 1988) and primary school students (Krinzinger et al., 2009). For example, Wigfield and Meece asked students as young as sixth grade to fill out a math anxiety questionnaire and an attitude questionnaire that assess students' expectations for success and perceived ability in math. They found that higher math anxiety was associated with reduced perceptions of ability and future expectations of success in mathematics. A similar pattern of results was found in a different study with fourth graders whose math anxiety was shown to be negatively related to mathematics grades and academic ability in math (Chiu & Henry, 1990). Indeed, math anxiety can be *experienced* at every age during schooling (Bush, 1991; Krinzinger et al., 2009; Meece et al., 1990; Suinn, Taylor, & Edwards, 1988; Wigfield & Meece, 1988). This is because math anxiety is thought to originate early in schooling.

One issue that is less clear, however, is whether math anxiety is actually related to math achievement early in elementary school. For instance, Krinzinger et al. (2009) found that young children do indeed posses math anxiety that is negatively associated with how much they like doing math, but they did not find an association between math anxiety and calculation ability. These findings should be alarming nonetheless as levels of math anxiety do not remain stable across schooling but increase with age (Brush, 1981; Meece, 1981). Therefore, even though it is unclear whether math anxiety is associated with math achievement early in elementary school, it seems highly likely that math anxiety will eventually emerge as a source of math difficulty in a child's academic career. Moreover, as children advance in schooling, math anxiety can begin to deter students from taking advanced elective courses in mathematics that would better prepare them for a college career.

Understanding the early emergence of math anxiety is critical as early interventions may be able to deter a pattern of math avoidance and change children's attitudes toward math during an age when children's attitudes are malleable (Tobias, 1995; Townsend & Wilton, 2003). For this reason, we conducted our own investigation of math anxiety among first and second grade children (Ramirez, Gunderson, Levine, & Beilock, 2009). As with previous research, we were interested in investigating if math anxiety is related to young children's math achievement. However, we also wanted to investigate this relationship as a function of the WM, which, similar to the choking and ST phenomena, seems critical in understanding performance.

We first constructed an age appropriate measure of math anxiety (Child Math Anxiety Questionnaire (CMAQ)), which we adapted from a previously published measure for middle school children (MARS-E—Suinn et al., 1988) (see Figure 2).

We began by measuring children's math anxiety. A few days later, we returned to test children's WM using the total digit span task that is a composite of the forward and backward span tests of the *Wechsler Intelligence Scale for Children*—third edition (WISC-III) (Wechsler, 1991). We also tested children's math achievement and reading achievement using the *Woodcock–Johnson III Applied Problems Subtest* (Woodcock, McGrew, & Mather, 2001).

Replicating past work with adults (Beilock & Carr, 2005), we found that math anxiety was indeed negatively related to math achievement, but only for those children with high WM (Highs). Importantly, we

Figure 2 A representation of the smiley scale slider that was used to measure children's responses to the CMAQ (Ramirez et al., 2009).

found that our measure of math anxiety was not related to reading achievement.

One way to understand our results is to recognize that problem solving strategies are quite different among children with high versus low WM (Barrouillet & Lépine, 2005; Geary, Hoard, Byrd-Craven, & DeSoto, 2004; Imbo & Vandierendonck, 2007) and that strategies that are advantageous in nonanxious populations can backfire on anxious ones. For example, low WM children typically rely on less sophisticated strategies such as finger and verbal counting, while high WM children show a greater reliance on more sophisticated strategies such as direct retrieval (Barrouillet & Lépine, 2005). However, retrieval strategies are not consistently used until the fourth grade upward (Ashcraft, 1982; Geary et al., 2004) when children have had the experience of using the repeated algorithms that build up strong problem–answer associations in memory (Siegler & Shrager, 1984). Prior to the fourth grade, children who use a retrieval strategy are often more successful than those who do not, but they must use this strategy in the face of ongoing interference from competing answers (Barrouillet & Lépine, 2005).

Hence, it is possible that math anxiety impacts the efficacy with which high WMs (or Highs) use retrieval strategies. Math anxiety may make high WM children more prone to retrieval interference, resulting in slower, less efficient, and error-prone retrieval processes (Barrouillet & Lépine, 2005). Math anxiety may also encourage high WMs to adopt unsuccessful backup strategies for retrieval, such as guessing (Beilock & DeCaro, 2007). Of course, since we did not ask children to report their problem solving strategies, this is speculation at present. However, as mentioned above, our previous work with adults examining the impact of performance pressure on the problem solving strategies of high versus low WM students supports this interpretation (Beilock & Carr, 2005; Beilock & DeCaro, 2007).

4.3. What gives rise to math anxiety?

Having shown that math anxiety is not only present at a young age (Krinzingeret al., 2009) but is also associated with poor performance in math (Ramirez et al., 2009), it seems imperative to examine the developmental origins of math anxiety and negative math attitudes. This is because children do not just pick up attitudes from thin air. Negative attitudes toward mathematics are likely driven by cultural and educational factors that have a long-term and consistent presence in a child's academic and emotional development (Tiedemann, 2000b; Yee & Eccles, 1988).

Take, for instance, the influence that a parent's own attitude has on their children's performance. Parental attitudes have been shown to predict student's math attitudes much better than their children's own past math achievement (Eccles, et al., 1990; Midgley, Feldlaufer, & Eccles, 1989; Simpkins, Davis-Kean, & Eccles, 2006; Yee & Eccles, 1988). While parents are a consistent influence in a child's life, teachers and the classroom environment also likely play an important role in shaping how a child approaches math. Indeed, when math anxious students are asked to speculate on the source of their math anxiety, they typically link their fear of math to a particular elementary teacher who responded angrily when he/she asked for help, seemed insensitive toward their struggle with math (Jackson & Leffingwell, 1999), or who embarrassed them in front of their peers for not being able to complete a math problem (Chapline, 1980; Chavez & Widmer, 1982; Wood, 1988). Fiore (1999) referred to this teacher response as math abuse (as cited by Brady & Bowd, 2005). It is easy to imagine why math abuse would cause students to develop math anxiety at a young age. What is not so clear is the source of such abuse and insensitivity.

One explanation is that early elementary school teachers are themselves anxious about math and that these negative feelings about math are passed onto their students (Beilock et al., 2010; Harper & Daane, 1998; Jackson & Leffingwell, 1999; Vinson, 2001; Wood, 1988). This explanation seems rational in light of the research findings suggesting that elementary education majors (who will become elementary teachers) have the highest levels of math anxiety of any college major (Hembree, 1990; Kelly & Tomhave, 1985; Nisbet, 1991; Trujillo & Hadfield, 1999; Watson, 1987). As discussed in the ST section, in a recently published study, we showed that teachers may pass on their math insecurities to their students (Beilock et al., 2010).

Of course, it is likely that there exist a variety of pedagogical methods by which teachers can transmit their math anxiety. After all, past studies have shown that math anxiety is positively related to feelings of apprehension at the prospect of teaching math (Brady & Bowd, 2005) and negatively related to teachers' perception of their ability to teach math effectively (Swars, Daane, & Giesen, 2010; Wenta, 2000). This might help explain why elementary school teachers who score high on a measure of mathematics anxiety have been found to spend less time planning mathematics lessons and use mathematics instruction time for non-mathematics-related activities more often than their less math anxious colleagues (Swetman, Munday, & Windham, 1993).

Feelings of apprehension about teaching math may also force teachers to entertain alternative answers to a lesser degree (Ball, 1990), spend less time in continued question and discussion after receiving a correct answer from a student (defined as *extended discourse*; Schleppenbach, Perry, Miller, Sims, & Fang, 2007), be more focused on expected responses and less likely to attend to student questions (Stigler, Fernandez, & Yoshida, 1996), and have high expectations of success but do little to provide motivational support (Turner et al., 2001). Avoidance strategies like those outlined above are a quite common experience among math anxious individuals (Brady & Bowd, 2005; Jackson & Leffingwell, 1999). In fact, in one case, a student reported that the teacher gave him or her a passing grade "on the condition that they refrain from taking further mathematics courses" (Brady & Bowd, 2005, p. 34). Such avoidance strategies at the hands of math anxious teachers can wreck havoc on a student's math competency and lead students to experience stress in future situations that involve math. It is no wonder that math avoidance is a hallmark of students with math anxiety (Ashcraft & Kirk, 2001; Hembree, 1990).

Though the impact of math anxiety can be far reaching, the silver lining in the research outlined above is that it allows researchers to identify the precise ways in which teachers and others may pass on their insecurities about math to children. Such knowledge is imperative for the development of effective strategies that will help teachers, students and others stave off the negative effects of math anxiety.

5. Bringing It All Together to Alleviate Suboptimal Performance in the Classroom

Having outlined the mechanisms and consequences associated with poor performance in high-pressure situations, math anxiety, and ST, one big question remains: What can we do with this knowledge to thwart poor performance?

5.1. Interventions reducing the burden of high-pressure situations and math anxiety

We and others have targeted worries associated with stressful situations as one way to alleviate poor performance (DeCaro et al., 2010; Kamann & Wong, 1993; Park, Ramirez, & Beilock, 2011; Ramirez & Beilock, 2011). We reasoned that if worries about the situation and its consequences co-opt the WM needed for task performance, then interventions that serve to alleviate such worries may help boost performance.

To do this, we (Ramirez & Beilock, 2011) turned to an effective therapeutic technique in the clinical literature termed expressive writing in which individuals are asked to repeatedly write about a traumatic or emotional experience over the course of many weeks. Expressive writing has been shown to work as a powerful technique for improving physical and psychological health (Smyth, 1998). More importantly, previous research has also shown that expressive writing can be quite effective at decreasing ruminations and increasing WM (Joormann & Tran, 2009; Klein & Boals, 2001). Hence, we reasoned that if expressive writing is an effective technique for reducing worries in a clinical domain, then giving students the opportunity to express their thoughts prior to a math exam might alleviate worries and prevent choking under pressure.

To test this, we asked students across two laboratory studies to complete a baseline math test in a low-pressure situation. After completing this initial math pretest, students were given a set of instructions designed to put them in a high-pressure environment. As mentioned earlier in the chapter (Beilock & Carr, 2005), the high-pressure scenario consisted of a monetary incentive, peer pressure, and social evaluation. Students then took another math test. However, before this second pressure-filled math test, students were asked to either expressively write, write about their previous day in an unemotional manner, or sit quietly (control group) for 10 min.

Students who were asked to expressively write were told to "write as openly as possible about their thoughts and feelings regarding the math problems they were about to perform," while those who were asked to write about an unrelated event were told to "write about their previous day in an unemotional, factual manner." Control students were simply told to sit quietly, while the experimenter retrieved some materials that would be used in a later portion of the experiment. After the 10-min period, we asked all the students to complete the pressure-filled math posttest.

We found that students who wrote about the their previous day in an unemotional manner or sat quietly for 10 min "choked" under pressure— that is, their accuracy in the posttest was significantly lower than their accuracy in the pretest. However, the students who were allowed to express their thoughts and concerns actually improved their performance in the posttest relative to the pretest.

If it is indeed true that expressive writing can aid students by reducing the impact of worries on performance, then students who are most prone to worry during math exams (math anxious students) and exams in general (test anxious students) should benefit the most from expressive writing. We investigated this in a series of follow-up studies. Specifically, we invited individuals with both high and low math anxiety to complete a math test (Park, Ramirez, & Beilock, 2011). We found that among students who sat quietly for 10 min before a math exam, those with high math anxiety performed significantly worse than students with low math anxiety. However, among students who engaged in our expressive writing manipulation for a 10-min period, those with high math anxiety performed comparable to those students with low math anxiety.

We have also taken our intervention into the school setting where, in two separate studies, we measured students test anxiety 6 weeks prior to their final biology exam (Ramirez & Beilock, 2011). Ten minutes prior to their final biology exam, we asked students to either expressively write or sit quietly. Our results showed that while test anxiety was negatively related to final exam performance among control students (who did not write), this association was not present among those who expressively wrote prior to taking their final exam. These results suggest that expressive writing can help stave off the effects of both math anxiety and general test anxiety.

Yet another way to thwart the negative impact of performance worries is to encourage students to talk out loud their problem solving procedure as they complete a difficult math exam. We (DeCaro et al., 2010) reasoned that explicitly directing WM resources toward the step-by-step execution of the math problems can prevent negative worries from disrupting the WM that is key to solving difficult math problems.

To test this, students were given a math pretest in a low-pressure practice situation. Students then completed a math posttest after being given our high-pressure scenario. Prior to the posttest, students were asked to either solve the problems quietly or say out loud their problem solving procedure. As predicted, students who were instructed to work on the problems quietly performed worse in the posttest relative to the pretest. But students who talked through the problem steps performed at the same level in the posttest as they did in the pretest.

Thus, stopping the ruminative process by means of writing or redirecting the WM to problem procedures seem to be quite effective at ensuring that stressful situations do not impact academic test performance. While some of these interventions have not been directly tested among math anxious students or those experiencing ST, given the similarities in the mechanisms of failure across these varied phenomena, we speculate that these interventions will prove useful in a variety of situations.

It is important to note that though our work specifically focused on protecting students from the harmful effects of performance-related worries, we would not advocate that these interventions are replacements for the more important task of changing the teaching practices and math anxiety of teachers and parents. This seems particularly important considering previous work that suggests that teachers can pass on their insecurities about math onto their students. Hence, reducing math anxiety at the teacher level should have a "trickle down" effect as well as positive impact on student learning.

The good news is that teachers are willing to set aside their fears regarding math to improve their knowledge and teaching practices (Trujillo & Hadfield, 1999) and there are a number of studies that suggest effective ways to treat math anxiety. Some studies have shown that interventions designed to treat the affective component of math anxiety (feelings of dread and nervous reactions) can be quite successful at reducing the math anxiety that adults experience—especially in education settings (Hendel & Davis, 1978; Hoy & Woolfolk, 1990). Variations of systematic desensitization treatments (i.e., walking patients through imagined encounters with stressors and providing patients with relaxation techniques) have also consistently been found to be effective at reducing math anxiety (Foss & Hadfield, 1993; Schneider & Nevid, 1993; Walter & Jeffrey, 1993; Zettle, 2003). Though the majority of these studies were conducted in adult populations, we speculate that these treatments could be applied toward treating math anxiety in children as well.

In addition, previous work suggests that exercises combining brief therapeutic interventions and math training may be the most effective at reducing math anxiety in teachers (Hembree, 1990). The benefits of such interventions should be particularly useful in helping math anxious teachers develop more confidence in their ability to teach math (Swars et al., 2010) which could thus change the instructional practices that make students math anxious (Battista, 1994; Chapline & Newman, 1984; Sovchik, Meconi, & Steiner, 1983; Troutman, 1978). For example, past work has shown that providing teachers with pedagogical workshops that encourage teachers to teach beyond simple algorithms and engage in extended discourse can change the attitude and problem solving approach that their own students hold toward mathematics (Simon & Schifter, 1993). Other work has shown that providing teachers with professional development centered on spatial knowledge and problem solving lessens teachers' spatial anxiety across the school year and improves their students' spatial learning (Krakowski, Ratliff, Levine, & Gomez, 2010). We speculate that these types of professional development activities are likely to work with math as well.

5.2. Interventions for reducing stereotype threat

Considering the wide interest that stereotype research has enjoyed, it should come as no surprise that a variety of recommendations for improving how students perform under ST have been put forth. Below we outline some interventions that are aimed specifically at reducing the impact of negative self-relevant stereotypes.

If highlighting an existing self-relevant stereotype is the catalyst to creating a ST environment, then eliminating the practice of reporting demographic information (e.g., personal information such as sex, racial identity, and SES) prior to a test should prevent students from dwelling on negative expectations of success. Interestingly, this assumption has actually been tested by Danaher and Crandall (2008) who reanalyzed data collected by Stricker and Ward (2004) in which students were asked to report demographic information either before or after taking a standardized test. Using less conservative decision criteria, Dahaner and Crandall were able to show that soliciting identity information at the conclusion rather than at the opening of a test reduced the difference in how men and women performed by 33%. Such a finding highlights the profound impact that existing negative stereotypes can have on high-stakes test performance.

However, for many students, such test-relevant interventions may be too late as they may enter the testing situation with a history of underperforming. It is for this reason that Cohen et al. (Cohen, Garcia, Apfel, & Master, 2006; Cohen, Garcia, Purdie-Vaughns, Apfel, & Brzustoski, 2009) were interested in finding an efficient way to increase the self-integrity of academically stigmatized students across the school year. To do this, Cohen et al. conducted two field studies where roughly half of the students were asked to affirm the values that were most important to them and write an essay that explained why these values were important to them (self-affirmation condition). The other half of students were asked to indicate their values they deemed least important to them and write an essay that expressed why those values might be important to others (control condition). This intervention was administered at the beginning of the school year and it took only 15 min to complete. The authors found that African-American students in the self-affirmation condition actually performed .3 grade points better during the semester than those in the control condition. These effects were not found among EA students.

Interestingly, these effects were also long lasting, as a follow-up study showed that the AA students assigned to the self-affirmation condition continued showing superior performance even 2 years after the initial study (Cohen et al., 2009). Since we have previously discussed how the consequences of ST are not limited to AA, it is important to point out that neither are the interventions that are meant to reduce ST. In subsequent studies using similar methodology, researchers have shown that self-affirmation exercises can reduce the gender gap in STEM disciplines as well (Miyaki et al., 2010). These results suggest that while ST may have far-reaching consequences on intellectual achievement, there exist simple strategies to reduce the psychological burden of negative societal stereotypes.

The work presented above suggests that the degree to which students are affected by ST can be reduced by moving the specific period when students report demographic information in a high-stakes exam (e.g., after the exam rather than before) and encouraging students to self-affirm their values at the beginning of the school year as a way of keeping negative societal expectations at bay. The impact of negative stereotypes can also be reduced by changing how students identify themselves.

Individuals have multiple social identities that are sometimes associated with competing expectations of success (Rydell, McConnell, & Beilock, 2009). One early study that attempted to investigate the effect of competing identities looked at Asian-American females who share a negatively stereotyped gender identity ("women") and a positively stereotyped ethnic identity ("Asian"; Shih, Pittinsky, & Ambady, 1999). Shih et al. asked Asian-American female students to complete a math task after being asked to respond to a survey that was meant to highlight their gender identity, ethnic identity, or neither. Their results showed that while students performed poorly when their gender identity was highlighted, they performed moderately when no identity was highlighted and performed the best when their ethnic identity was highlighted. Encouraging students to look at themselves beyond their stigmatized status seems to hold promise in helping students maintain good performance. However, Shih's study raises the question: What would happen if both identities were highlighted (as is often common in real-world academic contexts)?

We (Rydell et al., 2009) addressed this question in a study that explored whether we could deemphasize contextually threatening situations by highlighting positive identities concurrently. We found that while reminding female students of their gender before taking a math test can cause poor performance, reminding female students about their gender in combination with their status as high-achieving college students can disarm the negative consequences of ST. Indeed, other work has also shown that taking a more complex view of oneself (by creating an elaborate concept map of oneself) can encourage students to see themselves beyond stereotypes and ensure that students perform at their best (Gresky, Ten Eyck, Lord, & McIntyre, 2005).

Another route by which to influence ability beliefs and change how students perform under threat is to provide strong role models that run counter to stereotypes (Dasgupta & Asgari, 2004; McIntyre, Paulson, & Lord, 2003; McIntyre et al., 2005). For example, Marx and Roman (2002) showed that women perform just as well as men when a test is administered by a female proctor but not when a test is administered by a male proctor. Importantly, they also found that the students' perceptions of how successful the female proctor was in mathematics impacted performance, such that female proctors had a more positive impact on women's math performance if the students perceived these proctors to be highly competent in math.

A series of naturalistic experiments further demonstrate the power of strong role models. In one study, researchers wondered whether exposure to female professors in a math and science course might influence the STEM achievement of undergraduate women (Carrell, Page, & West, 2009). To test this, researchers tracked a group of men and women in the U.S. Air Force Academy who were randomly assigned to math and science classes that varied only on one factor—the gender of the professor. Their results showed that professor's gender had a powerful effect on a number of outcome variables for female students, including class performance, likelihood of taking future courses in math and science, and likelihood of pursuing a degree in a STEM field (Carrell, Page & West, 2009). These results were not found among male students who, presumably, do not encounter negative societal expectations of success in math and science.

6. CONCLUSION

The way in which emotional factors combine with memory and attention processes to produce skilled performance is of fundamental importance to the understanding of human cognition. Yet, it is only recently that the interplay of emotion and cognitive control has received much attention in human performance research. Findings from this emerging area suggest that high-pressure or negative emotion-inducing situations can fundamentally alter skilled performance—preventing or inhibiting the recruitment of the appropriate cognitive resources necessary for optimal skill execution. Moreover, these types of unwanted skill failures are often most likely to occur for those with the most to lose. In terms of minorities (e.g., AA in the classroom) or underrepresented groups (e.g., women in math), for example, just being aware of a negative performance stereotype concerning how one's social group should perform can inhibit performance in stereotype-relevant skill domains.

In this chapter, we bring work together from cognitive psychology, social psychology, developmental psychology, and education in an attempt to understand the interplay of emotion and cognition in education, asking questions about how a variety of performance phenomena (from choking under pressure to ST to math anxiety) alter the cognitive processes that support performance—processes that under less emotion-inducing situations would be readily available for execution. Though the phenomena we describe in this chapter originate from different sources, they share common cognitive mechanisms by which poor performance occurs. Knowledge of how a diverse set of stressful academic situations impacts performance is imperative for designing effective performance environments that ensure that all students perform up to their potential in school.

REFERENCES

Ambady, N., Shih, M., Kim, A., & Pittinsky, T. L. (2001). Stereotype susceptibility in children: Effects of identity activation on quantitative performance. *Psychological Science, 12*(5), 385–390.

Aronson, J., Lustina, M. J., Good, C., Keough, K., Steele, C. M., & Brown, J. (1999). When White men can't do math: Necessary and sufficient factors in stereotype threat. *Journal of Experimental Social Psychology, 35*(1), 29–46.

Ashcraft, M. H. (1982). The development of cognitive arithmetic: A chronometric approach. *Developmental Review, 2*(3), 213–236.

Ashcraft, M. H., & Faust, M. W. (1994). Mathematics anxiety and mental arithmetic performance: An exploratory investigation. *Cognition and Emotion, 8*(2), 97–125.

Ashcraft, M. H., & Kirk, E. P. (2001). The relationships among working memory, math anxiety, and performance. *Journal of Experimental Psychology: General, 130*(2), 224–237.

Ashcraft, M. H., & Krause, J. A. (2007). Working memory, math performance, and math anxiety. *Psychonomic Bulletin & Review, 14*(2), 243–248.

Ashcraft, M. H., & Ridley, K. S. (2005). Math anxiety and its cognitive consequences: A tutorial review. In J. I. D. Campbell ed.), (pp. 315–327)). New York: Psychology Press.

Baddeley, A. D., & Hitch, G. (1974). Working memory. In G. A. Bower ed.), (pp. 647–667). New York: Academic Press.

Ball, D. L. (1990). The mathematical understandings that prospective teachers bring to teacher education. *The Elementary School Journal, 90*(4), 449–466.

Barrouillet, P., & Lépine, P. (2005). Working memory and children's use of retrieval to solve addition problems. *Journal of Experimental Child Psychology, 91*(3), 183–204.

Battista, M. T. (1994). Teacher beliefs and the reform movement in mathematics education. *Phi Delta Kappan, 75*, 462–470.

Beilock, S. L., & Carr, T. H. (2001). On the fragility of skilled performance: What governs choking under pressure? *Journal of Experimental Psychology: General, 130*(4), 701–725.

Beilock, S. L., & Carr, T. H. (2005). When high-powered people fail: Working memory and "choking under pressure" in math. *Psychological Science, 16*(2), 101–105.

Beilock, S. L., & DeCaro, M. S. (2007). From poor performance to success under stress: Working memory, strategy selection, and mathematical problem solving under pressure. *Journal of Experimental Psychology: Learning, Memory, & Cognition, 33*(6), 983–998.

Beilock, S. L., Gunderson, E. A., Ramirez, G., & Levine, S. C. (2010). Female teachers' math anxiety affects girls' math achievement. *Proceedings of the National Academy of Sciences, 107*(5), 1060–1063.

Beilock, S. L., Kulp, C. A., Holt, L. E., & Carr, T. H. (2004). More on the fragility of performance: Choking under pressure in mathematical problem solving. *Journal of Experimental Psychology: General, 133*(4), 584–600.

Beilock, S. L., Rydell, R. J., & McConnell, A. R. (2007). Stereotype threat and working memory: Mechanisms, alleviation, and spill over. *Journal of Experimental Psychology: General, 136*(2), 256–276.

Bogomolny, A. (1996). Modular arithmetic. Retrieved March 1, 2000, from: http://www.cut-the-knot.com/blue/Modulo.shtml.

Brady, P., & Bowd, A. (2005). Mathematics anxiety, prior experience and confidence to teach mathematics among pre-service education students. *Teachers and Teaching: Theory and Practice, 11*(1), 37–46.

Brown, R. P., & Lee, M. N. (2005). Stigma consciousness and the race gap in college academic achievement. *Self & Identity, 4*(2), 149–157.

Brown, R. P., & Pinel, E. C. (2003). Stigma on my mind: Individual differences in the experience of stereotype threat. *Journal of Experimental Social Psychology, 39*(6), 626–633.

Brush, L. R. (1981). Some thoughts for teachers on mathematics anxiety. *Arithmetic Teacher, 29*(4), 37–39.

Bush, W. S. (1991). Factors related to changes in elementary students' mathematics anxiety. *Focus on Learning Problems in Mathematics, 13*(2), 3343.

Bussey, K., & Bandura, A. (1984). Influence of gender constancy and social power on sex-linked modeling. *Journal of Personality and Social Psychology, 47*(6), 1292–1302.

Cadinu, M., Maass, A., Frigerio, S., Impagliazzo, L., & Latinotti, S. (2003). Stereotype threat: The effect of expectancy on performance. *European Journal of Social Psychology, 33* (2), 267–285.

Cadinu, M., Maass, A., Rosabianca, A., & Kiesner, J. (2005). Why do women underperform under stereotype threat? Evidence for the role of negative thinking. *Psychological Science, 16*(7), 572–578.

Carrell, S. E., Page, M. E., & West, J. W. (2009). Sex and science: How professor gender perpetuates the gender gap. *Quarterly Journal of Economics, 125*, 1101–1144.

Chapline, E. B. (1980). TEAM: Program development and evaluation. Paper presented at the meeting of the American Educational Research Association, Boston, MA.

Chateignier, C., Dutrevis, M., Nugier, A., & Chekroun, P. (2009). French-Arab students and verbal intellectual performance: Do they really suffer from a negative intellectual stereotype? *European Journal of Psychology of Education, 24*(2), 219–234.

Chavez, A., & Widmer, C. C. (1982). Math anxiety: Elementary teachers speak for themselves. *Educational Leadership, 39*(5), 387–388.

Chipman, S. F., Krantz, D. H., & Silver, R. (1992). Mathematics anxiety and science careers among able college women. *Psychological Science, 3*(5), 292–295.

Chiu, L. -H., & Henry, L. L. (1990). The development and validation of the mathematics anxiety rating for children. *Journal of Measurement and Evaluation in Counseling and Development, 23*(3), 121–212.

Cohen, G. L., Garcia, J., Apfel, N., & Master, A. (2006). Reducing the racial achievement gap: A social-psychological intervention. *Science, 313*(5791), 1307–1310.

Cohen, G. L., Garcia, J., Purdie-Vaughns, V., Apfel, A., & Brzustoski, P. (2009). Recursive processes in self-affirmation: Intervening to close the minority achievement gap. *Science, 324*(5925), 400–403.

Croizet, J., & Claire, T. (1998). Extending the concept of stereotype threat to social class: The intellectual underperformance of students from low socioeconomic backgrounds. *Personality and Social Psychology Bulletin, 24*(6), 588–594.

Croizet, J., Després, G., Gauzins, M., Huguet, P., Leyens, J., & Méot, A. (2004). Stereotype threat undermines intellectual performance by triggering a disruptive mental load. *Personality and Social Psychology Bulletin, 30*(6), 721–731.

Danaher, K., & Crandall, C. S. (2008). Stereotype threat in applied settings re-examined. *Journal of Applied Social Psychology, 38*(6), 1639–1655.

Dasgupta, N., & Asgari, S. (2004). Seeing is believing: Exposure to counterstereotypic women leaders and its effect on automatic gender stereotyping. *Journal of Experimental Social Psychology, 40*(5), 642–658.

DeCaro, M. S., Rotar, K. E., Kendra, M. S., & Beilock, S. L. (2010). Diagnosing and alleviating the impact of performance pressure on mathematical problem solving. *The Quarterly Journal of Experimental Psychology: Human Experimental Psychology, 63*(8), 1619–1630.

Desert, M., Preaux, M., & Jund, R. (2009). So young and already victims of stereotype threat: Socio-economic status and performance of 6 to 9 years old children on Raven's progressive matrices. *European Journal of Psychology of Education, 24*(2), 207–218.

Eccles, J. S., Jacobs, J. E., & Harold, R. D. (1990). Gender role stereotypes, expectancy effects, and parents' socialization of gender differences. *Journal of Social Issues, 46*(2), 183–201.

Engle, RW. (2002). Working memory capacity as executive attention. *Current Directions in Psychological Science, 11*(1), 19–23.

Faust, M. W. (1992). *Analysis of physiological reactivity in mathematics anxiety.* Unpublished doctoral dissertation, Bowling Green State University, Bowling Green, Ohio.

Faust, M. W., Ashcraft, M. H., & Fleck, D. E. (1996). Mathematics anxiety effects in simple and complex addition. *Mathematical Cognition*, 2(1), 25–62.

Fennema, E. (1989). The study of affect and mathematics: A proposed generic model for research. In D. B. McLeod, and V. M. Adams, Eds.), *Affect and mathematical problem solving: A new perspective* (pp. 205–219). New York: Springer-Verlag.

Fennema, E., Peterson, P. L., Carpenter, T. P., & Lubinski, C. A. (1990). Teachers' attributions and beliefs about girls, boys, and mathematics. *Educational Studies in Mathematics*, 21(1), 55–69.

Fiore, G. (1999). Math-abused students: Are we prepared to teach them? *Mathematics Teacher*, 92(5), 403–406.

Foss, D. H., & Hadfield, O. D. (1993). A successful clinic for the reduction of mathematics anxiety among college students. *College Student Journal*, 27(2), 157–166.

Geary, D. C., Hoard, M. K., Byrd-Craven, J., & DeSoto, M. C. (2004). Strategy choice in simple and complex addition: Contributions of working memory and counting knowledge for children with mathematical disability. *Journal of Experimental Child Psychology*, 88(2), 121–151.

Geary, D. C., & Widaman, K. F. (1992). Numerical cognition: On the convergence of componential and psychometric models. *Intelligence*, 16(1), 47–80.

Gimmig, D., Huguet, P., Caverni, J. -P., & Cury, F. (2006). Choking under pressure and working-memory capacity: When performance pressure reduces fluid intelligence. *Psychonomic Bulletin & Review*, 13(6), 1005–1010.

Gonzales, P. M., Blanton, H., & Williams, K. J. (2002). The effects of stereotype threat and double-minority status on the test performance of Latino women. *Personality and Social Psychology Bulletin*, 28(5), 659–670.

Good, C., Aronson, J., & Harder, J. A. (2008). Problems in the pipeline: Stereotype threat and women's achievement in high-level math courses. *Journal of Applied Developmental Psychology*, 29(1), 17–28.

Gresky, D. M., Ten Eyck, L. L., Lord, C. G., & McIntyre, R. B. (2005). Effects of salient multiple identities on women's performance under mathematics stereotype threat. *Sex Roles*, 53(9/10), 703–716.

Harper, N. J., & Daane, C. J. (1998). Causes and reduction of math anxiety in preservice elementary teachers. *Action in Teacher Education*, 19(4), 29–38.

Hembree, R. (1990). The nature, effects, and relief of mathematics anxiety. *Journal for Research in Mathematics Education*, 21(1), 33–46.

Hendel, D. D., & Davis, S. O. (1978). Effectiveness of an intervention strategy for reducing mathematics anxiety. *Journal of Counseling Psychology*, 25(5) 429–234.

Hopko, D. R., Ashcraft, M. H., Gute, J., Ruggiero, K. J., & Lewis, C. (1998). Mathematics anxiety and working memory: Support for the existence of a deficient inhibition mechanism. *Journal of Anxiety Disorders*, 12(4), 343–355.

Hoy, W. K., & Woolfolk, A. E. (1990). Socialization of student teachers. *American Educational Research Journal*, 27(2), 279–300.

Imbo, I., & Vandierendonck, A. (2007). Do multiplication and division strategies rely on executive and phonological working memory resources? *Memory & Cognition*, 35(7), 1759–1771.

Inzlicht, M., & Ben-Zeev, T. (2000). A threatening intellectual environment: Why females are susceptible to experiencing problem-solving deficits in the presence of males. *Psychological Science*, 11(5), 365–371.

Inzlicht, M., McKay, L., & Aronson, J. (2006). Stigma as ego depletion: How being the target of prejudice affects self-control. *Psychological Science*, 17(3), 262–269.

Joormann, J., & Tran, T. B. (2009). Rumination and intentional forgetting of emotional material. *Cognition & Emotion*, 23(6), 1233–1246.

Jackson, C., & Leffingwell, R. (1999). The role of instructors in creating math anxiety in students from kindergarten through college. *Mathematics Teacher, 92*(7), 583–587.

Kamann, M. P., & Wong, B. Y. L. (1993). Inducing adaptive coping self-statements in children with learning disabilities through self-instruction training. *Journal of Learning Disabilities, 26*(9), 630–638.

Keller, J. (2007). Stereotype threat in classroom settings: The interactive effect of domain identification, task difficulty and stereotype threat on female students' maths performance. *British Journal of Educational Psychology, 77*(2), 323–338.

Kelly, W., & Tomhave, W. (1985). A study of math anxiety and math avoidance in pre-service elementary teachers. *Arithmetic Teacher, 32*(5), 51–53.

Klein, K., & Boals, A. (2001). Expressive writing can increase working memory capacity. *Journal of Experimental Psychology: General, 130*(3), 520–533.

Koenig, A. M., & Eagly, A. H. (2005). Stereotype threat in men on a test of social sensitivity. *Sex Roles, 52*(7/8), 489–496.

Krakowski, M., Ratliff, K. R., Levine, S. C., & Gomez, L. (2010). Fostering spatial learning in the classroom: Integrating psychological research with educational practice. Paper presented at the American Educational Research Association, Denver, CO.

Krinzinger, H., Kaufmann, L., & Willmes, K. (2009). Math anxiety and math ability in early primary school years. *Journal of Psychoeducational Assessment, 27*(3), 206–225.

Levy, B. (1996). Improving memory in old age through implicit self stereotyping. *Journal of Personality and Social Psychology, 71*(6), 1092–1107.

Leyens, J. -P., Désert, M., Croizet, J. -C., & Darcis, C. (2000). Stereotype threat: Are lower status and history of stigmatization preconditions of stereotype threat? *Personality and Social Psychology Bulletin, 26*(10), 1189–1199.

Lyons I. M., & Beilock, S. L. (2010). Mathematics anxiety: Separating the math from the anxiety. Poster presented at the annual Psychonomics meeting in St. Louis, MO.

Marx, D. M., & Roman, J. S. (2002). Female role models: Protecting women's math test performance. *Personality and Social Psychology Bulletin, 28*(9), 1183–1193.

Marx, D. M., Stapel, D. A., & Muller, D. (2005). We can do it: The interplay of construal orientation and social comparison under threat. *Journal of Personality and Social Psychology, 88*(3), 432–446.

Mattarella-Micke, A., Mateo, J., Kozak, M. N., Foster, K., & Beilock, S. L. (in press). Choke or thrive? The relation between salivary cortisol and math performance depends on individual differences in working memory and math anxiety. *Emotion.*

McIntyre, R. B., Lord, C. G., Gresky, D. M., Ten Eyck, L. L., Frye, G. D. J., & Bond Jr., C. F. (2005). A social impact trend in the effects of role models on alleviating women's mathematics stereotype threat. *Current Research in Social Psychology, 10*, 116–136.

McIntyre, R. B., Paulson, R., & Lord, C. (2003). Alleviating women's mathematics stereotype threat through salience of group achievements. *Journal of Experimental Social Psychology, 39*(1), 83–90.

Meece, J. (1981). Individual differences in the affective reactions of middle and high school students to mathematics: A social cognitive perspective. Unpublished doctoral dissertation, University of Michigan, Ann Arbor, MI.

Meece, J. L., Wigfield, A., & Eccles, J. S. (1990). Predictors of math anxiety and its consequences for young adolescents' course enrollment intentions and performances in mathematics. *Journal of Educational Psychology, 82*(1), 60–70.

Midgley, C., Feldlaufer, H., & Eccles, J. S. (1989). Student/teacher relations and attitudes toward mathematics before and after the transition to junior high school. *Child Development, 60*(4), 981–992.

A. Miyake, and P. Shah, Eds.),1999. New York: Cambridge University Press.

Miyaki, A., Kost-Smith, L. E., Finkelstein, N. D., Pollock, S. J., Cohen, G. L., & Ito, T. A. (2010). Reducing the gender achievement gap in college science: A classroom study of values affirmation. *Science*, *330*(6008), 1234–1237.

National Education Association (2003). *Status of the American Public School Teacher.* Retrieved from: http://www.nea.org/assets /docs/Status_of_the_American_ Public_School_Teacher_2000-2001.pdf.

Nisbet, S. (1991). A new instrument to measure preservice primary teachers' attitudes to teaching mathematics. *Mathematics Education Research Journal*, *3*(2), 34–56.

Park, D., Ramirez, G., & Beilock, S. L. (2011). Put your math burden down: Expressive writing for the highly math anxious. Poster presented at the Midwestern Psychological Association, Chicago, IL.

Perry, D. G., & Bussey, K. (1979). The social learning theory of sex differences: Imitation is alive and well. *Journal of Personality and Social Psychology*, *37*(10), 1699–1712.

Pinel, E. C. (1999). Stigma consciousness: The psychological legacy of social stereotypes. *Journal of Personality and Social Psychology*, *76*(1), 114–128.

Ployhart, R. E., Ziegert, J. C., & McFarland, L. A. (2003). Understanding racial differences on cognitive ability tests in selection contexts: An integration of stereotype threat and applicant reactions research. *Human Performance*, *16*(3), 231–259.

Ramirez, G., & Beilock, S. L. (2011). Writing about testing worries boosts exam performance in the classroom. *Science*, *331*(6014), 211–213.

Ramirez, G., Gunderson, E. A., Levine S. C., & Beilock, S. L. (2009). The influence of math anxiety on young children's math achievement. Poster presented at the Midwestern Psychological Association, Chicago, IL.

Regner, I., Smedding, A., Gimming, D., Thinus-Blanc, C., Monteil, J. -M., & Huguet, P. (2010). Individual differences in working memory moderate stereotype threat effects. *Psychological Science*, *20*(10), 1–3.

Richardson, F. C., & Woolfolk, R. L. (1980). Mathematics anxiety. In I. G. Sarason ed.), (pp. 271–288). Hillsdale, NJ: Erlbaum.

Rydell, B. J., McConnell, A. R., & Beilock, S. L. (2009). Multiple social identities and stereotype threat: Imbalance, accessibility, and working memory. *Journal of Personality & Social Psychology*, *96*(5), 949–966.

Schleppenbach, M., Perry, M., Miller, K. F., Sims, L., & Fang, G. (2007). The answer is only the beginning: Extended discourse in Chinese and U.S. mathematics classrooms. *Journal of Educational Psychology*, *99*(2), 380–396.

Schmader, T. (2002). Gender identification moderates stereotype threat effects on women's math performance. *Journal of Experimental Social Psychology*, *38*(2), 194–201.

Schmader, T., & Johns, M. (2003). Converging evidence that stereotype threat reduces working memory capacity. *Journal of Personality and Social Psychology*, *85*(3), 440–452.

Schmader, T., Johns, M., & Forbes, C. (2008). An integrated process model of stereotype threat effects on performance. *Psychological Review*, *115*(2), 335–356.

Schneider, W. J., & Nevid, J. S. (1993). Overcoming math anxiety: A comparison of stress inoculation training & systematic desensitization. *Journal of College Student Development*, *34*(4), 283–288.

Shih, M., Pittinsky, T., & Ambady, N. (1999). Stereotype susceptibility: Identity salience and shifts in quantitative performance. *Psychological Science*, *10*(1), 80–83.

Siegler, R. S., & Shrager, J. (1984). Strategy choices in addition and subtraction: How do children know what to do? In C. Sophian ed.), (pp. 229–293). Hillsdale, NJ: Erlbaum.

Simon, M. A., & Schifter, D. (1993). Toward a constructivist perspective: The impact of a mathematics teacher inservice program on students. *Educational Studies in Mathematics*, *25*(4), 331–340.

Simpkins, S. D., Davis-Kean, P. E., & Eccles, J. S. (2006). Math and science motivation: A longitudinal examination of the links between choices and beliefs. *Developmental Psychology, 42*(1), 70–83.

Smyth, J. M. (1998). Written emotional expression: Effect sizes, outcome types, and moderating variables. *Journal of Consulting and Clinical Psychology, 66*(1), 174–184.

Sovchik, R. J., Meconi, L. J., & Steiner, E. (1983). Mathematics anxiety of preservice elementary mathematics methods students. *School Science and Mathematics, 81*(8), 643–648.

Spencer, S. J., Steele, C. M., & Quinn, D. M. (1999). Stereotype threat and women's math performance. *Journal of Experimental Social Psychology, 35*(1), 4–28.

Steele, C. M. (1997). A threat in the air: How stereotypes shape intellectual identity and performance. *American Psychologist, 52*(6), 613–629.

Steele, C. M., & Aronson, J. (1995). Stereotype threat and the intellectual test performance of African-Americans. *Journal of Personality and Social Psychology, 69*(5), 797–811.

Stigler, J. W., Fernandez, C., & Yoshida, M. (1996). Traditions of school mathematics in Japanese and American elementary classrooms. In L. P. Steffe., P. Nesher., P. Cobb.., G. A. Goldin, and B. Greer, Eds.), Hillsdale, NJ: Lawrence Erlbaum Associates.

Stricker, L. J., & Ward, W. C. (2004). Stereotype threat, inquiring about test takers' ethnicity and gender, and standardized test performance. *Journal of Applied Social Psychology, 34*(4), 665–693.

Suinn, R-M. (1972). Mathematics anxiety rating scale, MARS. Rocky Mountain Behavioral Sciences Institute, Fort Collins, CO.

Suinn, R. M., Taylor, S., & Edwards, R. W. (1988). Suinn mathematics anxiety rating scale for elementary school students (MARS-E): Psychometric and normative data. *Educational and Psychological Measurement, 48*(4), 979–986.

Swars, S. L., Daane, C. J., & Giesen, J. (2010). Mathematics anxiety and mathematics teacher effeminacy: What is the relationship in elementary preservice teachers? *School Science and Mathematics, 106*(7), 306–315.

Swetman, B., Munday, R., & Windham, R. (1993). Math-anxious teachers: Breaking the cycle. *College Student Journal, 22*(4), 421–427.

Tiedemann, J. (2000a). Gender-related beliefs of teachers in elementary school mathematics. *Educational Studies in Mathematics, 41*(2), 191–207.

Tiedemann, J. (2000b). Parents' gender stereotypes and teachers' beliefs as predictors of children's concept of their mathematical ability in elementary school. *Journal of Educational Psychology, 92*(1), 144–151.

Tiedemann, J. (2002). Teachers' gender stereotypes as determinants of teacher perceptions in elementary school mathematics. *Educational Studies in Mathematics, 50*(1), 49–62.

Tobias, S. (1995). Overcoming math anxiety. W. W. Norton, New York.

Townsend, M., & Wilton, K. (2003). Evaluating change in attitude towards mathematics using the 'then–now' procedure in a cooperative learning program. *British Journal of Educational Psychology, 73*(4), 473–487.

Trbovich, P. L., & LeFevre, J. A. (2003). Phonological and visual working memory in mental addition. *Memory & Cognition, 31*(5), 738–745.

Troutman, J. (1978). Cognitive predictors of final grades in finite mathematics. *Educational and Psychological Measurement, 38*(2), 401–404.

Trujillo, K. M., & Hadfield, O. D. (1999). Tracing the roots of mathematics anxiety through in-depth interviews with preservice elementary teachers. *College Student Journal, 33*(2), 219–232.

Turner, M. L., & Engle, R. W. (1989). Is working memory capacity task dependent? *Journal of Memory and Language, 28*(1), 127–154.

Turner, J. C., Midgler, C., Meyer, D. K., Gheen, M., Anderman, E. M., & Kang, Y. (2001). The classroom enviroment and students' reports of avoidance strategies in mathematics. *Journal of Educational Psychology, 94*(1), 88–106.

Vinson, B. M. (2001). A comparison of preservice teachers' mathematics anxiety before and after a methods class emphasizing manipulatives. *Early Childhood Education Journal, 29*(2), 89–94.

Walter, S. J., & Jeffrey, N. S. (1993). Overcoming math anxiety: A comparison of stress inoculation training and systematic desensitization. *Journal of College Student development, 34*(4), 283–288.

Watson, J. (1987). The attitudes of pre-service primary teachers toward mathematics: Some observations. *Research in Mathematics Education in Australia.*, 48–56.

Wechsler, D. (1991). Wechsler Intelligence Scale for Children—Third Edition. The Psychological Corporation, San Antonio, TX.

Wenta, R. G. (2000). Efficacy of pre-service elementary mathematics teachers. Unpublished doctoral dissertation, Indiana University, Bloomington, IN.

Wigfield, A., & Meece, J. (1998). Math anxiety in elementary and secondary school students. *Journal of Educational Psychology, 80*(2), 210–216.

Wood, E. F. (1988). Math anxiety and elementary teachers: What does research tell us? *For the Learning and Mathematics, 8*(1), 8–13.

Woodcock, R. W., McGrew, K. S., & Mather, N. (2001). Woodcock-Johnson III Tests of Achievement. Riverside Publishing, Itasca, IL.

Yee, D. K., & Eccles, J. S. (1988). Parent perceptions and attributions for children's math achievement. *Sex Roles, 19*(5), 317–333.

Zettle, R. D. (2003). Acceptance and commitment therapy vs. systematic desensitization in treatment of mathematics anxiety. *The Psychological Record, 53*(2), 197–215.

CHAPTER SIX

THERE IS NOTHING SO PRACTICAL AS A GOOD THEORY

Robert S. Siegler, Lisa K. Fazio *and* Aryn Pyke

Contents

Abstract

Children from low-income families begin school with less mathematical knowledge than peers from middle-income backgrounds. This discrepancy has long-term consequences: Children who start behind usually stay behind. Effective interventions have therefore been sought to improve the mathematical knowledge of preschoolers from impoverished backgrounds. Some curriculum-based interventions have met with impressive success; two disadvantages of such interventions, however, are that they are quite costly in terms of the time and resources they require and their multifaceted lessons make it impossible to determine why they work. In this chapter, we describe a theoretical analysis that motivated the development of a simple, brief, and inexpensive intervention that involved playing a linear number board game. Roughly an hour of playing this game produced improvements in numerical magnitude comparison, number line estimation, counting, numeral identification, and ability to learn novel arithmetic problems by preschoolers from low-income backgrounds. The gains were greater than those produced by playing a parallel nonnumerical game or engaging in

Psychology of Learning and Motivation, Volume 55

ISSN 0079-7421, DOI 10.1016/B978-0-12-387691-1.X0001-4

© 2011 Elsevier Inc.

All rights reserved.

other numerical activities. Detailed analyses of learning patterns indicated that this theoretically motivated, game-based intervention exercises most of its effects by enhancing and refining children's representations of numerical magnitudes.

1. INTRODUCTION

When children enter kindergarten, they already differ greatly in mathematical knowledge. These early differences have large and lasting consequences. Initial knowledge predicts subsequent success in many domains (Bransford, Brown, & Cocking, 1999), but the relation between early math knowledge and subsequent math achievement is particularly strong and persistent (e.g., roughly twice as strong as the relation between early and later reading achievement; Duncan et. al, 2007). Limited mathematical knowledge has large, deleterious economic and occupational consequences in adulthood (McCloskey, 2007; Rivera-Batiz, 1992).

Children from low-income families are particularly at risk for difficulties learning mathematics. They tend to begin school with less numerical knowledge than their classmates from middle- or high-income households, and over the course of schooling, they fall steadily further behind (e.g., N. C. Jordan, Kaplan, Olah, & Locuniak, 2006). Again, similar patterns are present in other areas such as reading, but the differences in mathematical knowledge tend to be greater (Case, Griffin, & Kelly, 1999).

Recognition of these problems has led a number of researchers to devise programs intended to improve the mathematical knowledge of preschoolers from low-income families and thus to reduce the gap between them and children from more affluent backgrounds. However, these large-scale interventions are costly, both financially and in the time needed to train teachers to implement them. Because these interventions are so multifaceted, they also yield limited information regarding how to improve future interventions and future theories of numerical cognition.

In this chapter, we briefly describe the early development of numerical knowledge, differences between the numerical knowledge of preschoolers from low-income and middle-income backgrounds, and three broad-based curricular interventions that have been found to improve that knowledge. We then present a theoretical analysis that suggests that underdeveloped knowledge of numerical magnitudes is a key source of the mathematical difficulties of children from low-income backgrounds. Next, we describe an intervention, based on the theoretical analysis, designed to improve young children's knowledge of numerical magnitudes. Finally, we present evidence regarding the effectiveness of the intervention and discuss general implications of the findings.

2. Development of Mathematical Knowledge

2.1. Early mathematical abilities

Even infants possess a rough sense of numerical magnitudes. For example, 6-month olds can discriminate sets of dots or other geometric shapes differing in number by 50% (e.g., three versus two dots; six versus four dots), and 9-month olds can discriminate sets differing by 33% (e.g., four versus three dots) (Brannon, Suanda, & Libertus, 2007). Infants of this age can also do a form of nonverbal arithmetic; for example, they look longer when the addition of one object to an object that the infants had seen hidden behind a screen appears to yield one or three objects rather than two (Wynn, 1992). The tasks on which infant numerical competence has been demonstrated share two characteristics: they are nonverbal, and they can be performed with an approximate sense of numerical magnitude rather than requiring an exact sense (although two dots differ from one by only a single dot, the set sizes also differ by 100%.)

Between ages 2 and 5 years, children begin to link verbally stated numbers to nonverbal quantities and also to form exact representations of numerical magnitudes. Thus, by the start of kindergarten, the large majority of children in the United States can perform basic mathematical tasks such as reading small numerals, naming simple shapes, and counting to 10 (U.S. Department of Education, 2000). In fact, many preschoolers can count to 100 (Miller, Smith, Zhu, & Zhang, 1995; Siegler & Robinson, 1982).

Reciting the number words in the correct order, however, does not mean that children understand the purpose of counting or that the final number in a count of objects signifies the set size. There is a substantial gap in time between when children learn the counting sequence and when they understand that the purpose of counting is to determine the number of objects. Thus, when asked to count five items, young preschoolers often say, "one, two, three, four, five" but cannot answer the question, "How many are there?" except by again counting "one, two, three, four, five" (Le Corre, Van de Walle, Brannon, & Carey, 2006; Schaeffer, Eggleston, & Scott, 1974). Similarly, many preschoolers who can count six objects flawlessly have no idea whether "5" or "6" indicates a larger quantity (Le Corre & Carey, 2007; Sarnecka & Carey, 2008; Siegler & Robinson, 1982). It is only around the age of 4 years that children understand that the purpose of counting is to establish the number of objects in a set, and it is only around 5 years that they know the relative magnitudes of the numbers 1–10 (Gelman & Gallistel, 1978; Siegler & Robinson, 1982).

Another skill that children begin to learn before the start of formal schooling is arithmetic. As noted previously, infants can perform nonsymbolic arithmetic problems, but it is not until 4 or 5 years that most children can solve verbal arithmetic problems with sums of 5 or less (e.g., "What is 2 + 2?"). Children solve these problems using a variety of strategies: retrieval of answers from memory, counting on fingers, counting without referring to fingers, and putting up fingers and recognizing how many are there (Siegler & Robinson, 1982). Preschoolers are adaptive in their choices among these strategies, using more time-consuming strategies more often on relatively difficult problems that they cannot solve using quicker strategies (Siegler & Shrager, 1984).

2.2. Development of numerical knowledge in low- and middle-income populations

Numerous studies have shown that children from low-income households lag behind in mathematical knowledge from the preschool period onward (N. C. Jordan et al., 2006; N. C. Jordan, Kaplan, Ramineni, & Locuniak, 2009; Klibanoff, Levine, Huttenlocher, Vasilyeva, & Hedges, 2006; Starkey, Klein, & Wakeley, 2004; Stipek & Ryan, 1997). At kindergarten entry, children from low-income families score 1.3 standard deviations lower than peers from more affluent backgrounds on tests of basic math skills (Duncan & Magnuson, in press). Similarly, kindergartners from working class families lag a full 12 months behind peers from middle-class backgrounds in their ability to perform basic addition (Hughes, 1981), and only 33% of kindergarteners whose families are currently or have at some point been on welfare can read numerals and count beyond 10, skills that are usually present among kindergartners in general (U.S. Department of Education, 2000).

Preschoolers and kindergartners from low-income families also have great difficulty with story problems (e.g., "Mary had three apples and gave Bill two apples. How many apples does Mary have now?"). Moreover, unlike children from middle-income families, they show minimal improvement over the course of kindergarten in solving such problems (N. C. Jordan et al., 2006).

These early deficits are important because early math achievement is highly predictive of later math achievement (Aunola, Leskinen, Lerkkanen, & Nurmi, 2004; Duncan & Magnuson, in press; Duncan et al., 2007; N. C. Jordan et al., 2009). Children's numerical competence in kindergarten predicts their rate of growth in mathematical ability through third grade, even after controlling for income (N. C. Jordan et al., 2009). Math achievement test scores upon entering kindergarten are also strongly predictive of scores at the end of fifth grade (Duncan & Magnuson, in press; Duncan et al., 2007) and even in high school (Stevenson & Newman, 1986). These results suggest that if children from low-income backgrounds entered kindergarten with skills similar to those of middle-income peers, the differences observed in later elementary school might be considerably reduced or eliminated.

2.3. Differences in exposure to math of preschoolers from different economic backgrounds

Differences in mathematical knowledge among preschoolers and kindergartners from different economic backgrounds reflect differences in mathematical activities at home and in school. Middle-income parents report more numerical activities in the home than do low-income parents (N. C. Jordan et al., 2006; Starkey & Klein, 2000). Middle-class parents are also more likely to incorporate math during play (Tudge & Doucet, 2004) and present more complex number tasks (Saxe, Guberman, & Gearhart, 1987). Especially important, parental reports of mathematical activities with their children correlate with the children's mathematical skills (Blevins-Knabe & Musun-Miller, 1996). The greater mathematical experience that children from middle-class families receive at home likely facilitates their mathematics achievement in school.

Teachers also affect preschoolers' mathematical knowledge. Preschool students in classrooms with a relatively large amount of math-related talk learn more mathematics during the school year than preschoolers in classrooms where the teacher rarely mentions math (Klibanoff et al., 2006). The quality of the preschool also affects how much children learn. Preschools that primarily serve children from low-income backgrounds tend to be of lower quality and to be less effective in promoting academic skills (Early et al., 2010; LoCasale-Crouch et al., 2007; Pianta et al., 2005). The effect of low-quality preschools becomes even more crucial, given that low-income parents tend to believe that most of children's exposure to mathematics should come from the school rather than from the home (Holloway, Rambaud, Fuller, & Eggers-Pierola, 1995; Starkey & Klein, 2000). The divergent experiences at home and at school of children from different economic backgrounds suggest that one way of improving the mathematical skills of children from low-income households is to increase exposure to mathematical concepts in preschool and kindergarten. In the next section, we discuss several interventions that provide such additional exposure.

3. EFFECTS OF LARGE-SCALE MATH CURRICULA

Over the years, many large-scale interventions have been implemented in an attempt to improve the mathematical skills of preschoolers from low-income backgrounds (Arnold, Fisher, Doctoroff, & Dobbs, 2002; Case et al., 1999; Clements & Sarama, 2008; Griffin, Case, &

Siegler, 1994; Pagani, Jalbert, & Girard, 2006; Sophian, 2004; Starkey & Klein, 2000; Starkey et al., 2004). These multifaceted interventions demonstrate that children from low-income backgrounds can become considerably more proficient in math if given proper support. Below, we review three of the interventions whose effectiveness has received the most empirical support: Number Worlds (e.g., Griffin, 2003), Building Blocks (e.g., Clements & Sarama, 2008), and Pre-K Mathematics (e.g., Starkey et al., 2004)

The Number Worlds curriculum (formerly called Rightstart, Griffin et al., 1994) focuses on teaching children the underlying concept of number before moving on to formal addition and subtraction. As such, the program ensures that children have a good conceptualization of addition, subtraction, and numerical magnitudes using real objects (e.g., four blocks) before introducing symbolic representations (e.g., the numeral 4). There is also an emphasis on encouraging children to connect different representations of number. For example, children should understand that the numeral 4, the phrase "four cars," and a picture of four dots all refer to the same number of objects (Griffin, 2003). Within the curriculum, children spend approximately 20 min each school day involved in small-group math activities, mostly hands-on games. These sessions are facilitated by the teacher who encourages conversation during the games by asking questions such as "How many do you have," "What number are you on," and "Who is farther along." The children also sing songs about numbers, work with money, and engage in many other numerical activities.

In a study in which kindergartners from low-income backgrounds participated in 40 sessions of the Number Worlds curriculum, 87% passed a simple test of numerical skills. In contrast, only 25% of kindergartners from similar backgrounds who received classroom lessons typical for their preschool passed the same test (Griffin & Case, 1996; Griffin et al., 1994). Children who received the intervention remained more advanced at the end of first grade (despite receiving the intervention only during kindergarten), and their teachers rated them at the end of first grade as having better number sense than peers who did not receive the intervention during kindergarten. In fact, despite participants beginning kindergarten with much less number knowledge than children from middle-class backgrounds, those participants who were present for the entire school year finished kindergarten with number knowledge equivalent to that of children from middle-income backgrounds who received a different mathematics curriculum (Griffin & Case, 1997).

A second successful preschool curriculum, Building Blocks (Clements & Sarama, 2007), features small-group and whole-group activities, computer games, and family activities to be done at home. The curriculum provides experience with a wide variety of aspects of mathematics, including numbers, patterns, and geometry. Children spend at least 1 h per week for 26 weeks focused on math (Clements & Sarama, 2007, 2008). The curriculum takes into account typical learning trajectories, with the activities becoming more difficult as the children's mathematical thinking becomes more advanced. These learning trajectories are based on descriptive studies of typical developmental sequences and help teachers understand the changes that typically occur in children's thinking with age and mathematical experience (Sarama & Clements, 2002, 2004).

In a large randomized trial (Clements & Sarama, 2008), children in 35 lower and middle-class preschool classrooms received one of three approaches: Building Blocks, another research-based preschool mathematics curriculum, and the curriculum used in that classroom the previous year. Children who received the Building Blocks curriculum improved their math skills more than children who received the previous year's curriculum and more than children who received the comparison curriculum.

A third highly successful preschool math curriculum, Pre-K Mathematics, was developed by Starkey, Klein, and colleagues (Starkey & Klein, 2000; Starkey et al., 2004). It combines school-based activities with activities for parents and children to do at home. In the school-based part of the intervention, children participate in small-group activities for 20 min twice a week throughout the school year. Home activities link to the small-group activities in school; parents are provided with manipulatives to use in each activity and are given instructions on how to perform them.

Children from low-income families who participated in Pre-K Mathematics showed equivalent mathematical knowledge at the end of the program to age peers from middle-income backgrounds who did not participate (Starkey et al., 2004). In addition, two large studies demonstrated that combining the Pre-K Mathematics curriculum with the Building Blocks software led to large gains in mathematical knowledge compared to control classrooms that continued using the same curricula as the previous year (Klein, Starkey, Clements, Sarama, & Iyer, 2008; Sarama, Clements, Starkey, Klein, & Wakeley, 2008).

Although these interventions are effective, they are very costly in terms of time and resources. In addition to the money that preschools must spend to purchase the curricula, teacher training requires substantial time. In a test of the Building Blocks curriculum, teachers received 34 h of group training and 16 h of in-class coaching (Clements & Sarama, 2008). In studies of Number Worlds, teachers received assistance from the researchers twice a week throughout the school year (Griffin & Case, 1997). Similarly, teachers who implemented Pre-K Mathematics participated in 8 days of workshops over the course of the school year, along with on-site training at least once per month (Klein et al., 2008;

Starkey et al., 2004). It is unclear whether these interventions can be effective without such large amounts of teacher support. In the absence of strict guidance, teachers tend to modify the curricula in ways that make them less effective (Griffin, 2007; Griffin & Case, 1997).

The high costs of implementing these preschool curricula were one motivation for our efforts to develop a briefer, more focused intervention. A second motivation for developing the intervention, at least as important, was to test whether a theory of early numerical development would translate into effective instruction. Because the intervention suggested by the theory was brief and entailed virtually no expense, the two goals could be pursued within a single theory-based instructional procedure.

4. THEORETICAL BACKGROUND OF A TARGETED INTERVENTION

Learning mathematics crucially depends on mastery of previously presented content. In elementary and middle school mathematics, one important type of foundational knowledge is often referred to as "number sense." However, the number sense construct has been used to refer to such a heterogeneous range of abilities that it is difficult to specify what it means, much less to improve it. For example, the National Mathematics Advisory Panel (2008) defined number sense to include skill at identification of the numerical value associated with small quantities; counting; proficiency in estimating numerical magnitudes; principled understanding of place values and of how to compose and decompose whole numbers; knowledge of the commutative, associative, and distributive laws; and ability to apply those laws to solve problems. All these are important aspects of mathematical knowledge, but it is difficult to see what they have in common beyond being important, early developing aspects of numerical knowledge.

After reviewing the literature on number sense, Siegler and Booth (2005) concluded that the core competence within it was the ability to translate accurately among alternative representations of numerical magnitudes. Among the indices of the quality of numerical magnitude representations are accuracy of estimates of discrete quantities (e.g., "About how many people attended the play"), accuracy of estimates of continuous physical dimensions ("About how long is that school bus"), and accuracy of judgments of the plausibility of answers to arithmetic problems ("About how much is 12×18") (Crites, 1992; Siegel, Goldsmith, & Madson, 1982). The first two examples involve spatial to numerical translations; the third example involves a translation between two numerical representations.

A large amount of evidence with both children (e.g., Case, 1978) and adults (Dehaene, 1997) indicates that knowledge of numerical magnitudes is represented as a mental number line, in which number symbols (e.g., "4") are connected with nonverbal representations of quantity. The nonverbal representations of quantity appear to be largely spatial (e.g., de Hevia & Spelke, 2010), though other sensory modalities are also mapped onto the symbolic representations of numerical magnitudes (e.g., K. E. Jordan, Suanda, & Brannon, 2008; Lourenco & Longo, 2010). Behavioral and neural data with both children and adults support the mental number line construct (Ansari, 2008). Some of the evidence comes from studies of numerical magnitude comparison, in which the greater the difference between two numbers, the faster the people's identification of their relative sizes (e.g., Holyoak & Mah, 1982; Moyer & Landauer, 1967). Another large body of evidence comes from studies of the SNARC (spatial–numerical association of response codes) effect, the tendency of people in societies with left-to-right orthographies to respond faster in choice situations when the smaller of two numbers is on the left and the larger is on the right (e.g., Dehaene, Bossini, & Giraux, 1993). A third type of evidence is that brain damaged patients with left hemifield neglect displace rightward their bisections of numerical ranges, for example, estimating that the midpoint between 11 and 19 is 17, as would follow from their neglecting the left side (11–15) of a left-to right number line between 11 and 19 (Zorzi, Priftis, & Umilta, 2002). Yet a fourth type of evidence is that the horizontal, intraparietal sulcus (HIPS) area, an area central to numerical magnitude representations, shows greater activation when tasks demand fine discriminations between magnitudes than when coarse discriminations are adequate, as would be expected from the mental number line construct (Ansari, 2008; Hubbard, Piazza, Pinel, & Dehaene, 2005).

Although the hypothesis that people represent numerical magnitudes on a mental number line is widely accepted, investigators disagree on the form of the representation. Some investigators (e.g., Dehaene, 1997) have proposed that the representation is compressive, with the distance between successive whole numbers at the low end of the number line being larger than the distance between successive whole numbers at the high end of the line. Other investigators (e.g., Brannon, Wusthoff, Gallistel, & Gibbon, 2001) have proposed that magnitude representations increase linearly with numerical size, but with increasing noise as the numbers increase (the accumulator model). Yet others (e.g., Case, 1992) have proposed that after age 5 or 6, means of the representation of each number increase linearly but without increasing variability around each mean.

Number line estimation has proved to be an especially useful task for examining the form of the mental number line and for comparing alternative theoretical predictions. This task involves presenting a horizontal line with a number at each end (e.g., 0 and 100) and no other intervening marks or numbers. The goal is to estimate the location on the number line of a third number (e.g., "Where would 34 go?"). Then, the estimates of different numbers are considered together, and the function that best relates the presented number to the numerical equivalent of its estimated position on the number line is identified.

This number line estimation task has a number of advantages. The task can be used with any real number: whole numbers, fractions, decimals, and negative numbers. It is also nonroutine for both children and adults; therefore, performance on it reflects people's underlying knowledge, rather than their familiarity with a practiced procedure. It is also quick and easy to administer and maps in a transparent way to the issues of whether the form of numerical representation is linear, logarithmic, or some other pattern, and whether representations of numbers become increasingly noisy with increasing numerical magnitudes. Another advantage is that the number line task yields several measures of the quality of estimation: percent absolute error (the distance of the child's estimate from the correct position), variance accounted for by the function that most accurately relates the number presented to the child's estimate of its position on the number line, and the slope of the best fitting linear function (Booth & Siegler, 2006).

As shown in Figure 1 and discussed in Siegler and Opfer (2003), examining the relationship between the number that was presented and the estimate of that number's position on the number line allowed discrimination among the three theoretical patterns described previously. Adults' number line estimates closely approximated the linear function of $y = x$ (estimated magnitude = actual magnitude) (Figure 2). Second graders, however, did not generate linearly increasing estimation patterns with slopes of 1.00. Instead, their estimates tended to follow a logarithmic function. At all four ages, the variability of estimates was unrelated to the size of the number being estimated, thus arguing against the accumulator model.

The same transition from a logarithmic to a linear distribution of estimates has been found at a variety of ages, as children gain experience

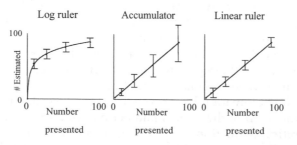

Figure 1   Means and variability on number line task predicted by three models of numerical representations.

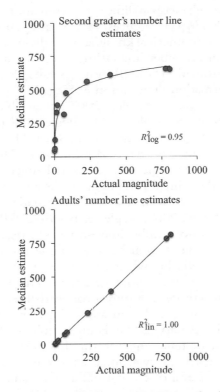

Figure 2 Logarithmic pattern of estimates on 0–1000 number line task generated by second graders and linear pattern of estimates on the same task generated by adults. Adapted from Siegler and Opfer (2003).

with an increasing range of numbers. For the 0–10 range, 3- and 4-year olds tend to produce a logarithmic pattern of number line estimates, whereas 5- and 6-year olds tend to generate a linear pattern (Berteletti, Lucangeli, Piazza, Dehaene, & Zorzi, 2010). For 0–100, kindergarteners usually produce a logarithmic function and second graders a linear one (Siegler & Booth, 2004). For 0–1000, a corresponding logarithmic to linear transition is seen between second and fourth grade (Booth & Siegler, 2006), and for 0–10,000, a parallel transition occurs between third and sixth grade (Thompson & Opfer, 2010).

This logarithmic to linear transition is not unique to the number line estimation task. Children undergo parallel changes at the same ages on numerosity estimation (generating approximately N dots on a computer screen), measurement estimation (drawing a line of approximately N units), numerical categorization (saying whether a number is very small, small, medium, big, or very big), and memory for numbers (Booth & Siegler, 2006; Laski & Siegler, 2007; Thompson & Siegler, 2010).

This increasing reliance on linear representations seems to play a central role in individual differences, as well as age-related differences, in the development of numerical knowledge. Individual differences in the linearity of children's number line estimates predict differences in their linearity on other estimation tasks (Booth & Siegler, 2006), their memory for numerical information (Thompson & Siegler, 2010), their categorization of numbers (Laski & Siegler, 2007), their ability to learn new arithmetic facts (Booth & Siegler, 2008; Siegler & Ramani, 2009), and their overall math achievement test scores (Geary, Hoard, Byrd-Craven, Nugent, & Numtee, 2007; Siegler & Booth, 2004). These relations tend to be substantial; for example, the relation between the linearity of numerical magnitude estimates and math achievement test scores ranges from $r = 0.40$ to $r = 0.60$ from first to fourth grade (Booth & Siegler, 2006, 2008; Geary et al., 2007; Siegler & Booth, 2004).

Why might linearity of number line estimates be related to these varied mathematical skills? The relation between numerical magnitude representations and arithmetic knowledge provides an example that can be used to explain the relation more generally. The presentation of an arithmetic problem activates not only a rote verbal representation of the answer to the problem, but also an approximate representation of the answer's magnitude (Ansari, 2008; Hanich, Jordan, Kaplan, & Dick, 2001). An approximate representation that has more activation strength concentrated in the correct answer and the few numbers around it is more likely to generate retrieval of the correct answer, and to generate close misses in cases where errors are made, than an approximate representation in which activation strength is more widely distributed among different numbers. Approximate representations in which strength is concentrated in the correct answer and the few numbers around it are also more likely to allow rejection of implausible answers and recalculation in cases where implausible answers are retrieved.

This analysis is supported by performance on verification tasks. Presented an arithmetic problem and a potential answer, both adults and children reject false answers whose magnitudes are distant from the correct answer $(3 + 8 = 17)$ more quickly than false answers with magnitudes similar to the correct answer $(3 + 8 = 13,)$ supporting the interpretation that both approximate and exact answers are activated by arithmetic problems. Children who are better at math show this effect more strongly (e.g., Ashcraft, 1992), showing both that people vary in the range of numbers activated by arithmetic problems and that the variation is related to more general mathematical proficiency, including arithmetic proficiency. Moreover, accurate magnitude representations scaffold further arithmetic learning: manipulations that help children gain linear representations of numerical magnitude also help them learn correct answers to novel addition problems (Booth & Siegler, 2008; Siegler & Ramani, 2009).

Individual differences in the quality of magnitude representations can be detected from early ages. For example, kindergartners who are less accurate at number line estimation obtain lower achievement test scores at the end of their kindergarten year (Siegler & Booth, 2004) and first graders who have been identified as having math difficulties are less accurate at number line estimation than classmates without math difficulties (Geary et al., 2007). These findings, together with the strong relations between the quality of magnitude representations and many other aspects of early mathematical understanding, suggested that targeting an intervention to improve magnitude representations might yield far-reaching gains in mathematical knowledge.

5. FROM THEORY TO PRACTICE: DEVELOPING A BOARD GAME INTERVENTION

What experiences might facilitate a child's development of a linear representation of numerical magnitude? Counting experience likely contributes, but such experience appears insufficient: Children can often count perfectly in a numerical range at least a year before they even know the ordering of numerical magnitudes in that range, much less possess an equal interval scale of the magnitudes (Le Corre et al., 2006; Ramani & Siegler, 2008; Schaeffer et al., 1974). Thus, young children may "lack an understanding of the concrete significance of the verbal [counting] string" (Petitto, 1990, p. 70).

If counting is insufficient, what other experiences might scaffold a linear representation of numerical magnitudes? Experiences that provide redundant cues to numerical magnitudes can be especially effective in helping children represent and discriminate the magnitudes (e.g., K. E. Jordan et al., 2008). One activity that provides such redundant cues is playing linear, numerical board games—that is, board games with linearly arranged, consecutively numbered, equal-sized spaces, such as the first row of Chutes and Ladders. As noted by Siegler and Booth (2004), the greater the number in the current square, the greater (a) the distance the child has moved the token, (b) the number of discrete moves the child has made, (c) the number of number words the child has said and heard, and (d) the amount of time since the game began. Consistent with the view that these cues to numerical magnitude are useful, Ramani and Siegler (2008) found that preschoolers who reported having played Chutes and Ladders produced number line estimates that were more accurate and more closely followed a linear function than peers who reported never having played the game.

Of course, correlation is not causation. Therefore, to experimentally test the benefits of playing such games, Siegler and Ramani (2008) devised a number board game similar to the first row of Chutes and Ladders (the row with the numbers 1–10.) As shown in Figure 3, this linear physical representation transparently reflects the ratio characteristics of the number system. Just as 6 is twice as large as 3, the position of the "6" square is twice as far from the start position as the position of the "3" square; it takes twice as much time to reach the "6" square; and the child needs to say twice as many number words and make twice as many hand movements with the token to reach "6." In combination, the auditory, visuospatial, kines-thetic, and temporal cues to the magnitudes of the numbers 1–10 were expected to provide a robust, multimodal foundation for a linear repre-sentation of numerical magnitudes in that range.

Children who played the linear board game were required to name the number in each square that they traversed during the game; thus, if they were on the "3" square and spun "2," they needed to count "4, 5." This meant that the child needed to encode the number in the square, some-thing that preschoolers do not do automatically (Berch, Foley, Hill, & Ryan, 1999) but that seems crucial for correlating the number's identity with its magnitude.

5.1. Assessing the benefits of the numerical board game

Siegler and Ramani (2008) provided the first test of the effects of playing the linear numerical board game. They randomly assigned 36 preschoo-lers from low-income backgrounds to play one of the two games depicted in Figure 3—the number board game or the color board game. Each game board featured 10 horizontally arranged, equal-sized squares of various colors. The color version and the number version of the game were almost identical, the only difference being that in the number game, the numbers 1–10 were listed consecutively from left to right, one num-ber per square. On each turn, the child spun a spinner and moved his or her token the indicated number of squares (one or two). For each square traversed, the child was required to state its color (in the color game) or its

Figure 3   Game boards for the linear number game (left) and the color game (right). Siegler, R. S. (2009). Improving the numerical understanding of children from low-income families. *Child Development Perspectives, 3*, 118–124.

number (in the number game). If a child erred or could not name the numbers or colors in the squares, the experimenter would do so and the child would repeat the names. Children participated in four 15- to 20-min sessions over a 2-week period; thus, each child participated in roughly 1 h of game play in total.

This brief experience playing the number board game had a dramatic impact on the children's mathematical knowledge. From pretest to posttest, the percent variance in children's number line estimates that was accounted for by the best fitting linear function increased from 15% to 61% for children who played the number board game, whereas it was 18% on both pretest and posttest for children who played the color board game. Thus, the number board game proved effective at enhancing knowledge of numerical magnitudes, and these benefits did not arise from the incidental properties of the intervention that were shared by the number and color games (e.g., 1:1 correspondence between the number spun and the number of movements of the token that the child made, social interaction with an adult experimenter in a game context, observing a linear array of squares that were not explicitly associated with numbers, or exposure to mathematics in preschool).

This initial demonstration of the potential of the numerical board game to improve children's numerical knowledge led Ramani and Siegler (2008) to conduct a more ambitious study that examined the generality over tasks and over time of the benefits of playing the number board game. First, consider generality over tasks. Whereas Siegler and Ramani (2008) examined only effects of the number board game on number line estimation, Ramani and Siegler (2008) compared the effects of playing the number and color board games on four tasks: number line estimation, magnitude comparison ("Which number is bigger, N or M"), numeral identification ("What number is on this card"), and counting (from 1 to 10). Based on the interpretation that the improvement in number line estimation in the prior study reflected improved representations of numerical magnitudes, playing the number game was expected to enhance performance on numerical magnitude comparison as well as on number line estimation, a result that would not be expected if the improved number line performance was due to the superficial resemblance between the numeral board game and the number line task. The number board game was also expected to increase numeral identification ability and counting, because it provides practice and feedback on these skills.

Now consider generality over time. To assess whether the benefits of playing the number board game endured over time, children's learning was assessed not only on a posttest administered immediately after the fourth game playing session, but also on a follow-up test 9 weeks after the final game playing session. Presumably, if the game playing produced changes in numerical representations, the effects would endure rather than only influencing immediate performance.

The results of the study can be summarized in a single sentence. Children who played the number board game improved on all four tasks from pretest to posttest, and the gains were maintained over the 9-week follow-up period. Viewing the same results from a different perspective, performance in the two experimental conditions was comparable on the pretest, but children who played the number board game were superior on all four tasks on both the posttest and the follow-up. These results, which have been replicated by Whyte and Bull (2008) with a sample of children from England, indicate that the number board game provides distinctive benefits for low-income children that are otherwise not afforded by their numerical experiences in preschool.

In the third study of the series, Siegler and Ramani (2009) addressed three additional issues. One was whether playing the number board game enhanced children's ability to learn novel arithmetic problems. The refinements in children's representations of numerical magnitude produced by playing the numerical board game were expected to enhance children's arithmetic learning skills. A prior behavioral study showed that the accuracy of first graders' number line estimates on a pretest predicted their ability to learn answers to arithmetic problems (Booth & Siegler, 2008). Other studies that examined neural functioning showed that presenting arithmetic problems activates an approximate representation of the answer's magnitude as well as a rote verbal representation of the answer (Hanich et al., 2001). Thus, to the extent that the linear board game facilitates magnitude understanding, it was also expected to facilitate learning of previously unknown answers to arithmetic problems. Improved magnitude representations were also expected to influence the errors that were made in the direction of the errors being closer to the correct answer.

A second purpose of the study was to test the representational mapping hypothesis, an idea proposed by Siegler and Ramani (2009) that learning is enhanced when the physical form of the learning materials parallels the desired mental representation. In the present situation, this implied that a linear game board would yield greater learning than other game board configurations because the linear board mapped more transparently onto the mental number line. A mental number line is not the only useful representation of magnitude. Magnitudes are sometimes depicted using circular representations (e.g., clocks, scales, speedometers, etc.), and adults can generate and use internal circular representations to answer questions about numerical magnitudes if asked to do so (Bachtold, Baumuller, & Brugger, 1998). To examine the effects of the linearity of the number game board on children's learning, Siegler and Ramani (2009) compared effects of playing the game with a linear board to the effects of playing the same game with a circular board. Half of the children in the circular board condition played the game in the clockwise direction and half in the counterclockwise direction; the circular boards are shown in Figure 4.

The linear and circular board games shared several cues to numerical magnitude: the amount of time needed to reach various numbers on the board, the number of hand movements required to reach them, and the number of number words said and heard in the process of reaching them. However, the circular board did not provide linear visuospatial cues to the magnitudes associated with each number. To the extent that such visuo-spatial cues to number are particularly salient, as they have been hypothesized to be based on both neural and behavioral evidence (de Hevia & Spelke, 2010), the linear board game was expected to lead to better magnitude understanding than the circular game.

A third goal of the study was to test whether other numerical experiences, in particular the types of numerical experiences that children most often encounter in preschool, would be just as helpful as playing the number board game. The most common numerical experiences in preschool are verbal counting, object counting, and numeral identification (Ginsberg & Russell, 1981; Saxe et al., 1987). It seemed likely that these activities contribute to knowledge of counting and numeral identification, but they did not seem likely to enhance children's knowledge of numerical magnitudes. As noted earlier, counting accurately from 1 to 10 does not lead quickly to understanding numerical magnitudes in that range. In addition, a prior intervention that focused on counting and numeral identification did not increase knowledge of numerical magnitudes

Figure 4 Game boards for the clockwise (left) and counterclockwise (right) versions of the circular number game.

(Malofeeva, Day, Saco, Young, & Ciancio, 2004). Thus, relative to counting and identifying numbers, playing the number board game was expected to lead to superior performance on posttest tasks that reflect magnitude understanding (magnitude comparison, number line estimation, and arithmetic).

To pursue these three goals—examining transfer to arithmetic, comparing the effects of circular and linear boards, and testing whether other numerical activities were as useful as playing the number board game— Siegler and Ramani (2009) randomly assigned children to one of three conditions: playing the linear number board game, playing the circular number board game, or engaging in the numerical control activities. The first four sessions were much like those in Ramani and Siegler (2008): children received a pretest on number line estimation, magnitude comparison, numeral identification, counting, and simple arithmetic; played the game or engaged in other numerical activities; and received a posttest at the end of the fourth session on the same tasks as on the pretest. However, this study also involved a fifth session during the following week, in which each child received three feedback trials on each of two addition problems that they answered incorrectly on the pretest and then were tested on those two problems and on two nontrained addition problems.

As shown in Figure 5, playing the linear board game produced much greater gains in accuracy of magnitude comparison and number line estimation than the other two conditions did. Both linear and circular games yielded greater improvements in numeral identification than did the numerical control activities. Performance on counting was at ceiling in all conditions, so no differential effects of condition were observed.

Especially striking, playing the linear board game increased children's learning from subsequent experience with addition problems beyond that in the other two conditions. On the trained problems (but not on the untrained ones), children who had played the linear game prior to the arithmetic training produced more correct answers on the posttest (45%) than children who had played the circular game (30%) or children who were earlier engaged in the numerical control activities (28%). Furthermore, even when they answered incorrectly, children who earlier played the linear game produced closer misses (smaller absolute error) than those produced by their peers in the other two conditions. These findings suggest that playing the linear board game affords an enhanced understanding of magnitude that helps to constrain the range of plausible answers to arithmetic problems. It also adds evidence for the position that visuospatial cues are crucial for understanding numerical magnitudes. The other cues were present in the circular board game, but playing that game had little effect on knowledge of numerical magnitudes.

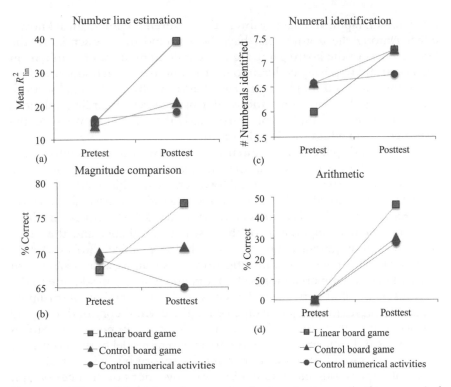

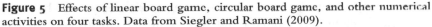

Figure 5 Effects of linear board game, circular board game, and other numerical activities on four tasks. Data from Siegler and Ramani (2009).

6. CONCLUSIONS

Children differ greatly in their mathematical knowledge at the beginning of kindergarten. These early individual differences are maintained, and indeed steadily increase, over the course of schooling. These and the related finding that early and later mathematical knowledge is closely related to social class have led to large-scale and small-scale interventions intended to improve the mathematical knowledge of children from low-income backgrounds.

Several large-scale interventions have produced very encouraging results, but these interventions are also expensive to implement. In part for this reason, and in part to test whether theoretical understanding of numerical development could lead to an effective, inexpensive intervention, Siegler and Ramani developed a linear numerical board game and tested its effects on the mathematical knowledge of preschoolers from impoverished backgrounds. Playing the number board game produced large, broad, rapid, and stable gains in the children's mathematical knowledge. Among the features that have been found to be essential to the effectiveness of the board game are a linear configuration of numbers on the board and requiring children to say the number in each square as they move their token through that square (Laski, 2008). In this final section, we briefly reflect on implications of this research regarding relations between theory and application, particularly the relation between cognitive theory and educational applications.

Theory and application are often viewed as two categories into which research can be classified; within this view, some investigations contribute to theory and others to practice. However, as the historian of science Donald Stokes noted in his classic book *Pasteur's Quadrant*, the relation between theory and application is better viewed as a 2 × 2 matrix, in which one dimension is importance of the research for theory and the other dimension is importance of the research for practice (Stokes, 1997). Stokes cited Pasteur's classic investigations of smallpox as an example of research that was important for both theory and practice; in addition to the obvious practical importance of Pasteur's studies for eradicating smallpox, the research provided crucial evidence for the germ theory of disease and was foundational for the fields of microbiology and immunology. Stokes cited Niels Bohr's formulation of the solar system model of the atom as an example of research that was important for theory but without obvious practical implications and Thomas Edison's inventions of the phonograph as an example of research that had great practical importance but little theoretical significance. (Stokes was too polite, or circumspect, to cite research that was of little importance theoretically or practically, though examples are not hard to find.) As this analysis illustrates, there is no inherent opposition between "theoretical research" and "applied research"; indeed, the same research programs have often made major contributions to both.

In a cognitive context, the relation between research on the mental number line and research on the number game application illustrates the symbiotic relation that often arises between theory and application. To the best of our knowledge, the mental number line construct originated as Moyer and Landauer's (1967) explanation for their classic demonstration of distance effects in numerical magnitude comparison. It has continued to be a theoretically central construct ever since in both adult cognitive psychology (e.g., Dehaene, 1997) and cognitive development (e.g., Case & Okamoto, 1996). The mental number line construct has been equally central as a target of instruction, both in the teaching of arithmetic (Resnick, 1983) and as a central conceptual structure for organizing a wide range of numerical acquisitions (Case & Griffin, 1990).

In the present context, as in Case's and Resnick's work, the relation between theory and application flowed in both directions. The theoretical question of how children form initial linear representations of numerical magnitudes led to the idea that board games might play an important role. The theoretical analysis of how correlational patterns that emerge while playing board games could contribute to linear magnitude representations provided a mechanism that might underlie the relation. The theoretical construct of the mental number line suggested that a linear organization of the number board game would be most effective for improving those representations.

The benefits flowed from application to theory as well. The experiment contrasting the effects of playing the game with linear and circular boards indicated that linear visuospatial cues are especially important for forming linear numerical magnitude representations, more important than temporal, tactile, and auditory cues, which the two types of boards shared. The applied studies also broadened theory in the area by indicating a mechanism through which linear representations can arise—real-world experience playing board games. In addition, findings from the board game studies raised new theoretical questions, such as how children who do not play board games form linear representations of numerical magnitudes, whether experience playing board games from right to left would produce mental number lines extending from right to left, and whether mental number lines can be formed from noisier data about numerical magnitudes than produced in the present board game context.

More generally, we believe that there are a variety of intellectual benefits to pursuing research in Pasteur's Quadrant. One of the most important benefits of studying thinking in applied contexts is that it focuses attention on real-world experiences that shape the thinking we see in the laboratory. In the study of cognitive development, the role of board games in shaping numerical representations is just one example; three others are studies documenting the role of exposure to nursery rhymes in gaining phonological awareness (Maclean, Bryant, & Bradley, 1987), the role of fairy tales in providing base cues for problem solving (Chen, Mo, & Honomichl, 2004), and the role of selling girl scout cookies in helping children gain record keeping and organizational skills (Rogoff, Topping, Baker-Sennett, & Lascasa, 2002). In addition, many of the most important aspects of cognitive development beyond the first few years of life are shaped by experiences that occur in school. To the extent that the field of cognitive development ignores the role of knowledge that is gained in school, it has little chance of understanding intellectual development beyond the age of school entry.

The relation is no less important in adult cognitive psychology. Studies of adult cognition also rest on knowledge gained in school. This is true not only for areas taught in school, such as mathematics and science, but also of "basic" competencies such as memory and categorization. Cross-cultural studies of differences in memory and categorization between schooled and unschooled populations illustrate the extent of the influence of schooling on these basic processes (Cole, Gay, Glick, & Sharp, 1971; Shweder et al., 2006). More generally, efforts to bring together theory and application lead researchers to study the environments that help create the thought patterns that we take for granted as basic human endowments, but that actually vary considerably across times, places, cultures, and individuals. Thus, yet another advantage of striving to work in Pasteur's Quadrant is that it leads to a focus on the environments that shape cognition, a focus that promises both to deepen our theoretical understanding and to yield effective applications.

ACKNOWLEDGMENTS

The research described in this paper was funded in part by grants R305A080013 and R305H050035 from the Institute of Education Sciences, in addition by support from the Teresa Heinz Chair at Carnegie Mellon University.

REFERENCES

Ansari, D. (2008). Effects of development and enculturation on number representation in the brain. *Nature Reviews Neuroscience, 9*, 278–291.
Arnold, D. H., Fisher, P. H., Doctoroff, G. L., & Dobbs, J. (2002). Accelerating math development in head start classrooms. *Journal of Educational Psychology, 94*, 762–770.
Ashcraft, M. H. (1992). Cognitive arithmetic: A review of data and theory. *Cognition, 44*, 75–106.
Aunola, K., Leskinen, E., Lerkkanen, M., & Nurmi, J. (2004). Developmental dynamics of math performance from preschool to grade 2. *Journal of Educational Psychology, 96*, 699–713.
Bächtold, D., Baumüller, M., & Brugger, P. (1998). Stimulus–response compatibility in representational space. *Neuropsychologia, 36*, 731–735.
Berch, D. B., Foley, E. J., Hill, R. J., & Ryan, P. M. (1999). Extracting parity and magnitude from Arabic numerals: Developmental changes in number processing and mental representation. *Journal of Experimental Child Psychology, 74*, 286–308.
Berteletti, I., Lucangeli, D., Piazza, M., Dehaene, S., & Zorzi, M. (2010). Numerical estimation in preschoolers. *Developmental Psychology, 46*, 545–551.
Blevins-Knabe, B., & Musun-Miller, L. (1996). Number use at home by children and their parents and its relationship to early mathematical performance. *Early Development and Parenting, 5*, 35–45.
Booth, J. L., & Siegler, R. S. (2006). Developmental and individual differences in pure numerical estimation. *Developmental Psychology, 41*, 189–201.
Booth, J. L., & Siegler, R. S. (2008). Numerical magnitude representations influence arithmetic learning. *Child Development, 79*, 1016–1031.
Brannon, E. M., Suanda, S. H., & Libertus, K. (2007). Temporal discrimination increases in precision over development and parallels the development of numerosity discrimination. *Developmental Science, 10*, 770–777.
Brannon, E. M., Wusthoff, C. J., Gallistel, C. R., & Gibbon, J. (2001). Numerical subtraction in the pigeon: Evidence for a linear subjective number line. *Psychological Science, 12*, 238–243.

Bransford. J.D., Brown. A.L, and Cocking. R.R., (Eds.), (1999). *How people learn: Brain, mind, experience, and school.* Washington, DC: National Academy Press.

Case, R. (1978). Intellectual development from birth to adulthood: A neo-Piagetian approach. In R. S. Siegler (Ed.), *Children's thinking: What develops?* Hillsdale, NJ: Erlbaum.

Case, R. (1992). *The mind's staircase: Exploring the conceptual underpinnings of children's thought and knowledge.* Hillsdale, NJ: Erlbaum.

Case, R., & Griffin, S. (1990). Child cognitive development: The role of central conceptual structures in the development of scientific and social thought. In C. Hauert (Ed.), *Developmental psychology: Cognitive, perceptuo-motor and neuropsychological perspectives* Oxford, England: North-Holland.

Case, R., Griffin, S., & Kelly, W. M. (1999). Socioeconomic gradients in mathematical ability and their responsiveness to intervention during early childhood. In D. P. Keating, and G. Hertzman, (Eds.), *Developmental health and the wealth of nations* (pp. 125–149). New York: Guilford.

Case, R., & Okamoto, Y. (1996). The role of central conceptual structures in the development of children's thought. *Monographs of the Society for Research in Child Development, 61,* (Nos. 1-2).

Chen, Z., Mo, L., & Honomichl, R. (2004). Having the memory of an elephant: Long-term retrieval and the use of analogues in problem solving. *Journal of Experimental Psychology: General, 133,* 415–433.

Clements, D. H., & Sarama, J. (2007). Effects of a preschool mathematics curriculum: Summative research on the building blocks project. *Journal for Research in Mathematics Education, 38,* 136–163.

Clements, D. H., & Sarama, J. (2008). Experimental evaluation of the effects of a research-based preschool mathematics curriculum. *American Education Research Journal, 45,* 443–494.

Cole, M., Gay, J., Glick, J., & Sharp, D. (1971). *The cultural context of learning and thinking.* New York: Basic Books.

Crites, T. (1992). Skilled and less skilled estimators' strategies for estimating discrete quantities. *The Elementary School Journal, 92,* 601–619.

de Havia, M. D., & Spelke, E. S. (2010). Number-space mapping in human infants. *Psychological Science, 21,* 653–660.

Dehaene, S. (1997). *The number sense: How the mind creates mathematics.* New York: Oxford University Press.

Dehaene, S., Bossini, S., & Giraux, P. (1993). The mental representation of parity and number magnitude. *Journal of Experimental Psychology: General, 122,* 371–396.

Duncan, G. J., Dowsett, C. J., Claessens, A., Magnuson, K., Huston, A. C., & Klebanov, P., et al., (2007). School readiness and later achievement. *Developmental Psychology, 43,* 1428–1446.

Duncan, G. J., & Magnuson, K. (in press). The nature and impact of early achievement skills, attention skills, and behavior problems. In R. M. Murnane & G. J. Duncan (Eds.), *Social inequalities and educational disadvantage.* Washington, DC: Brookings Institution.

Early, D., Iruka, I. U., Ritchie, S., Barbarin, O., Winn, D. C., & Crawford, G. M., et al., (2010). How do pre-kindergarteners spend their time? Gender, ethnicity, and income as predictors of experiences in pre-kindergarten classrooms. *Early Childhood Research Quarterly, 25,* 177–193.

Geary, D. C., Hoard, M. K., Byrd-Craven, J., Nugent, L., & Numtee, C. (2007). Cognitive mechanisms underlying achievement deficits in children with mathematical learning disability. *Child Development, 78,* 1343–1359.

Gelman, R., & Gallistel, C. R. (1978). *The child's understanding of number.* Cambridge, MA: Harvard University Press.

Ginsberg, H. P., & Russell, R. L. (1981). Social class and racial influences on early mathematical thinking. *Monographs of the Society for Research in Child Development, 46*(6) Serial No. 69.

Griffin, S. (2003). Number Worlds: A research-based mathematics program for young children. In D. H. Clements, and J. Sarama, (Eds.), *Engaging young children in mathematics: Standards for early childhood mathematics education* (pp. 325–342). Mahwah, NJ: Lawrence Erlbaum Associates.

Griffin, S. (2007). Early intervention for children at risk of developing mathematical learning difficulties. In D. B. Berch, and M. M. Mazzocco, (Eds.), *Why is math so hard for some children? The nature and origins of mathematical learning difficulties and disabilities* (pp. 373–396). Baltimore, MD: Brookes Publishing.

Griffin, S., & Case, R. (1996). Evaluating the breadth and depth of training effects when central conceptual structures are taught. *Society for Research in Child Development Monographs, 59,* 90–113.

Griffin, S., & Case, R. (1997). Re-thinking the primary school math curriculum: An approach based on cognitive science. *Issues in Education, 3,* 1–49.

Griffin, S., Case, R., & Siegler, R. S. (1994). Rightstart: Providing the central conceptual prerequisites for first formal learning of arithmetic to students at risk for school failure. In K. McGilly (Ed.), *Classroom lessons: Integrating cognitive theory and classroom practice* (pp. 25–49). Cambridge, MA: MIT Press.

Hanich, L. B., Jordan, N. C., Kaplan, D., & Dick, J. (2001). Performance across different areas of mathematical cognition in children with learning difficulties. *Journal of Educational Psychology, 93,* 615–626.

Holloway, S. D., Rambaud, M. F., Fuller, B., & Eggers-Pierola, C. (1995). What is "appropriate practice" at home and in child care?: Low-income mother's views on preparing their children for school. *Early Childhood Research Quarterly, 10,* 451–473.

Holyoak, K. J., & Mah, W. A. (1982). Cognitive reference points in judgments of symbolic magnitude. *Cognitive Psychology, 14,* 328–352.

Hubbard, E. M., Piazza, M., Pinel, P., & Dehaene, S. (2005). Interactions between number and space in parietal cortex. *Nature Reviews Neuroscience, 6,* 435–448.

Hughes, M. (1981). Can preschool children add and subtract? *Educational Psychology, 1,* 207–219.

Jordan, K. E., Suanda, S. H., & Brannon, E. M. (2008). Intersensory redundancy accelerates preverbal numerical competence. *Cognition, 108,* 210–221.

Jordan, N. C., Kaplan, D., Olah, L. N., & Locuniak, M. N. (2006). Number sense growth in kindergarten: a longitudinal investigation of children at risk for mathematics difficulties. *Child Development, 77,* 153–175.

Jordan, N. C., Kaplan, D., Ramineni, C., & Locuniak, M. N. (2009). Early math matters: Kindergarten number competence and later mathematics outcomes. *Developmental Psychology, 45,* 850–867.

Klein, A., Starkey, P., Clements, D. H., Sarama, J., & Iyer, R. (2008). Effects of a pre-kindergarten mathematics intervention: A randomized experiment. *Journal of Research on Educational Effectiveness, 1,* 155–178.

Klibanoff, R. S., Levine, S. C., Huttenlocher, J., Vasilyeva, M., & Hedges, L. V. (2006). Preschool children's mathematical knowledge: The effect of teacher "math talk.". *Developmental Psychology, 42,* 59–69.

Laski, E. V. (2008). *Internal and external influences on learning: A microgenetic analysis of the acquisition of numerical knowledge from board games (Unpublished doctoral dissertation).* Pittsburgh, PA: Carnegie Mellon University.

Laski, E. V., & Siegler, R. S. (2007). Is 27 a big number? Correlational and causal connections among numerical categorization, number line estimation, and numerical magnitude comparison. *Child Development, 76,* 1723–1743.

Le Corre, M., & Carey, S. (2007). One, two, three, four, nothing more: An investigation of the conceptual sources of the verbal counting principles. *Cognition, 105*, 395–438.

Le Corre, M., Van de Walle, G., Brannon, E. M., & Carey, S. (2006). Re-visiting the competence/performance debate in the acquisition of the counting principles. *Cognitive Psychology, 52*, 130–169.

LoCasale-Crouch, J., Konold, T., Pianta, R., Howes, C., Burchinal, M., & Bryant, D., et al., (2007). Observed classroom quality profiles in state-funded pre-kindergarten programs and associations with teacher, program, and classroom characteristics. *Early Childhood Research Quarterly, 22*, 3–17.

Lourenco, S. F., & Longo, M. R. (2010). General magnitude representation in human infants. *Psychological Science, 21*, 873–881.

Maclean, M., Bryant, P., & Bradley, L. (1987). Rhymes, nursery rhymes, and reading in early childhood. *Merrill-Palmer Quarterly: Journal of Developmental Psychology, 33*, 255–281.

Malofeeva, E., Day, J., Saco, X., Young, L., & Ciancio, D. (2004). Construction and evaluation of a number sense test with head start children. *Journal of Educational Psychology, 96*, 648–659.

McCloskey, M. (2007). Quantitative literacy and developmental dyscalculias. In D. B. Berch, and M. M. Mazzocco, (Eds.), *Why is math so hard for some children? The nature and origins of mathematical learning difficulties and disabilities* (pp. 415–429). Baltimore, MD: Paul H Brookes Publishing.

Miller, K. F., Smith, C. M., Zhu, J., & Zhang, H. (1995). Preschool origins of cross-national differences in mathematical competence: The role of number-naming systems. *Psychological Science, 6*, 56–60.

Moyer, R. S., & Landauer, T. K. (1967). Time required for judgments of numerical inequality. *Nature, 215*, 1519–1520.

National Mathematics Advisory Panel. (2008). *Foundations for Success: The Final Report of the National Mathematics Advisory Panel*. Retrieved from http://www2.ed.gov/about/bdscomm/list/mathpanel/index.html.

Pagani, L. S., Jalbert, J., & Girard, A. (2006). Does preschool enrichment of precursors to arithmetic influence intuitive knowledge of number in low income children? *Early Childhood Education Journal, 34*, 133–146.

Petitto, A. L. (1990). Development of number line and measurement concepts. *Cognition and Instruction, 7*, 55–78.

Pianta, R., Howes, C., Burchinal, M., Bryant, D., Clifford, R., & Early, D., et al., (2005). Features of pre-kindergarten programs, classrooms, and teachers: Do they predict observed classroom quality and child–teacher interactions. *Applied Developmental Science, 9*, 144–159.

Ramani, G. B., & Siegler, R. S. (2008). Promoting broad and stable improvements in low-income children's numerical knowledge through playing number board games. *Child Development, 79*, 375–394.

Resnick, L. B. (1983). Mathematics and science learning: A new conception. *Science, 220*, 477–478.

Rivera-Batiz, F. L. (1992). Quantitative literacy and the likelihood of employment among young adults in the United States. *Journal of Human Resources, 27*, 313–328.

Rogoff, B., Topping, K., Baker-Sennett, J., & Lascasa, P. (2002). Mutual contributions of individuals, partners, and institutions: Planning to remember in Girl Scout cookie sales. *Social Development, 11*, 266–289.

Sarama, J., & Clements, D. H. (2002). Building blocks for young children's mathematical development. *Journal of Educational Computing Research, 27*, 93–110.

Sarama, J., & Clements, D. H. (2004). Building blocks for early childhood mathematics. *Early Childhood Research Quarterly, 19*, 181–189.

Sarama, J., Clements, D. H., Starkey, P., Klein, A., & Wakeley, A. (2008). Scaling up the implementation of a pre-kindergarten mathematics curriculum: Teaching for understanding with trajectories and technologies. *Journal of Research on Educational Effectiveness*, *1*, 89–119.

Sarnecka, B. W., & Carey, S. (2008). How counting represents number: What children must learn and when they learn it. *Cognition*, *108*, 662–674.

Saxe, G. B., Guberman, S. R., & Gearhart, M. (1987). Social processes in early number development. *Monographs of the Society for Research in Child Development*, *52*(2).

Schaeffer, B., Eggleston, V. H., & Scott, J. L. (1974). Number development in young children. *Cognitive Psychology*, *6*, 357–379.

Shweder, R. A., Goodnow, J. J., Hatano, G., LeVine, R. A., Markus, H. R., & Miller, J. (2006). The cultural psychology of development: One mind, many mentalities. In R. M. Lerner, & W. Damon, (Eds.), *Handbook of child psychology, 6th Ed., Vol. 1, Theorectical models of human development* (pp. 716–792). Hoboken, NJ: Wiley.

Siegel, A. W., Goldsmith, L. T., & Madson, C. M. (1982). Skill in estimation problems of extent and numerosity. *Journal for Research in Mathematics Education*, *13*, 211–232.

Siegler, R. S., & Booth, J. L. (2004). Development of numerical estimation in young children. *Child Development*, *75*, 428–444.

Siegler, R. S., & Booth, J. L. (2005). Development of numerical estimation: A review. In J. I. D. Campbell (Ed.), *Handbook of mathematical cognition* (pp. 197–212)). Boca Raton, FL: CRC Press.

Siegler, R. S., & Opfer, J. E. (2003). The development of numerical estimation: Evidence for multiple representations of numerical quantity. *Psychological Science*, *14*, 237–243.

Siegler, R. S., & Ramani, G. B. (2008). Playing linear numerical board games promotes low-income children's numerical development. *Developmental Science*, *11*, 655–661.

Siegler, R. S., & Ramani, G. B. (2009). Playing linear number board games—but not circular ones—improves low-income preschoolers' numerical understanding. *Journal of Educational Psychology*, *101*, 545–560.

Siegler, R. S., & Robinson, M. (1982). The development of numerical understandings. H. W. Reese, and L. Lipsitt, (Eds.), *Advances in Child Development and Behavior 16*, (pp. 242–312). New York: Academic Press.

Siegler, R. S., & Shrager, J. (1984). Strategy choice in addition and subtraction: How do children know what to do. In C. Sophian (Ed.), *Origins of cognitive skills* (pp. 229–293). Hillsdale, NJ: Erlbaum.

Sophian, C. (2004). Mathematics for the future: Developing a Head Start curriculum to support mathematics learning. *Early Childhood Research Quarterly*, *19*, 59–81.

Starkey, P., & Klein, A. (2000). Fostering parental support for children's mathematical development: An intervention with Head Start families. *Early Education & Development*, *11*, 659–680.

Starkey, P., Klein, A., & Wakeley, A. (2004). Enhancing young children's mathematical knowledge through a pre-kindergarten mathematics intervention. *Early Childhood Research Quarterly*, *19*, 99–120.

Stevenson, H. W., & Newman, R. S. (1986). Long-term prediction of achievement and attitudes in mathematics and reading. *Child Development*, *57*, 646–659.

Stipek, D. J., & Ryan, R. H. (1997). Economically disadvantaged preschoolers: Ready to learn but further to go. *Developmental Psychology*, *33*, 711–723.

Stokes, D. (1997). *Pasteur's quadrant: Basic science and technological innovation*. Washington, DC: Brookings Institution Press.

Thompson, C. A., & Opfer, J. E. (2010). How 15 hundred is like 15 cherries: Effect of progressive alignment on representational changes in numerical cognition. *Child Development*, *81*, 1768–1786.

Thompson, C. A., & Siegler, R. S. (2010). Linear numerical magnitude representations aid children's memory for numbers. *Psychological Science, 21*, 1274–1281.

Tudge, J. R. H., & Doucet, F. (2004). Early mathematical experiences: observing young Black and White children's everyday activities. *Early Childhood Research Quarterly, 19*, 21–39.

U.S. Department of Education, NCES. (2000). *America's kindergartners*. Retrieved from http://www.nces.ed.gov/pubsearch/pubsinfo.asp?pubid = 2000070.

Whyte, J. C., & Bull, R. (2008). Number games, magnitude representation, and basic number skills in preschoolers. *Developmental Psychology, 44*(2), 588–596.

Wynn, K. (1992). Addition and subtraction by human infants. *Nature, 358*, 749–750.

Zorzi, M., Priftis, K., & Umiltà, C. (2002). Neglect disrupts the mental number line. *Nature, 417*, 138–139.

CHAPTER SEVEN

THE POWER OF COMPARISON IN LEARNING AND INSTRUCTION: LEARNING OUTCOMES SUPPORTED BY DIFFERENT TYPES OF COMPARISONS

Bethany Rittle-Johnson *and* Jon R. Star

Contents

Abstract

Comparison is a powerful learning process that has been leveraged to improve learning in a variety of domains. We identify five different types of comparisons that have been used in past research and develop a framework for describing them and the learning outcomes they support. For example, comparing multiple methods for solving the same problem, with a focus on which method is better for solving a particular problem, can improve procedural flexibility. We include a review of our own efforts to design and evaluate educational materials that leverage different types of comparisons to support mathematics learning in classrooms, including our

Psychology of Learning and Motivation, Volume 55

ISSN 0079-7421, DOI 10.1016/B978-0-12-387691-1.00007-7

© 2011 Elsevier Inc.

All rights reserved.

ongoing effort to encourage use of comparison throughout the Algebra I curriculum. In the context of this classroom work, two new comparison types emerged. Overall, we illustrate how cognitive science research helped guide the design of effective educational materials and how educational practice revealed new ideas to test and incorporate into theories of learning.

1. INTRODUCTION

Comparison is a powerful learning process that has been leveraged to improve learning in a variety of domains. As Goldstone, Day, and Son (2010, p. 103) noted: "Comparison is one of the most integral components of human thought. . . .. Furthermore, research has demonstrated that the simple act of comparing two things can produce important changes in our knowledge." Indeed, comparison aids learning of a broad range of topics, ranging from preschoolers learning new words (e.g., Namy & Gentner, 2002), elementary school children learning estimation methods (Star & Rittle-Johnson, 2009), to business school students learning contract negotiation skills (e.g., Gentner, Loewenstein, & Thompson, 2003).

The diversity of topics for which comparison aids learning is exciting, but limited efforts have been made to synthesize across studies to gain a more comprehensive understanding of how comparison aids learning. Such an understanding is critical for revising theories of learning and designing effective educational materials that leverage comparison. A primary purpose of this chapter is to develop a framework of different types of comparisons and the learning outcomes each supports, with a focus on research in problem-solving domains. A second purpose is to review our own efforts to design and evaluate educational materials that leverage different types of comparisons to support mathematics learning in classrooms.

First, we review previous research on comparison, developing a framework for classifying different types of comparisons. We focused on studies that examined the impact of comparison on problem-solving domains, with occasional supportive evidence from nonproblem-solving domains. Most of these studies used brief interventions that were conducted in a controlled laboratory setting. Next, we present evidence from our classroom-based research on using different types of comparisons to support mathematics learning. Finally, we outline our ongoing efforts to support mathematics teachers in their use of comparison throughout the school year.

2. COMPARISON TYPES USED IN PAST RESEARCH

We used the existing literature on how comparison supports learning in problem-solving domains to develop the framework in Table 1. Most past research can be classified as using one of five comparison types, identified in the columns of the table. Four characteristics that distinguish the comparison types, as well as a sample reflection prompt, are indicated in the rows of the table. The first distinction is the comparison goal, ranging from when one can use a solution method to what concept the examples share (row 2). The second distinction is the features of the examples being compared (row 3). Often, the examples are *worked examples*—a problem statement along with a step by step solution to the problem. The to-be-compared worked examples can vary in (a) whether the problem is the same or different and (b) whether the solution method is the same or different. Alternatively, rather than using worked examples, the examples can be instances of the same concept. The third distinction is the focus of the comparison, ranging from a focus on how one problem differs from another to why one method works and one does not (row 4).

The fourth distinction is the learning outcomes typically supported by the comparison (row 5). For example, consider problem comparison (column 2). Comparing different problems solved using the same solution method, with a focus on when a particular method can be used, has been shown to support transfer of the method to new problems (e.g., Gick & Holyoak, 1983). In contrast, comparing different correct methods for solving the same problem, with a focus on the efficiency of the methods (i.e., correct method comparison, column 4), has been shown to support procedural flexibility (e.g., Rittle-Johnson & Star, 2007). Thus, a variety of things can be compared for a variety of reasons, each supporting a different learning outcome. In the final row of the table, we provide a sample reflection prompt used in past research to help illustrate each type of comparison. Note that this framework and review of the literature is not meant to be exhaustive, but rather is meant to capture key features of existing studies on comparison in problem-solving domains. Next, we provide details on each type of comparison.

2.1. Problem Comparison

One of the earliest studied types of comparison is comparing two different problems solved with the same method (i.e., problem comparison—see column 2 in Table 1). The goal is to support learning of a general solution method. This type of comparison has been well studied in the analogical learning literature. For example, adults were asked to read stories about two problems solved with the same method and to "list all the important

Table 1 Distinctions Between Five Types of Comparisons Used in Past Research.

Distinction	Comparison type				
	Problem	Problem category	Correct method	Incorrect method	Concept
Comparison goal	When can you use it?	How do these problems differ?	Which is better?	Which is correct?	What concept do they share?
Features of examples	Different problems, solved with the same method	Problems from different categories, solved with different methods	Same problem solved with two different correct methods	Same problem solved with a correct and an incorrect method	Different examples of the same concept
Focus of comparison	When a method can be used based on similarities in the method across problems	How one problem differs from another	When and why one method is more efficient or easier	Why one method works and one does not	What key idea the examples share
Learning outcome supported	Solve new problems using the target method (i.e., transfer)	Distinguish between easily confusable problem categories	Know multiple methods and use most appropriate method (i.e., procedural flexibility)	Make misconception errors less often and use correct methods more often	Know key concept(s)
Sample reflection prompt	"List all the important similarities you can think of in the *methods* used to capture the fortress and put out the fire." (from Catrambone & Holyoak, 1989)	"What is the distinguishing characteristic between the combinations and permutations formulas?" (based on VanderStoep & Seifert, 1993)	"_____'s way is better on this problem because:" (from Rittle-Johnson & Star, 2009)	"How do you know which way is correct?" (from Durkin, 2009)	"How is the equal sign like the greater than and less than symbols?" (based on Hattikudur & Alibali, 2010)

similarities you can think of in the *methods* [emphasis in original] used to capture the fortress and put out the fire." (Catrambone & Holyoak, 1989, p. 1156). These participants were much more likely to use the illustrated solution method to solve a new problem than were participants who studied the same examples, but were not encouraged to compare them. In general, illustrating how the same method can be used to solve two isomorphic problems and prompting for comparison leads to spontaneous transfer of the method to a new problem (Catrambone & Holyoak, 1989; Gick & Holyoak, 1983). Furthermore, carefully crafted comparison prompts lead to better learning than just presenting the examples side by side or giving generic prompts to compare the two examples (Catrambone & Holyoak, 1989; Gentner et al., 2003).

This type of comparison can support learning of curricular content, at least in adults. In a series of studies, business school students read two different problem scenarios illustrating the same contract negotiation method. They compared the examples by identifying their similarities or summarized each example individually. Students who compared were much more likely to use the illustrated negotiation method to solve a new problem scenario, including in an interactive, contract negotiation setting (Gentner et al., 2003; Loewenstein & Gentner, 2001; Loewenstein, Thompson, & Gentner, 1999, 2003; Thompson, Gentner, & Loewenstein, 2000).

Comparing problems is thought to support transfer by helping people abstract the key features of the method so that it is not tied to overly narrow problem features. For example, in many of the studies described above, people who compared worked examples were more likely to describe the solution to the example problems in general terms, rather than being tied to the specifics of the problem context (Catrambone & Holyoak, 1989; Gentner et al., 2003; Gick & Holyoak, 1983). In addition, explicitly stating the general method *after* students had compared two example problems improved transfer; stating the general method without use of comparison did little to improve transfer (Gick & Holyoak, 1983).

There are some limits on when comparing problems aids transfer. Reed (1989) had college students compare two algebra word problems and their solutions or study the same examples sequentially. Across three experiments, comparing the problems and their solutions did not support transfer of the solution methods to new problems. Reed (1989) suggested that complex multistep methods may be more difficult to learn via problem comparison than simpler methods such as the one learned in Gick and Holyoak (1983). Learning complex methods at the appropriate level of generality to solve a range of problems is perhaps too difficult to learn from comparing a single pair of problems, at least without additional instructional support. Nevertheless, comparing the similarities in different problems solved with the same method often helps people learn a more general solution method that they can transfer appropriately to new problems.

2.2. Problem Category Comparison

A second type of comparison that has been studied in the analogical learning literature also involves comparison of different problems (see column 3 of Table 1). In this comparison type, the different problems are not isomorphic, but rather are from different, but easily confusable, problem categories. Thus, the problems need to be solved using different methods. The goal is to notice how the problems differ in order to distinguish between easily confusable problem categories.

For example, college students were asked to compare examples of algebra word problems from different categories or to study the examples one at a time (Cummins, 1992). Across three experiments, those who compared were better able to sort new examples by problem category and to describe their structural features. Similarly, college students (a) were shown worked examples of a combination and a permutation problem and were provided with instruction that compared the two problem categories or (b) were presented with the same two worked examples, without comparison (VanderStoep & Seifert, 1993). Again, those given the comparisons were better able to correctly categorize problems and justify their choices.

It is not simply the act of comparison, but rather comparing examples of different problem categories that seems to help learners distinguish between the categories. In a recent classroom study, middle school students compared an example from each of two easily confusable problem categories (i.e., a positive and a negative feedback loop) or compared two examples of the same problem category (e.g., two positive feedback loops) (Day, Goldstone, & Hill, 2010). Those who compared the two types of feedback loops were better able to classify new examples as positive versus negative feedback loops.

Problem solving requires correctly categorizing problems, and this can be particularly difficult when problem categories share some key features. Comparing examples of different problem categories, with attention to the distinguishing features of each category, can help people learn to better distinguish them.

2.3. Correct Method Comparison

Rather than comparing different problems, people can also compare different methods for solving the same problem. This type of comparison has been described in observational studies of mathematics teaching. Expert mathematics teachers often have students compare multiple methods for solving the same problem (e.g. Ball, 1993; Lampert, 1990), as do teachers in high performing countries such as Japan (Richland, Zur, & Holyoak, 2007). This emphasis on sharing and comparing methods was formalized in the National Council of Teachers of Mathematics ("Curriculum focal points for prekindergarten through grade 8 mathematics") (2000).

These observational studies do not link the practice of comparing methods to measured student outcomes. In this section, we focus on comparing correct methods for solving the same problem (i.e., correct method comparison; see column 4 in Table 1); in the next section, we focus on comparing a correct method to an incorrect method (i.e., incorrect method comparison; see column 5 in Table 1).

Comparing correct methods can focus attention on when and why one method is better for solving a particular problem, and this focus should support procedural flexibility (e.g., Rittle-Johnson & Star, 2007). Procedural flexibility incorporates the knowledge of multiple methods as well as the ability to choose the most appropriate method based on specific problem features (Kilpatrick, Swafford, & Findell, 2001; Star, 2005; Verschaffel, Luwel, Torbeyns, & Van Dooren, 2009). Procedural flexibility supports efficient problem solving and is also associated with greater accuracy solving novel problems and with a greater understanding of domain concepts (e.g., Blöte, Van der Burg, & Klein, 2001; Carpenter, Franke, Jacobs, Fennema, & Empson, 1998; Hiebert et al., 1996). Asking students to compare two correct methods for solving a problem and asking them to reflect on which is better for solving a given problem (e.g., is more efficient) should be particularly well suited to supporting procedural flexibility. We confirmed this hypothesis in our classroom studies on comparison, described in Section 3.

2.4. Incorrect Method Comparison

In addition to comparing correct methods for solving a problem, expert mathematics teachers capitalize on students' incorrect methods and compare them with correct methods (Fraivillig, Murphy, & Fuson, 1999; Huffred-Ackles, Fuson, & Sherin Gamoran, 2004; Stigler & Hiebert, 1998). Identifying why one method works and one does not should help reduce misconceptions and support more frequent use of correct methods (see column 5 of Table 1).

Support for the value of incorrect method comparison comes from a recent experimental study on fourth- and fifth-grade students learning about decimal magnitude (Durkin, 2009). Students either compared 12 examples of an incorrect method for placing a decimal on a number line to a correct method or compared 12 examples of two different correct methods. Those who compared incorrect and correct methods were more accurate at placing decimals on number lines at posttest than students who studied only correct methods. They also made fewer misconception errors and had better retention of decimal concepts after a 2-week delay. Similarly, elementary school children who were prompted to explain six correct and incorrect solutions to problems such as 4 + 5 + 8 = 4 + _ solved more equations correctly at posttest than students who studied only correct examples, although comparison was not supported explicitly (Siegler, 2002) (see also Curry, 2004; Huang, Liu, & Shiu, 2008).

Supporting evidence for the value of comparing correct and incorrect examples comes from studies on scientific refutation texts. In refutation texts, two possible solutions are presented to example problems—one based on a correct scientific concept and one based on a common misconception (e.g., solution to a motion problem using a correct Newtonian mechanics concept vs. using an incorrect concept)—and the incorrect solution is identified and refuted. Refutation texts have been shown to reduce misconception errors and improve use of correct scientific concepts more than expository texts that do not include or refute incorrect solutions (Alvermann & Hague, 1989; Diakidoy, Kendeou, & Ioannides, 2003; van den Broek & Kendeou, 2008).

Studying incorrect examples is thought to reduce the strength of those incorrect ways of thinking (e.g., Siegler, 2002). Because incorrect ways of thinking continue to coexist and compete for selection over correct ways of thinking, it is important to reduce their strength and thus their probability of being used. Comparing incorrect methods to correct ones should help strengthen correct methods and weaken incorrect ones. This type of comparison should also promote noticing of conflicting ideas (van den Broek & Kendeou, 2008) and focus attention on the distinguishing features of the correct examples, including the relevant concepts (Durkin, 2009). Thus, contrasting incorrect examples with correct ones can help reduce misconception errors and increase use of correct methods.

2.5. Concept Comparison

Although problems or solutions are most often compared in problem-solving domains, people can also learn from comparing multiple examples of the same concept (column 6 in Table 1). Identifying what concept the examples share should help people understand that concept better.

We could find only one study that evaluated the benefit of concept comparison in a problem-solving domain. Elementary school students compared the equal sign to the greater than and less than symbols or learned about the equal sign by itself in a brief lesson. Students who compared the symbols, which indicate the relation between the values on either side of it, developed a better relational understanding of the equal sign (e.g., accepted that $6 + 4 = 5 + 5$ is true) (Hattikudur & Alibali, 2010).

Studies on concept development, particularly categorization, also indicate a benefit of comparing examples of the same concept. Numerous studies have found that showing preschoolers two examples of a category (e.g., of an object property like texture), rather than only one example of the category, greatly improves their ability to identify a new instance of the category (e.g., Graham, Namy, Gentner, & Meagher, 2010; Namy & Gentner, 2002; Waxman & Klibanoff, 2000).

Gentner and Markman (1997) have proposed that comparing two examples of a concept promotes structural alignment between the representations of each example, highlighting their common structure, especially their shared relational structures. For example, comparing the equal sign with the greater than and less than signs may highlight the common role the three share, indicating the relation between quantities on either side of it. Overall, comparing examples of the same concept can help people learn that concept, although evidence for this claim in problem-solving domains is limited.

2.6. Summary of Prior Research

Research on the benefits of comparison for learning in problem-solving domains clearly indicates that comparison aids learning across a variety of outcomes, subject matters, and age groups. As summarized in Table 1, at least five different types of comparisons have been studied in previous research. The different types of comparisons vary in how the to-be-compared examples differ and in the focus of the comparisons. In turn, each type of comparison supports a different learning outcome.

The amount and nature of evidence in support of the effectiveness of each type of comparison varies substantially. For example, there is extensive research with adults indicating that problem comparison supports transfer, both on laboratory tasks and from homework assignments. This research has focused on fairly simple solution methods, and none of it has been done with children or in a school setting. In contrast, correct method comparison is supported by skilled mathematics teachers, but the impact of this type of comparison on learning had not been evaluated in previous research. Finally, in the vast majority of experimental research on comparison, the comparison intervention was brief, typically lasting 5–10 min, often involving a single comparison episode, and occurred in a laboratory setting. Even the studies with elementary school children were conducted one-on-one outside the classroom (e.g., Durkin, 2009; Hattikudur & Alibali, 2010; Siegler, 2002).

3. OUR SHORT-TERM CLASSROOM RESEARCH ON COMPARISON

In our own research, our goal was to evaluate how comparison supports learning of school mathematics within a classroom setting. We redesigned two to three math lessons on a particular topic in several different ways and implemented these lessons during students' mathematics classes. Thus, students were accountable for learning the material, and we needed to design materials that were feasible to use in a classroom setting. In a series of five studies, we evaluated the effectiveness of comparing correct methods because this is the type of comparison most often advocated within mathematics education. In two of these studies, we also evaluated the effectiveness of comparing problems. See Table 2 for an overview of each study.

Before we could evaluate the effectiveness of using comparison in mathematics classrooms, we needed to modify the methods used in prior comparison research to make them feasible for use in classrooms. We maintained two common features of experimental research on comparison—the use of worked examples and prompts for explanations. Worked examples are commonly used in textbooks, so they are familiar to students, and using worked examples ensured exposure to multiple solution methods for all students. Furthermore, prompting learners to generate explanations while studying worked examples improves learning from the examples (Atkinson, Derry, Renkl, & Wortham, 2000). Thus, for each condition, we created a packet of worked examples with appropriate explanation prompts. We also included practice problems.

Unlike in past research on comparison, we had students work with a partner. Working with a partner provides a familiar context for students to generate explanations (e.g., comparisons), and students who collaborate with a partner tend to learn more than those who work alone (e.g., Johnson & Johnson, 1994; Webb, 1991). Our condition manipulation occurred at the partner level—pairs of students were randomly assigned to condition within the same classroom. This unique methodology allowed us to experimentally evaluate an instructional manipulation in a familiar classroom context (i.e., partner work), while avoiding the need for a much larger number of classrooms that would have been necessary if we had randomly assigned classrooms to condition.

Finally, we used principles from the comparison literature to maximize the potential impact of our comparison materials. First, worked examples were presented side by side to help students align the two examples (e.g.,

Table 2 Summary of Design Features and Outcomes from Our Experimental Studies on Using Comparison to Support Mathematics Learning

	Rittle-Johnson and Star (2007)	Star and Rittle-Johnson (2009)	Rittle-Johnson, Star, and Durkin (2009)	Rittle-Johnson, Star, and Durkin (2010)	Rittle-Johnson and Star (2009)
Design features					
Instructional conditions	Compare methods or sequential	Compare methods or sequential	Compare methods, sequential, or compare-problem-types	Compare methods, sequential, or delayed-compare-methods	Compare methods, compare-equivalent-problems, or compare-problem-types
Target task	Linear equations	Computational estimation	Linear equations	Linear equations	Linear equations
% Children familiar with a target method at pretest	96%	79%	20% (59% if broader criteria)	25% (56% if broader criteria)	69%
Condition(s) with highest performance					
Conceptual knowledge	Same (poor measure)	Depends on prior knowledge for retention	Depends on prior knowledge	Same (poor measure)	Compare methods
Procedural knowledge	Compare methods	Same	Depends on prior knowledge	Compare methods and sequential for retention	Same
Flexibility knowledge	Compare methods	Compare methods	Depends on prior knowledge	Compare methods and sequential	Compare methods
Flexible use	Compare methods	Compare methods	Depends on prior knowledge	Compare methods	Compare methods and compare-problem-types

find the similarities in the examples) (Richland & Holyoak, 2005). Second, the solution steps were labeled using common labels because common labels facilitate alignment of examples and subsequent learning from comparison (e.g., Namy & Gentner, 2002). Third, we included explicit prompts to identify similarities and differences because this is encouraged by expert mathematics teachers (Fraivillig et al., 1999; Huffred-Ackles et al., 2004; Lampert, 1990) and improves learning from comparison (Catrambone & Holyoak, 1989; Gentner et al., 2003). Finally, we provided some direct instruction to supplement learners' comparisons, as this has been found to improve learning from comparison (Gick & Holyoak, 1983; Schwartz & Bransford, 1998; VanderStoep & Seifert, 1993). Schwartz and Bransford (1998) suggested that comparison helps prepare students to learn from direct instruction, but is often not sufficient on its own. All our materials and papers are available at http://gseacademic.harvard.edu/contrastingcases.

3.1. Correct Method Comparison in Mathematics Classrooms

Our initial studies focused on comparing multiple methods for solving the same problem. All the methods were correct, but they varied in which was most appropriate and efficient for solving a particular problem. Students studied pairs of worked examples and were prompted to compare them (*compare methods condition*) or studied the same examples one at a time and were prompted to reflect on them individually (*sequential condition*). Our comparison prompts focused student attention on recognizing that both methods adhered to domain principles, but that a particular method was more efficient for solving a particular problem.

We hypothesized that the compare methods condition would support procedural flexibility better than the sequential condition. We assessed procedural flexibility in two ways: (a) students' flexibility knowledge (e.g., success in solving problems in multiple ways when prompted, evaluation of nonstandard solution methods) and (b) their flexible use of methods (i.e., spontaneous choice of the most efficient method to solve a particular problem). Comparing methods should highlight the accuracy and efficiency of multiple solution methods and facilitate knowledge and use of these methods. We also explored whether comparing methods would support better conceptual or procedural knowledge, as procedural flexibility is associated with both types of knowledge (e.g., Blöte et al., 2001; Carpenter et al., 1998; Hiebert et al., 1996).

In a majority of our studies, middle school students learned about multistep equation solving. The National Council of Teachers of Mathematics (2006) recommends linear equation solving as a Curriculum Focal Point for Grade 7. Regrettably, students often memorize rules and do not learn flexible and meaningful methods for solving equations (Kieran, 1992). Consider the equation $3(x + 2) = 6$. Two possible first steps are to distribute the 3 or to divide both sides by 3, and the latter approach is arguably more efficient because it reduces the number of computations and steps needed to solve the equation.

In Rittle-Johnson and Star (2007), seventh-grade students ($N = 70$) in pre-algebra classes learned about solving multistep linear equations during three class periods. Pairs of students were randomly assigned to compare methods or study the same examples sequentially (see Figure 1 for an example of materials for each condition). As predicted, those who

A. Compare Methods Condition

Shanequa's Solution:		Jill's Solution:	
$\frac{1}{2}(x + 1) = 8$		$\frac{1}{2}(x + 1) = 8$	
$x + 1 = 16$		$\frac{1}{2}x + \frac{1}{2} = 8$	
$x = 15$	*Subtract on both*		
		$\frac{1}{2}x = 7\frac{1}{2}$	*Subtract on both*
		$x = 15$	*Multiply on both*

Label the first step for each solution in the blank space provided above.

1. Shanequa and Jill solved the problem differently, but they got the same answer. Why?

2. Why might you choose to use Shanequa's way?

B. Sequential Condition

Jill's Solution:	
$\frac{1}{2}(x + 1) = 8$	
$x + 1 = 16$	
$x = 15$	*Subtract on both*

Label the first step in the blank space provided above.

1. When Jill subtracted on both sides, what number did she subtract? Why did she subtract that number?

-----*NEXT PAGE*-----

Shanequa's Solution:	
$\frac{1}{2}(x + 3) = 14$	
$\frac{1}{2}x + \frac{3}{2} = 14$	
$\frac{1}{2}x = 12\frac{1}{2}$	*Subtract on both*
$x = 25$	*Multiply on both*

Label the first step in the blank space provided above.

1. Do you think the solution method used on this problem is a good one? Why?

Figure 1 Sample pages from the compare methods and sequential conditions in Rittle-Johnson and Star (2007).

compared methods gained greater procedural flexibility. They also had greater success in solving equations (i.e., procedural knowledge). The two groups did not differ in conceptual knowledge, although the reliability of the measure was poor and was not closely aligned with the concepts students were likely to learn from the comparisons.

Students' explanations during the intervention confirmed that those who compared methods often compared the similarities and differences in solution steps across examples and evaluated their efficiency and accuracy; these students were also more likely to use alternative methods when solving practice problems during the intervention. In turn, frequency of making explicit comparisons during the intervention and frequency of using alternative methods on the practice problems were each predictive of learning outcomes. Overall, comparing methods helped students differentiate important characteristics of examples (e.g., efficiency) and consider multiple methods.

We found parallel results for 157 fifth- and sixth-grade students learning about estimating answers to multiplication problems (e.g., About how much is 37 × 29?) (Star & Rittle-Johnson, 2009). Comparing methods supported greater procedural flexibility, and it also aided retention of conceptual knowledge *if* students had above average knowledge of estimation at pretest. Overall, the similarity of the findings was striking given the large differences in the domains, including whether there was a single correct answer and what features of the methods were needed to be considered (e.g., efficiency vs. proximity to the correct answer).

Theories of analogical learning help to explain how comparing methods aids learning (Gentner, 1983; Hummel & Holyoak, 1997). In both the studies, most students were familiar with one of the solution methods at pretest. When students are familiar with one method, they can learn new methods via analogy to the familiar one. Students can make inferences about the new method by identifying its similarities and differences with a known method and making projections about how the new method works based on its alignment with the known method. For example, students who compared methods identified how the unfamiliar methods were similar to and different from the method that they already knew; in turn, these types of comparative explanations predicted learning (Rittle-Johnson & Star, 2007).

Our subsequent research revealed potential limitations on when comparing methods is effective. In particular, students' prior knowledge can impact whether they are prepared to learn from comparing methods. Indeed, if students are not familiar with one of the methods, they cannot learn new methods via analogy to a known method.

To test the importance of prior knowledge, we worked with 236 seventh- and eighth-grade students whose schools did not use a pre-algebra curriculum and thus had had limited experience solving equations

(Rittle-Johnson, Star, & Durkin, 2009). Students who did not attempt algebraic methods at pretest (i.e., novices) benefited most from studying examples sequentially, rather than from comparing methods. The novices in the compare methods condition seemed overwhelmed during the intervention—they completed less of the intervention materials and were less successful in implementing nonstandard methods when prompted. In contrast, students who attempted algebraic methods at pretest learned more from comparing methods.

A follow-up study suggested that slowing the pace of instruction allowed novices to learn from comparing methods (Rittle-Johnson et al., 2010). We worked with 198 eighth-grade students who had little prior instruction on equation solving, so we modified the materials from Rittle-Johnson et al. (2009) to cover less content in more time by focusing on fewer problem types, cutting the number of examples and explanation prompts, and adding 30 min to the intervention time. Condition did not interact with use of algebra at pretest in this study. Regardless of students' prior knowledge, comparing methods supported more flexible use of procedures than sequential study, including on a 1-month retention test. On other outcome measures, the compare methods and sequential groups learned a comparable amount.

In this study, we also explored the effectiveness of delaying comparison of methods. Students studied one method on the first day, and on the second day, they compared it with alternative methods. The goal was to develop knowledge of one solution method before comparing it with alternatives. However, students learned the least in this condition, relative to always comparing methods or always studying the examples sequentially. We expected delayed comparison of methods to be effective for novices and suspect that alternative instantiations of this approach could be beneficial. For example, it may be beneficial to delay comparison of multiple methods, but not to delay introduction of multiple methods (e.g., initially study multiple methods sequentially and then compare them).

There were some advantages to immediately comparing methods and no disadvantages in this study, suggesting that novices were able to learn from comparing two unfamiliar methods when the pace of instruction was slowed down. On the basis of theories of analogical learning, these novices learned via mutual alignment. During mutual alignment, people notice potentially relevant features in two unfamiliar examples by identifying their similarities and then focusing attention on and making sense of these similarities (Gentner et al., 2003; Kurtz, Miao, & Gentner, 2001). Indeed, novices who compared methods often made comparisons between the two examples, focusing on comparing problem features, solution steps, answers, and the relative efficiency of the methods. Given adequate support, novices seemed able to learn by making analogies between two unfamiliar methods. However, learning via mutual alignment appears to be more difficult, and thus require more instructional support, than learning an unfamiliar method via analogy to a known method.

Overall, comparing methods supports procedural flexibility and sometimes conceptual and procedural knowledge as well (see Table 2). It can be used early in the learning process, but it must be carefully supported and the advantages are less substantial.

3.2. Problem Comparison in Mathematics Classrooms

We became interested in the effectiveness of alternative types of comparison for supporting mathematics learning. Given the potential benefits of problem comparison for supporting transfer, we explored the effectiveness of using this type of comparison in mathematics classrooms.

In past research, the goal of comparing problems was to learn *when* a particular method could be used. The focus has been on comparing equivalent problems solved with the same method. Thus, in our *compare-equivalent-problems* condition, students compared two equivalent equations that varied only in the particular numbers and variables (e.g., $3(x + 2) = 6$ and $5(x + 3) = 15$); the two equations were solved using the same method. Prompts focused on the similarities in the solution steps and when a particular solution step could be used. In the context of solving equations, a second variation of comparing problems emerged that may better focus attention on when particular solution steps can be used. In the *compare-problem-types* condition, students compared problems with different problem features solved using similar, although not identical, methods. For example, they compared solutions with $3(x + 2) = 6$ and $3(x + 2) + 5(x + 2) = 16$. Prompts focused on both similarities and differences in the solution methods due to different problem features.

In Rittle–Johnson and Star (2009), we worked with 162 seventh- and eighth-grade students who had previous experience solving equations. They were randomly assigned to the compare–equivalent–problems, compare–problem–types, or compare methods condition and worked on the materials with a partner during three math classes. Frequency of exposure to different solution methods was the same across conditions. Students who compared methods gained greater procedural flexibility and conceptual knowledge than students in either compare problem condition. Students in all three conditions made similar gains in procedural knowledge, including success transferring the methods to new problem types. These findings suggest that for mathematics learning, comparing methods supports transfer as well as comparing problems, and it supports procedural flexibility and conceptual knowledge better than comparing problems.

In Rittle-Johnson et al. (2009), described above, we also included a compare–problem-types condition. Recall that in this study, students had little previous experience with equation solving. For students who attempted to use algebra at pretest, the compare–problem-types condition was less effective than the compare methods condition and was not more effective than the sequential condition. However, for students who did not use algebra at pretest, the compare–problem-types condition was more effective than the compare methods condition, although it was not more effective than the sequential condition.

Overall, our comparing problems conditions have not been especially effective in supporting learning relative to comparing methods or sequential study of examples (see Table 2). These findings corroborate concerns raised by Reed (1989) that for complex multistep methods, comparing problems may not effectively support transfer. Our findings also suggest that comparing problems solved with complex methods does not support procedural flexibility or conceptual understanding as well as comparing methods. However, we are not ready to abandon comparing problems for supporting mathematics learning. Problem comparison seems particularly useful in helping people recognize the relevance of a method for solving new problems, so it may be more helpful for supporting learning in tasks where this is particularly difficult.

3.3. Summary of Our Mathematics Classroom Studies

Designing classroom studies pushed our thinking about different types of comparisons, what learning outcomes each supports, and when learners are prepared to learn from comparison. We have evaluated two types of comparisons in mathematics classrooms — correct method comparison and problem comparison. Comparing correct methods consistently supported procedural flexibility across studies for students who knew one of the solution methods at pretest (see Table 2). For these students, comparing methods sometimes supported greater procedural knowledge (Rittle-Johnson & Star, 2007; Rittle-Johnson et al., 2009) or greater conceptual knowledge (Rittle-Johnson & Star, 2009; Rittle-Johnson et al., 2009; Star & Rittle-Johnson, 2009). For novices, who did not know one of the solution methods at pretest, comparing methods was helpful only after we slowed the pace of the lesson, aiding flexible use of the methods. Overall, comparing methods can help a variety of students learn, but its advantages are more substantial if students have sufficient prior knowledge. How best to develop this prior knowledge is an important topic for future research.

We have evaluated comparing problems in only two studies, and it has been generally less effective than comparing methods, especially for students with prior knowledge in the domain. It may be more effective for learning other mathematical topics and merits additional research. Finally, although we did not isolate the impact of other types of comparisons, we have prompted students in all conditions to occasionally make problem category comparisons. For example, a few reflection prompts included a new equation and asked students if a particular methods could be used to solve it (typically, it could not). Perhaps as a result, we have seen few instances of students attempting to apply a particular method inappropriately (i.e., having difficulty distinguishing problem categories).

4. OUR YEARLONG STUDY ON USING COMPARISON IN ALGEBRA I CLASSROOMS

Given the promise of comparison for supporting mathematics learning, we wanted to evaluate the effectiveness of teachers using comparison throughout the school year. In collaboration with Kristie Newton, we are currently conducting a randomized controlled trial, evaluating whether using comparison throughout the Algebra I curriculum will improve student learning. The need to design a yearlong, teacher led classroom intervention encouraged us to consider a wider range of comparison types, and two new types emerged. In this section, we discuss the materials we developed, particularly the types of comparisons we supported, and then overview our study design.

4.1. Materials: Types of Comparisons

On the basis of the promise of our worked example-based approach to supporting comparison, we developed a set of supplementary materials of worked example pairs (WEPs) that could be used in conjunction with any Algebra I curriculum. They were designed to maximize their potential impact based on previous research. A sample WEP is shown in Figure 2. As before, the two worked examples were presented side by side. To facilitate processing of the examples, we included thought bubbles, where two students (Alex and Morgan) described their solution methods. We used common language in these descriptions as much as possible to help facilitate alignment of the examples.

All WEPs included explanation prompts. To help build consistency across examples and scaffold appropriate reflection, we included three types of explanation prompts for each WEP. *Understand* prompts, such as "How did Alex solve the equation?," were meant to ensure that students understood each worked example individually. *Compare* prompts, such as "What are some similarities and differences between Alex's and Morgan's ways," were meant to encourage comparison of the two worked examples. Understand and compare prompts were similar across comparison

Which is Correct?

Alex and Morgan were asked to solve $45y + 90 = 60y$

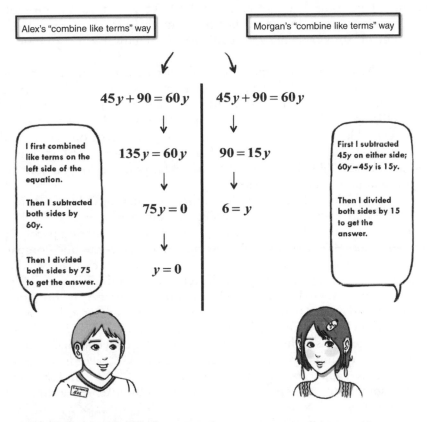

Alex's "combine like terms" way

Morgan's "combine like terms" way

I first combined like terms on the left side of the equation.

Then I subtracted both sides by 60y.

Then I divided both sides by 75 to get the answer.

$$45y + 90 = 60y$$
$$\downarrow$$
$$135y = 60y$$
$$\downarrow$$
$$75y = 0$$
$$\downarrow$$
$$y = 0$$

$$45y + 90 = 60y$$
$$\downarrow$$
$$90 = 15y$$
$$\downarrow$$
$$6 = y$$

First I subtracted 45y on either side; 60y − 45y is 15y.

Then I divided both sides by 15 to get the answer.

* How did Alex solve the equation?
* How did Morgan solve the equation?
* Why did Alex combine the terms on the left as a first step?
* Why did Morgan subtract 45y as a first step?
* Which way is correct, Alex's or Morgan's way? How do you know?
* Can you state a general rule about combining like terms that describes what you have learned from comparing Alex's and Morgan's ways of solving this type of problem?

3.2.2

Figure 2 Sample worked example pair from our Algebra I scale-up project, illustrating a *which-is-correct* comparison.

types and were meant to prepare students to reflect on the final, *make connection* prompts. The make connection prompts varied by comparison type and were designed to encourage reflection on the instructional goal for that comparison type. Our pilot work revealed that sometimes teachers skipped or inadequately addressed the make connection prompts (often due to time constraints), so we added a takeaway page for each WEP. On the takeaway page, the fictitious students Alex and Morgan identified the comparison goal for that WEP. This was meant to promote a summary statement by the teacher. Some direct instruction is needed to supplement student-generated comparisons (Schwartz & Bransford, 1998).

Initially, a team of six experienced Algebra I teachers, including Star, generated over 140 WEPs based on their intuitions of how comparison could support learning in as many Algebra I lessons as possible. Some of the WEPs focused on comparing methods and others focused on comparing problems. However, sometimes the comparison goals and expected learning outcomes were different from those identified in previous research. Table 3 presents the four main types of comparisons we supported in our Algebra I materials.

First, consider different goals for comparing methods. As in our previous research, we included correct method comparisons with the goal of identifying when and why one method was better for solving particular problems (i.e., *Which is better?*). We also added incorrect method comparisons (i.e., *Which is correct?*). For example, in Figure 2, Alex made a common error of treating $45y$ and 90 as like terms and combining them to get $135y$. The goal was to help students learn a correct method for combining like terms and reduce their use of a common, incorrect method. Finally, a new goal for comparing methods emerged that we called *why-does-it-work?* The goal was to help students understand a conventional solution method. For example, given the task of expanding $(x^4)^2$, a comparison was made between application of the power rule ($x^{(4 \times 2)}$ or x^8) and the more cumbersome, but conceptually transparent, method of expanding and then squaring ($x^4 \times x^4$, $(x \times x \times x \times x) \times (x \times x \times x \times x)$, or x^8). Students are asked to reflect on why different steps lead to the same answer. The goal was not for students to adopt the more cumbersome method. Rather, it was for students to understand the power rule. This is in contrast to the which-is-better comparisons, where the goal was to learn when and why one method is better for solving particular types of problems.

Second, consider problem comparisons. A novel comparison goal for comparing problems emerged, which was to reflect on *how do they differ?* On these WEPs, the solution method was not central. Rather, the focus was on the relations between the different problems and their answers and what these relations revealed about underlying concepts. For example, Alex graphed the equation $y = x^2$ and Morgan graphed the equation $y = -x^2$. Students were prompted to consider how the negative coefficient affected the graph of the quadratic function. Thus, the goal was to support understanding of a key concept, such as the

Table 3 Distinctions Between the Types of Comparisons Used in Our Yearlong Algebra I Classroom Study.

Distinction	Comparison type			
	Correct method		Incorrect method	Problem
Comparison goal	Which is better?	Why does it work?	Which is correct?	How do they differ?
Features of examples	Same problem solved with two different correct methods	Same problem solved with two different correct methods	Same problem solved with a correct and an incorrect method	Different problems. Focus is not on solution methods
Focus of comparison	When and why a method is more efficient or easier	Conceptual rationale revealed in one method that is less apparent in the other method	Why one method works and one does not	What relations between problems and answers reveal about underlying concept
Learning outcomes supported	Know multiple methods and use most appropriate method (i.e., procedural flexibility)	Know why methods work	Make misconception errors less often and use correct method more often	Understand concept
Sample worked example pair	Solving the proportion $4/5 = 24/n$ by finding equivalent fractions or by cross-multiplying	Expanding the expression $(x^4)^2$ by applying the power rule $(x^{(4 \times 2)})$ or by expanding and then squaring	Solving $45y + 90 = 60y$ by first subtracting $45y$ from both sides or by incorrectly combining $45y + 90$	Graphing the equations $y = x^2$ and $y = -x^2$
Sample *make connection* prompt	Can you make up a general rule for when Alex's way is better and when Morgan's way is better?	Even though Alex and Morgan did different first steps, why did they get the same answer?	Can you state a general rule about combining like terms?	How does changing the sign of the coefficient of x^2 affect the graph of the quadratic function?

meaning of coefficients. Only one of our WEPs focused on *when can you use it* (not included in Table 3, but see Table 1, column 2). This was not intentional, but rather reflects what emerged when teachers had the goal of comparing problems in mind.

The need to design comparison materials to support learning throughout the school year pushed us to generate a broader range of comparison types. The two new comparison types, *how do they differ* and *why does it work*, are novel ways to instantiate comparing concepts (last column of Table 1). In the context of the Algebra I curriculum, comparing examples of the same concept was most naturally done by comparing problems or comparing methods, but with a focus on the underlying concepts. Future research will be needed to isolate the effect of these two types of comparisons on specific learning outcomes, particularly conceptual knowledge. Emergence of new ideas that should be tested and integrating into theories of learning are one clear benefit of bridging between cognitive science and education, highlighting that the benefits are not unidirectional from theory to practice. As championed by Ann Brown, educational practice provides important new ideas for theoretical research (Brown, 1997).

4.2. Implementation and Evaluation

We formalized an instructional routine that should maximize the effectiveness of using our comparison materials. Each WEP had three types of reflection prompts (understand, compare, and make connections described above) meant to culminate in a discussion of the learning goal for the pair. Teachers were encouraged to have students study and discuss the WEP in small groups before discussing them as a class. Teachers then led a whole–class discussion, ending with the takeaway message for that comparison type. Teachers were given considerable latitude in determining which WEPs to use, when to use them, and how much time in a class period to allot for each WEP. On average teachers typically spent about 15 min on each WEP. Teachers were asked to use our materials about twice a week so that this instructional routine would become familiar and part of the norms in their classrooms.

To support effective use of our comparison materials, teachers were provided with 1 week (35 h) of professional development in the summer. This professional development focused on the different types of comparisons and the learning goals supported by each. Teachers spent time reading and talking about the collection of WEPs and about our instructional model more generally. In addition, teachers worked in groups to develop practice lessons that were implemented and then debriefed by the group. For more information about the professional development, see Newton, Star, and Perova (2010).

During 2009–2010, we piloted our materials with 13 Algebra I teachers. Each time teachers used our materials, they were asked to call and report on what WEP they had used, how they had used it, and their impressions on the strengths and weaknesses of the materials. Teachers also videotaped their use of our materials every other week so that we could examine teacher's implementation. The pilot teachers were generally positive about the materials and typically used our materials once or twice a week. Overall, we were very encouraged by the feasibility of teacher implementation of our materials.

In summer 2010, we began our randomized controlled trial, with 50 teachers using our comparison materials for the 2010–2011 school year (with an equal number serving as control teachers). We will evaluate the fidelity of implementation, using both teacher surveys and classroom observations, and student learning outcomes, using a standardized test of algebra knowledge and a researcher-designed measure that focuses on procedural flexibility (since standardized tests do not assess procedural flexibility). We are optimistic that supporting diverse types of comparisons in the classroom will improve mathematics learning across a variety of outcomes. We will also gain insights into whether differences in teacher implementation, including their choices of the types of comparisons to use and how they are supported, influence student learning.

5. Conclusions and Future Directions

Comparison is a fundamental part of human cognition and a powerful learning mechanism. It permeates our everyday lives and has been shown to improve learning in a broad range of domains. We have developed a framework for identifying different types of comparisons and comparison goals and the learning outcomes supported by each type. The evidence for the effectiveness of some types of comparisons is strong, while the evidence for others is preliminary. A majority of the evidence comes from brief laboratory experiments, but our own work indicates that comparison can support learning in mathematics classrooms. Our current efforts to infuse comparison throughout the Algebra I curriculum have revealed new comparison goals that merit additional attention. Our hope is that highlighting different types of comparisons and comparison goals, which have largely remained implicit in past research, will guide future research efforts to flesh out how different types of comparisons support different learning outcomes as well as guide the design of effective educational materials.

Future research also needs to pay careful attention to individual differences that influence learning from comparison. For example, people with low prior knowledge have difficulty comparing which of two novel solution methods is better and need careful scaffolding. We suspect that other individual differences, such as working memory capacity and views toward mathematics, will impact the effectiveness of different types of comparisons as well.

We conclude this chapter with some general advice about bridging between cognitive science and education. First, bridging between the two usually requires collaboration between cognitive scientists and education researchers. The necessary expertise is simply too great for one person. Our combined expertise has allowed us to do research that ranges from microgenetic analyses of learning processes to a yearlong classroom scale-up project. Second, it can be challenging to identify a promising instructional practice given the myriad of possibilities. Looking for convergence across the cognitive science and education literatures highlights particularly promising ones to pursue. For example, comparison emerged as a learning process espoused in both literatures. Third, conducting experimental research in classrooms naturally constrains the research to at least some typical classroom conditions. Our unique approach of randomly assigning pairs of students to conditions allowed us to gather experimental evidence on the effectiveness of an instructional approach with a reasonable number of classrooms. Finally, cognitive science does not only inform educational practice; educational practice reveals new constraints and new ideas that need to be tested and incorporated into theories of learning.

ACKNOWLEDGMENTS

Research and Preparation of this chapter was funded in part by NSF Grant #DRL-0814571 and IES Grant #R305H050179.

REFERENCES

Alvermann, D. E., & Hague, S. A. (1989). Comprehension of counterintuitive science text: Effects of prior knowledge and text structure. *Journal of Educational Research, 82*(4), 197–202.
Atkinson, R. K., Derry, S. J., Renkl, A., & Wortham, D. (2000). Learning from examples: Instructional principles from the worked examples research. *Review of Educational Research, 70*(2), 181–214.
Ball, D. L. (1993). With an eye on the mathematical horizon: Dilemmas of teaching elementary school mathematics. *The Elementary School Journal, 93*, 373–397.
Blöte, A. W., Van der Burg, E., & Klein, A. S. (2001). Students' flexibility in solving two-digit addition and subtraction problems: Instruction effects. *Journal of Educational Psychology, 93*(3), 627–638.
Brown, A. L. (1997). Transforming schools into communities of thinking and learning about serious matters. *American Psychologist, 52*, 399–413.
Carpenter, T. P., Franke, M. L., Jacobs, V. R., Fennema, E., & Empson, S. B. (1998). A longitudinal study of invention and understanding in children's multidigit addition and subtraction. *Journal for Research in Mathematics Education, 29*(1), 3–20.

Catrambone, R., & Holyoak, K. J. (1989). Overcoming contextual limitations on problem-solving transfer. *Journal of Experimental Psychology: Learning, Memory, and Cognition, 15*(6), 1147–1156.

Cummins, D. (1992). Role of analogical reasoning in the induction of problem categories. *Journal of Experimental Psychology: Learning, Memory, and Cognition, 18*(5), 1103–1124.

Curry, L. (2004). The effects of self-explanations of correct and incorrect solutions on algebra problem-solving performance. In K. Forbus., D. Genter, and T. Regier, (Eds.), *Proceedings of the twenty-sixth annual conference of the cognitive science society* (pp. 1548) Mahwah, NJ: Erlbaum.

Day, S., Goldstone, R. L., & Hill, T. (2010). The effects of similarity and individual differences on comparison and transfer. In S. Ohlsson, and R. Catrambone, (Eds.), *Cognition in flux: Proceedings of the 32nd annual meeting of the cognitive science society* (pp. 465–470). Austin, TX: Cognitive Science Society.

Diakidoy, I. -A. N., Kendeou, P., & Ioannides, C. (2003). Reading about energy: The effects of text structure in science learning and conceptual change. *Contemporary Educational Psychology, 28*(3), 335–356.

Durkin, K. (2009). The effectiveness of comparing correct and incorrect examples for learning about decimal magnitude (Master's thesis). Vanderbilt University, Nashville, TN.

Fraivillig, J. L., Murphy, L. A., & Fuson, K. (1999). Advancing children's mathematical thinking in everyday mathematics classrooms. *Journal for Research in Mathematics Education, 30*, 148–170.

Gentner, D. (1983). Structure-mapping: A theoretical framework for analogy. *Cognitive Science, 7*(2), 155–170.

Gentner, D., Loewenstein, J., & Thompson, L. (2003). Learning and transfer: A general role for analogical encoding. *Journal of Educational Psychology, 95*(2), 393–405.

Gentner, D., & Markman, A. B. (1997). Structure mapping in analogy and similarity. *American Psychologist, 52*, 45–56.

Gick, M. L., & Holyoak, K. J. (1983). Schema induction and analogical transfer. *Cognitive Psychology, 15*(1), 1–38.

Goldstone, R. L., Day, S., & Son, J. (2010). Comparison. In B. Glatzeder., V. Goel A. von Müller, (Eds.), *Towards a theory of thinking Vol. II*, (pp. 103–122). Heidelberg, Germany: Springer Verlag.

Graham, S. A., Namy, L. L., Gentner, D., & Meagher, K. (2010). The role of comparison in preschoolers' novel object categorization. *Journal of Experimental Child Psychology, 107*(3), 280–290.

Hattikudur, S., & Alibali, M. W. (2010). Learning about the equal sign: Does comparing with inequality symbols help? *Journal of Experimental Child Psychology, 107*(1), 15–30.

Hiebert, J., Carpenter, T. P., Fennema, E., Fuson, K. C., Human, P., & Murray, H., et al., (1996). Problem solving as a basis for reform in curriculum and instruction: The case of mathematics. *Educational Researcher, 25*(4), 12–21.

Huang, T. -H., Liu, Y. -C., & Shiu, C. -Y. (2008). Construction of an online learning system for decimal numbers through the use of cognitive conflict strategy. *Computers & Education, 50*(1), 61–76.

Huffred-Ackles, K., Fuson, K., & Sherin Gamoran, M. (2004). Describing levels and components of a math-talk learning community. *Journal for Research in Mathematics Education, 35*(2), 81–116.

Hummel, J. E., & Holyoak, K. J. (1997). Distributed representations of structure: A theory of analogical access and mapping. *Psychological Review, 104*(3), 427–466.

Johnson, D. W., & Johnson, R. T. (1994). *Learning together and alone: Cooperative, competitive and individualistic learning*, 4th ed. Allyn & Bacon, Boston, MA.

Kieran, C. (1992). The learning and teaching of school algebra. In D. Grouws (Ed.), *Handbook of research on mathematics teaching and learning* (pp. 390–419). New York: Simon & Schuster.

Kilpatrick, J., Swafford, J. O, and Findell, B, (2001) (Eds.), *Adding it up: Helping children learn mathematics* Washington DC: National Academy Press.

Kurtz, K., Miao, C. -H., & Gentner, D. (2001). Learning by analogical bootstrapping. *The Journal of the Learning Sciences, 10*, 417–446.

Lampert, M. (1990). When the problem is not the question and the solution is not the answer: Mathematical knowing and teaching. *American Educational Research Journal, 27*, 29–63.

Loewenstein, J., & Gentner, D. (2001). Spatial mapping in preschoolers: Close comparisons facilitate far mappings. *Journal of Cognition and Development, 2*(2), 189–219.

Loewenstein, J., Thompson, L., & Gentner, D. (1999). Analogical encoding facilitates knowledge transfer in negotiation. *Psychonomic Bulletin and Review, 6*(4), 586–597.

Loewenstein, J., Thompson, L., & Gentner, D. (2003). Analogical learning in negotiation teams: Comparing cases promotes learning and transfer. *Academy of Management Learning and Education, 2*(2), 119–127.

Namy, L. L., & Gentner, D. (2002). Making a silk purse out of two sow's ears: Young children's use of comparison in category learning. *Journal of Experimental Psychology: General, 131*(1), 5–15.

National Council of Teachers of Mathematics. (2000). Principles and standards for school mathematics. National Council for Teachers of Mathematics, Reston, VA.

National Council of Teachers of Mathematics. (2006). Curriculum focal points for prekindergarten through grade 8 mathematics. National Council for Teachers of Mathematics, Reston, VA.

Newton, K. J., Star, J. R., & Perova, N. (2010). Learning by teaching: Using a model teaching activity to help teachers learn to use comparison in algebra. In P. Brosnan., D. B. Erchick, and L. Flevares, (Eds.), *Proceedings of the 32nd annual meeting of the North American chapter of the international group for the Psychology of Mathematics Education* Columbus, OH: Ohio State University.

Reed, S. K. (1989). Constraints on the abstraction of solutions. *Journal of Educational Psychology, 81*(4), 532–540.

Richland, L.E., & Holyoak, K.J. (2005). Learning and transfer by analogy: Cross-cultural insights. Paper presented at the annual meeting of American Education Research Association, Montréal, Québec.

Richland, L. E., Zur, O., & Holyoak, K. J. (2007). Cognitive supports for analogies in the mathematics classroom. *Science, 316*(5828), 1128–1129.

Rittle-Johnson, B., & Star, J. R. (2007). Does comparing solution methods facilitate conceptual and procedural knowledge? An experimental study on learning to solve equations. *Journal of Educational Psychology, 99*(3), 561–574.

Rittle-Johnson, B., & Star, J. R. (2009). Compared with what? The effects of different comparisons on conceptual knowledge and procedural flexibility for equation solving. *Journal of Educational Psychology, 101*(3), 529–544.

Rittle-Johnson, B., Star, J. R., & Durkin, K. (2009). The importance of prior knowledge when comparing examples: Influences on conceptual and procedural knowledge of equation solving. *Journal of Educational Psychology, 101*(4), 836–852.

Rittle-Johnson, B., Star, J., & Durkin, K. (2010). *Developing procedural flexibility: When should multiple solution methods be introduced?* Paper presented at the Annual meeting of the American Educational Research Association, Denver, CO.

Schwartz, D. L., & Bransford, J. D. (1998). A time for telling. *Cognition and Instruction, 16*(4), 475–522.

Siegler, R. S. (2002). Microgenetic studies of self-explanation. In N. Garnott J. Parziale, (Eds.), *Microdevelopment: transition processes in development and learning* (pp. 31–58). Cambridge, MA: Cambridge University Press.

Star, J. R. (2005). Reconceptualizing procedural knowledge. *Journal for Research in Mathematics Education, 36*, 404–411.

Star, J. R., & Rittle-Johnson, B. (2009). It pays to compare: An experimental study on computational estimation. *Journal of Experimental Child Psychology, 101*, 408–426.

Stigler, J. W., & Hiebert, J. (1998). Teaching is a cultural activity. *American Educator, 22*(4), 4–11.

Thompson, L., Gentner, D., & Loewenstein, J. (2000). Avoiding missed opportunities in managerial life: Analogical training more powerful than individual case training. *Organizational Behavior and Human Decision Processes, 82*(1), 60–75.

van den Broek, P., & Kendeou, P. (2008). Cognitive processes in comprehension of science texts: The role of co-activation in confronting misconceptions. *Applied Cognitive Psychology. Special Issue: Advances in text comprehension: Model, process and development, 22*(3), 335–351.

VanderStoep, S. W., & Seifert, C. M. (1993). Learning "how" versus learning "when": Improving transfer of problem-solving principles. *Journal of the Learning Sciences, 3*(1), 93–111.

Verschaffel, L., Luwel, K., Torbeyns, J., & Van Dooren, W. (2009). Conceptualizing, investigating, and enhancing adaptive expertise in elementary mathematics education. *European Journal of Psychology of Education, 24*(3), 335–359.

Waxman, S. R., & Klibanoff, R. S. (2000). The role of comparison in the extension of novel adjectives. *Developmental Psychology, 36*(5), 571–581.

Webb, N. M. (1991). Task-related verbal interaction and mathematics learning in small groups. *Journal for Research in Mathematics Education, 22*(5), 366–389.

CHAPTER EIGHT

THE UBIQUITOUS PATTERNS OF INCORRECT ANSWERS TO SCIENCE QUESTIONS: THE ROLE OF AUTOMATIC, BOTTOM-UP PROCESSES

Andrew F. Heckler

Contents

Psychology of Learning and Motivation, Volume 55

ISSN 0079-7421, DOI 10.1016/B978-0-12-387691-1.00008-9

© 2011 Elsevier Inc.

All rights reserved.

Abstract

Nonexperts often exhibit regular and persistent patterns of errors when answering questions about science concepts. Typically, these patterns are considered to be due to high-level mental structures such as concepts or mental models that are different from the relevant expert concepts. Here, I consider the systematic influence of automatic, bottom-up processes on answering patterns to science questions. General evidence of the existence of top-down and bottom-up processes is surveyed from a variety of areas in cognitive science. Specifically, it is found that patterns of incorrect answering are a significant empirical driving force behind many investigations in learning and performance, and many of these areas invoke the need for bottom-up mechanisms to explain observations. The application of some of these mechanisms to the area of student answering of science questions is discussed. In particular, it is hypothesized that patterns of incorrect answering on a broad class of science questions are strongly influenced by the phenomenon of *competition* between relevant and irrelevant information in the questions. I investigate the particular cases in which the outcomes of this competition are mediated by the relative *processing times* and allocation of *attention* to relevant and irrelevant information in questions. These mechanisms result in predictable patterns of response choice, response time, and eye gaze fixations, and I discuss some studies suggesting that these mechanisms are at work when students answer specific physics questions. If, as suggested, automatic, bottom-up processes play a role in performance on science tasks, then this has important implications for models of understanding and learning science.

1. INTRODUCTION

This chapter revolves around what could be regarded as the most important empirical finding of science education to date, namely, that people often answer simple scientific questions incorrectly, yet in regular, patterned ways. More specifically, following Piaget's numerous demonstrations that children often answer ostensibly simple questions incorrectly, thousands of empirical studies have established that when conceptual questions about simple natural phenomena are posed to students, their answers are often contrary to scientists' answers, remarkably similar to those of other students, and resistant to traditional instruction (for lists, see Kind, 2004; McDermott & Redish, 1999; Pfundt & Duit, 2000). For example, students often believe, even after traditional instruction, that an upward traveling ball must have a net upward force acting on it (Clement, 1982).

Thus, we find ourselves in a fortuitous situation: we have numerous replicable empirical observations of how students respond to specific science questions, sometimes in great detail. If patterns in the responses are found, one can consider two general ways in which these findings can be useful.[1] First, information about students' answering patterns can help to inform instruction. An example of this is the several-decades demonstrated success in physics curriculum design and implementation done at the University of Washington, in which students' incorrect answering patterns have become a fundamental starting point for instructional methods (e.g., McDermott, 2001).

Second, patterns in the empirical data can be used to help build models of hypothesized mechanisms that *cause* the response patterns and perhaps student responses more generally. Ideally, these models can help us to make *predictions* of answering patterns to novel sets of questions. Furthermore, these models of causal mechanisms may also make predictions of how students would respond to specific types of instruction, and as such the models may also prove useful for designing instruction to help students answer difficult questions correctly.

In this chapter, I will concentrate more on the second approach, namely, investigating models of basic mechanisms that can not only help to explain *why* there are patterns of incorrect answers to science questions but can also *predict* answer patterns. While most existing explanations of answering patterns involve higher level mental structures such as *misconceptions*, I will consider the possibility that a number of bottom-up, automatic mechanisms can play a significant role in the generation of answering patterns.

The general idea that both bottom-up and top-down mechanisms are at work in learning and answering questions related to physical phenomena is hardly new. Some researchers have investigated and discussed this topic, even going back to Piaget. Nonetheless, the investigation of the potentially important role of bottom-up mechanisms in student answering patterns has been relatively ignored (especially in the science education arena) and is consequently an underexplored topic ripe for rigorous investigation. Therefore, in this chapter I will explore some of the past work on the influence of bottom-up processes on answering patterns and I will focus on the particular phenomenon of *competition*.

Specifically, I propose that answering patterns are often strongly influenced by competition between relevant and irrelevant information present in a science question. I will examine how competition manifests itself

---

[1] In addition to the two uses mentioned here, it may also be useful to build phenomenological models that reproduce observed response patterns for given questions, with minimal assumptions about the causes of the patterns.

in two interrelated ways. First, in most cases, the relevant variables in science are not easily observable (e.g., density determines floating) and, as a result, they are less likely to automatically engage *attention* than some of the irrelevant variables (e.g., size does not determine floating). In addition, the relevant information in science is often more difficult to process than irrelevant information and, as a result, more relevant information is *processed slower*. For example, there are data (described below) suggesting that students' well-known preference for utilizing *height* rather than *slope* on a graph is strongly influenced by the fact that in typical contexts height is inherently processed *faster* than slope.

The outcome of the competition mediated by these mechanisms may not only influence and thus help predict response choices but they may also imply patterns in other response metrics, such as processing time (e.g., response times) and attention (e.g., eye gaze) to specific features of a posed question. Thus, the hypothesized role of many of these mechanisms has the virtue of being testable by a number of different measurement modalities.

This investigation of the role of basic, automatic mechanisms in answering science questions stands in contrast to most existing explanations in science education that focus on higher level structures or processes, such as *concepts* or *explicit reasoning*, as causes of incorrect answering patterns. Nonetheless, the more bottom-up mechanisms proposed here are likely to complement higher level explanations.

2. THE GENERAL STRUCTURE OF ANSWERING PATTERNS AND THE CRITICAL ISSUE OF SIMILARITY

Because the central theme of this chapter is about patterns in student answering to science questions, it is worth considering the often ignored yet important issue of how one comes to claim or establish the existence of a *pattern in answering*. The empirical data of student responses to a set of questions itself are in a sense "raw" data. The question of whether there are any patterns in these raw data is, strictly speaking, a judgment based on an arbitrary (though perhaps reasonable) definition of *pattern*. Such a definition inevitably involves assumptions about the *similarity* of responses and of questions. Therefore, in this section, I will discuss the necessity of including explicitly constructed and acknowledged assumptions with any claims of patterns. The intention of the discussion is to reveal that the issue of *patterns* is fundamental to building a consistent, predictive theory of student responses, is far from resolved, and is certainly a fertile area for further empirical and theoretical investigation beyond the scope of this paper.

I will consider two main categories of patterns in answering: between-student and within-student answering, since these two kinds of answering patterns require fundamentally different explanations[2] (see also Siegler (1981) and discussions within about Piaget's view on this).

2.1. Between-student answering patterns

As is commonly defined, a between-subject pattern is the phenomenon of many subjects exhibiting similar performance on the same task. In science education, this phenomenon occurs when a specific question is posed to a number of students and many of them often answer incorrectly in ways that are judged to be similar (see the next section for a discussion about the similarity of responses). For example, when asked what is inside the bubbles formed in boiling water, a significant number of students answer that the bubbles are filled with air, when in fact the correct answer is that they are filled with water vapor (Osborne & Cosgrove, 1983).

Between-student answering patterns can be explained in a general way (though somewhat vaguely) by the fact that students are biologically similar, namely, they have similar cognitive processes and perhaps even similar "innate knowledge" (e.g., see Carey, 2009; Carey & Spelke, 1996), and students have similar everyday experiences, including experiences of the natural world and social experiences (e.g., Driver, Asoko, Leach, Mortimer, & Scott, 1994; Gelman, 2009), which shape their actions.

2.2. Within-student answering patterns

Within-student answering patterns require a different kind of explanation than between-student patterns. A within-student answering pattern of interest occurs when a specific set of questions, *judged to be similar* in some important way, is posed to a student, and the student provides answers that are *judged to be similar*. Therefore, determining within-student patterns is not straightforward, since it necessitates a *judgment of similarity* of both questions and responses. Since similarity is always a judgment based on a (presumably reasonable) choice of criteria, there is no one "correct" measure of similarity of questions and of responses, but there are certainly some measures that are more useful than others, depending on the task at hand. It is especially important to distinguish between a judgment of similarity of questions and responses on the basis of expert knowledge rather than on the basis of the student (i.e., answerer) point of view.

Judging the similarity of questions and responses based on an expert point of view is often necessary from an instructional point of view, since

---

[2]Note there are other ways to search for patterns using a purely psychometric approach (e.g., C. Reiner, Proffit, & Salthouse, 2005).

the goal of instruction is for students to recognize similarity and apply consistency as experts do. In fact, the assessment of a particular concept or skill could be seen as the practice of constructing questions that are similar from an expert's point of view in that they test knowledge of that particular concept or skill. In this case, instructors often look for only one kind of pattern: the pattern of correct answering. That is, the pattern that matches the expert point of view. However, not only is there useful information in patterns of incorrect answers, but students often do not use the same bases for judging similarity between questions that experts do (cf. Chi, Feltovich, & Glaser, 1981). Therefore, the interpretation of a pattern or lack of a pattern in answering from an expert scientist's point of view may be misleading, and even instructionally counterproductive. Instead, examining why *students* judge the similarity between questions can be helpful information for instruction (e.g., see Driver & Easley, 1978; Elby, 2001; Hammer, 1996a, 1996b).

Furthermore, since we are investigating the origin of within-student answering patterns, examining *student* judgment of similarity of questions (rather than expert similarity judgment) is warranted. In particular, we are interested in causes of answering patterns (any proposed pattern that has no cause could be regarded as arbitrary and not scientifically useful), and students are presumed to be the cause. Therefore, I will make the general assumption that a set of questions is answered in a similar manner by a particular student because the questions are for some reason being treated by the *student* in a similar manner. That is, within-student patterns occur because the questions are *judged to be similar by the student*, either implicitly or explicitly. For example, a student could perceive two questions as being about the same thing (e.g., force and motion) and thus apply a coherent impetus theory (i.e., misconception) to both questions. On the other hand, two questions could also be treated as similar because some automatic cognitive mechanism (of which the student in not necessarily consciously aware of) is processing both questions in a similar manner. Specific examples of such mechanisms will be discussed in Section 7.

Still, any claim of the existence of a within-student answer pattern caused by student-judged similarity of a set of questions must be based on an *inference* about the basis upon which the student is judging similarity. This inference is inevitably made by the person who is claiming the existence of a pattern. For example, is an explicit rule or concept (such as impetus theory) used by the student to judge similarity of two questions, or is it some bottom-up perceptual similarity? This is an important point because any claim of a within-student pattern is not solely an empirical observation but necessarily also depends on an assumption about the student's basis for similarity judgment. A typical assumption is that the students base their judgment of similarity of questions on some particular naïve concept. However, if the identification of the concept used by the student is incorrect or the student's responses are based on some other mechanism that does not involve an explicit concept (such as an automatic bottom-up mechanism), then any claimed pattern may be less meaningful. Alternatively, incorrect assumptions about a student's basis for judging similarity may result in a failure to recognize the presence of a within-student pattern of answering.

In short, any claimed within-student pattern in answers practically entails some assumption about the student's implicit or explicit judgment of similarity among the questions. Of course, any claim of within-student answering patterns also depends on the nature of the judged similarity in the *responses*. Such a judgment is usually done by the one who is making claims of answering patterns and is inevitably related to the assumptions of the student's bases for judging similarity of questions. In addition, one can measure and compare not only the content of the responses but also the other factors, such as time to respond and allocation of attention.

Therefore, the task of claiming within-student patterns on a given set of questions must critically include a detailed characterization, via comparative measurements or other analysis, of the bases upon which one is claiming similarity of both the questions and the answers. Ultimately, a careful description of the nature of the similarities will help to provide insight and clarity about the mechanisms underlying these answer patterns.

In practice, the issue of determining the basis of similarity judgments necessary for claiming patterns of answers has been implicit and relatively straightforward. It is common to find that questions and student responses are grouped into a few readily recognizable (by experts and even many students) and robust categories that include the correct response and a couple of prevalent incorrect response types (e.g., Bao & Redish, 2006). For example, Siegler (1976) found that when students are given balance task problems, one category of responses is to choose the side with the larger mass as winning, regardless of the length of the lever arm. In some cases, Chi (2005) points out that responses have been categorized in terms of past scientific theories, such as the impetus theory for force and motion questions. In order to account more for the student perspective, many researchers have carefully studied student responses and constructed reasonable categories of student responses that are specific to the domain. For example, Vosniadou and Brewer (1992) categorized student models of the earth according to various specific student models (flat, hemisphere, round, etc.). Chi (2005) has also pointed out another way to categorize responses in a more domain general manner, by looking for students' tendencies to answer according to ontological categories.

Nonetheless, it is important to keep in mind that these above examples of claims of student answering patterns necessarily make assumptions about how students interpret and answer the questions. We will discuss such assumptions in more detail in Section 3.

2.3. Summary

While between-student and within-student answering patterns tend to empirically occur simultaneously, both require different explanations. For the former, one must explain why *students* are similar; for the latter, one must explain why *questions* are similar. Both must characterize how *responses* are similar, though one can compare more than just the content of a response and look to other metrics such as response time.

From a general viewpoint, between-student patterns are somewhat trivially explained by the fact that students have similar biology and have many similar daily experiences. However, it is still a challenge to explain why many students tend to choose a specific answer to a specific question.

Explaining within-student answering patterns requires an explicit characterization and demonstration of the basis upon which *students* (rather than experts) are perceiving—either implicitly or explicitly—the similarity of questions.

3. EXISTING EXPLANATIONS FOR INCORRECT ANSWER PATTERNS TO SCIENCE QUESTIONS

In this section, I will briefly review major existing explanations of incorrect answer patterns for science questions. I will focus on explanations of results from students that are typically between 10 and 20 years of age. There is also a significant amount of work on the development of concepts in young children that can be relevant to incorrect answering patterns on science questions (e.g., Carey, 2009; Gelman, 2009), though I will not discuss this here.

3.1. Misconceptions

The most widely assumed explanation for incorrect answer patterns stems from the abductive inference that the patterns are caused by somewhat coherent and generally applied "misconceptions" or "naïve theories" cued by the question and constructed by students from their everyday experience (e.g., Carey, 1985; Driver & Erickson, 1983; McCloskey, 1983; Vosniadou, 1994; Wellman & Gelman, 1992). A student, for example, might (incorrectly) answer that a ball traveling on a curved track would continue to travel in a curve after leaving the track because he/she has developed a coherent theory predicting that when objects are moving in a curved path, they will continue to move in a curved path, even in the absence of external forces (McCloskey, Caramazza, & Green, 1980). Note that this explanation directly addresses the case of within-student answer patterns. Since it is also found that many students exhibit the same consistent answer patterns (i.e., between-student patterns), presumably these students have all formed the same misconception because they have derived it from everyday experiences common to all students.

The term *misconception* is frequently used in the literature, and it is important to note that the term actually describes an *inference* about the cause of patterns of incorrect answering rather than an empirical observation of student answering. Clearly, it is logically valid that *if* students held coherent, incorrect theories (i.e., misconceptions) and *if* they consistently applied these theories, then they would likely answer relevant questions in patterned incorrect ways (following the pattern of the misconception and its consistent application). However, it is not necessary to have a misconception in order to produce patterns of incorrect answers: the pattern may also be due to other causes. Thus, I will sometimes refer to patterns of incorrect answering as *misconception-like* answers.

The misconceptions explanation has been critiqued because it was recognized that the model of student-held coherent yet incorrect theories was not universally valid at least in its strictest interpretation in two ways. First, when students were asked questions about or relevant to their putative theories, the theories themselves were often highly fragmented, incomplete, and logically inconsistent certainly from the point of view of the expert and often even from the perspective of the student (e.g., diSessa, Gillespie, & Esterly, 2004; for a discussion, see Keil, 2010). Second, student answering was shown to often be fairly sensitive to context; thus, within-student patterns of incorrect answers could be disrupted by simply making small changes to the context of the question. For example, on the question concerning objects moving in a curved path, Kaiser, Jonides, and Alexander (1986) found that significantly many students answered that water would come out of a curved hose in a straight line, and significantly less answered that a ball would come out a of curved tube in a straight line.

Of course, this critique of the misconceptions explanation could be at least partially addressed by the fact that the questions judged to be similar by an expert may not be perceived as similar by the student, therefore a lack of a pattern could be expected. Furthermore, there are many examples in which students do consistently answer incorrectly in ways that are consistent with them holding an incorrect concept for a significant set of questions. However, in some cases, the answering is so fragmented even with small changes in question context that it is difficult to imagine that the student holds a robust theory that is applied to many situations.

3.2. Knowledge in pieces or resources

In light of the demonstrated sensitivity of student answering to the context of some questions, others have suggested that rather than cuing coherent theories, questions with different contexts instead cue different (and often incorrect) combinations of "pieces of knowledge." In this way, within-student patterns of incorrect answers could be disrupted. Between-student patterns were still observed for a given question, and this could be explained because students have many of the same experiences; thus, a given question will often cue similar combinations of pieces of knowledge, resulting in student responding with similar incorrect answers. The pieces of knowledge represent basic phenomena such as "force as mover" (diSessa, 1993) or relations such as "more x means more y" (e.g., Stavy & Tirosh, 2000). A perhaps more general version of the pieces of knowledge explanation claims that questions may cue incorrect "resources" that students use to answer a question (e.g., Hammer, 2000). These resources can be wide ranging and include factual knowledge, basic relations, procedural knowledge, and epistemological beliefs. An especially powerful aspect to the knowledge in pieces model is the notion that student often have "untapped" knowledge and skills that can be used to improve their learning and performance (e.g., Hammer & Elby, 2003). To support this, there is evidence that students sometimes have the correct knowledge available to answer correctly, but this knowledge is often not cued (Hammer, Elby, Scherr, & Redish, 2005; Heckler, 2010; Sabella & Redish, 2007).

Finally, it should be noted that a more comprehensive version of the knowledge in pieces explanation is in fact extended to include loosely bound collections of pieces of knowledge that can form something resembling a coherent concept, thus explaining the presence of within-student patterns in some cases (e.g., diSessa & Sherin, 1998).

3.3. Ontological categories

Somewhat independent of the misconceptions and knowledge in pieces explanations is a third prominent explanation for incorrect patterns in answering. Some researchers (e.g., Chi, 2005; Reiner, Slotta, Chi, & Resnick, 2000) provide arguments and evidence for a "domain general" mechanism for misconception-like answering patterns, as opposed to "theory-specific" or "domain-specific" explanations of misconceptions and knowledge in pieces. The domain general process they investigate is the incorrect categorizing of the ontological nature of certain physical variables or phenomena (e.g., Chi, Slotta, & de Leeuw, 1994). For example, students commonly (incorrectly) believe that force is a substance in the sense that objects "have" a force (Reiner et al., 2000). Like the misconceptions explanation, this explanation can account for within-student answering patterns.

3.4. Summary

The explanations involving student-held concepts, theories, or models tend to naturally explain the presence of within-student patterns, while explanations involving more fragmented knowledge in pieces explanation tend to naturally explain the absence of within-student patterns that might be expected if students held coherent misconceptions. Both kinds of explanations have been modified to explain the presence or lack of answer patterns to some degree, though there is still debate about the validity of each explanation (e.g., see diSessa, Gillespie, & Esterly, 2004).

The existing explanations of coherent yet incorrect concepts or theories, incorrect ontologies, or knowledge in pieces all account for within-student patterns for at least some sets of questions. However, since each explanation is different, they may also identify and explain different patterns of answering. For example, the misconceptions explanation tends to be quite domain specific and will tend to search for and identify patterns within a specific domain, whereas the ontological category explanation is more domain general; consequently, this kind of approach will tend to search and identify patterns that are more domain general. On the other hand, these different explanations all appear to agree on the general reason for between-student patterns, namely, that whatever mechanism is responsible for the within-student patterns is common to all students.

Finally, a caveat: I have focused here on incorrect answer patterns specifically to science questions, yet there is also significant work on pattern of incorrect answers to more general questions, of which science is a subset. In particular, I refer to the field of heuristics and biases and the pioneering work of Tversky and Kahnemann (1974). I will address this in Section 6.1.

4. THE INSUFFICIENCY OF EXISTING EXPLANATIONS

While explanations discussed above are useful in the examination of student answering patterns, this section discusses three limitations of these explanations. Section 5 then describes an empirical example highlighting these limitations and the need for the inclusion of a more bottom–up mechanistic explanation.

4.1. Limitation 1: patterns are typically assumed to be caused by high-level mental structures and processes

I would like to emphasize that the critical question addressed in this chapter is "What causes student incorrect answer patterns to science questions?" This is a question about an *empirical observation* that allows a broad range of possible explanations. In contrast, the typical approach to the empirical evidence is to assume that the patterns are caused by "higher level" mental structures such as concepts, schemas, mental models, or loose collections of pieces of knowledge (e.g., Carey, 1985; Driver & Erickson, 1983; McCloskey, 1983; Novak, 2002; J. P. Smith, diSessa, & Roschelle, 1993; Vosniadou, 1994).[3] These approaches tend instead to ask questions such as "What are the student concepts that explain the answer patterns?" or "How are incorrect concepts learned?" These questions are not directly about empirical observations of answering patterns, rather they are questions about *inferences* about the observations. In short, the typical approach to the empirical observation of incorrect answering pattern is to *already assume* the cause of the patterns, namely, that they are a result of some high-order mental structure such as concepts or mental models.

The origin of this assumption may be traced back to Piaget (1952/ 1936, 1972/1970), who argued that scientific knowledge cannot be learned from sensory information alone, but rather requires explicit higher order thinking and interaction with the world in order to form high-level mental schemas necessary for scientific knowledge (see also Driver et al., 1994; Leach & Scott, 2003; Taber, 2010; Vosniadou, 1996).[4] Therefore, the argument goes: since higher level structures of knowledge are needed to understand science, such mental structures are needed to answer science questions in a correct and consistent manner.

However, the topic of this chapter is not directly about the origins or nature of scientific knowledge, it is about the origins of incorrect answering patterns to science questions. While one might agree that answering science questions consistently correctly may require correct higher level mental structures, answering incorrectly in patterned ways does *not* necessarily require a higher level mental structure. The patterns could be caused or strongly influenced by more basic, bottom-up processes that are implicit and relatively unknown to the answerer.

In other words, even if we assume that consistently correct answering occurs if and only if the answerer holds the correct concept (let us ignore

---

[3] Some models, such as Vosniadou's (1994) framework theory, include lower level unconscious aspects to the proposed mental structure.
[4] Note that there is also much discussion about the difference between individual cognition and social cognition (e.g., Leach & Scott, 2003), which we will not discuss here.

the possibility of false positives for simplicity), it still does not logically follow that incorrect answering patterns imply an incorrect concept.[5] Rather, incorrect answering only implies the *absence of a correct concept*, which could imply either the presence of an incorrect concept or the *absence* of any concept at all. For example, misconception-like answers could stem from implicit, automatic, and relatively unconscious processes that direct the student toward "undesired" answers in regular ways and may have little to do with consistently applied explicit concepts. One might claim that a pattern in answering requires some regularity in mental structure. This may be true, but it does not require a high-level mental structure—regularity in answering could be due to more basic processes. Therefore, most explanations of patterns of incorrect answers assume only one cause, namely, high-level mental structures; here, I would like to consider another influence (if not an alternative cause), namely, bottom-up processes.

Finally, the lack of a clear operational definition of high-level *mental structures* (e.g., a scientific concept) severely limits scientific progress of the high-level mental structures approach to explaining incorrect answering patterns to science questions (cf. diSessa & Sherin, 1998; diSessa et al., 2004). If one is to argue that mental structures such as concepts or mental models cause answering patterns, it is critical to establish a robust, unambiguous definition of such structures based on empirical observations characterizing the extent to which a student has a particular mental structure. Constructing such a definition will be a challenge. For example, if one cannot decisively claim that high-level mental structures are the sole cause of answering patterns, then one cannot use answering patterns as a sufficiently decisive empirical measure of the existence of high-level mental structures. This is related to the argument discussed earlier that any claim of the existence of patterns practically requires some assumption of the cause of the patterns, which may or may not be due to high-level mental structures.

4.2. Limitation 2: current explanations have limited predictive power

As mentioned in the introduction, one of the main scientific reasons for constructing a causal explanation of an empirical phenomenon is to make specific predictions about other, related empirical phenomena. There is

---

[5]Perhaps it should not be surprising that such a compelling, complementary, converse idea was also assumed. That is, if correct answering patterns result from correct concepts, then one might also imagine that incorrect answering patterns result from incorrect concepts or misconceptions. This "counterpart concept," so to speak, may be especially compelling given the strong evidence that prior knowledge interfered with learning the correct concept. The symmetric picture is completed with the assumption that this interfering prior knowledge is none other than a misconception.

value in post hoc explanations of existing empirical evidence, though an explanation increases in usefulness (a) the more it can be generalized to predict other situations and (b) the more specific the predictions can be about any given situation. This also implies that the more scientifically useful a model is, the more testable it is.

Current explanations of misconception-like answering patterns do have some predictive power, though the predictions are quite limited. One reason for this is because most current explanations are done *post hoc*. For example, the well-known phenomenon of incorrect answering to force and motion problems was not *predicted*. Rather, it was empirically *discovered* (e.g., Clement, 1982; Viennot, 1979) and then later explained as being due to students having an incorrect impetus theory of force and motion. This explanation could not be generalized to predict student answer patterns for questions about other physics topics such as simple circuits. It might be argued that since it is to be expected that students construct many concepts in the course of everyday life, the misconception model predicts that, in general, incorrect answer patterns are likely to be found for many other topics, though it cannot predict which topics or what those patterns will be.

There are, however, some specific predictions that the misconceptions model does make about students answering questions, specifically about force and motion questions. In its strictest interpretation, the model predicts that a subpopulation of students will answer all force and motion questions with an impetus motion model. Scientifically, there is an advantage to this model: it makes a specific prediction. As it turns out, the model's predictions are marginally successful in that they do predict some observed patterns, but other times the prediction of patterns are incorrect; thus, the model does not hold up to all empirical observations. Nonetheless, this test should be considered scientific progress: the model made a prediction, and the prediction was empirically tested. The picture for the predictive power of the ontological category model is very similar to that of the misconception model, and it too has succeeded in making some specific predictions but has failed at least one test of its strictest interpretation (Gupta, Hammer, & Redish, 2010).

The resources or knowledge in pieces models, which include the cuing of much finer-grained mental structures, have similar limitations of predictiveness as the misconceptions model in that the resources model also employs post hoc explanations for specific answer patterns (due to cuing of "incorrect" resources) rather than specific predictions of answer patterns. However, because the model is so flexible, there has yet to be any specific, testable predictions for this model (to the knowledge of the author), though there have been some preliminary attempts (e.g., diSessa et al., 2004; Elby, 2000). In order to achieve more scientific progress with such a model, more effort must be made to deduce testable predictions from it.[6]

In sum, current high-level mental structure explanations, such as the misconceptions model, do make a limited number of specific predictions about answering patterns to some specific questions. The misconception model predictions have been somewhat accurate in specific domains, though they have very limited predictive power and scientific usefulness in their current state. If more scientific progress is to be made in this area, mental structure theories models need to make significantly more specific, testable predictions about answering patterns that apply to a range of questions. This will likely entail the incorporation of specific mechanisms and quantifiable models, which tend to be missing in current models.

4.3. Limitation 3: current explanations rarely consider response data beyond the response content

The overwhelming majority of studies on student responses to science questions investigate the content of the student responses, such as the correctness of the response, the patterns of answer choices in a multiple choice test, the explanations in an interview, and the solution method in a problem solving task. However, there are a number of other response measurements that can be extremely useful, including response time, eye tracking, gesturing, and measurements of brain activity. Some of these modes will be discussed in Sections 6 and 7. Indeed, this is a growing area of activity that will provide much needed empirical data useful for testing models.

Since these additional response metrics tend to measure rapid, bottom-up processes of which the answerer is unaware, they will allow the testing of models that include bottom-up as well as top-down processes. A challenge for models such as the misconceptions model or the knowledge in pieces model will be to make testable predictions of such measurements.

5. Example: The Case of Competing Relevant and Irrelevant Information

In light of the general limitations discussed in the previous section of existing high-level mental structure explanations of student answering patterns to science questions, I would like to point out a particular

---

[6]However, the resources model has proved useful in other ways (e.g., Hammer 1996), namely, for orienting strategies for instruction. The interest here is in the scientific value of the model in terms of predicting answering patterns, which is not the same. The scientific liability of current models is to be distinguished from the *instructional* usefulness of models such as the misconception model or the resources model.

limitation. This limitation can be framed in terms of the notion of *competition*.

Explanations employing high–level mental structures typically assume that a specific question activates a specific mental structure in the student, be it a coherent theory, mental model, an ontological frame, or loosely bound pieces of knowledge, and this activated structure in turn leads to a specific response. However, these explanations do not (currently) include specific mechanisms that explain (or predict) *which* specific mental structure will be cued as opposed to another. For example, if a number of concepts and resources are plausibly relevant to the student for a given question posed, then why are only particular ones used in a given case? Since these explanations to not provide a specific mechanism responsible for activating one "plausible" concept over another in a given case, they will not be able to explain why a particular answer was chosen. Furthermore, if more than one concept is activated, then how is an answer choice determined? Does this mechanism for determining the answer choice result in a pattern of answers?

This limitation can also be described in terms of the *information* that is presented by the question and perceived by the student. Presumably, the student will often attend to both relevant and irrelevant information (as judged by an expert). What is the mechanism that determines which information is attended to or used to determine the answer? In other words, if a question presents a variety of information relevant to various competing mental structures, then what determines the outcome of the competition, and ultimately the student response?

To illustrate this point, consider the known difficulties students have with understanding the relation between electric field (E) and electric

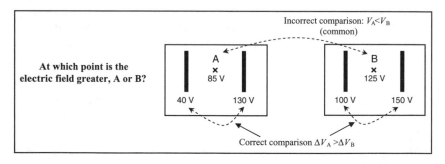

Figure 1 Undergraduate physics students compared the electric fields between the two sets of plates at the indicated voltages. For a series of eight questions, about 50% of the students consistently and incorrectly chose the point with the greater *value* of the voltage at the point between the plates (here, "B"). Less than 40% consistently chose the correct answer, which is found by taking the *difference* between the voltages of the plates. This misconception–like answering pattern could be considered as due to *competition* between relevant and irrelevant information.

potential (V), which is measured in *volts* (e.g., Maloney, O'Kuma, Hieggelke, & Van Heuvelen, 2001). For example, Figure 1 presents some data collected in my lab that are typical of the confusion in the relation between E and V. Thirty-five undergraduate physics students were shown a diagram of two sets of metal plates held at indicated voltages, and they were asked to determine which point midway between each set had a greater electric field (magnitude). The task was given post relevant instruction, so the students were reasonably familiar with these diagrams. This is a fairly simple and straightforward question in which a student may apply the idea that the magnitude of the electric field is proportional to the gradient of the electric potential, $E = |dV/dx|$. For this task, since the separation between each set of plates is the same, this simplifies to the idea that the point with the greater electric field is the one for which the *difference* in electric potential between the plates is the greatest. Instead, about 50% of students post instruction consistently and incorrectly chose the point with the greatest *value* of electric potential. Why is there often a consistent preference for the value of the potential rather than the *difference* in values between two plates?

Let us consider two possible scenarios that highlight the insufficiency of the misconception and knowledge in pieces explanations mentioned above, thus illustrating the need for a more specific mechanism that can explain and predict an answer preference resulting in a pattern of errors. The first scenario is centered around the notion that the students have learned the (incorrect) concept "the value of electric potential at a point predicts electric field," but have not learned the correct concept "gradient of electric potential predicts electric field," and this explains their patterns in answering. However, the question still remains as to specifically *why* the potential–field association was learned and why the potential gradient–field association was not learned.

The second possible scenario is based on the possibility that many students may have in fact learned both the association of electric potential with electric field and potential gradient with field, but there is nonetheless a preference for one because of the nature of the specific question. In this example (as well as many others), potential and difference in potential *compete*, and the former often wins. From the misconceptions perspective, students hold both the correct and incorrect concepts, but there is no explanation (or prediction) specifying why many students consistently choose the scientifically incorrect concept over the correct one for this question. Likewise, in terms of knowledge in pieces, one might claim that the question cued a basic relation such as "more is more." However, this basic relation could be applied to both the value of the electric potential and the difference in electric potential (more potential is more field, or more difference in potential is more field), and the knowledge in pieces approach also does not specify why one "more is more" was preferred over the other.

In sum, existing explanations of patterns of incorrect answering on science questions do not provide specific predictions or mechanisms that determine why, for a given specific topic, there may be a preference for learning a scientifically incorrect concept relevant to that topic rather than a correct one, or if students have learned both correct and incorrect concepts, why students choose one over the other when responding to a specific question.

It may be possible to modify mental structure models to explain and predict the outcomes of competition. Nonetheless, in the following sections, I describe some specific bottom-up mechanisms that can naturally help to explain and predict the outcome of competition between competing relevant and irrelevant information in at least some questions, namely, that many students tend to base their decision on the dimension that is processed the fastest or garners the most attention, even if it is incorrect. First I will briefly review some previous work that has examined the role of bottom-up mechanisms relevant to science learning and performance.

6. Bottom-Up Versus Top-Down Processing: Evidence from Answer Patterns

The idea that there are two kinds of cognitive systems involved in learning and performance has been discussed in the field of psychology for over 100 years (e.g., James, 1950/1890; Johnson-Laird, 1983; Neisser, 1963; Piaget, 1926; Shiffrin & Schneider, 1977; Vygotsky, 1987/1934). There are a number of recent studies demonstrating that higher and lower order processes interact significantly in decision making and reasoning (Alter, Oppenehimer, Epley, & Eyre, 2007; Evans 2003, 2008; Glöckner & Betsch, 2008; Kahneman & Frederick, 2002; Sloman, 1996), category learning (Kloos & Sloutsky, 2008; Maddox & Ashby, 2004), memory and recall (Poldrack & Packard, 2003), and language learning (e.g., Smith, Jones, & Landau, 1996).

Some of the evidence of two mental processing systems stems from the observation that for many tasks there appears to be two distinct ways to arrive at a response, and in many cases these two paths lead to different responses (cf. the *Criterion S* of Sloman, 1996). One kind of response tends to be fast, implicit, intuitive, automatic, and relatively effortless and is ascribed to being a result of System 1 processes. The other response tends to be slower, explicit, and effortful and is thought to come from a System 2 process (e.g., Evans, 2008; Kahneman & Frederick, 2002; Stanovich & West, 2000).

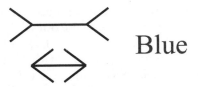

Blue

A bat and a ball cost
$1.10 in total. The bat
costs $1 more than the
ball. How much does
the ball cost?

Figure 2   Examples of tasks that provide evidence of two different systems at work in the course of solution: one automatic and implicit and the other deliberate and explicit. In these cases, the different systems lead to different answers. In particular, the fast, automatic system leads to "incorrect" answers, thus implying that one can construct a pattern of incorrect answers with similar tasks. The first task is an optical illusion in which one is to compare the lengths of the horizontal lines. The second task is the well-known Stroop task, in which one is to name the color of the letters. On the third task, constructed and studied by Kahneman and Frederick (2002), most college students answer (incorrectly) "10 cents."

An optical illusion is a classic case; an example, as pointed out by Sloman (1996), is the Muller-Lyer illusion (see Figure 2). In this case, the System 1 "perceptual" response is fast and clearly conflicts with the System 2 response that comes from reasoning that would include a concrete measurement. Other examples of two systems at work, some of which are presented in Figure 2, include the Stroop effect (e.g., MacLeod, 1991), belief bias (e.g., Evans, 2003), relapse errors (Betsch, Haberstroh, Molter, & Glöckner, 2004), and perseveration (Brace, Morton, & Munakata, 2006). Of course, these empirical phenomena are not all proposed to be caused by the same mechanism, but all of them have been explained in terms of a dual system similar to System 1 and System 2.

While there are some issues about the ambiguity of the meaning of System 1 and System 2 processes (e.g., see Evans, 2008), there are a number of studies testing predictions resulting from models that assume dual interacting systems at work in learning and performance in reasoning (DeNeys, 2006), relapse errors (Betsch et al., 2004), Stroop effect (Cohen, Dunbar, & McClelland, 1990; Kane & Engle, 2003), and category learning (Sloutsky, Kloos, & Fisher, 2007; Zeithamova & Maddox, 2006). There is further evidence building in neurological findings, showing that different areas of the brain are active during the putative engagement of the two different systems (e.g., Goel, Buchel, Frith, & Dolan, 2000).

A related line of compelling evidence of the existence of nontrivial implicit knowledge and skills is the field of *implicit learning* (e.g., Reber, 1989). In short, humans can unconsciously learn fairly complex rules that are applicable to novel (though somewhat limited) tasks (e.g., Berry & Dienes, 1993; Reber, 1993). For example, people can learn to remember strings of letters better if the strings have fairly complex statistical structure compared to remembering a random sequence, even though the learners are unaware that they are learning any structure. In addition, they can recognize new strings that are similar in structure to the ones they learned, though they are unable to report why they are similar. Evans, Clibbins, Cattani, Harris, & Dennis (2003) provide evidence of the learning in multicue judgment tasks involves both implicit and explicit knowledge, and this may help to explain why experts typically cannot fully explain their knowledge of rules used in tasks, because some of this knowledge is in fact implicit.

Finally, there is an illuminating difference between cognitive science studies on dual systems and science education studies on student answering to science questions. The above empirical studies, such as the Stroop effect, or optical illusions reveal a pattern of incorrect answering, yet the patterns of answering in this case are usually seen as evidence of automatic processes rather than evidence of a high-level mental structure such as a misconception.[7] For example, one would not claim that the Stroop effect is the result of a misconception. In contrast, in science education research, the patterns of incorrect answers to science questions have been taken as evidence of high-level mental structures such as misconceptions.

6.1. Heuristic and biases

The study of judgment and rational choice has a rich history in cognitive science and is related to the topic of incorrect answer patterns to science questions. This is partly because the study of judgment and choice is partially driven by the empirical observation that people often make systematic errors in judgment and choice. For example, in a series of classic studies, Tversky and Kahneman (1974) demonstrated that people tend to make general kinds of systematic errors in questions that require some level of quantitative or probabilistic judgment. For example, people have biases in judgments of the relative sizes of populations due to retrievability from memory. When verbally given a list of male and females, people tend to judge the list has more of one gender if more of names of that gender in the list are famous names.

Based on earlier work by Simon (1955), these patterns have often been explained in terms of *bounded rationality*, namely, that people make rational decisions that automatically include real-world constraints such as limited time and limited access to information. This idea in turn has led to explanations of systematic errors as due to the use of *heuristics*. That is, the hypothesis is that people use fast and efficient heuristics to make

---

[7]There are exceptions: one might attribute errors in syllogistic reasoning as the result of a mental model (Johnson-Laird, 1983), though this explanation makes assumptions of implicit processes as well (Evans, 2000).

judgments and choices. While in most cases this process is quite successful, in other cases the use of heuristics can lead to biases that cause systematic errors. For example, Goldstein and Gigerenzer (2002) discuss the *recognition heuristic*: if two alternatives are provided and one must choose only one based on some criterion and only one of the alternatives is recognized (familiar), then assume that the recognized one has a higher value of the criterion. The common task used to demonstrate the use of this heuristic is the case in which people are given the names of two cities in the world and asked to choose the one with the higher population. People often choose the city name that they recognize. For reviews of the topic of heurisitics and biases, see, for example, Gigerenzer (2008), Kahneman (2003), and Gilovich and Griffin (2002).

Evidence for the existence of heuristics has typically come from the recognition that, empirically, a given strategy or heuristic is used in many kinds of relevant problems by many people. See Gigerenzer (2008) for a number of examples of heuristics that are empirically well supported. In addition, there has been some progress in establishing testable predictions from the somewhat detailed models of heuristics that bolster the scientific usefulness of the heuristics hypothesis (e.g., see Bergert & Nosofky, 2007; Gigerenzer & Brighton, 2009).

There are two main reasons for bringing up the topic of heuristics. First, since the notion of heuristics was applied to explain patterns of incorrect answering, the pervasive use of heuristics may be an alternative or complementary explanation of misconception-like answers to science questions. Second, the heuristics tends to be regarded as an automatic, bottom-up process rather than an analytic explicit reasoning process (e.g., Evans, 2008; Kahneman, 2003). Therefore, if misconception-like answers to science questions are influenced by bottom-up processes, then heuristics models may be candidates for such processes.

In Section 7, I briefly mention how this may be applied to a specific example, but clearly the application of the hypothesis of general use of heuristics to answering science questions has potential to be a rich area for study in more detail.

6.2. Studies on bottom-up processes in science learning and performance

While the overwhelming majority of studies on student responses to science questions have focused on higher level mental structures, there have been a small number of studies investigating evidence of more implicit lower level processes taking place when students answer questions about natural phenomena.

The phenomenon of *representational momentum* is an example. If a student observes an image of an object undergoing implied or apparent motion and the object then suddenly disappears, the immediate memory of the last position of the object is shifted forward from the actual last position, as if to imply a continuing motion of the object (Freyd & Finke, 1984). This phenomenon is called representational momentum because most have interpreted the results as evidence that the perceptual system internalizes physical principles of motion and creates a representation of the motion that manifests itself, for example, in distorted memories (Freyd, 1987, 1992; Hubbard, 1995, 1998). The effect is small and short-lived but reliable, and the observers are not aware of the distortion; thus, it could be considered as implicit knowledge.

Interestingly, the implicitly projected paths do not always follow Newtonian motion. For example, Freyd and Jones (1994) found that for a ball exiting a circular tube, the perceptually preferred paths were in a continuing spiral rather than a straight line. They argued that this may help to explain why some students explicitly choose the incorrect spiral path when the question is posed explicitly. That is, there may be some influence of the implicit knowledge on the explicit answering. Similarly, Kozhevnikov and Hegarty (2001) found that even experts' implicit knowledge as measured by representational momentum is non-Newtonian, even though their explicit answers are Newtonian. Although it would appear that this implicit knowledge is difficult to change (however, see Courtney & Hubbard, 2008), they propose that it may still affect answering even of experts under certain constraints such as time limitations.

There are other kinds of studies demonstrating students "saying one thing, but doing another" on science-related tasks that would suggest that there are implicit and explicit systems separately influencing performance. For example, Piaget (1976), as pointed out by Oberle, McBeath, Madigan, & Sugar (2006), found that children could hit targets by appropriately letting go a string attached to an object that they were twirling in circles above their heads, but when asked in a paper and pencil task when the ball should be released, they answered incorrectly (i.e., they answered when the string was aligned with the target). Likewise, Oberle et al. asked students to compare the times it would take to two objects of either the same mass and different size or same size and different mass to fall the same (fairly large) height in the realistic scenario when air resistance is explicitly included. They found that students often answered that the objects would fall at the same rate. However, when the students were asked to physically drop two balls such that they would land at the same time, they found that students would drop the balls at *different* times, contrary to their explicit answers, They attributed this difference in answering to two different systems, namely, a perceptual system based on everyday perceptual experience and a higher level conceptual system.

There are also a number of studies investigating the student responses to the motions of objects, demonstrating that although many students may answer incorrectly on questions about motion represented by static displays, they often answer very accurately when the motions are animated (see Rohrer, 2003). For example, when given a choice of trajectories of a ball leaving a curved tube, students will answer correctly more often when given an animation compared to a static diagram (Kaiser, Proffitt, & Anderson, 1985). However, the benefit of animation decreases with increased complexity of motion (Kaiser, Proffitt, Whelan, & Hecht, 1992). This difference in responding has been interpreted as due to the static diagrams cuing explicit (incorrect) reasoning knowledge based on, for example, impetus models and the animated format cuing implicit perceptual knowledge that is based on common experience.

Finally, there are a number of studies on learning that indicate the existence and importance of low-level implicit automatic processes relevant to mathematics concepts. For example, in a study on 8–10-year-old children learning to solve simple addition problems, Siegler and Stern (1998) found that the time to solution was a reliable measure of the solvers' implicit use of a shortcut strategy. They found a bimodal distribution of times to solution with the solvers using the shortcut strategy solving the problem faster. Over a period of weeks, students became better at solving the problems and, perhaps most interestingly, many students started to use the shortcut strategy (as measured by time to solution) before they were explicitly aware of it as verbally reported by the solver. This suggests that there is a process of unconscious strategy discovery.

Furthermore, some researchers have investigated how math learning may be influenced by the phenomenon of perceptual learning, which is lower level, unconscious learning that results in an increase in the ability to extract information simply through experience (no explicit feedback is required). Kellman, Massey, and Son (2010) have found that simple perceptual learning tasks improve performance on higher level math tasks, for example, by increasing the learner's ability to focus on relevant rather than irrelevant dimensions. Goldstone, Landy, and Son (2010) provide evidence for the argument that the low-level perceptual system can adapt (i.e., learn) to achieve specific purposes, such as automatic recognition of symbols or diagrams in math and science, and this learned automaticity at least partially explains continual success on math and science tasks. Both of these examples highlight the educational possibilities of tapping into low-level processes and making required tasks automatic in order to improve math and science performance.

In sum, there are a small number of studies that provide evidence for the idea that automatic bottom–up processes can influence student learning and answering on science and math questions. Some of these studies used other modes of measurement such as response time and nonverbal responses that can help to support the claim that automatic processes are involved. In the next section, I will describe how a large class of science questions involve competing dimensions, and automatic bottom-up processes may at least partially cause the known misconception-like answering patterns to these questions.

7. THE PHENOMENON OF COMPETITION IN SCIENCE QUESTIONS

Section 5 described an example in which competing relevant and irrelevant information (from the perspective of an expert) was present in a science question, and many students consistently based their answer on the irrelevant information. In this section, I will discuss in more detail the phenomenon of *competition* between relevant and irrelevant information in science questions, and the outcomes of this competition as mediated by the low-level mechanisms of relative processing time and allocation of attention. The phenomenon of competition in science questions and its role in misconception-like answering patterns is described in three points:

First, it is assumed that students may consider—either implicitly or explicitly—a number of dimensions (e.g., variables or features) when answering science questions. I would like to emphasize that the dimensions considered by a novice are not always the same dimensions considered by an expert. Novice students may utilize dimensions not scientifically valid according to experts because the students may nonetheless perceive these dimensions as relevant. For example, when determining the period of a pendulum, many students may consider both the mass and length of the pendulum (see Figure 3), yet only the length is scientifically relevant.

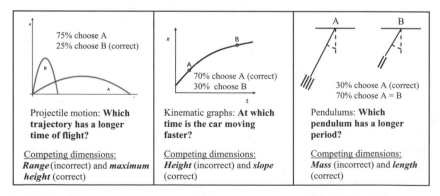

Figure 3 Examples of physics questions with competing dimensions. The indicated student response percentages were collected in pilot studies, with $N > 40$ in for each question.

Second, I propose that for a significant number of science questions, *competition* between relevant and irrelevant dimensions in a question plays a significant role in incorrect answering patterns. To illustrate the pervasiveness of this phenomenon, Figures 1 and 2 as well as Table 1 present a few examples of competing relevant and irrelevant dimensions for questions that have well-known misconception-like answering patterns. It would not be difficult to provide dozens of such examples. Note that collaborators and I have conducted interviews with some students answering these questions to support the validity of the questions.

Third, I propose that well-known mechanisms may at least in part predict and explain the outcomes of competition and the resulting patterns of student answers. These mechanisms are discussed in the next section. It is important to note that we are not explaining the cause of competition itself. Rather, we will help to explain and predict the *outcome* of two competing dimensions.

7.1. Relative processing times of relevant and irrelevant dimensions

I would like to consider the hypothesis that, when there are competing plausible dimensions upon which to base an answer for a given science question, students tend to choose the dimension that is *processed the fastest*. This hypothesis is somewhat similar to the fast heuristic model of "take the best," which chooses the first discriminating attribute to make a decision (e.g., Gigerenzer & Goldstein, 1996; see also Bergert & Nosofsky, 2007). Note that the dimensions of interest need only to be plausible from the perspective of the student; thus, both relevant and irrelevant dimensions may compete.

This hypothesis stems from evidence that if there is competition between relevant and irrelevant information in a question, then the outcome can be influenced by the relative time to process the relevant and irrelevant dimensions. Perhaps the best known method demonstrating this phenomenon is the Stroop effect (e.g., MacLeod, 1991), though the story likely also involves the more general concept of automaticity of processes (Cohen, Dunbar, & McClelland, 1990; Macleod & Dunbar, 1988). The Stroop effect occurs when a well-learned cue that is technically irrelevant to a task nonetheless competes with the relevant cues and interferes in task performance. The classic example is the color–word task, for example, spelling out the word "blue" in red-colored letters and asking participants to name the color of the letters (see Figure 4). Accuracy is typically lower and response times higher when the color of the letters conflicts with the word compared to when the color matches the word. Furthermore, the interfering dimension (word) is typically

Table 1   Examples of Science Concepts with Competing Relevant and Irrelevant Dimensions

Target dimension	Correct predictive dimension/relation	Incorrect/incomplete competing dimension	Common incorrect answer	Correct relationship
Force	Acceleration	Velocity	Greater velocity means greater net force	Greater acceleration means greater net force
Time of flight	Maximum height of projectile	Range of projectile	Both the range and height determine time of flight	Only height determines time of flight
Speed	Slope on x versus t graph	Height on x versus t graph	Higher point on graph means higher speed	Slope on graph determines speed
Period	Length of pendulum	Mass of pendulum	Mass and length determine period	Length only determines period
Electric field	Electric potential gradient	Electric potential	Higher potential means higher electric field	Higher potential gradient means higher electric field
Sliding distance	Initial velocity	Mass	Both initial velocity and mass determine sliding distance	Only initial velocity determines sliding distance
Torque (balance)	(Mass × distance)	Mass	Greater mass (force) means greater torque	Force and position determine torque
Mass	(Volume × density)	Volume	Bigger objects have more mass	Volume and density determine mass
Amount of thermal energy	(Temperature × mass)	Temperature	Higher temperature objects have more thermal energy	Temperature and mass determine total thermal energy
Energy dissipation	(I^2R)	Resistance	Higher resistance means higher energy dissipation	Resistance and current determine energy dissipation

processed with similar or shorter times than the relevant dimension (color).

Some physics questions can be considered similar to the Stroop task in that they have two competing dimensions that in some cases lead to conflicting answers and in other cases lead to the same answer. For example, consider the well-known difficulties students have in answering questions about graphs (Beichner, 1994; McDermott, Rosenquist, & van Zee, 1987; Mokros & Tinker, 1987). Students often interpret graph as a physical picture and there is a general confusion about the meaning of height and slope of a graph. In particular, when students are presented with a position versus time graphs for an object (see Figure 4) and asked, "At which point does the object have a higher speed?" many incorrectly answer according to the higher point (incorrect) rather than the greater slope (correct) (McDermott et al.). The graph questions in Figure 4 ask students to compare the speeds (i.e., slopes) at two points on a graph. For this question, the relevant dimension is *slope* and the irrelevant dimension is *height*. One may construct graphs in which the higher point has the higher slope (aligned) or when the higher point has the lower slope (conflicting). Students will often consistently choose the higher point in both cases, basing their answers on the irrelevant dimension of height rather than slope. Consequently, one finds that many students answer the aligned questions correctly and the conflicting question incorrectly (Heckler, Scaife, & Sayre, 2010).

Let us now consider the previously mentioned hypothesis that, among competing plausible dimensions, students tend to choose the dimension

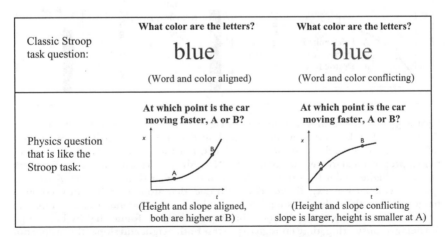

Figure 4 Analogy between a physics question and the Stroop task. Both involve competing dimensions (word vs. color, or height vs. slope), with faster times or higher accuracy for the aligned case.

that is *processedthefastest*. For the example of the graph question above, the hypothesis would predict that since height is often preferred over slope, height is processed inherently faster than slope.

In a recent study, collaborators and I confirmed the predictions of this hypothesis (Heckler & Scaife, 2010; Heckler et al., 2010). In this study (see Figure 5), we used response time as a proxy for processing time, and in speeded comparison task, we found that students could compare the heights of two points significantly faster than the slopes of two points. Furthermore, we found students, as expected, often consistently choose the point with the higher value than the point with greater slope. Perhaps most interestingly, we found that when a short (3 s) delay is imposed on answering, long enough for student to process both dimensions, the students' accuracy significantly improved. Thus, the students were capable of answering correctly, but instead they tend to answer *quickly*, and it may be this preference for answering quickly that drives students to choose the dimension that is processed the fastest.

It is worth noting that the above study also found that students answering incorrectly also answered faster. Thus, there is more than just patterns to the response content; however, there are also patterns to the response *times*. Response times on questions have been investigated in the past to eliminate the effect of guessing, thus improving the accuracy of the tests (Bridgeman et. al, 2004; Schnipke & Scrams,

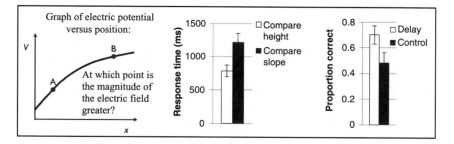

Figure 5 Competition via different processing times of relevant and irrelevant dimensions. Similar to the kinematics graph in Figure 3, the question above (figure left) elicits slope–height confusion in students. For the question above, the electric field is proportional to the slope of the line. Nonetheless, 55% of students consistently chose the higher point (incorrect) rather than the higher slope (correct). A separate speeded comparison experiment demonstrated that students inherently compare heights faster than slopes, supporting the idea that students might simply be choosing the faster processed dimension. In addition, we found that by imposing a 3-s delay on answering, time enough to process both height and slope, the proportion of correct responses increased (figure right). This supports the idea that students can answer correctly, but instead they tend to answer *quickly* (Heckler, Scaife, & Sayre, 2010).

1997; van der Linden, 2008), or to detect cheating (van der Linden & van Krimpen-Stoop, 2003). However, for the questions used in this study, students answered in patterned ways, and thus they are not guessing (e.g., see Heckler et al., 2010).

In sum, some patterns in responses to science questions may arise from lower level implicit decision criteria (e.g., answer quickly) rather than from some higher level conceptual understanding. The influence of this lower level process can be significant enough to mask a student's overall ability to determine the correct answer. The hypothesis that students will tend to base their answer on the plausible information that is processed the fastest makes testable predictions about response *times* as well as response choices. Not only is there some existing evidence to support this hypothesis, but there are also many possibilities of testing it further by designing experiments that include the capture of response time data as well as response choice data.

7.2. High salience of irrelevant cues: attentional learning

Competition can also be manifested in terms of allocation of attention. When two or more cues are present, it is often the case that one of them captures most of the attention. This phenomenon of *cue competition* is fundamental to a wide range of learning and behavior. For example, decades of studies in category learning have identified two major factors that determine which cues are learned and which are ignored among a multitude of competing cues in the environment: learners tend to learn cues that are relatively salient, predictive, or both (e.g., see Edgell, Bright, Ng, Noonan, & Ford, 1992; Hall, 1991; Trabasso & Bower, 1968). There are a number of successful models that can explain the trade-off between the salience and predictiveness of a dimension in terms of *learned attention* (e.g., Kruschke, 2001; Mackintosh, 1975). In our recent work, collaborators and I have provided evidence that when low-salient cues repeatedly compete with high-salient cues, the low-salient cues are learned to be ignored, even if they are more predictive than the high-salient cues (Heckler, Kaminski, & Sloutsky, 2008; 2011). This *learned inattention* to low-salient yet predictive information may contribute to the students' difficulties in correctly answering science questions and learning science concepts.

How can attentional learning lead to incorrect answering on science questions? Science concepts involve highly predictive cues, but these predictive cues can be of relatively low salience. For example, the acceleration of an object uniquely predicts the net force on that object, yet acceleration is often less salient than velocity (e.g., Schmerler, 1976), and students often infer the net force on an object from the velocity of the object rather than its acceleration (e.g., Clement, 1982; Halloun &

Hestenes, 1985). Thus, people's natural preference for attending to more salient cues can be problematic in science learning and performance, because these more salient cues may prevent attention to more predictive but less salient cues.

From this perspective, it is reasonable to expect that answering patterns to science questions may be strongly influenced by the format (i.e., surface features) of the question itself. This is reminiscent of a study by Chi et al. (1981), who found that novices tend to be distracted by surface features of questions rather than the underlying structure.

Therefore, I would like to consider the hypothesis that many students may simply base their response on the most salient and plausibly relevant features of a science question, even if these salient features may in fact be unrelated or contrary to the relevant scientific concept. With several competing features, the most salient one tends to automatically capture attention, with little opportunity for alternative less salient features to be considered.

For example, Figure 6 presents two questions that are based on the slope–height confusion on graph questions mentioned earlier. After relevant instruction, introductory undergraduate physics students were shown the above position versus time graphs of two cars and asked, "When are the speeds of the cars the same?" The speeds are the same at the time(s) when the slopes are the same. The score for the graph with the parallel lines is near perfect, presumably because the sameness of the slopes of the lines captured the attention. In this case then, attention was given to the relevant dimension of *slope*. However, for the crossed–lines graph, many students chose the time at which the lines intersected, presumably because this point captures attention more than the time at which the lines

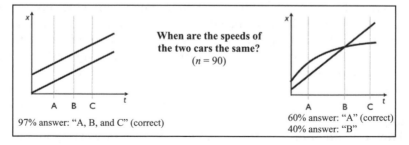

Figure 6 Hypothesized manipulation of attention on kinematics graph questions. For these questions, only the slopes of the lines at any given point are relevant, the relative heights (i.e., values) of the point on lines are irrelevant. In the parallel line graphs, almost all students answered "correctly" presumably allocating most attention to the fact that the *slopes* of the lines are equal. However, in the crossed line graph, many students presumably allocated most attention to the point at which the lines cross (*values* are equal).

have the same slope. Therefore, this is consistent with the hypothesis that students answer according to the features of the question that capture the most attention. In the case of the crossed lines, the irrelevant dimension of the *values* of the lines captured attention and led many students to the incorrect response.

One advantage of the hypothesis that bottom-up attentional allocation can play a role in incorrect answering patterns is that it can potentially be measured and tested independent of student response choices. For example, one can operationally define overt eye gaze (as measured by an eye tracker) as a measure of attention (cf. Rehder & Hoffman, 2005). Specifically, the dimension that results in the first and longest fixations is considered as the one capturing the most attention (and is the most salient). In the example in Figure 6, one would expect, for example, that attention would be fixed on the intersection of the lines on the second graph.

Note that the term *salience* is used in many contexts, and it is important to use the term consistently. Informally speaking, the salience of a cue or dimension is usually defined as the quality of standing out or being more noticeable compared to other cooccurring dimensions. Salience is often more formally regarded empirically as a quality of a cue or dimension that, separate from relative predictiveness, affects attention to (e.g., Kim & Cave, 1999; Lamy, Tsal, & Egeth, 2003) and the learning of (e.g., Edgell et al., 1992; Hall et al., 1977; Kruschke & Johansen, 1999; Trabasso & Bower, 1968) a cue relative to other present cues. Therefore, one may operationally define salience in a number of ways. For example, one may define the salient dimension as the one that attracts the most attention, as measured by eye tracking.

It is also important to keep in mind that the attention to a cue or dimension depends on the context. For example, the relative attention to two given cues can depend on the presence or absence of other cues; thus, changing the perceptual or conceptual format of the context may change the relative attention to two cues. Furthermore, attention (or salience) depends on bottom-up mechanisms operating at the level of perceptual features as well as on top-down mechanisms operating at the level of cognitive strategies, for example, controlling a search task (e.g., Egeth & Yantis, 1997). Therefore, our measures of relative attention to specific dimensions should be regarded as specific to particular questions and tasks. Nonetheless, the mechanism of attention to salient dimensions and its possible effect on student answering is general.

In a number of recent studies on enhancing multimedia learning, eye tracking results have shown that participants are distracted by irrelevant features and tend to look at more relevant areas of diagrams after instruction (Canham & Hegarty, 2010) and at relevant areas of animations if they are highlighted (Boucheix & Lowe, 2010), or if they are experts (Jarodzka,

Scheiter, Gerjets, & Van Gog, 2010). Nonetheless, more studies are needed that specifically focus on expert and novice attention to relevant and irrelevant features in physics problems known to elicit misconception-like responses. That is, the irrelevant features are more than just randomly distracting. There may be previously learned attention to incorrect dimensions that must eventually be overcome. An example of a related study is a study on spatial visualization ability and physics problem solving ability by Kozhevnikov, Motes, and Hegarty (2007) who found that students who made "graph-as-picture" misconception-like descriptions tended to look at the axes less than those students who accurately describe kinematics graphs questions; however, the eye tracking data were more ambiguous about differences between students looking at the lines in the graphs.

In sum, salient yet scientifically irrelevant features of a question compete for attention with less salient yet relevant features, and this may play an important role in incorrect student answering patterns. One may be able to observe the potential role of allocation of attention in the answering of science questions by measuring attention via eye tracking during the course of responding to question tasks. Since allocation of attention is controlled by both bottom-up and top-down processes, the challenge will be designing experiments to separate out these two kinds of processes in order to determine the extent to which automatic attentional mechanisms may be influencing response choices. Furthermore, there are a number of models of attention and attentional learning that may be applicable to misconception-like answering and may offer ways to test such models.

8. SUMMARY AND GENERAL DISCUSSION

Why do people often answer simple scientific questions incorrectly in regular, patterned ways? This simply posed, powerful question is the driving force behind this chapter. It is one of those simple yet deeply important questions found in science like "what makes stars shine?" or "what causes cancer?" It is a question that can lead to a deeper understanding of how people think and learn and how they interact with the world.

While there is general agreement on the existence of patterns of incorrect answering to science concept questions, there is less agreement about the causes of such patterns. The phenomenon of answering patterns is certainly not monolithic and likely arises from a number of mechanisms. As discussed in Section 2, a critical issue about incorrect answering patterns is that a cause for the patterns must first be assumed in order to identify a practically relevant pattern, and then it must be based on similarities in questions perceived by the *answerer* rather than the expert who poses them.

In the field of science education, prevalent explanations for incorrect answering patterns have focused on high-level mental structures, such as misconceptions and explicit thinking. These explanations have been useful for instruction, but they have very limited predictive power. This lack of predictive power is largely due to the lack of specific models and mechanisms. Furthermore, while these explanations do not exclude the possible influence of automatic, bottom-up processes, they rarely explicitly include them.

On the other hand, in the field of cognitive science, patterns of incorrect answering on a variety of tasks both inside and outside the domain of science have also been a major empirical driving force for investigations in areas such as category learning, language learning, reasoning, decision making, and judgment. However, in these cases, models explaining the patterns of answers often include either (or both) implicit or explicit processes, and this approach has yielded some specific predictive models that have demonstrated some success.

Therefore, in this chapter, the potential role of bottom-up processes in incorrect answering patterns to science questions was explored. In particular, the phenomenon of *competition* was investigated as it relates to the answering of science questions because this phenomenon highlights the limitations of high-level mental structure models and the need for bottom-up mechanisms to explain patterns of incorrect answering.

Two examples of bottom-up mechanisms that can predict the outcome of competing dimensions were examined: relative processing time and allocation of attention to relevant and irrelevant dimensions. First, it is hypothesized that students tend to choose the dimension that is processed the fastest. Second, it is hypothesized that students tend to choose the dimension that captures the most attention (and is plausibly relevant). While specific examples of each mechanism were discussed, it still remains an open question as to how these two mechanisms may be related or interact. Data on response choices supported the predictions of the two mechanisms. For the processing time mechanism, patterns in data of the response times also supported the hypothesized mechanism. Therefore, one advantage to this proposed mechanism is that it makes testable predictions on response measures in addition to the response choice.

8.1. The relevance to science education

The multiple choice questions discussed here, as well as many of the questions used in research on science misconceptions, are similar to science questions commonly found in textbooks and classroom tests. The fact that responses to these questions may be strongly influenced by automatic bottom-up processes in many students has double-edged implications. First, it calls into question the presumed validity of these questions, since they were meant to test the extent to which students have explicit understanding of a particular scientific concept. However, these and similar questions, such as those used on well-vetted concept inventories, (e.g., Ding, Chabay, Sherwood, & Beichner, 2006; Hestenes, Wells, & Swackhammer, 1992), *have* often been validated through student interviews to ensure that the large majority of students can explicitly explain their answer choice. That is to say, these multiple choice questions do often reflect students' explicit understanding as interpreted by their explanations.

Therefore, the second implication of the influence of bottom-up processes on answering patterns is to call into question what is meant by *understanding* of a concept. *Any* claim about "student understanding" or "what a student is thinking" can only be operationally defined by or inferred from student performance on a task, be it the response to an informal question in class, to a multiple choice question on a test, or the success on a semester-long group project. If, as is suggested in this chapter and in the work on dual systems discussed in Section 6, the performance on these tasks is inevitably influenced by unconscious, automatic, bottom-up processes, then our understanding of *understanding a science concept* must include both explicit reasoning and automatic, bottom-up processes. One might say that both "System 1" and "System 2" are a necessary part of what we operationally mean by understanding a science concept, as they both may influence performance on any task relevant to the science concept. Indeed, a significant portion of expert science knowledge may be implicit (cf. Evans, Clibbins, Cattani, Harris, & Dennis, 2003).

If bottom-up processes do play an important role in understanding of a science concept, then this suggests that one should utilize methods of instruction that align these process with goals of explicit reasoning (cf. Brace et al., 2006; Goldstone et al., 2010; Kellman et al., 2010). For example, students may be better able to understand the meaning of tangent slopes on a graph if they can process them as quickly as positions on a graph. Or if one is to reason that velocity is not in the direction of force, this may be facilitated if such examples were highly available in memory due to repeated practice examples.

The goal of this chapter was to investigate the potential role of automatic, bottom-up processes in the well-known phenomenon of patterns of incorrect answering to science concept questions. It seems clear that bottom-up processes can play an important role in student answering, and disregarding such processes risks ignoring a plausible opportunity to improve our understanding of learning and understanding of scientific concepts.

ACKNOWLEDGMENTS

This research is supported by the Institute of Education Sciences, U.S. Department of Education, through grant R305H050125.

REFERENCES

Alter, A. L., Oppenehimer, D. M., Epley, N., & Eyre, R. N. (2007). Overcoming intuition: Metacognitive difficulty activates analytic reasoning. *Journal of Experimental Psychology: General, 136,* 569–576.

Bao, L., & Redish, E. F. (2006). Model analysis: Representing and assessing the dynamics of student learning. *Physical Review Special Topics: Physics Education Research, 2,* 010103-1–010103-16.

Beichner, R. J. (1994). Testing student interpretation of graphs. *American Journal of Physics, 62,* 750–762.

Bergert, F. B., & Nosofsky, R. M. (2007). A response-time approach to comparing generalized rational and take-the-best models of decision making. *Journal of Experimental Psychology: Learning, Memory, and Cognition, 33,* 107–129.

Berry, D. C., & Dienes, Z. (1993). *Implicit learning.* Hove, UK: Erlbaum.

Betsch, T., Haberstroh, S., Molter, B., & Glöckner, A. (2004). Oops – I did it again: When prior knowledge overrules intentions. *Organizational Behavior and Human Decision Processes, 93,* 62–74.

Boucheix, J. -M., & Lowe, R. K. (2010). An eye-tracking comparison of external pointing cues and internal continuous cues in learning with complex animations. *Learning and Instruction, 20,* 123–135.

Brace, J. J., Morton, J. B., & Munakata, Y. (2006). When actions speak louder than words. Improving children's flexibility in a card-sorting task. *Psychological Science, 17,* 665–669.

Bridgeman, B., Cline, F., & Hessinger, J. (2004). Effect of extra time on verbal and quantitative GRE scores. *Applied measurement in Education, 17,* 25–37.

Canham, M., & Hegarty, M. (2010). Effects of knowledge and display design on comprehension of complex graphics. *Learning and Instruction, 20,* 155–166.

Carey, S. (1985). *Conceptual change in childhood.* Cambridge, MA: MIT Press.

Carey, S. (2009). *The origin of concepts.* New York: Oxford University Press.

Carey, S., & Spelke, E. (1996). Science and core knowledge. *Philosophy of Science, 63,* 515–533.

Chi, M. T. H. (2005). Commonsense conceptions of emergent processes: Why some misconceptions are robust. *The Journal of the Learning Sciences, 14,* 161–199.

Chi, M. T. H., Feltovich, P. J., & Glaser, R. (1981). Categorization and representation of physics problems by experts and novices. *Cognitive Science, 5,* 121–152.

Chi, M. T. H., Slotta, J. D., & de Leeuw, N. (1994). From things to processes: A theory of conceptual change for learning science concepts. *Learning and Instruction, 4,* 27–43.

Clement, J. (1982). Students' preconceptions in introductory mechanics. *American Journal of Physics, 50,* 66–71.

Cohen, J. D., Dunbar, K., & McClelland, J. L. (1990). On the control of automatic processes: A parallel distributed processing account of the Stroop effect. *Psychological Bulletin, 97,* 332–361.

Courtney, J. R., & Hubbard, T. L. (2008). Spatial memory and explicit knowledge: An effect of instruction on representational momentum. *The Quarterly Journal of Experimental Psychology, 61*, 1778–1784.

Deneys, W. (2006). Dual processing in reasoning: Two systems but one reasoned. *Psychological Science, 17*, 428–433.

Ding, L., Chabay, R., Sherwood, B., & Beichner, R. (2006). Evaluating an electricity and magnetism assessment tool: Brief electricity and magnetism assessment. *Physical Review Special Topics: Physics Education Research, 2*, 010105-1–010105-7.

diSessa, A. A. (1993). Toward an epistemology of physics. *Cognition and Instruction, 10* (2–3), 105–225.

diSessa, A. A., Gillespie, N. M., & Esterly, J. B. (2004). Coherence versus fragmentation in the development of the concept of force. *Cognitive Science, 28*, 843–900.

diSessa, A. A., & Sherin, B. L. (1998). What changes in conceptual change. *International Journal of Science Education, 20*, 1155–1191.

Driver, R., & Easley, J. (1978). Pupils and paradigms: a review of literature related to concept development in adolescent science students. *Studies in Science Education, 5*, 61–84.

Driver, R., Asoko, H., Leach, J., Mortimer, E., & Scott, P. H. (1994). Constructing scientific knowledge in the classroom. *Educational Researcher, 23*, 5–12.

Driver, R., & Erickson, G. (1983). Theories-in-action: Some theoretical and empirical issues in the study of students' conceptual frameworks in science. *Studies in Science Education, 10*, 37–60.

Edgell, S. E., Bright, R. D., Ng, P. C., Noonan, T. K., & Ford, L. A. (1992). The effects of representation on the processing of probabilistic information. In B. Burns (Ed.), New York: Elsevier Science.

Egeth, H. E., & Yantis, S. (1997). Visual attention: Control, representation, and time course. *Annual Review of Psychology, 48*, 269–297.

Elby, A. (2000). What students' learning of representations tells us about constructivism. *Journal of Mathematical Behavior, 19*, 481–502.

Elby, A. (2001). Helping physics students learn how to learn. *American Journal of Physics, 69*, S54–S64.

Evans J. St. B. T. (2000). In J.A. Garcia- Madruga et al. (Eds.), *Mental models in reasoning* (pp. 41-56). Madrid: UNED.

Evans, J. St. B. T. (2003). In two minds: Dual process accounts of reasoning. *Trends in Cognitive Sciences, 7*, 454–459.

Evans, J. St. B. T. (2008). Dual-processing accounts of reasoning, judgment, and social cognition. *Annual Review of Psychology, 59*, 255–278.

Evans, J. St. B. T., Clibbins, J., Cattani, A., Harris, A., & Dennis, I. (2003). Explicit and implicit processes in multicue judgment. *Memory & Cognition, 31*, 608–618.

Freyd, J. J. (1987). Dynamic mental representations. *Psychological Review, 94*, 427–438.

Freyd, J. J. (1992). Dynamic representations guiding adaptive behavior. In D. Meyer, and S. Kornblum, (Eds.), (pp. 309–323). Dordrecht: Kluwer.

Freyd, J. J., & Finke, R. A. (1984). Representational momentum. *Journal of Experimental Psychology: Learning, Memory, & Cognition, 10*, 126–132.

Freyd, J. J., & Jones, K. T. (1994). Representational momentum for a spiral path. *Journal of Experimental Psychology: Learning, Memory, & Cognition, 20*, 968–976.

Gelman, S. A. (2009). Learning from others: Children's construction of concepts. *Annual Review of Psychology, 60*, 115–140.

Gigerenzer, G. (2008). Why heuristics work. *Perspectives on Psychological Science, 3*, 20–29.

Gigerenzer, G., & Brighton, H. (2009). Homo heuristicus: Why biased minds make better inferences. *Topics in Cognitive Science, 1*, 107–143.

Gigerenzer, G., & Goldstein, D. G. (1996). Reasoning the fast and frugal way: Models of bounded rationality. *Psychological Review, 103*, 650–669.

Gilovich, T., & Griffin, D. W. (2002). Heuristics and biases then and now. In T. Gilovich., D. W. Griffin, and D. Kahneman, (Eds.), (pp. 1–18). Cambridge, UK: Cambridge University Press.

Glöckner, A., & Betsch, T. (2008). Modeling option and strategy choices with connectionist networks: Towards an integrative model of automatic and deliberate decision making. *Judgment and Decision Making, 3*, 215–228.

Goel, V., Buchel, C., Frith, C., & Dolan, R. J. (2000). Dissociation of mechanisms underlying syllogistic reasoning. *Neuroimage, 12*, 504–514.

Goldstein, D. G., & Gigerenzer, G. (2002). Models of ecological rationality: The recognition heuristic. *Psychological Review, 109*, 75–90.

Goldstone, R. L., Landy, D. H., & Son, J. Y. (2010). The education of perception. *Topics in Cognitive Science, 2*, 265–284.

Gupta, A., Hammer, D., & Redish, E. F. (2010). The case for dynamic models of learners' ontologies in physics. *The Journal of the Learning Sciences, 19*, 285–321.

Hall, G. (1991). *Perceptual and associative learning*. New York: Oxford University Press.

Hall, G., Mackintosh, N. J., Goodall, G., & Dal Martello, M. (1977). Loss of control by a less valid or less salient stimulus compounded with a better predictor of reinforcement. *Learning and Motivation, 8*, 145–158.

Halloun, I. A., & Hestenes, D. (1985). Common-sense concepts about motion. *American Journal of Physics, 53*, 1056–1065.

Hammer, D. (1996 a). Misconceptions or p-prims: How may alternative perspectives of cognitive structure influence instructional perceptions and intentions? *The Journal of the Learning Sciences, 5*, 97–127.

Hammer, D. (1996b). More than misconceptions: Multiple perspectives on student knowledge and reasoning, and an appropriate role for education research. *American Journal of Physics, 64*, 1316–1325.

Hammer, D. (2000). Student resources for learning introductory physics. *American Journal of Physics, 68*, S59.

Hammer, D., & Elby, A. (2003). Tapping epistemological resources for learning physics. *The Journal of the Learning Sciences, 12*, 53–90.

Hammer, D., Elby, A., Scherr, R., & Redish, E. F. (2005). Resources, framing, and transfer. In J. Mestre (Ed.), (pp. 89–119). Charlotte, NC: Information Age.

Heckler, A. F. (2010). Some consequences of prompting novice students to construct force diagrams. *International Journal of Science Education, 32*, 1829–1851.

Heckler, A. F., Kaminski, J.A., & Sloutsky, V.M. (2008). Learning associations that run counter to biases in learning: Overcoming overshadowing and learned inattention. *Proceedings of the 30th Annual Conference of the Cognitive Science Society* (pp. 511–516). Austin, TX: Cognitive Science Society.

Heckler, A. F., Kaminski, J.A., & Sloutsky, V.M. (2011). Salience, learned inattention and recovery from overshadowing (in preparation).

Heckler, A. F., & Sayre, E. C. (2010). What happens between pre- and post-tests: Multiple measurements of student understanding during an introductory physics course. *American Journal of Physics, 78*, 768–777.

Heckler, A. F., & Scaife, T.M. (2011). Processing time and competition between relevant and irrelevant dimensions on science questions.(in preparation).

Heckler, A. F., Scaife, T. M., & Sayre, E. C. (2010). Response times and misconception-like responses to science questions. In S. Ohlsson, and R. Catrambone, (Eds.), (pp. 139–144). Austin, TX: Cognitive Science Society.

Hestenes, D., Wells, M., & Swackhammer, G. (1992). Force concept inventory. *The Physics Teacher, 30*, 141–158.

Hubbard, T. L. (1995). Environmental invariants in the representation of motion: Implied dynamics and representational momentum, gravity, friction, and centripetal force. *Psychonomic Bulletin & Review, 2,* 322–338.

Hubbard, T. L. (1998). Representational momentum and other displacement in memory as evidence for nonconscious knowledge of physical principles. In S. Hameroff., A. Kaszniak, and A. Scott, (Eds.), (pp. 505–512). Cambridge, MA: MIT Press.

James, W. (1950). *The principles of psychology.* New York: Dover Original published 1890.

Jarodzka, H., Scheiter, K., Gerjets, P., & Van Gog, T. (2010). In the eyes of the beholder: How experts and novices interpret dynamic stimuli. *Learning and Instruction, 20,* 146–154.

Johnson-Laird, P. N. (1983). *Mental models.* Cambridge, MA: Harvard University Press.

Kahneman, D. (2003). A perspective on judgment and choice: Mapping bounded rationality. *American Psychologist, 58,* 697–720.

Kahneman, D., & Frederick, S. (2002). Representativeness revisited: Attribute substitution in intuitive judgement. In T. Gilovich., D. Griffin, and D. Kahneman, (Eds.), (pp. 49–81). Cambridge, UK: Cambridge University Press.

Kaiser, M. K., Jonides, J., & Alexander, J. (1986). Intuitive reasoning about abstract and familiar physics problems. *Memory & Cognition, 14,* 308–312.

Kaiser, M. K., Proffitt, D. R., & Anderson, K. A. (1985). Judgments of natural and anomalous trajectories in the presence and absence of motion. *Journal of Experimental Psychology: Learning, Memory, and Cognition, 11,* 795–803.

Kaiser, M. K., Proffitt, D. R., Whelan, S. M., & Hecht, H. (1992). Influence of animation on dynamical judgments. *Journal of Experimental Psychology: Human Perception & Performance, 18,* 669–689.

Kane, M. J., & Engle, R. W. (2003). Working-memory capacity and the control of attention: The contributions of goal neglect, response competition, and task set to Stroop interference. *Journal of Experimental Psychology: General, 132,* 47–70.

Keil, F. C. (2010). The feasibility of folk science. *Cognitive Science, 34,* 825–862.

Kellman, P. J., Massey, C. M., & Son, J. Y. (2010). Perceptual learning modules in mathematics: Enhancing students' pattern recognition, structure extraction, and fluency. *Topics in Cognitive Science, 2,* 285–305.

Kim, M. -S., & Cave, K. R. (1999). Top-down and bottom-up attentional control: On the nature of the interference of a salient distractor. *Perception and Psychophysics, 61,* 1009–1023.

Kind, V. (2004). Beyond appearances: Students' misconceptions about basic chemical ideas: A report prepared for the Royal Society of Chemistry (2nd ed.). London: Education Division, Royal Society of Chemistry. Retrieved December 8, 2009 from http://www.rsc.org/education/teachers/learnnet/pdf/LearnNet/rsc/miscon.pdf.

Kloos, H., & Sloutsky, V. M. (2008). What's behind different kinds of kinds: Effects of statistical density on learning and representation of categories. *Journal of Experimental Psychology: General, 137,* 52–72.

Kozhevnikov, M., & Hegarty, M. (2001). Impetus beliefs as default heuristics: Dissociation between explicit and implicit knowledge about motion. *Psychonomic Bulletin & Review, 8,* 439–453.

Kozhevnikov, M., Motes, M. A., & Hegarty, M. (2007). Spatial visualization in physics problem solving. *Cognitive Science, 31,* 549–579.

Kruschke, J. K. (2001). Toward a unified model of attention in associative learning. *Journal of Mathematical Psychology, 45,* 812–863.

Kruschke, J. K., & Johansen, M. K. (1999). A model of probabilistic category learning. *Journal of Experimental Psychology: Learning Memory and Cognition, 25,* 1083.

Lamy, D., Tsal, Y., & Egeth, H. E. (2003). Does a salient distractor capture attention early in processing? *Psychonomic Bulletin and Review, 10,* 621–629.

Leach, J., & Scott, P. (2003). Individual and sociocultural views of learning in science education. *Science and Education, 12,* 91–113.

Mackintosh, N. J. (1975). A theory of attention: Variations in the associability of stimuli with reinforcement. *Psychological Review, 82,* 276–298.

MacLeod, C. M. (1991). Half a century of research on the Stroop effect: An integrative review. *Psychological Bulletin, 109,* 163–203.

Macleod, C. M., & Dunbar, K. (1988). Training and Stroop-like interference: Evidence for a continuum of automaticity. *Journal of Experimental Psychology: Learning, Memory and Cognition, 14,* 126–135.

Maddox, W. T., & Ashby, F. G. (2004). Dissociating explicit and procedural-learning based systems of perceptual category learning. *Behavioural Processes, 66,* 309–332.

Maloney, D. P., O'Kuma, T. L., Hieggelke, C. J., & Van Heuvelen, A. (2001). Surveying students' conceptual knowledge of electricity and magnetism. *American Journal of Physics, 69,* S12–S23.

McCloskey, M. (1983). Naive theories of motion. In D. Gentner, and A. L. Stevens, (Eds.), (pp. 299–324). Hillsdale, NJ: Lawrence Erlbaum Associates, Inc.

McCloskey, M., Caramazza, A., & Green, B. (1980). Curvilinear motion in the absence of external forces: Naïve beliefs about the motion of objects. *Science, 210,* 1139–1141.

McDermott, L. C. (2001). Physics education research: The key to student learning. *American Journal of Physics, 69,* 1127–1137.

McDermott, L. C., & Redish, E. F. (1999). RL-PER-1: Resource letter on physics education research. *American Journal of Physics, 67,* 755–767.

Mcdermott, L. C., Rosenquist, M. L., & van Zee, E. (1987). Student difficulties in connecting graphs and physics: Examples from kinematics. *American Journal of Physics, 55,* 503.

Mokros, J. R., & Tinker, R. F. (1987). The impact of microcomputer-based labs on children's ability to interpret graphs. *Journal of Research in Science Teaching, 24,* 369–383.

Neisser, U. (1963). The multiplicity of thought. *British Journal of Psychology, 54,* 1–14.

Novak, J. D. (2002). Meaningful learning: The essential factor for conceptual change in limited or inappropriate propositional hierarchies leading to empowerment of learners. *Science Education, 86,* 548–571.

Oberle, C. D., McBeath, M. K., Madigan, S. C., & Sugar, T. G. (2006). The Galileo bias: A naive conceptual belief that influences people's perceptions and performance in a ball-dropping task. *Journal of Experimental Psychology: Learning, Memory, and Cognition, 31,* 643–653.

Osborne, R., & Cosgrove, M. (1983). Children's conceptions of the changes of state of water. *Journal of Research in Science Teaching, 20,* 825–838.

Piaget, J. (1926). *The language and thought of the child.* London: Routledge & Kegan Paul.

Piaget, J. (1952). *The origins of intelligence in children.* New York: International University Press Original published 1936.

Piaget, J. (1972). *Psychology and epistemology: Towards a theory of knowledge* (A. Wells, Trans.). Harmondsworth: Penguin.(Original published 1970).

Piaget, J. (1976). *The grasp of consciousness* (S. Wedgwood, Trans.). Cambridge, MA: Harvard University Press (Original published 1974).

Pfundt, H., & Duit, R. (2000). *Bibliography: Students' alternative frameworks and science education, 5th ed. Kiel, Germany: Institute for Education Science.*

Poldrack, R. A., & Packard, M. G. (2003). Competition among multiple memory systems: Converging evidence from animal and human brain studies. *Neuropsychologia, 41,* 245–251.

Reber, A. S. (1989). Implicit learning and tacit knowledge. *Journal of Experimental Psychology: General, 118,* 219–235.

Reber, A. S. (1993). *Implicit learning and tacit knowledge.* Oxford: Oxford University Press.

Rehder, B., & Hoffman, A. B. (2005). Eye tracking and selective attention in category learning. *Cognitive Psychology, 51*, 1–41.

Reiner, C., Proffit, D. R., & Salthouse, T. (2005). A psychometric approach to intuitive physics. *Psychonomic Bulletin and Review, 12*, 740–745.

Reiner, M., Slotta, J. D., Chi, M. T. H., & Resnick, L. B. (2000). Naïve physics reasoning: A commitment to substance-based conceptions. *Cognition and Instruction, 18*, 1–34.

Rohrer, D. (2003). The natural appearance of unnatural incline speed. *Memory & Cognition, 31*, 816–826.

Sabella, M. S., & Redish, E. F. (2007). Knowledge organization and activation in physics problem solving. *American Journal of Physics, 75*, 1017–1029.

Schmerler, J. (1976). The visual perception of accelerated motion. *Perception, 5*, 167–185.

Schnipke, D. L., & Scrams, D. J. (1997). Modeling item-response times with a two-state mixture model. *Journal of Educational Measurement, 34*, 213–232.

Shiffrin, R. M., & Schneider, W. (1977). Controlled and automatic human information processing: II. Perceptual learning, automatic attending, and a general theory. *Psychological Review, 84*, 127–190.

Siegler, R. S. (1976). Three aspects of cognitive development. *Cognitive Psychology, 8*, 481–520.

Siegler, R. S. (1981). Developmental sequences within and between concepts. *Monographs of the Society for Research in Child Development, 46*, 1–84.

Siegler, R. S., & Stern, E. (1998). Conscious and unconscious strategy discoveries: A microgenetic analysis. *Journal of Experimental Psychology: General, 127*, 377–397.

Simon, H. A. (1955). A behavioral model of rational choice. *Quarterly Journal of Economics, 69*, 99–118.

Sloman, S. A. (1996). The empirical case for two systems of reasoning. *Psychological Bulletin, 119*, 3–22.

Sloutsky, V. M., Kloos, H., & Fisher, A. V. (2007). When looks are everything: Appearance similarity versus kind information in early induction. *Psychological Science, 18*, 179–185.

Smith, J. P., diSessa, A. A., & Roschelle, J. (1993). Misconceptions reconceived: A constructivist analysis of knowledge in transition. *The Journal of the Learning Sciences, 3*, 115–163.

Smith, L. B., Jones, S. S., & Landau, B. (1996). Naming in children: A dumb attentional mechanism? *Cognition, 60*, 143–171.

Stanovich, K. E., & West, R. F. (2000). Individual differences in reasoning: Implications for the rationality debate. *Behavioral and Brain Sciences, 23*, 645–665.

Stavy, R., & Tirosh, D. (2000). *How students (mis-) understand science and mathematics: Intuitive rules.* New York: Teachers College Press.

Taber, K. S. (2010). Constructivism and direct instruction as competing instructional paradigms: An essay review of Tobias and Duffy's Constructivist instruction: Success or failure? Education Review, 13(8) Pages 1–45. Retrieved September 20, 2010 from http://www.edrev.info/essays/v13n8index.html.

Trabasso, T., & Bower, G. H. (1968). *Attention in learning: Theory and research.* New York: Wiley.

Tversky, A., & Kahneman, D. (1974). Judgment under uncertainty: Heuristics and biases. *Science, 185*, 1124–1131.

van der Linden, W. J. (2008). Using response times for item selection in adaptive testing. *Journal of Educational and Behavioral Statistics, 33*, 5–20.

van der Linden, W. J., & van Krimpen-Stoop, E. M. L. A. (2003). Using response times to detect aberrant response patterns in computerized adaptive testing. *Psychometrika, 68*, 251–265.

Viennot, L. (1979). Spontaneous reasoning in elementary dynamics. *European Journal of Science Education, 1*, 205–221.

Vosniadou, S. (1994). Capturing and modeling the process of change. *Learning and Instruction, 4*, 45–69.

Vosniadou, S. (1996). Towards a revised cognitive psychology for new advances in learning and instruction. *Learning and Instruction, 6*, 95–109.

Vosniadou, S., & Brewer, W. F. (1992). Mental models of the earth: A study of conceptual change in childhood. *Cognitive Psychology, 24*, 535–585.

Vygotsky, L. S. (1987). Thinking and speech. In R. W. Rieber & A. S. Carton (Eds.), *The collected works of L. S. Vygotsky, Vol. 1: Problems of general psychology.* New York: Plenum Press.(Original published 1934).

Wellman, H. M., & Gelman, S. A. (1992). Cognitive development: Foundational theories of core domains. *Annual Review of Psychology, 43*, 337–375.

Zeithamova, D., & Maddox, W. T. (2006). Dual-task interference in perceptual category learning. *Memory & Cognition, 34*, 3878–398.

CHAPTER NINE

CONCEPTUAL PROBLEM SOLVING IN PHYSICS

Jose P. Mestre, Jennifer L. Docktor, Natalie E. Strand *and* Brian H. Ross

Contents

Psychology of Learning and Motivation, Volume 55

ISSN 0079-7421, DOI 10.1016/B978-0-12-387691-1.00009-0

© 2011 Elsevier Inc.

All rights reserved.

Abstract

Students taking introductory physics courses focus on quantitative manipulations at the expense of learning concepts deeply and understanding how
they apply to problem solving. This proclivity toward manipulating equations leads to shallow understanding and poor long-term retention. We
discuss an alternative approach to physics problem solving, which we call
conceptual problem solving (CPS), that highlights and emphasizes the role
of conceptual knowledge in solving problems. We present studies that
explored the impact of three different implementations of CPS on conceptual learning and problem solving. One was a lab-based study using a
computer tool to scaffold conceptual analyses of problems. Another was
a classroom-based study in a large introductory college course in which
students wrote conceptual strategies prior to solving problems. The third
was an implementation in high school classrooms where students identified
the relevant principle, wrote a justification for why the principle could be
applied, and provided a plan for executing the application of the principle
(which was then used for generating the equations). In all three implementations benefits were found as measured by various conceptual and problem solving assessments. We conclude with a summary of what we have
learned from the CPS approach, and offer some views on the current and
future states of physics instruction.

1. INTRODUCTION

Learning a physical science well requires not only the ability to solve
quantitative problems but also to have an understanding of the concepts,
their relations, and how they are used to help solve problems. In physics,
instructors know, and research has documented, that students tend to
focus on quantitative problem solving at the expense of learning concepts
(Bagno & Eylon, 1997; Larkin, 1979; 1981b; 1983; Larkin & Reif, 1979;
Tuminaro & Redish, 2007; Walsh, Howard, & Bowe, 2007). Perhaps
because homework and exams in undergraduate physics courses largely
demand quantitative solutions to problems, students spend time searching
for and manipulating equations to get answers. This is not a bad strategy
for getting good grades, but it is a poor strategy for gaining deep conceptual understanding (Kim & Pak, 2002). Without a conceptual framework
that integrates and gives meaning to equations and problem solving
procedures, there is very little residual learning of introductory physics
several weeks after a course is over. There is a clear need to devise
instructional strategies that elevate the importance of conceptual understanding, and that help students integrate conceptual knowledge with
problem solving processes.

This chapter discusses several research studies exploring conceptual problem solving (CPS) in physics. Broadly speaking what we mean by *CPS* is integrating the solving of the problem with an analysis of the underlying concept being used. The problem solving takes place guided by the conceptual analysis. We begin by discussing the central role of problem solving in physics, how experts and novices differ in their approach to problem solving, and why CPS is important in physics teaching and learning.

1.1. Problem solving in physics

The beauty of physics lies in its parsimony—a small number of major principles can be used to solve a wide range of problems encompassing a wide range of contexts (Larkin, 1981b). Yet, beginning physics students do not perceive physics this way, but rather view physics as embodied in many equations—too many to be memorized. Although it is true that equations play a central role in physics both in terms of how they instantiate principles and concepts and how they are used in problem solving, to physicists equations are not viewed as things to be memorized. Experts can construct these equations easily on-the-fly by understanding the principles/concepts and the context in which they need to be applied. This ability is the hallmark of expertise in physics and takes years to achieve (Larkin, McDermott, Simon, & Simon, 1980).

Further, some aspects of physics problem solving at the introductory level often remain tacit, or at least are not made highly visible in the problem solving instruction provided by expert instructors (Reif & Heller, 1982). Next we describe what that tacit knowledge is, how experts use it to their advantage, and how novices circumvent using it.

1.2. Expert problem solving in introductory physics

Here we will deal with how experts solve problems in introductory physics, not how they solve novel problems that they have not seen before. It has been known for quite some time that experts focus on the major principles/concepts when asked for an approach needed to solve a problem or when asked to categorize problems according to similarity of solution (Chi, Feltovich, & Glaser, 1981; de Jong & Ferguson-Hessler, 1986; Hardiman, Dufresne, & Mestre, 1989). How do experts go about deciding which principles/concepts are fruitful to apply to a physics problem? The problem's context (e.g., story line, objects and how they are configured, variables/quantities given, quantity asked for) contains information that helps the expert decide if a particular principle/concept can be applied, and the specific form of the equation needed to instantiate the principle/concept to the particular problem context. The expert *selects* a likely principle/concept, *justifies* that it can be applied, and for the expert the principle is chunked with *procedures*/equations for applying it (Larkin, 1979). It is the justification process for applying the major principle/concept based on the question asked and the problem's story line that often remains tacit in traditional instruction (Larkin, 1981a).

For example, conservation of mechanical energy is a major idea in mechanics, and is relatively easy to apply in problem solving—one simply sets the mechanical energy (made up of the sum of potential and kinetic energies) in some initial state equal to the mechanical energy is some final state, and solves for whatever unknown is asked for in the particular problem under consideration. The hard part, and what often remains tacit, is how to decide if conservation of mechanical energy is a useful principle to select (Larkin, 1981a). To apply conservation of mechanical energy requires that no external nonconservative forces do work on the system under consideration. If some external force does work on the system, then the work-energy theorem (another major idea in mechanics related to conservation of mechanical energy) should be applied, not conservation of mechanical energy. Thus, an expert reading a problem that initially appears amenable to the application of conservation of energy checks the problem context to make sure that there are no external nonconservative forces doing work; if there aren't, then conservation of mechanical energy is a good bet; if there are external nonconservative forces doing work, then the expert can switch seamlessly to considering the work-energy theorem as a viable alternative. To determine whether there are external nonconservative forces doing work, the expert looks for additional contextual cues such as whether there is friction, tension forces due to strings or ropes, or external agents pushing or pulling (Anzai & Yokoyama, 1984; de Jong & Ferguson-Hessler, 1991; Savelsbergh, de Jong, & Ferguson-Hessler, 2002). Looking for these clues in the problem that lead to this decision is not trivial and can be very difficult for novices.

Finding such *justifications* for applying certain major ideas is something that experts do all the time, and something that most novices do not know how to do well, if at all. Examining justifications for applying a particular concept/principle in a problem context is a very useful expert skill and permeates mechanics, and indeed all of physics problem solving. In addition, successful problem solvers can generate an organized solution plan for how to apply principles (Finegold & Mass, 1985; Priest & Lindsay, 1992).

1.3. Novice problem solving in introductory physics

Novices can become rather proficient at physics problem solving, and eventually after much practice show the kind of top-down CPS approach described in the previous section (Eylon & Reif, 1984). But, this transition is difficult, especially since equation-based approaches such as means-ends analysis (Larkin, 1983; Larkin et al., 1980; Newell & Simon, 1972; Simon

& Simon, 1978) tend to yield successful solutions a good portion of the time. The expert is able to use a top-down approach—the problem context and surface features trigger a possible principle/concept to select, then the context is checked to ensure there is an adequate justification for applying this principle/concept, and then the equation(s) needed to instantiate the principle/concept is generated (Larkin, 1983). The novice, however, uses the problem context to find equations that contain the variables in the problem. Then the novice tries to reduce the "distance" between the initial state and the goal state. For example, a problem asking for the velocity of a block after it has slid down a frictionless ramp might bring up equations with velocity, distance and time, with the solver looking to find enough equations for which the values are given or can be calculated in order to end up with the velocity of interest. Means-ends analysis is not as haphazard as it might sound—it often yields correct answers because novices can also rely on other clues to narrow their search for equations, such as which section of the book/course is currently being covered or what problems analogous to this one s/he has previously seen or solved.

1.4. Operational definition of conceptual problem solving

We have broadly defined CPS above as a general approach for physics problem solving by which solvers integrate the *selection* of a principle/concept, its *justification*, and generate *procedures* for applying the principle/concept. The central thesis of the chapter is that teaching learners to use CPS provides both a deeper understanding of the domain and can even help in solving problems. In the sections that follow, we describe three studies that explore the value of different implementations of CPS with both college undergraduates and high school students. We begin with a study that compared a top-down approach for solving problems to a novice equation-centered approach. We then describe a teaching experiment conducted in a large undergraduate course that highlighted the role of principles, justifications, and procedures in problem solving. Finally, we describe an approach to implement CPS in high school physics instruction that allows for flexibility on the part of teachers. In all three cases, findings demonstrate that CPS is effective for helping students achieve a better understanding of how concepts relate to problem solving, as measured by a variety of assessments.

2. A Computer-Based Tool for Conceptual Problem Solving

Given students' proclivity toward means-ends analysis as the preferred method for solving physics problems, one must think of ways of structuring and scaffolding students' problem solving activities in order to elevate the usefulness of principles and concepts in problem solving. Experienced physics instructors will attest that simply telling students to use concepts more in their problem solving is typically met with blank stares. Our first attempt at CPS tried to structure the problem solving process so that it started with an analysis of a problem in terms of principles/concepts and general procedures for applying them *before* any equations were even considered. In this approach equations were actually the result of the conceptual analysis—that is, equations emerged naturally as a direct result of the conceptual analysis.

2.1. The hierarchical analysis tool (HAT)

Our earliest attempt at evaluating the usefulness of CPS made use of a computer-based tool called the hierarchical analysis tool (HAT) (Dufresne, Gerace, Hardiman, & Mestre, 1992; Mestre, Dufresne, Gerace, Hardiman, & Touger, 1993). The HAT was a menu-driven tool that allowed its user to perform analyses of mechanics problems based on principles and procedures by making selections from a series of menus. Each menu asked the user to make a selection that became more specific as the analysis proceeded. At the first menu the user was asked to select one of four major principles that could be used for solving the problem under consideration. Subsequent menus asked the user to make decisions that allowed further specification of the principle, leading to procedures for applying the principle. If, and only if, the analysis was performed correctly an equation was generated that was tailor-made to solve the problem under consideration. It is important to note that the term "tool" is to be taken seriously since the HAT never provided feedback on whether or not the analysis was appropriate after each menu selection was made. If the user made an inappropriate decision, the next menu presented would be consistent with the previous set of menu selections, but the analysis would head in a direction that was inappropriate for solving the particular problem. Hence, the HAT was an internally consistent decision-making tree that allowed a top-down analysis of problems based on principles and procedures.

Figure 1 contains a problem and Figure 2 contains the set of menus and selections appropriate for its analysis. This is a problem that could be solved by applying work and energy concepts, which would be the appropriate selection at the first menu. The second menu relates to the issue described in the previous section, namely that before deciding whether the work–energy theorem or conservation of mechanical energy should be applied, one needs to decide if there are external forces doing work (designated as a nonconservative system). In this case, an external force (friction) does work on the system making conservation of mechanical energy inappropriate and the work-energy theorem appropriate. At

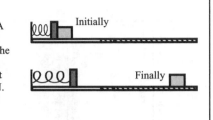

One end of a horizontal spring
(k = 5N/m) is connected to a wall. A
small block is used to compress the
spring 0.5 m and is then released. The
block eventually moves away from
the spring and into a region where it
experiences a frictional force of 2 N.
Where does the block come to rest?

Figure 1 Sample problem analyzed by HAT menus. [Reprinted from Dufresne et al. (1992). Reprinted by permission of Taylor & Francis, Ltd.]

menu level 3, the user is asked to identify the external force doing work on the system so that the appropriate work term can be constructed. In menus 4–6, procedural questions are asked that allow the construction of appropriate terms in the work–energy theorem equation appearing in menu 8. Hence the selections made in menus 4–6 specified the three terms in the work–energy theorem equation, namely the work done by the nonconservative force (friction), and the initial and final mechanical energies of the system.

Additional scaffolding features are contained in the last line at the bottom of menus 1–7, which allowed the user to back up if she or he felt that they had made a wrong choice along the way, to return to the first menu to restart the analysis, to enter a glossary and look up an unfamiliar term (e.g., nonconservative force), to list previous selections to see the previous choices made during the analysis to that point, or to give up and quit. The HAT was a tool and not a tutor; if the user made inappropriate selections along the way, the resulting equation in menu 8 would be consistent with the menu selections made (i.e., menu 8 would contain equations constrained by the previous choices made), which would not be appropriate for solving the problem under consideration.

2.2. Implementation of the HAT

A series of experiments was conducted in the lab using pre-post performance on various dependent measures to compare a group of students using the HAT to solve 25 problems over 5-h long sessions against three other groups solving the same 25 problems under different conditions: (1) using a *textbook* as an aid, (2) using a computer-based *"equation sorting tool"* that consisted of a searchable database of over 170 equations found in an introductory mechanics textbook; the database could be searched by surface attributes of problems (e.g., "pulley problems"), by variable names

1

Which principle applies to this part of the problem solution?
1. Newton's second law or kinematics
2. Angular momentum
3. Linear momentum
4. Work and energy

Please enter your selection: [4]
(B)ackup   (M)ain menu   (G)lossary   (L)ist selections   (Q)uit

2

Describe the system in terms of its mechanical energy
1. Conservative system (conservation of energy)
2. Nonconservative system

Please enter your selection: [2]
(B)ackup   (M)ain menu   (G)lossary   (L)ist selections   (Q)uit

3

Describe the nonconservative forces acting on the body.
1. Friction
2. Applied force
3. Friction and applied force
4. There are no nonconservative forces acting on this body

Please enter your selection: [1]
(B)ackup   (M)ain menu   (G)lossary   (L)ist selections   (Q)uit

4

Describe the changes in mechanical energy. Consider only the energy of one body at a time at some initial and final state.
1. Change in kinetic energy
2. Change in potential energy
3. Change in potential and kinetic energy

Please enter your selection: [2]
(B)ackup   (M)ain menu   (G)lossary   (L)ist selections   (Q)uit

5

Describe the changes in potential energy.
1. Changes in gravitational potential energy
2. Changes in spring potential energy
3. Changes in gravitational and spring potential energy

Please enter your selection: [2]
(B)ackup   (M)ain menu   (G)lossary   (L)ist selections   (Q)uit

6

Describe the boundary conditions
1. No initial gravitational potential energy
2. No final gravitational potential energy
3. Initial and final gravitational potential energy

Please enter your selection: [2]
(B)ackup   (M)ain menu   (G)lossary   (L)ist selections   (Q)uit

7

Is there another body in the system which has not been examined?
1. Yes
2. No

Please enter your selection: [2]
(B)ackup   (M)ain menu   (G)lossary   (L)ist selections   (Q)uit

8

The Energy Principle states that the work done on the system by all nonconservative forces is equal to the change in the mechanical energy of the system: $W_{nc} = E_f - E_i$
According to your selections,
$W_{nc} = -fd$
$E_f = 0$ and $E_i = 1/2(kx^2)$
Please press any key to continue

9

Work and Energy
1. Problem solved
2. Return to Main Menu to continue solution
3. Review previous solution screens

Please enter your selection:

Figure 2   Sample HAT menus. [Reprinted from Dufresne et al. (1992). Reprinted by permission of Taylor & Francis, Ltd.]

(e.g., "velocity"), by physics terms (e.g., "energy"), or by combinations of sequential searches using any of these three, and (3) using *no aid* whatsoever. Subjects in all experiments were undergraduates who had completed a mechanics course 2 months prior to the start of the study with a grade of B or better (the grade requirement ensured subjects had learned a reasonable amount of the material in the course since our experiment did not strive to teach them the material from scratch). Details of the studies can be found in Dufresne et al. (1992) and Mestre et al. (1993).

2.3. Dependent measures

Across different experiments, the impact of the CPS modeled by the HAT was measured using two types of problem categorization as well as a problem solving test.

2.3.1. Three-Problem Categorization Task

In one of the experiments a three-problem categorization task was used pre- and posttreatment (Hardiman et al., 1989), with each item consisting of a *model problem* and two *comparison problems*. The task was to choose which of the two comparison problems was solved most like the model problem. The following is a sample item (Hardiman et al., 1989):

> *Model Problem*: A 90 kg mass is connected to a light horizontal spring of force constant 60 N/m and placed on a surface with coefficient of static friction 0.4. If the free end of the spring is slowly moved away from the mass, what distance may the free end be pulled before the mass begins to move?
>
> *Comparison Problem (Surface-Feature Match)*: A 50 kg mass with an initial horizontal velocity of 5 m/s passes over a rough surface of length 0.5 m and coefficient of kinetic friction 0.2. After leaving the rough surface, it collides with a light horizontal spring of force constant 120 N/m. Find the maximum compression of the spring.
>
> *Comparison Problem (Deep Structure Match)*: A 60 kg block is placed on a frictionless inclined plane of angle 25°. The block is attached to a hanging mass by a light string over a frictionless pulley. Find the minimum value of the hanging mass so that the system remains in equilibrium.

The surface features (objects in the problem) and deep structure (concept/principle needed for solution) of the two comparison problems were manipulated so that a comparison problem could match the model problem in one of four ways: (a) surface features, (b) deep structure, (c) both surface features and deep structure, or (d) neither surface features nor deep structure. Performance was determined according to how well a subject could pick the comparison problem that matched the model problem on deep structure (one, and only one, of the two comparison problems always matched the model problem on this dimension). Note that this task did not allow determination of the reasoning used by subjects in making their decisions; subjects may have answered an item correctly by using surface-feature reasoning, principle-based reasoning, or some combination, but whatever reasoning was used remained hidden. The reasoning used was explored using a two-problem categorization task described next.

2.3.2. Two-Problem Categorization Task

In another experiment a two-problem task was used pre- and posttreatment with each item consisting of two problems (Hardiman et al., 1989). The subject was asked to decide whether or not the two problems would be solved with a similar approach and to provide a written reason for their answers. The two problems could match in the same four ways described in the three-problem task of the previous section. Performance on each item was based on two criteria, yielding two measures for each item: (a) Whether or not the subject used principle-based reasoning and (b) whether or not the categorization made was correct.

2.3.3. Problem Solving

Two problem solving tests were developed, consisting of four problems solvable by each of the following concepts: Newton's second law ($F = ma$), conservation of energy, conservation of momentum, and conservation of angular momentum. Half of the subjects received one of the tests prior to treatment, and the other test posttreatment, with the two exams counterbalanced. The exams were graded on the basis of three different criteria: (a) As is typically done in grading problems on physics exams (partial credit, holistic), (b) based on whether the final answer is correct (1 point) or incorrect (0 point), and (c) based on evidence of whether a correct principle was being applied (1 point if either a statement made in the solution identified the correct principle or if the correct equation(s) was applied, 0 otherwise).

2.4. Findings from the HAT Studies

2.4.1. Three-Problem Categorization Performance

The experiment that used the three-problem categorization task compared the HAT with the equation sorting tool and the textbook conditions. The HAT group showed a significant improvement relative to the other two groups. Ability to select which of the two comparison problems was solved most like the model problem improved by 10% after treatment for the HAT group, remained constant for the equation sorting tool group, and decreased by 4% for the textbook group. Findings suggested that use of the HAT resulted in enhanced ability to categorize problems according to solution similarity, but no determination could be made concerning whether this improvement was due to increased accuracy in identifying principles needed to solve problems, or increased consideration of principles, or some mix of the two.

2.4.2. Two-Problem Categorization Performance

The experiment that used the two-problem task compared the HAT against a control condition in which subjects solved the treatment problems with no aid. The HAT group significantly increased their principle-based categorization by 35% from pre- to posttreatment, whereas the control group increased by 23%. However, this greater use of principle-based categorization by the HAT group did not result in better performance in comparison to the control group on correct categorizations; the pre- and postscores of the HAT group on correct categorizations made were 58% and 55%, respectively, and 67% and 64% for the control group. Thus, although the HAT treatment resulted in its users using principle-based categorizations more often than the control group, this increase in consideration of principles did not result in ability to use principles to make accurate categorization decisions. It is possible that HAT led to an understanding that principles should be used more but not to any better ability to select the principle from the problems' context.

2.4.3. Problem Solving Performance

The experiment that assessed problem solving performance compared the HAT against the no-aid control condition. Although both groups improved in their problem solving from pre- to post-tests, the HAT group significantly outperformed the control group (see Table 1). Whether measured by holistic physics-exam-style grading, final-answer grading, or correct-principle grading, the HAT intervention led to higher performance.

Table 1 Performance on the Problem Solving Test

	Holistic grading		Final-answer grading		Principle grading	
	Pre (%)	Post (%)	Pre (%)	Post (%)	Pre (%)	Post (%)
HAT	33	88	28	73	40	95
Control	37	77	32	58	42	80

The test was graded three different ways: (a) holistic, physics exam style; (b) score based on final answer only; and (c) score based on whether the appropriate principle was being applied. [Reprinted from Dufresne et al. (1992). Reprinted by permission of Taylor & Francis, Ltd.]

2.5. Conclusions from the HAT Studies

Across the different experiments, there were clear benefits for the students learning with the HAT tool. The categorization results were mixed, but suggest some increase in the understanding that principles should be used to make the categorization choices and, in one experiment, improved performance in making this selection. Problem solving showed a large improvement for HAT learners, suggesting that learning to conceptually analyze the problems before applying equations is a helpful instructional strategy. Although the HAT tool is a simple one, guiding learners to conceptually analyze problems before solving them seems to improve their understanding and problem solving.

3. A CLASSROOM-BASED INTERVENTION OF CONCEPTUAL PROBLEM SOLVING AT A UNIVERSITY

Unlike the lab-based HAT studies described above, the study described in this section was conducted in the messy environment of a large (~150 students) introductory calculus-based mechanics course for science and engineering majors. Given the propensity of novice physics students to rely on equation-based approaches for solving problems, an attempt was made to integrate an intervention in the course that not only illustrated a top down conceptual approach to solving problems but that also allowed students to actively practice it. The intervention consisted of *strategy writing*, to be described next.

3.1. Strategy writing

Leonard, Dufresne, and Mestre (1996) devised an instructional intervention, *strategy writing*, based on expert analyses of problems (see Chi et al., 1981). A strategy was defined for students as a prose paragraph that discussed qualitatively the "what, why, and how" of a problem's solution. More specifically, students were told that a strategy should (a) *select* the principle(s)/concept(s) that could be applied to solve a problem, (b) provide a *justification* for why the principle(s)/concept(s) could be applied, and (c) describe a *procedure* for applying the principle(s/concept(s) to generate a solution. (Note that the second component of the strategy is the illusive tacit knowledge described earlier.) As we hope the reader can see, this is nearly identical to our operational definition of CPS provided earlier. Other than this general description of what was meant by strategy, the only other guidance given to students on how to write a good strategy was to tell them to apply the following test to the quality of a strategy they might write: If a student who is stuck solving a problem is provided with a

Problem: A block of wood having a mass of 0.5 kg is at rest on a level floor. A lump of putty having a mass of 200 g is thrown at the block so that it is traveling horizontally the instant it hits and sticks to the block. The block and putty slide 1 m along the rough floor. If the coefficient of kinetic friction is 0.2, what was the original speed of the putty?

Strategy: The lump of putty has a totally inelastic collision with the block (i.e., it sticks to the block after the colision). Momentum is conserved in this collision since there are no external forces exerted on the system during the collision. Then, the block with putty attached slide on a rough surface and eventually stop. Here we must use the work-energy theorem, since a nonconservative force, friction, does work on the system and changes its kinetic energy from some initial value to 0. In summary, apply conservation of momentum to the collision, and the work-energy theorem to the sliding portion of the problem, and solve for the original speed of the putty.

Figure 3 Homework problem with an instructor-generated strategy.

quality strategy, he or she should be able to start and make substantial progress toward generating a solution to the problem. Students were also told that strategies were qualitative descriptions and that no equations should be present in strategies. Figure 3 contains a homework problem and a sample instructor-generated strategy.

3.2. Implementation of strategy writing

Strategy writing was implemented in two of the teaching components of the course, the lecture and discussion sections. In the lecture, the instructor modeled strategy writing whenever a sample problem was worked out (about once per lecture); the strategy would be developed a piece at a time, followed by generation of the solution based on the strategy. Instructors in the discussion section would also reinforce strategy writing. Students were encouraged to practice strategy writing when solving the weekly homework sets, but the homework sets were not collected so it could not be ascertained whether or not students did homework or practiced strategy writing when they did homework; solutions to every problem in each homework set was posted on a bulletin board and put on reserve in the library, and the solution to each problem contained an instructor-generated strategy. The incentive for practicing strategy writing in homework assignments was three hour exams comprised of both multiple choice items and a single problem of medium-hard difficulty requiring a strategy separate from a solution (heretofore, the "work-out problem"); this problem counted for 25% of the exam grade with the strategy accounting for half of the credit.

3.3. Dependent measures

3.3.1. Student Strategies on Exams

The strategies that students wrote for the work-out problem on the three exams provided evidence of their ability to write coherent strategies, which in turn displayed how well they could integrate conceptual knowledge in a problem solving context. Writing strategies in exams was a high-stakes situation given that they accounted for 13% of the grade on each exam. Although the context in which strategies were written served a summative assessment function, students' strategies also provided diagnostic information about their conceptual deficits and hence could be used as formative assessments to target individual students' difficulties for instructional remediation.

3.3.2. Multiple Choice Categorization Task

A five-item multiple choice categorization task was devised and administered to students in the final exam (which was all multiple choice). Each item presented a standard "textbook" physics problem and asked students to select from among five principles/concepts the one that could be applied to solve the problem in the most efficient manner possible. One of the problems used is shown in Figure 4.

Instructions: The following questions consist of problems that you don't need to solve. Below are five choices labeled A–E containing one or more major concepts studied in the course. Your job is to decide which major concept(s) needs to be applied to solve each problem in the most efficient manner and make the appropriate selection. Use the same set of five multiple choices for all questions, and you may use each choice, A–E, once, more than once, or not at all.

Problem: A mass M is connected to a string of length L to form a simple pendulum, with the other end of the string attached to the ceiling. If the mass has speed v at the bottom of the swing, what is the tension in the rope at that point? Consider the string to be massless.

Multiple choices:
    (A) Newton's second law
    (B) Work-energy theorem or conservation of mechanical energy
    (C) Linear momentum or conservation of linear momentum
    (D) Conservation of linear momentum followed by conservation of
         mechanical energy
    (E) Angular momentum or conservation of angular momentum

Figure 4   Sample multiple choice categorization task. [Reprinted from Leonard et al. (1996). Reprinted by permission of the American Association of Physics Teachers.]

In order to compare categorization performance of the strategy class to a standard class, the same five categorization problems were placed in the final exam of the same course taught by a different instructor.

3.4. Findings from the strategy writing study

3.4.1. Student Strategies

As might be expected, students varied greatly in their ability (and willingness) to write strategies. The important point we want to make here is that the good strategies indicate a deep conceptual analysis of physics that is not usually seen in traditional instruction. Figure 5 contains two strategies generated by two students for the problem shown from the third hour exam (additional student-generated strategies can be found in Leonard et al., 1996). The first strategy is very good and contains all three elements described earlier. The student states the major principle needed in the first line (conservation of mechanical energy). The next three sentences describe a procedure

---

Problem:
A disk of mass, $M = 2$ kg, and radius, $R = 0.4$ m, has string wound around it and is free to rotate about an axle through its center. A block of mass, $m = 1$ kg, is attached to the end of the string and the system is released from rest with no slack in the string. What is the speed of the block after it has fallen a distance, $d = 0.5$ m. Don't forget to provide a strategy and a solution.

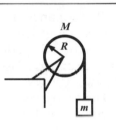

Good student strategy:
I would use conservation of mechanical energy to solve this problem. The mass m has some potential energy while it is hanging there. When the block starts to accelerate downwards the potential energy is transformed into rotational kinetic energy of the disk and kinetic energy of the falling mass. equating the initial and final states; and using the relationship between v and ω the speed of m can be found. Mechanical energy is conserved even with the nonconservative tension force because the tension force is internal to the system. (pulley, mass, rope)

Poor student strategy:
In trying to find the speed of the block I would try to find angular momentum kinetic energy, use gravity, I would also use rotational kinematics and moment of inertia around the center of mass for the disk.

Figure 5 This is a problem and two student-generated strategies from a mid-semester exam. The first strategy is very good and the second is lacking. [Reprinted from Leonard et al. (1996). Reprinted by permission of the American Association of Physics Teachers.]

by which conservation of mechanical energy can be applied to the problem, identifying relevant quantities (types of kinetic and potential energies present in initial and final states), and needed relationships (that velocity and angular velocity are related). The last sentence provides the justification for why mechanical energy is applicable; the student identifies a nonconservative force (tension) and correctly states that since this force is internal to the system conservation of mechanical energy still applies.

In contrast, the second strategy is not very useful since it does not pass the litmus test provided earlier, namely a student that is stuck solving this problem would not be helped by reading this strategy (on the contrary, s/he would likely end up more confused). The poor strategy in Figure 5 is essentially a shopping list of terms covered in the course, and it is evident that this student understands little of the course's content. About one-third of strategies written on exams were very good and displayed solid understanding of how concepts, justifications and procedures for solving problems; another one-third wrote reasonably good strategies showing substantial understanding, with the remaining third writing poor strategies displaying significant deficits.

3.4.2. Performance on Categorization Items

Strategy writing led to substantial improvement in categorizing items. The overall performance on the five categorization problems for the nonstrategy class was 48% ($N = 376$), whereas for the strategy class it was 70% ($N = 148$), a highly significant difference (chance is 20%). The strategy class outperformed the nonstrategy students on all five questions, with the performance differences ranging from 14% to 40%.

Another way to look at the effect is examining it across the distribution of students in each class. Each class was divided into quartiles based on final-exam performance. Not surprisingly, the categorization performance was correlated with this performance. Most interestingly, however, the categorization performance of the lowest quartile in the strategy class was equivalent to that of the highest quartile students in the nonstrategy class. The strategy writing not only improved overall group performance but it also improved performance across the whole distribution of students.

3.5. Conclusions from the strategy writing study

We wish to highlight two aspects of the results of this study. First, although strategy writing was not done well by all learners, the good strategies were *really* good explanations—they showed a deep understanding of the physical concepts that one would not usually get from traditional instruction. Second, being taught to write these strategies had very large effects on the categorization performance. The focus on strategy writing taught these students to analyze the underlying concept of the problem. Even students who did not learn to write good strategies still learned to analyze the underlying concepts.

4. A Classroom-Based Intervention of Conceptual Problem Solving at Several High Schools

The previous two implementations of CPS were done with high fidelity, the HAT studies in a controlled lab environment and the strategy writing implemented by a set of lecture and discussion instructors who agreed to follow a common regimen for an entire semester. In high schools there are numerous constraints that work against high fidelity implementation. Those include varying levels of teacher expertise in physics and teachers' teaching styles, and time pressure to cover content and to administer mandated tests. All of these constraints limit the amount of time that can be spent experimenting with new instructional techniques as well as the amount of time available to administer assessments to measure impact. Because of these constraints, a high school environment offers a good testing ground for CPS's robustness as a viable approach since its implementation would likely vary considerably in fidelity. There are also adaptation challenges in terms of structuring CPS in ways that offered students more scaffolding than would be needed with a college audience.

4.1. Structured strategies and two-column solutions

The adaptation of CPS into high school classrooms combines two elements of previous research: strategy writing described in the previous section, and accompanying two-column solutions described below (Smith, Mestre, & Ross, 2010). The high school adaptation began with a conceptual analysis similar to strategy writing but more structured so that students (and teachers) had a clear idea of what was expected of them. The strategy portion had three parts: Principle, Justification, and Plan, with the three parts presented sequentially and clearly labeled. The strategy was followed by a two-column solution, which consisted of the steps from the plan in the left column, and the right column consisting of equations or mathematics that go along with each step in the plan. A sample problem with its accompanying strategy is provided in Figure 6 and the accompanying two-column solution is provided in Figure 7.

Problem: A 2275 kg car (car 1) going 28 m/s rear-ends an 875 kg compact car (car 2) going 16 m/s in the same direction on an icy road. The two cars stick together after the collision. What is the speed and direction of the two cars immediately after the collision?

Principle:
Conservation of momentum: the momentum of the system in the initial state is equal to the momentum of the system in the final state.

Justification:
There is zero net external force exerted on the two car system during the collision (we assume that the icy road is frictionless). Therefore, the impulse on the system is zero and the change in momentum of the system of two cars is also zero.

Plan:
1. Draw a picture and assign symbols for quantities in the problem. Choose a coordinate system.
2. Write an equation for conservation of momentum in the horizontal direction. Expand this equation to include the momentum of car 1 and the momentum of car 2 before and after they collide.
3. Solve for the final velocity of the two cars stuck together. Substitute values and calculate a numerical answer.

Figure 6   Sample problem and written strategy.

4.2. Implementation of conceptual problem solving in high schools

Since CPS is a framework for teaching problem solving and not a curriculum, it is relatively undemanding for instructors to implement into their teaching, and can be adapted by the instructor to fit his or her instructional style. It does not require any changes to the order in which physics topics are taught or the way in which concepts are introduced; rather, instructors follow a strategic approach when teaching problem solving. The teachers were provided with a large bank of problems with strategies and two-column solutions, which had been written and reviewed by the authors, and were free to pick problems that they wished to use to match their content coverage. Teachers were also free to use their own problems.

4.2.1. Participating Schools and Teachers

Four high schools participated in the study, but one school is excluded from this discussion due to irregularities with the implementation and assessment procedures. The remaining schools (and CPS teachers at those schools) will be referred to as A, B, and C. The teachers who agreed to use the CPS approach met with researchers during the summer prior to

Plan step	Equation(s) used in step
1. Draw a picture and assign symbols for quantities in the problem. Choose a coordinate system.	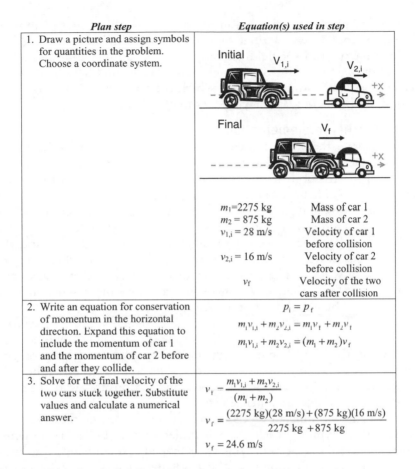 $m_1 = 2275$ kg — Mass of car 1 $m_2 = 875$ kg — Mass of car 2 $v_{1,i} = 28$ m/s — Velocity of car 1 before collision $v_{2,i} = 16$ m/s — Velocity of car 2 before collision v_f — Velocity of the two cars after collision
2. Write an equation for conservation of momentum in the horizontal direction. Expand this equation to include the momentum of car 1 and the momentum of car 2 before and after they collide.	$p_i = p_f$ $m_1 v_{1,i} + m_2 v_{2,i} = m_1 v_f + m_2 v_f$ $m_1 v_{1,i} + m_2 v_{2,i} = (m_1 + m_2) v_f$
3. Solve for the final velocity of the two cars stuck together. Substitute values and calculate a numerical answer.	$v_f = \dfrac{m_1 v_{1,i} + m_2 v_{2,i}}{(m_1 + m_2)}$ $v_f = \dfrac{(2275 \text{ kg})(28 \text{ m/s}) + (875 \text{ kg})(16 \text{ m/s})}{2275 \text{ kg} + 875 \text{ kg}}$ $v_f = 24.6$ m/s

Figure 7 Sample solution formatted as two columns.

implementation to discuss key aspects of the approach and receive implementation guidelines. At every school the CPS approach was compared to "traditional" problem solving practices that emphasize equations and mathematical procedures. At School A this comparison was made between a single teacher's classes over multiple years, at School B there were multiple classes taught by the same teacher, and at School C there were two different teachers (a CPS teacher and a control teacher). To ensure flexibility, only non–Advanced Placement physics courses were used in this study.

There were differences in the teachers' knowledge of physics and their teaching experience. The student populations at each school varied as well. For example, School A was a small suburban high school with an experienced physics teacher and an affluent, high-achieving student population. School B was a rural high school at which the teacher was teaching physics (out-of-field) for only the second time, and the student population was primarily low income. School C is a high school in a small city with a diverse student body at which the teacher has a strong background in physics but typically teaches math classes.

4.2.2. Teacher Implementation

As stated above, the high school teachers were given minimal guidance on how to implement the CPS approach during problem solving instruction. They had the freedom to select problems from the samples they were provided, to decide how to model the approach for students, to structure in-class activities, and to choose how to assess students' understanding of the approach and assign grades. This flexibility was intended to permit teachers to adapt the approach to fit their instructional style and the specific needs of their students. Information about the teachers' implementation was drawn from researcher observations of their classes and self-descriptions of their teaching during a debriefing discussion with researchers at the conclusion of the study.

During the debriefing sessions, the CPS teachers reported that they devoted approximately two class periods to the approach for each 2- to 3-week unit during the fall semester (the units covered motion with constant acceleration, Newton's laws, work/energy, and impulse/momentum). In general they would provide students with instructions for writing a strategy, show an example, and then ask students to try it on their own or with other students working in groups while they provided in-class assistance and feedback. Typically each exam included one problem that required students to use the approach, which was graded and contributed to their semester grades. In addition to problem solving, class time was also spent on activities such as lecture, demonstrations, laboratories, and exams. Specific features of the teachers' implementations are described below.

Being an experienced teacher, Teacher A used his own established set of problems and required students to write strategies for between one-third and one-fourth of their assigned homework problems. He typically used the approach with more advanced problems (multiple steps, more advanced mathematics, or a combination of multiple principles) and utilized the two-column solution format in an informal way. In contrast, relatively inexperienced Teacher B relied exclusively on researchers' sample materials and copied the strategies word-for-word when writing on the board. Students were provided with blank worksheet templates for writing strategies and two-column solutions and frequently worked with a partner or small group. In the control section of the class Teacher B used the same problems but formatted them in an equation-focused way. Teacher C used a mix of the researchers' problems and his own, and primarily implemented the approach for later topics (momentum and energy) in conjunction with cooperative learning groups. He had students practice the first steps of strategy writing (principle and justification) for between four and six problems in a worksheet packet and only solve one or two problems completely to present to the rest of the class.

4.3. Dependent measures

In addition to the qualitative data obtained from observations and debriefing discussions with the teachers, the treatment and control classes were evaluated using an assortment of conceptual and problem solving measures. There were five different types of tests administered, but due to time constraints not every school gave every test. The time allotted for each test ranged from 15 to 25 min, for a total between 45 and 90 min. Three of the tests were more conceptual in nature, and two emphasized problem solving. A sample problem from each test is available in appendix.

4.3.1. Conceptual Tests

1. *Problem Categorization*: Three-problem categorization tasks similar to those used in Hardiman et al. (1989) but designed to be grade appropriate. Each task presents a "model" problem and students must select which of two alternatives would be solved most like the model problem. Problems are specifically designed to vary their match on superficial features (objects or context) or match on concepts and principles used to solve them. This assesses a student's principle-based categorization skills and use of representations.
2. *Conceptual Questions*: Free-response explanations for a realistic physical situation (School A) or conceptual questions in a multiple choice format (Schools B and C).
3. *Finding Errors*: Shown a worked-out solution that includes a physics error and asked to identify and describe the error in writing; the error was conceptual and not algebraic. This assesses a student's ability to evaluate problem solving strategies.

4.3.2. Problem Solving Tests

1. *Equation Instantiation*: Shown a problem and worked solution in symbolic form, and asked to assign/match the appropriate values for each quantity in the final expression. This assesses variable assignment and efficient equation use.
2. *Problem Solving*: Three to five standard free response problems. This assesses both how students access concepts and use equations.

Free-response conceptual questions (used at School A) and problem solving questions were scored by two researchers using agreed-upon rubrics, and then these scores were further discussed to reach a single consensus score. The problem solving questions were scored according to a rubric modified from Docktor (2009), which scores solutions on the categories of useful description, selecting a relevant physics concept or principle, applying the concepts to the specific conditions in the problem, executing mathematical procedures, and the overall communication of a logical reasoning pattern. The *finding errors* test was scored both for identifying a mistake in the sample solution and giving a correct explanation for the mistake.

4.4. Findings from high school implementations

4.4.1. Teacher Responses to the Approach

All teachers stated that they liked the general "philosophy" of the approach because it forced students to think about what they were doing and why, and it emphasized concepts rather than equations during problem solving. Some teachers reinforced this to students with statements such as "I want to change your thinking from 'which equation should I use' to 'what is the concept'" (Teacher C). However, the teachers acknowledged that the approach requires more writing than traditional problem solving and therefore required more class time. Each teacher accounted for this increased time in different ways: Teacher A only used the approach for a subset of problems, B didn't get through as many problems and modified the approach so students wrote their plan steps directly into the two-column solution, and Teacher C didn't require students to solve all problems completely. Teacher A also expressed some reservations that high school students could think about higher level concepts in this way; in particular, he felt that students have trouble developing a plan before actually trying to solve the problem because they might need to do a little trial and error before identifying what principle to use.

4.4.2. Performance on Dependent Measures

In general, the problem solving and conceptual measures administered to students showed a consistent advantage to the CPS classes over the control classes that were taught more traditionally. Conceptual questions and problem solving tests were given at all schools. The conceptual questions test showed a significant difference at two of the schools, a 10% difference at School A and a substantial 20% difference at School B. Although not statistically significant, School C also showed a difference of 11% in favor of CPS. The problem solving test showed consistent differences of 10–16%, but it was only statistically reliable at School C (16%).

The problem categorization test, equation instantiation test, and finding errors tests did not show any significant differences between groups at the three schools. However, there was a 12% difference in equation instantiation favoring CPS at School A, and an 11% difference in problem categorization at School B that show trends in the appropriate direction. The finding errors test was extremely difficult for these students and almost no one was able to correctly identify conceptual mistakes in a solution.

In addition to the quantitative measures, statements from some of the teachers indicated observable differences in students' performance. Teacher C commented that students were producing a higher quality of solutions and were engaging in richer discussions in their groups. More objectively, the class (compared to his previous class) had higher performance on an energy momentum unit test and on a district-wide physics assessment.

4.5. Conclusions from the high school study

Overall, the high school teachers responded favorably to using the CPS approach and their students showed a consistent 10–20% advantage on a common set of assessments compared to classes that were taught using traditional problem solving instruction. Out of the five different assessments administered, the approach was particularly influential on students' responses to conceptual questions and to their problem solving processes. Remember that this intervention required no change in the curriculum and no extra instruction time.

The instructional materials were intentionally flexible, and each teacher chose to implement strategy writing and two column solutions in a slightly different style. Teacher A had moderate success by using the approach somewhat informally with a subset of his own problems, whereas Teacher B produced substantial differences with an implementation that included the worksheet templates designed by researchers (the fidelity with which Teacher B implemented CPS was extremely close to what was originally intended by the designers). Teacher C chose to give students a great deal of practice selecting appropriate principles for problems without solving them completely, yet this still resulted in improved problem solving performance. All of these teachers routinely have students work in groups during class, and this was also true of class periods that included CPS.

The teachers also addressed several points to consider when implementing the approach. For example, in response to students' resistance to writing strategies they had to provide external motivation for following the framework such as points on homework or exams. Some teachers suggested CPS works best for later topics in mechanics (i.e., conservation laws) and for more complex problems that require planning, such as problems that involve a combination of multiple principles. The teachers acknowledge that identifying and justifying principles is a higher level problem solving skill that is difficult for students, and students need appropriate scaffolding to learn how to do this. A promising addition to the approach includes using synthesizing concept diagrams to emphasize the main ideas learned in a course (Bagno & Eylon, 1997).

5. CONCLUDING REMARKS

We have reviewed different implementations of CPS with university and high school students both in carefully controlled laboratory studies as well as in the messy environment of real college and high school class-rooms. The common feature across all of our implementations of CPS was the emphasis on conceptual analyses of problems, in particular attempting to illustrate how conceptual knowledge is used to solve pro-blems and to make more explicit some of the tacit knowledge used by experts in solving problems. For example, justifying why a particular principle could be applied to solve a problem by examining the problem's story line (question asked, context, objects in the problem and attributes present such as friction) is something that experts do naturally but is a skill that is not overtly taught in traditional instruction.

In all three implementations reviewed, students who practiced CPS showed advantages in conceptual measures as well as in problem solving. Also heartening is the fact that there is an element of robustness in CPS; despite the relatively short intervention in the three high schools (about eight 50-min classes over a 4-month period), and the wide variation in teachers' implementation, CPS students displayed benefits from the inter-vention. Additional good news is that CPS can be "blended" into a course without major curricular changes, redesign, or disruptions. However, CPS is an approach that demands more work from students than is typical in traditional physics classes (e.g., deep thinking about concepts; more writing of prose about abstract concepts and how they apply to problem solving—both uncommon in physics classes), which is likely to meet with more resistance from students than traditional instructional approaches to problem solving.

An interesting final question to entertain is What next? This, we believe, is a more meaningful question at the high school level than at the college level. Our early work exploring ways to help students gain conceptual understanding as well as similar early work by Larkin, Reif and their collaborators led many others to apply results from physics education research to the design of curricular reforms in introductory physics instruc-tion. Another catalyst to this reform was the availability of concept inven-tories (Hestenes, Wells, & Swackhamer, 1992; Thornton & Sokoloff, 1998) that measured students' understanding of basic physics concepts following instruction. Those revealed to the physics community that despite students earning reasonable grades in traditional courses, they emerged with major conceptual deficits (Hake, 1998). As a result, introductory physics instruction has witnessed various innovations that promote active learning in large lectures and that target conceptual understanding (Mazur, 1997; Sokoloff & Thornton, 2004). There have also been techniques developed for assuring that students come to class prepared with basic course content. For example, Just-in Time Teaching (JiTT) (Novak, Patterson, Gavrin, & Christian, 1999) is a technique where students answer web-delivered "quizzes" prior to class-time to show they have read the textbook. In a similar vein, web-delivered *multimedia learning modules* cover basic course content prior to class-time (Chen, Stelzer, & Gladding, 2010; Stelzer, Brookes, Gladding, & Mestre, 2010; Stelzer, Gladding, Mestre, & Brookes, 2009) and students receive credit for viewing them and answering a few questions about the content. Both of these instructional techniques have resulted in students coming to class better prepared so that instruction can focus on refining concepts and illustrating how they apply to problem solving. In addition, the advent of classroom polling technologies (otherwise known as "clickers"; see http://www.iclicker.com) have also allowed efficient, seamless, and anonymous formative assessment of students' conceptual knowledge in both small and large lecture classes, giving instructors opportunities to address students' conceptual deficiencies on the fly (Dufresne, Gerace, Leonard, Mestre, & Wenk, 1996). (For a review of these and other curricular and problem solving reforms, see a physics education research synthesis by Docktor & Mestre, 2011.)

At the high school level, physics instruction remains a challenge. One major difference between college and high school physics instruction is that two-thirds of high school physics teachers are teaching out of field (White & Tesfaye, 2010). This lack of domain expertise makes the need for CPS-like instruction in high school more important but less likely to occur. What teachers could use is a resource to help them implement CPS in ways that supplement problem solving instruction and that do not rely heavily on teacher support/expertise. One possibility is to develop a computer-based CPS tool that would allow students to practice CPS on their own. Such a technological tool might contain some features present in the HAT reviewed earlier, but with feedback and scaffolding features to provide pedagogical support to students. Teachers could assign problems for homework that required students to use the tool; classroom discussions of homework could also discuss the CPS approach. As students became better at implementing CPS, some of the scaffolding features could be removed (either under teacher control or software control based on degree of success with implementing CPS). Such a tool could also indirectly serve to increase the physics, and problem solving knowledge of teachers teaching out of field.

ACKNOWLEDGMENTS

Work in part supported by the Institute of Education Sciences of the US Department of Education under Award No. DE R305B070085. Any opinions, findings, and conclusions or recommendations expressed in this publication are those of the authors and do not necessarily reflect the views of the Institute of Education Sciences.

APPENDIX: SAMPLE QUESTIONS USED IN HIGH SCHOOL ASSESSMENTS

Categorization test question

Model Problem

A sled of mass 50 kg is on frictionless snow. A child pulls on the sled with a force of 11.0 N at an angle of 20° above the horizontal, as shown in the diagram. After moving a horizontal distance d, the sled is moving at a speed of 3 m/s. Find the distance d.

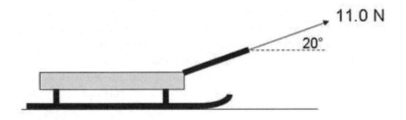

Circle which one of the two alternatives below would be solved most like the model problem.

Alternative 1

The compressed air in an air-gun pushes a plastic projectile 0.3 m with an average force of 44.5 N. What is the velocity of a 0.15-kg projectile fired with the gun?

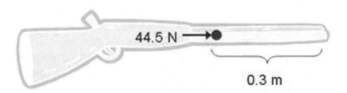

Alternative 2

A sled of mass 50 kg is on frictionless snow. A force F is applied at an angle of 20° above the horizontal, as shown in the diagram. As a result, the sled has a horizontal acceleration of 4 m/s². What is the magnitude of the applied force F?

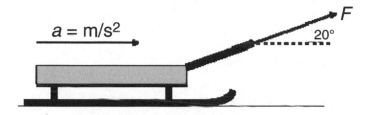

Multiple Choice Conceptual Question:
Two blocks of equal mass (box 1 and 2) slide down frictionless slopes whose vertical heights h are identical, as shown in the diagram. Both blocks start from rest and slide down to the bottom of the slope. Compare the kinetic energy of the blocks at the bottom of each slope. Which block has more kinetic energy, or are their kinetic energies the same, and why?

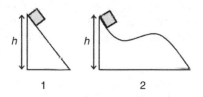

(a) The kinetic energies are the same. The blocks start from the same height, so they have the same gravitational potential energy at the top. No energy is lost along the slope. Therefore, they have the same amount of kinetic energy at the bottom.

(b) The kinetic energies are the same. The block on slope 2 has a longer distance to travel so it has more time to gain speed. But slope 1 is steeper, so the block has a greater acceleration. Therefore, they have the same amount of kinetic energy at the bottom.

(c) The kinetic energies are different, and the block on slope 1 has greater kinetic energy. Slope 1 is steeper, so the block gets to the bottom faster. Therefore it has a greater kinetic energy at the bottom.

(d) The kinetic energies are different, and the block on slope 2 has greater kinetic energy. Slope 2 is longer, so the block has more time to gain speed. Therefore it has a greater kinetic energy at the bottom.

Finding errors test question

A swimmer runs horizontally off a high diving board with a speed of 2.50 m/s, and lands in the water 1.2 s later. How high is the diving board?

Solution

Using motion under constant acceleration in the y-direction, we know the initial speed, time, and acceleration (gravity). Choose the origin to be at the water surface and the positive y-direction upward. Then solve for the height of the diving board.

$$y = v_i t + \frac{1}{2} at^2$$

$$y = v_i t + \frac{1}{2} gt^2$$

$$y = (2.5\,\text{m/s})(1.2\,\text{s}) + \frac{1}{2}(9.8\,\text{m/s}^2)(1.2\,\text{s})^2$$

$$y = 3.0\,\text{m} + 7.1\,\text{m} = 10.1\,\text{m}$$

Explain what is wrong with this solution and why it is incorrect.

EQUATION INSTANTIATION TEST QUESTION:

A 300 g air track cart traveling at 1.2 m/s collides with a 200 g cart traveling in the opposite direction at 0.8 m/s. The carts stick together after the collision. What is the speed of the carts after the collision?

$$m_1 \vec{v}_{1i} + m_2 \vec{v}_{2i} = (m_1 + m_2)\vec{v}_f$$

$$\Rightarrow \vec{v}_f = \frac{m_1 \vec{v}_{1i} + m_2 \vec{v}_{2i}}{(m_1 + m_2)}$$

Fill in the numbers below:

$$\vec{v}_f =$$

Problem solving test question:

A 40.0-kg child is standing on a bathroom scale in a downward moving elevator. The scale reads 440 N. What is the magnitude and direction of the acceleration of the elevator?

REFERENCES

Anzai, Y., & Yokoyama, T. (1984). Internal models in physics problem solving. *Cognition& Instruction*, 1(4), 397–450.

Bagno, E., & Eylon, B. (1997). From problem solving to knowledge structure: An example from the domain of electromagnetism. *American Journal of Physics*, *65*(8), 726–736.

Chen, Z., Stelzer, T., & Gladding, G. (2010). Using multimedia learning modules to better prepare students for introductory physics lecture. *Physical Review Special Topics – Physics Education Research*, *6*(010108), 1–5.

Chi, M. T. H., Feltovich, P., & Glaser, R. (1981). Categorization and representation of physics problems by experts and novices. *Cognitive Science*, *5*, 121–152.

de Jong, T., & Ferguson-Hessler, M. G. M. (1986). Cognitive structures of good and poor novice problem solvers in physics. *Journal of Educational Psychology*, *78*(4), 279–288.

de Jong, T., & Ferguson-Hessler, M. G. M. (1991). Knowledge of problem situations in physics: A comparison of good and poor novice problem solvers. *Learning and Instruction*, *1*, 289–302.

Docktor, J.L. (2009). *Development and validation of a physics problem-solving assessment rubric*. Unpublished doctoral dissertation, University of Minnesota, Twin Cities.

Docktor, J.L., & Mestre, J.P. (2011). A synthesis of discipline-based education research in physics. *Commissioned paper for the National Academies, National Research Council project on status, contributions, and future directions of discipline-based education research*. Washington, DC: National Academy Press. Retrieved February 16, 2011 from http://www7.nationalacademies.org/bose/DBER_Docktor_October_Paper.pdf.

Dufresne, R. J., Gerace, W. J., Hardiman, P. T., & Mestre, J. P. (1992). Constraining novices to perform expertlike problem analyses: Effects on schema acquisition. *The Journal of the Learning Sciences*, *2*(3), 307–331.

Dufresne, R. J., Gerace, W. J., Leonard, W. J., Mestre, J. P., & Wenk, L. (1996). Classtalk: A classroom communication system for active learning. *Journal of Computing in Higher Education*, *7*(2), 3–47.

Eylon, B. -S., & Reif, F. (1984). Effects of knowledge organization on task performance. *Cognition and Instruction*, *1*(1), 5–44.

Finegold, M., & Mass, R. (1985). Differences in the process of solving physics problems between good problem solvers and poor problem solvers. *Research in Science and Technology Education*, *3*, 59–67.

Hake, R. (1998). Interactive-engagement versus traditional methods: A six-thousand student survey of mechanics test data for introductory physics courses. *American Journal of Physics*, *66*, 64–74.

Hardiman, P. T., Dufresne, R., & Mestre, J. P. (1989). The relation between problem categorization and problem solving among experts and novices. *Memory & Cognition*, *17*(5), 627–638.

Hestenes, D., Wells, M., & Swackhamer, G. (1992). Force concept inventory. *The Physics Teacher*, *30*(3), 141–158.

Kim, E., & Pak, S. (2002). Students do not overcome conceptual difficulties after solving 1000 traditional problems. *American Journal of Physics*, *70*(7), 759–765.

Larkin, J. H. (1979). Processing information for effective problem solving. *Engineering Education*, *70*(3), 285–288.

Larkin, J. H. (1981a). Cognition of learning physics. *American Journal of Physics*, *49*(6), 534–541.

Larkin, J. H. (1981b). Enriching formal knowledge: A model for learning to solve textbook physics problems. In J. R. Anderson (Ed.), *Cognitive skills and their acquisition* (pp. 311–334). Hillsdale, NJ: Lawrence Erlbaum Associates, Inc.

Larkin, J. H. (1983). The role of problem representation in physics. In D. Gentner, and A. L. Stevens, (Eds.), *Mental models* (pp. 75–98). Hillsdale, NJ: Lawrence Erlbaum.

Larkin, J. H., McDermott, J., Simon, D. P., & Simon, H. A. (1980). Expert and novice performance in solving physics problems. *Science*, *208*(4450), 1335–1342.

Larkin, J. H., & Reif, F. (1979). Understanding and teaching problem solving in physics. *European Journal of Science Education, 1*(2), 191–203.

Leonard, W. J., Dufresne, R. J., & Mestre, J. P. (1996). Using qualitative problem-solving strategies to highlight the role of conceptual knowledge in solving problems. *American Journal of Physics, 64*(12), 1495–1503.

Mazur, E. (1997). *Peer instruction: A user's manual.* Upper Saddle River, NJ: Prentice Hall.

Mestre, J. P., Dufresne, R. J., Gerace, W. J., Hardiman, P. T., & Touger, J. S. (1993). Promoting skilled problem-solving behavior among beginning physics students. *Journal of Research in Science Teaching, 30*(3), 307–317.

Newell, A., & Simon, H. A. (1972). *Human problem solving.* Englewood Cliffs, NJ: Prentice-Hall, Inc.

Novak, G., Patterson, E., Gavrin, A., & Christian, W. (1999). *Just-in-time teaching: Blending active learning with web technology.* Upper Saddle River, NJ: Prentice Hall.

Priest, A. G., & Lindsay, R. O. (1992). New light on novice-expert differences in physics problems solving. *British Journal of Psychology, 83*(3), 389–405.

Reif, F., & Heller, J. I. (1982). Knowledge structure and problem solving in physics. *Educational Psychologist, 17*(2), 102–127.

Savelsbergh, E. R., de Jong, T., & Ferguson-Hessler, M. G. M. (2002). Situational knowledge in physics: the case of electrodynamics. *Journal of Research in Science Teaching, 39*(10), 928–951.

Simon, D. P., & Simon, H. A. (1978). Individual differences in solving physics problems. In R. S. Siegler (Ed.), *Children's thinking: What develops?* (pp. 325–361). Hillsdale, NJ: Erlbaum.

Smith, A. D., Mestre, J. P., & Ross, B. H. (2010). Eye-gaze patterns as students study worked-out examples in mechanics. *Physical Review Special Topics—Physics Education Research,* 6(020118), 1–9.

Sokoloff, D. R., & Thornton, R. K. (2004). *Interactive lecture demonstrations, active learning in introductory physics.* Hoboken, NJ: John Wiley & Sons, Inc.

Stelzer, T., Brookes, D., Gladding, G., & Mestre, J. (2010). Impact of multimedia learning modules on an introductory course on electricity and magnetism. *American Journal of Physics, 78,* 755–759.

Stelzer, T., Gladding, G., Mestre, J., & Brookes, D. (2009). Comparing the efficacy of multimedia modules with traditional textbooks for learning introductory physics content. *American Journal of Physics, 77,* 184–189.

Thornton, R. K., & Sokoloff, D. R. (1998). Assessing student learning of Newton's laws: The force and motion conceptual evaluation and the evaluation of active learning laboratory and lecture curricula. *American Journal of Physics, 66*(4), 338–352.

Tuminaro, J., & Redish, E. F. (2007). Elements of a cognitive model of physics problem solving: Epistemic games. *Physical Review Special Topics—Physics Education Research, 3* (020101), 1–22.

Walsh, L. N., Howard, R. G., & Bowe, B. (2007). Phenomenographic study of students' problem solving approaches in physics. *Physical Review Special Topics— Physics Education Research, 3*(020108), 1–12.

White, S., & Tesfaye, C.L. (2010). Who teaches high school physics? Results from the 2008-2009 nationwide survey of high school physics teachers. College Park, MD: American Institute of Physics. Retrieved February 15, 2011, from http://www.aip.org/statistics/trends/reports/hsteachers.pdf.

Index

Contents of Recent Volumes